The New England Small College
Athletic Conference

The New England Small College Athletic Conference

A History

DAN COVELL

Foreword by Stephen Hardy

McFarland & Company, Inc., Publishers
Jefferson, North Carolina

ISBN (print) 978-1-4766-8850-3
ISBN (ebook) 978-1-4766-4579-7

LIBRARY OF CONGRESS AND BRITISH LIBRARY
CATALOGUING DATA ARE AVAILABLE

Library of Congress Control Number 2022022480

© 2022 Dan Covell. All rights reserved

No part of this book may be reproduced or transmitted in any form or by any means, electronic or mechanical, including photocopying or recording, or by any information storage and retrieval system, without permission in writing from the publisher.

Front cover: Amherst plays Bates College in football at Garcelon Field on September 26, 2015 (Hovertover)

Printed in the United States of America

*McFarland & Company, Inc., Publishers
Box 611, Jefferson, North Carolina 28640
www.mcfarlandpub.com*

*To family, friends, and colleagues for their everlasting support,
to those who offered information and resources,
and to Sid Watson,
whose cooperation made possible the early study of this topic*

Contents

Foreword by Stephen Hardy	1
Introduction: "The Sweatiest of the Liberal Arts"	5
1. An Ideal Is Born: The Future NESCACs in the Emerging Intercollegiate Athletics Landscape	23
2. Establishing the Pentagonal Agreement: The Challenges of Formalization and Self-Interest	35
3. Alex Schulten, the 1.6 Rule, and the Artifice of the Ideal Image Exposed	55
4. The "Potted Ivy" Conference: From the Pentagonal Agreement to NESCAC	74
5. The New Conference Faces Immediate Challenges	101
6. "When All Hell Broke Loose": The Realities of Postseason Play	132
7. No Longer So Pure and Simple: Managing the AP-Era Ideal	159
8. Recruiting: The Realities of Athletics Resource Acquisition	186
Epilogue: The Cultivation of a New Image Era	210
Chapter Notes	231
Bibliography	247
Index	257

Foreword

BY STEPHEN HARDY

In October 1998, my wife and I enjoyed a splendid Saturday at Middlebury College, where our son Ben was co-captain of men's soccer. On that warm, blue-skyed morning his undefeated team played Amherst. A #1 national ranking was on the line. Across an expansive field complex, the same two schools' field hockey and football teams would face off, with the sun beaming toward the Green Mountains. There was a festival atmosphere—a typical weekend in the New England Small College Athletic Conference (NESCAC). It was, in a word, idyllic. After Middlebury's victory, we walked back toward the Field House, newly expanded with a glassy, state-of-the-art fitness facility. I put my arm around Ben and said, "Enjoy all of this, because life's downhill from here!"

Sports Illustrated has published several glowing tributes to the purity of the NESCAC product, from its founding in 1971. Dan Covell compares the reality to the ideal. He tells us the long history of athletics on NESCAC member campuses, beginning in the 1800s. It is solid research, based on extensive work in campus archives, media publications, and interviews, from which Covell provides many scenes where college presidents, athletic directors, trustees, coaches, faculty, players, parents, and others display glee, anger, smugness, and, above all, candor.

It's also a story of change over time. Most people forget that the NCAA had no separate "divisions" until the 1960s. In 1940, Williams football played Army—and lost by only one point. In 1950, Tufts advanced to the College World Series in Omaha, Nebraska. In 1962, Colby men's hockey was seeded third, *among all teams*, in the very first ECAC championship tournament. In 1972, Colby's women were founding members of ECAC *Division I* hockey.

It's a very different landscape today. By telling the story of NESCAC, Dan Covell shows how college athletics splintered and separated into new divisions and conferences. It's a story about the optimism and loftiness of strategy and the tedium of policy, the level where the sausage is actually made, especially in the areas of recruiting, admissions, and financial aid.

Covell remembers the 1951 Pentagonal Agreement, made by Amherst, Williams, Wesleyan, Bowdoin, and Dartmouth. It was the foundation of NESCAC. When I played at Bowdoin in the late 1960s, we heard many references to the Pentagonals. Among other things, the agreement prohibited athletically related financial aid. It restricted postseason play, a constant source of tension. It also limited recruiting—keeping coaches away from schools and homes. From the get-go, however, presidents wrote each other about reports of suspicious alumni "smokers" and banquets. As one president wrote to another in 1960: "it seems to me a little ridiculous to have a rule that coaches cannot go to schools and yet to let them travel around to meetings, large and small, where promising athletes are brought in for recruiting purposes." The distrust and carping did not subside after 1971.

Branding was a strategic item for NESCAC, long before it became a hot and overused concept in sports. Covell shows careful parsing of brand terms. What's "New England" about Hamilton and Union? Are we a "league" or a "conference"? Do we really want to be "Little Ivies"? What to do when the athletic director at the University of Maine at Portland-Gorham (now the University of Southern Maine) writes to complain about the acronym theft of *his* NESCAC—the New England *State* College Athletic Conference? He received no consideration. Thirty years later, he probably would have sued over trademark violation.

Some policies put presidents on the rack. For instance, what to do with endowed scholarship awards that included terms like "athletic proficiency" and were *intended* by their benefactors to attract and recruit good athletes? Since building endowments and cultivating donors were more central to overall strategy, the colleges danced delicately until 2004, when the NCAA's Division III membership voted to authorize audits of campus financial aid awards. Only then were the terms completely scrubbed from the language.

The most consequential changes were with post-season play. Covell skillfully shows how shifts in policy affected institutional strategy, which in turn made policy harder to enforce. In 1993, NESCAC first gave blanket approval for all teams (but football) to compete in national championships. By then, it was clear that member schools *needed* to compete nationally, *and win*, in order to stay prominent in the hearts and minds of stakeholders who gave money and built endowments. And to attract top athletes and their families. As one former AD tells Covell, "Once they opened that door everybody wants to win a national championship. I mean, that's what the competitor does. You want to be the best there is in the country."

Trinity staked its claim in squash. This meant getting international players and getting special admissions slots. By 2011, this produced 13 straight undefeated seasons and 244 straight match wins. Other NESCAC schools dominated various men's and women's sports. Women's tennis at Williams, men's and women's hockey at Middlebury, field hockey at Bowdoin, to name just a few. Success spawned more concern and criticism, including two influential books that attacked the "divide" between athletes and others on NESCAC campuses.

Covell clearly describes the actions and reactions to these internal and external threats. His concluding chapter outlines the most current challenges and opportunities in strategy and policy, especially vis-à-vis diversity goals. He is adept at finding the "telling" quote that captures a much bigger landscape. One of my favorites is from a longtime, highly successful, highly respected coach and AD: "My last five years as an AD I grew tired of meeting with parents and athletes who wanted a coach fired because the team didn't make the NCAAs. Many active coaches in NESCAC would happily go back to the old model." It's probably too late for that. But there's no harm in dreaming.

Stephen Hardy was graduated in 1970 from Bowdoin College, where he and his twin brother Erl were co-captains of men's hockey. He worked for 35 years as a professor at the University of Washington, Robert Morris University, and the University of New Hampshire, from which he retired in 2014 as professor of kinesiology and affiliate professor of history. His most recent publication is Hockey: A Global History.

Introduction

"The Sweatiest of the Liberal Arts"

> NESCAC, founded 23 years ago, is as pure as college athletics get.
>
> NESCAC firmly believes that athletics must be brought in line with academics, and not the other way around.
>
> NESCAC stands above the fray.
>
> —Douglas Looney, *Sports Illustrated* (1994)[1]

When *Sports Illustrated* published the article "Pure and Simple," by staff writer Douglas Looney, the magazine had just celebrated its fortieth anniversary, and while it had ceded some ground to the likes of burgeoning media giant ESPN, *SI* was still the "authoritative surveyor of the American sporting scene to its many readers."[2] Given the magazine's status and its dedication to covering sporting events and personalities of both national and international import, the overwhelmingly positive tone in the article was a tremendous boon for the cultivation of the ideal image of the New England Small College Athletic Conference, or NESCAC (while the acronym seems to call for a preceding article "the," it is referred to without it by the vast majority of stakeholders). The conference consists of eleven four-year primarily undergraduate institutions: Amherst College, Bates College, Bowdoin College, Colby College, Connecticut College, Hamilton College, Middlebury College, Trinity College, Tufts University, Wesleyan University, and Williams College. Collectively, they are widely acknowledged to be among the most prestigious institutions of higher education in America.

The tone and content of Looney's article couldn't have been more laudatory if drafted by a think tank of NESCAC publicists, so much so that one might take the author for an intercollegiate athletics naïf. Nothing could be further from the truth, as Looney, who had been writing for *SI* since the early 1980s, was an experienced investigative reporter. One of his most significant pieces, published in 1983, revealed disputes between University of Oklahoma head football coach Barry Switzer and standout running back Marcus Dupree, which "would start a storm of critical investigations into Switzer's program and would lead Switzer to the belief that *Sports Illustrated* had played a crucial role in his downfall at Oklahoma."[3] Perhaps Looney was smitten with the imagery he encountered in researching the NESCAC story, given what he'd seen and experienced covering the big-time. After all, following the publication of a critical piece on University of Colorado head football coach Chuck Fairbanks, Looney commented that he got a lot of negative letters but that "most of them are in crayon because they don't give these people sharp things."[4]

Until Looney's piece, *SI* portrayed NESCAC much like other national publications—that is, intriguing, endearing, charming, and a bit goofy, as seen in an *SI* article from 1993 announcing NESCAC's decision to allow teams to participate in National Collegiate Athletic Association (NCAA) Division III postseason competitions. The piece included a photo of four Williams men's basketball players, including seven-foot-three Eric Gingold—listed as the tallest Jew ever to play college basketball—posing in their team warm-ups in front of a barn with a dappled cow, a paean to the school's bovine logo. The article, part of *SI*'s annual college basketball preview, also ranked Williams eighth in its preseason Division III poll.[5]

Looney expanded on this perspective, first using a familiar trope to describe the idealized campus settings in which NESCAC athletics resided. "The Amherst College campus is too collegiate," he wrote, "the ambience too New England, the whole picture too Norman Rockwell. The grass is cut, and the flower beds are weeded. There is no trash. The sky is true blue." He cited the experiences of a Middlebury football player who "spent many a fall afternoon looking out over Vermont's Green Mountains, resplendent in the fall red produced by sugar maples, and pondering the Middlebury experience."[6] Looney then contrasted the idyllic campuses across NESCAC with the relative shabbiness of their athletics facilities, furthering the notion that this approach was "the perfect testimony to the NESCAC philosophy, which puts academics on a lofty perch and makes athletics an adjunct." To wit, "the [Williams football locker room] is a dump. It's way too small for all these bodies. The tile ceiling is ringed with water damage caused by a leaky roof; nine ceiling tiles are missing, and four more are hanging on in acts of faith. The walls are painted a sickly green. But that doesn't matter. The players act like players anywhere."[7]

While Looney conceded that "NESCAC schools aren't very good in most sports," he identified this perceived shortcoming as an attribute. "But they are not very good only if you measure the Colby football team, for example, against Miami's; the Bates basketball team against Arkansas's.

And such comparisons miss the point." He declared, "Insofar as sports are concerned, things are perfect, or pretty close to it," allowing Amherst (and former Trinity) president Tom Gerety to contextualize NESCAC in lofty philosophical terms: "Sports fulfill the natural drive to test oneself against others. It's our greatest ritual, short of war. I don't have much trouble justifying them, but that's only in this kind of setting. It seems everywhere else, sports are a distorting force." Gerety then sought to bring athletics into the liberal arts rubric when he commented, "Be it poetry, acting, philosophy or athletics, any youngster has more to give than what is called for in a traditional class." He concluded, "[Athletics is] the sweatiest of the liberal arts."[8]

Looney then examined NESCAC's operational approach to managing intercollegiate athletics. "NESCAC schools adhere to some basic guidelines," he wrote, noting that the schools followed NCAA Division III rules. "Then they go the spirit of the rules one better and do not try to slip a few desired athletes in with academic or need-based scholarships." Looney observed that NESCAC athletes, like all students, could apply for financial aid, but with no help from the athletic department. Bowdoin athletic director (AD) Sid Watson told Looney, "We can't tell a kid how much financial aid he's going to get, because we don't know ourselves." Looney also noted that NESCAC schools had all agreed to do no off-campus recruiting. "That's by far the most stringent recruiting rule in the land. Coaches can make phone calls and write letters and ask prospective student-athletes to visit the campus.... But there are no home visits, no recruiting trips to high schools, no recruiting calls." Next, Looney quoted Connecticut College president Claire Gaudiani, who insisted that NESCAC athletics "are showing that young adults can live their lives in a way that's closer to what many people think is the right way. We are making the right thing the normal thing." Looney stated, "This is not to say that these schools don't care about sports. Each, in varying ways, cares enormously.... But NESCAC schools will not do everything to achieve athletic success. Or even, in some ways, anything. If it happens, fine. If not, that's also fine."[9] The hard-bitten scribe in Looney chose not to look more closely at some of the actual practices and past recruiting issues that had brought conflict into the ranks, but perhaps if he had, he would have seen them as vastly minor indiscretions compared with the goings-on in the big-time he had witnessed.

Looney's piece—complete with more than a dozen full-color photos of NESCAC game action, including a two-page shot of a goal-line play run by Middlebury's offense during its 20–7 home win versus Wesleyan, and a full-page photo of the men's soccer and women's rugby games going on simultaneously on adjacent fields at Amherst—would serve as a landmark homage and ideal image touchstone for NESCAC stakeholders. Indeed, in 2016, a website devoted to the coverage of NESCAC athletics (managed by current NESCAC students) offered this assessment:

> Back in 1994, *Sports Illustrated* printed an article about the unique athletic landscape in the NESCAC that all incoming NESCAC student-athletes need to read. And even though we are 20 years, a financial crisis, a handful of recruiting violations and an internet boom away from those days, you'll find that a lot of Douglas Looney's words still ring true. ... [But] as each year goes by, the NESCAC begins to look more and more like other conferences around the country, hell-bent on recruiting, training year-round and winning at all costs.[10]

So what happened? Why is there now a website run by NESCAC students solely dedicated to covering NESCAC sports? Did Looney's intercollegiate athletics utopia really turn into just another group of schools operating athletics under a set of misguided principles? While accurate in large part, Looney's idyllic portrait failed to recognize there was another NESCAC ideal germinating, and in short order it would reach full flower. In 1993, the conference rescinded a ban on team postseason play, and soon multiple NESCAC teams were qualifying for NCAA Division III postseason play. Many won national championships (more than a hundred national team championships and several hundred individual championships by 2021), and Williams won recognition as the most successful NCAA Division III athletic program in the country twenty-two times. Only two other NESCAC schools had ever won this title, and Middlebury was one of them. Did this apparent divergence mean that NESCAC athletics had entered what Amherst's Gerety labeled a "distorted" realm and was no longer just a part of the educatory experience as the "sweatiest of the liberal arts"?

This book is a case study of how this group of private, academically selective liberal arts colleges in the American Northeast, which collectively created an educatory model for the country, experienced and responded to shifts in the competitive landscape of intercollegiate athletics beginning with the establishment of intercollegiate athletics programs in the late 1800s. From that point, several schools moved toward the creation of a loose alliance under the Pentagonal Agreement in the 1950s, which evolved to become NESCAC in 1971. Over the decades since, the group endeavored to manage a range of conflicts, including an image-altering decision relating to NCAA postseason championship participation, which has led to its current position as the perceived "gold standard" of the melding of intercollegiate athletics competitive excellence within the "small-time" framework of the primacy of high academic standards. This book will not only review how this evolution occurred but also seek to understand how and why these schools and their institutional decision makers cultivated this image, the institutional costs this pursuit exacted, and how this process serves as an instructive example in understanding small-college athletics conference development.

NESCAC and the American Intercollegiate Athletics Ideal

Although Hamilton is not in New England but in New York (but not in the town of Hamilton—that is the location of Colgate University), NESCAC membership can otherwise be accurately described as small (most with undergraduate enrollments between 1,800 and 2,000—Middlebury's is 2,420, Wesleyan's 2,850, and Tufts's 5,200) as well as highly selective (the mean combined SAT score for entering students in 2019 was just over 1320). The NESCACs are also among the wealthiest institutions in higher education, with the endowments of five member schools topping the $1 billion mark, led by $2.79 billion at Williams and $2.5 billion at Amherst.[11] The elite status of these schools has been in place for generations; as noted by one Dartmouth alumnus of the early 1960s, "They were aristocrats among colleges, abounding in prestige and excellence, part of the network of elite New England schools," and after one attended "Harvard or Wesleyan or Hamilton or Williams or Yale or Middlebury or Brown or Tufts or Bates or Bowdoin or Colby ... they'd go out to run the world."[12]

These factors also afforded the NESCACs periodic pop culture exposure: four top track sprinters from Bates were hired by United Press International to run copy from the ringside in the second Muhammad Ali–Sonny Liston fight in 1965 in Lewiston, Maine (only one runner was called upon since Ali famously knocked out Liston just seconds into the first round).[13] In the 1978 film *Animal House*, Faber College lothario Eric Stratton assumes the guise of "Frank Lyman from Amherst" to hit on unsuspecting female students at Emily Dickinson College. Meg Griffin touted her acceptance to Bowdoin in the long-running animated TV sitcom *Family Guy*. NESCAC is also home of alumni both famous and infamous, from U.S. presidents (Calvin Coolidge, Amherst; James Garfield, Williams; Franklin Pierce, Bowdoin) and political historians (Doris Kearns Goodwin, Colby) to pundits (Tucker Carlson and George Will, both Trinity) and political punch lines (Sean Spicer, Connecticut College). From the world of non-intercollegiate sport, the list includes broadcasters (Bryant Gumbel, Bates), Major League Baseball players (Jack Coombs, Colby) and executives (Ben Cherington, Amherst), National Basketball Association players (Duncan Robinson, Williams) and executives (Koby

Altman, Middlebury), National Hockey League players (Guy Hebert, Hamilton), Olympic athletes (marathoner Joan Benoit Samuelson, Bowdoin; rower Anita DeFrantz, Connecticut College; horse jumper Peter Wylde, Tufts), professional golfers (Jay Williamson, Trinity), and National Football League coaches (including enemies Bill Belichick and Eric Mangini, both Wesleyan).

Intercollegiate athletic participation is an important aspect of life on NESCAC campuses, as participation rates approach 50 percent of the student body at nine member schools, and many member schools sponsor more than thirty intercollegiate programs. But participation is not the endgame, as during the 2018–19 academic year, sixty-one NESCAC teams participated in NCAA team championships (winning seven) and thirteen individual sport participants claimed national championships. Team nicknames are also part of the conference's idealized image. In his 1994 piece, Looney wrote that the nicknames were "proof positive that NESCAC is not your normal, everyday college athletic conference." Excepting three rather prosaic monikers—the Cardinals (Wesleyan, which was once the more distinctive "Fighting Methodists" until a change in the early twentieth century), the Bobcats (Bates), and the Panthers (Middlebury)—the grouping's more esoteric nicknames include the Bantams (Trinity), the Camels (Connecticut College), the Continentals (Hamilton), the Ephs (Williams, from the school's founder Ephraim Williams), the Jumbos (Tufts, named for a stuffed elephant given to the school by circus magnate P.T. Barnum), the Mules (Colby, formerly the White Mules), the Polar Bears (Bowdoin, named for the exploits of alumnus and Arctic explorer Robert Peary, with white as the official school color), and the Mammoths (Amherst, née Lord Jeffs). Amherst made the switch in 2017 after students lobbied against the former mascot, which had been used in honor of Lord Jeffery Amherst, commander in chief of the British forces during the French and Indian War. While some alumni were resistant to the change (with some withholding donations in protest), Amherst maintained the nickname quirkiness in its replacement choice, an homage to the skeleton of a Columbian mammoth discovered by Amherst professor Frederic Brewster Loomis and brought to the college in 1925.[14] And when combined with Tufts's, what conference can claim two pachydermic nicknames?

"America Is Different": Intercollegiate Athletics and the American Higher Education Enterprise

> America is different. Its universities are unique in their efforts to please many constituencies—prospective students,

> donors, legislators, the general public.... The growth of intercollegiate sports aptly illustrates the strengths and weaknesses of a constituency-oriented system of higher education. With enthusiastic support from students, alumni, and even government officials, our colleges have developed athletic programs that have brought great satisfaction to thousands of athletes and millions of spectators. Few aspects of college life have done so much to win the favor of the public, build the loyalties of alumni, and engender lasting memories in the minds of student-athletes.
> —Derek Bok, former Harvard University president[15]

As Bok noted, the American model of intercollegiate athletics is indeed different. Nowhere else in the world do colleges and universities sponsor the breadth and depth of competitive athletics, in large part because American institutions of higher education have sought to integrate all facets of student life into the collegiate experience. From its earliest inception at Harvard College (now Harvard University), the school's founders intentionally chose the English collegiate system where students and masters lived, ate, studied, worshipped, and played together, rather than the European or Scottish model where students lived and boarded in the community.[16] This institutionalizing of all elements of student life would give rise to colleges' involvement in sponsoring, at least by virtue of its responsibility of in loco parentis, the extracurriculars, those nonacademic activities that were to emerge on college campuses.

In part due to this English influence on its model of education, the formation of American intercollegiate athletics was shaped by that country's Victorian-era amateur athletic code, the "fair play" ethos that "sportsmen" from the elite public schools brought to Oxford and Cambridge universities,[17] and this fair play ethos was "the watchword of the gentleman amateur," an amateur being anyone who did not play for pay.[18] But while the "Oxbridge" model was influential, American intercollegiate athletics "went in a different direction," where students "at elite eastern colleges proclaimed their allegiance to amateur athletics, but their athletics were riddled with professionalism."[19] From the very first contest between teams from different institutions (Harvard-Yale rowing matches in 1852), there have been conflicting notions on the merits of such competitions.

While students first initiated and organized athletics programs for health and fitness benefits in the mid–1800s, the focus quickly shifted from participation-based programs toward institution-maintained programs that sought to achieve primacy over rival institutions and, as noted by Frederick Rudolph, a Williams alumnus (Class of 1942) and longtime Williams faculty member, in his history of Williams College, "demanded the development of the means of victory."[20] This evolution led to the creation of the big-time athletic programs mentioned by Bok, as embodied today at many NCAA Division I institutions. Proponents of the big-time model cite the ability of these programs to create a sense of community among campus constituencies and to promote the institution in general, while critics complain that academic integrity is often sacrificed in the pursuit of athletic success and that institutional resources are misdirected away from academics to support athletics.

The Defining Characteristics of the NESCAC

> The ongoing struggle within NESCAC has always been between idealism versus realism.
> —John Casey, Tufts University head baseball coach and athletics administrator

One former NESCAC president captured the essence of the ideal image furthered by stakeholders, specifying a "notion of athletics in its purist form, of the student-athlete—in that order." This former president described participants as "students who come primarily to receive an education, and who compete in athletics for the love of the sport, and who recognize that what they will gain from the experience will have a great deal to do with the way they lead the rest of their lives." Ultimately, to this president, NESCAC athletics have "an intrinsic value ... that broadens our own understanding of what it means to be liberally educated." It is a view very much in sync with Gerety's "sweatiest liberal arts" ethos.

The founding members of what would become NESCAC were among the first institutions in the United States to develop intercollegiate athletic programs. These schools, referred to as New England "hilltop colleges," were similarly situated in rural locales throughout the region and attracted young men of mostly modest means from families who had never before sent a son to college. The decline in farming and local economic opportunities forced these young men to prepare for lives as teachers or clergy in the Congregational tradition.[21] In contrast, the students at Harvard, Princeton, and Yale tended to come from families of "mercantile wealth."[22] The similarities would give these schools a shared identity, of which their athletic fortunes would become part. This shared identity was not without some perceived variations and resulting recriminations, as evidenced by a Dartmouth student song penned around 1900: "I'll sing you a song of colleges and tell you where to go.... Amherst for you high-toned fops, Dartmouth for your men, for riches go to Williamstown." Likewise, "the first and only point of agreement between students of Amherst and Williams was their shared contempt for Dartmouth."[23] This was, no doubt, fueled by the fact that both schools alleged that Dartmouth used nonstudents, "ruffians off the streets of Hanover," in football games.[24] By 1960, according to a Dartmouth alumnus of the day, similarities reigned, as the men at these schools "would look, dress, and sound much the same ... *everyone* wore crewneck sweaters and maroon penny loafers."[25] Six decades later, some intraconference delineations developed, eliciting a snarky post on a contemporary website that claimed the prototypical Williams student was a "nerdy kid with an outdoorsy vibe ... definitely an eagle scout," a Bowdoin student was a "country club prepster ... 90% of wardrobe is polo shirts," a Wesleyan student was a "free spirit ... runs around naked a lot," a Colby student was "the kid that trys [*sic*] really hard to fit into a stereotype despite not really belonging to one," and a Connecticut College student was "the generic looking kid with super average abilities that you forget the name of within a day of graduating."[26]

These New England hilltop colleges delivered a curriculum imported from medieval European foundations and focused on teaching the seven liberal arts: grammar, rhetoric, logic, astronomy, arithmetic, geometry, and music. The concept of the "liberal arts college" was a newer American construct, when in the 1910s some educators began to argue that small liberal arts colleges offered an education distinct from those at emerging universities. This "liberal arts" approach to education was bolstered in part by the influential 1828 Yale Report, in which that school's president and a committee of faculty took the position that students should be required to study a range of topics to develop their minds broadly and sufficiently. There was also the sense that such a course of instruction would serve to inculcate moral character without sectarian or denominational interpretations.[27]

In the nineteenth century, therefore, "the New England college represented not a place, but a type of education.... The small colleges of the country took their guidance from the small colleges of New England," and across the country, these schools "were taken as the models, the very embodiment of what it should mean to go to college."[28] In the face of the overt specialization promoted by emerging universities, the future NESCACs signaled that they held fast to the notion of the all-around, well-rounded man (and this did mean "man," as many NESCACs did not move to coeducation until the late 1960s and early 1970s). In addition, early twentieth-century works of fiction such as Owen Johnson's *Stover at Yale*, identified as "the era's most iconic and influential sports novel,"[29] promulgated the notion that this type of system implemented its traditional character-building values through its athletics activities.[30] Former

Harvard president Abbott Lawrence Lowell took this notion further and ascribed this approach as a calling of sorts, commenting that "the elite"—those who attended these schools—"should be, if possible, both intellectually and physically superior. That among them some should be in mind and others in physique above the ordinary is not enough."[31] These factors would coalesce to define what is now known as a liberal arts education, and by the end of World War I, the terms "'college' and 'university' came into common parlance as if they were generically distinct concepts."[32]

Collectively, demographic and curricular similarities would, in time, give the hilltop colleges an enhanced shared identity on which their athletic fortunes would be based and would serve to reflect and reinforce the differences from big-time programs, virtually always sponsored by publicly funded "multiversities," distinguished by enrollments numbering in the tens of thousands, thousands of whom were graduate students, and oft-criticized for supporting faculties engaged in extensive and arcane research at the expense of undergraduate teaching. Even former University of California system president Clark Kerr, the generally acknowledged architect of the multiversity concept, wistfully lauded his time as an undergraduate at the small, liberal arts Swarthmore College as "the greatest transformational experience of my life.... I was trying to follow the [Swarthmore College president Franklin] Aydelotte ideal of the all-around student."[33]

Athletics in NESCAC would over time come to be defined by a series of perceived central, distinct, and enduring qualities and be promulgated as the "sweatiest of the liberal arts," a cultivated notion of an enterprise that was the philosophical opposite from that held by schools that packaged sport as popular entertainment, where true student-athletes achieved high levels of success within the NCAA Division III realm. As we will see, the foundation for what has become central and distinct about NESCAC began as American intercollegiate sport evolved into popular spectacle, when the schools that would compose the current membership opted to focus on fostering intercollegiate athletics on a scale targeted neither toward public entertainment nor linked with overt commercialism. The NESCAC ideal image also sought to portray school presidents as having ultimate control over the management and decision-making regarding conference athletics programs, a stark contrast to the perceptions of those who seemed to rule these factors in the big-time realm.

But was this image accurate? Were NESCAC decision makers really free to act regardless of stakeholder demands and competitive interests? The foundational tenets of NESCAC crystallized immediately after World War II, when American colleges and universities restarted their intercollegiate athletic programs after virtually all sports were suspended because of the armed conflicts. This resumption served as a significant launching point from which the intercollegiate athletic environment would experience numerous changes, especially among the schools seeking to compete in football, by far the sport with the greatest popular interest on the part of fans and stakeholder groups. This shift would become the basis for later managerial actions that sought to curtail the programmatic commercialization boom blossoming across the intercollegiate athletics landscape, sometimes without success. The advent of television, the post–World War II economic expansion experienced across the country, the rules changes such as open substitution, and the approval of spring practice sessions, which allowed for even greater specialization and skill refinement among participants, led many programs across the country to realize the commercial opportunities and increased stakeholder interests in the sport. This hastened the demarcation between the big-time programs and all the rest. The changes experienced in this period would lead the future NESCACs to adopt changes in the management of their football programs, the most significant of which was to seek closer affiliations with other similarly situated institutions in New England to protect their interests.

To this end, Amherst, Bowdoin, Dartmouth, Wesleyan, and Williams allied in the early 1950s under the Pentagonal Agreement for intercollegiate competition. In 1956, following Dartmouth's departure for the finally formalized Ivy League, the four remaining schools reaffirmed their association, identified in memorandum as the "agreement between Amherst, Bowdoin, Wesleyan and Williams concerning athletic policies," but nearly always referred to by stakeholders and participants by its now geometrically inaccurate original moniker. The reaffirmed agreement, modeled closely on the Ivy League's, outlined specific protocols for recruiting and admission of prospective athletes, as well as the recognition that athletic staff members were to be viewed as regular faculty members, with "responsibilities and duties ... commensurate with their dignity as members of the faculty and with the dignity of the institution they represent." The memo announcing this accord refers to "previous agreements" that had been "reviewed, confirmed and clarified," and that "the primary points ... rest not with the specific phrasing thereof, but rather with the underlying spirit and philosophy upon which the agreement is based."[34] This agreement, while a significant step in the cultivation of a shared intercollegiate athletics brand, would be ill-suited to address adequately the thornier issues endemic to the enterprise (namely, accusations of recruiting violations volleyed among the signatories almost from the very first days of the agreement's existence).

The limits of the Pentagonal Agreement notwithstanding, almost immediately other hilltop colleges in the region soon sought entrée to the assemblage. During the 1960s, hopefuls actively lobbied to join the Pentagonals, in part due to functional issues such as increasingly unworkable athletics schedules, as schools that had formerly been close competitors with nearby rivals (most future NESCACs often played local, larger public and private schools in other sports until the formation of the conference) were now finding that, owing to an increased emphasis on athletics at those larger schools (especially due to athletically related aid), it was no longer realistic to expect competitive equity.

Logistics aside, increased institutional prestige was the most important motivator to join the Pentagonals. The notion of the power of these schools to shape the concept of the American intercollegiate athletics ideal image was to some degree furthered by the fact that the group occupied a leadership position in the formation of intercollegiate athletics programs. This historical connection with the foundational big-time, coupled with a strong reputation for its academic programs, afforded a portrayal of the group as a scaled-down yet arguably purer version of the better-known Ivy League. The fact that virtually all decisions made within the Pentagonal realm were—for better or worse—made by presidents underscored the broader branding intent of these actions all the more.

In 1971, the Pentagonals would become NESCAC, bringing seven schools into the fold under a more detailed set of athletics administrative rules and procedures. The move served as a significant benchmark example of school administrators, college presidents in particular, who sought to exert influence for the practical benefit of their own institutions through the promotion of a collectively defined ideal image of intercollegiate athletics. The new agreement designated conference goals—the foundation of NESCAC's organizational identity—as "the largest feasible participation in a wide variety of sports well coached by quality people who remain genuinely interested in the students' personal growth and genuinely mindful of the educational goals of the enterprise." Williams president John Sawyer, dubbed by renowned sport historian (and former Bowdoin ice hockey co-captain) Stephen Hardy as "the architect of NESCAC more than anybody," noted that athletic programs could be defended only in budgetary terms "on the basis of very wide participation and the contribution it makes to their personal growth."[35] As outlined in Chapter 4, Sawyer was indeed the key factor, including how he influenced the list of new members, the steps in the negotiating process, and the crafting and defining of the language of NESCAC. This language codified NESCAC's organizational identity: that athletics were to be kept "in harmony" with institutional educational purposes, that student-athletes be representative of their institution's student body, and that presidents would have the ultimate authority over athletics. Original bylaws prohibited conference championships or standings to dissuade overt emphasis on competition, banned athletically related financial aid, strictly limited off-campus recruiting activities, did not require that conference members schedule other conference members, and set limits on lengths of playing seasons and the number of allowable athletic events. Institutional autonomy, freedom, and flexibility were also established as part of the conference's organizational identity. Former Middlebury AD Richard Coleman reinforced this ethos of member autonomy when he noted that NESCAC should be based on "mutual trust and confidence [rather] than a network of tight rules and regulations."[36]

"NESCAC Invented the Concept of Division III"

Big-time college athletics—those embodied by the highly visible NCAA Division I programs in sports such as football and men's basketball—are seen by many as inherently corrupt and exploitative since, it is argued, they compromise the stated mission of sponsoring institutions through overt commercialization and subversion of academic principles. Small-time athletics programs, by definition, do none of these things, and it is there, according to many, where actual students pursue sport as an avocation, not for professional gain but rather for the pure love of competition, and are coached and led by administrators who put first the well-being of the participants rather than the demands of miscellaneous stakeholder groups. Many also see this realm as keeping true to the Oxbridge ethos of amateurism, sportsmanship, and gentlemanly fair play. In fact, there are some who perceive professional league and tour sports more favorably than big-time college sport because the pros, whose participants unashamedly pay for play in the employ of owners seeking to maximize profits, are free of the hypocrisy of feigned amateurism and purported academic primacy touted by the big-time promoters.

So what, if anything, is central, distinct, and enduring about the small-time? Are the factors that influence the big-time not in play for them? For those who disavow the big-time and its trappings, the small-time is seen as an antidote, "virtually synonymous with the college spirit, in a mixture of competition, achievement, and leadership."[37] To many, the "small-time" concept is a compelling and seductive notion promoted largely by the small-time institutions themselves. Stories that further this positive brand image emerge with regularity in college publications across the country and, albeit less frequently, in the popular sport media platforms of the day. The general perception on the part of observers now is that since these schools appear to eschew the overt commercialism of the big-time, they must also be immune to the competitive pressures and expectations from stakeholders. Small-time means small stakes, it is reasoned, so why would these schools stoop to sully their image? Such perceptions have become an elemental part of the brand identity of the small, selective American liberal arts college.

Since NESCAC has become the most successful collective within the small-time realm of the NCAA's Division III, this success has become a substantial part of the current ideal image of the conference. Now that NESCAC schools win and win often, becoming the big-time of the small-time, athletics managers must grapple with the question of whether the "sweatiest liberal arts" notion is still valid and how important winning should be. As stated by a NESCAC president in the late 1990s, before NESCAC's athletic hegemony emerged, "NESCAC is a wonderful idea and remains a wonderful idea, although a somewhat conflicted one.... It was a brilliant concept in its origination, because at the time there was no such thing as Division III. Really, NESCAC invented the concept of Division III." This perspective captures the managerial attitude of the period: the expressed conflicts with what the extreme levels of success meant, the "idea of a self-limiting group of schools that agreed to relatively simple and relatively elegant limits on recruiting, on season length, and so on, and really tried to embrace the idea of the student-athlete." But this president understood that "the ironic source of our complexity," the fact NESCAC was drawn into a more competitive landscape, was because "we won. The NCAA created Division III, and we became integrated into Division III, and so rather than pure NESCAC against the impure NCAA, it became pure NESCAC juxtaposed against almost pure Division III."

Tufts's John Casey sagely observed that "the ongoing struggle within NESCAC has always been between idealism versus realism." Ultimately, the NESCAC's ideal image is a result of this struggle, waged among a range of internal and external stakeholders with varied perceptions of what is ideal, all of whom believed they had something to gain or lose in the struggle to shape it. And what was at stake? Through perspectives gleaned from memoranda, letters, documents, records, and publications, as well as observations from a wide variety of former and current NESCAC intercollegiate athletics stakeholders, this book examines the small-time sporting evolution of NESCAC, as driven by the individual and collective managerial actions and interactions of the membership in response to the developments of the ever-changing greater intercollegiate athletics environment, and provides context on how this evolution will likely continue. The following chapters move along chronologically, more or less, from the late 1700s to present day.

Chapter 1 documents how the future NESCACs were integral in

establishing the management, structure, and position of importance of intercollegiate athletics on American campuses in the latter half of the nineteenth and first decade of the twentieth centuries, but the evolution of the enterprise left them unable to compete at the increasingly commercialized highest level of competition. The impact of the 1929 Carnegie Report on the future NESCACs is also discussed.

Chapter 2 recounts how, as the competitive athletics divide widened following World War II, Amherst, Bowdoin, Wesleyan, and Williams responded by establishing a loosely structured athletics conference, based closely on that of the Ivy League. Nonetheless, the agreement failed to solve fully the competitive conflicts among schools, primarily in the area of recruiting of athletics prospects. The defining characteristics of athletic conferences are also presented and applied, as well as the ability of conferences to define shared identities among members.

Chapter 3 is an overview of how Bowdoin and other schools in the mid-1960s sought to cover its provision of athletically related aid in relation to NCAA academic eligibility legislation, and how these machinations impacted the participatory efforts of Bowdoin's standout hammer thrower, Alex Schulten. An overview of relevant NCAA academic eligibility legislation is provided.

As outlined in Chapter 2, the formation and maintenance of the Pentagonal Agreement was from the outset challenged by competitive interests from within, on the part of signatories, and from without, owing to continuing changes in the intercollegiate athletic environment. Pentagonal school presidents, who possessed varying degrees of familiarity and interest in issues and practices related to intercollegiate athletic management, attempted to maintain the operation of this loose confederation, often over the objections of their athletic directors, coaches, and student-athletes. Over the course of the 1960s, they cobbled together an expanded and more formalized configuration. The actual result of the process was the preservation of a substantial level of autonomy among members—for instance, there would be no requirement of round-robin scheduling—and continued presidential control over the operations of intercollegiate athletics to a level unmatched in any other such intercollegiate athletic conference or national governing body. Chapter 4 reviews this history, and the common reference to NESCAC as "the little Ivy League" is also discussed, as is the general antipathy toward it on the part of NESCAC stakeholders.

At the end of the 1960s, cultural changes impacting the nation influenced the operations of NESCAC athletics, including the move toward coeducation by the conference's formerly all-males schools. Chapter 5 addresses this shift as well as the impact of Title IX legislation. Recruiting violations in men's ice hockey at Union called into question how conference decision makers would handle internal disputes and led to Union leaving in 1978. The conference then opted to replace Union with Connecticut College in 1982 in a manner many conference stakeholders observed as haphazard and idiosyncratic. This chapter also includes a review of how influential national media outlets were now depicting NESCAC as the ideal version of intercollegiate athletics management and participation.

Chapter 6 provides a comprehensive review of conflicts concerning the ban of team sport participation in NCAA postseason play. The allowance of postseason team play in 1993 would soon lead to expectations from stakeholder groups to field championship-quality teams and to a concomitant escalation of recruiting and program intensity. This led to the transition from NESCACs Before Postseason (BP) era to the reality that NESCAC schools could compete for and win Division III national championships. This was the birth of the After Postseason (AP) era. For a brief period, NESCAC presidents considered rolling back the postseason participation opportunity, but stakeholder pushback was so strong that the scheme was abandoned. In its stead, the presidents made the long-avoided move to require full round-robin scheduling for all teams in all sports, removing a significant element of institutional managerial autonomy.

While national media outlets had expressed deep affection for NESCAC's BP-era image, AP-era NESCAC was seen as an even more intriguing concept, a mélange that combined the notion of the elite, academically inclined, small liberal arts schools nestled in picturesque New England locales with a newly established ability to achieve national athletic success. Chapter 7 explores the AP era and how it led certain NESCAC schools, namely Trinity with men's squash, to seek institutional advancement through athletics success. In 2003, the book *Reclaiming the Game: College Sports and Educational Values* was published; it contained research that concluded that NESCAC athletes have a significant advantage in the admissions process and graduate at a higher rate, but most get lower grades than the majority of their classmates, "bunch" in certain majors, and practices social self-segregation that distinguishes recruited athletes from students at large. That schools cooperated with the authors on data collection and shared information gave many the sense that they had been enlisted by NESCAC presidents to take on the role of athletics in their stead; the issues raised in their book could certainly help presidents confront problems on their campuses. The chapter also reviews the proposal promoted by certain NESCAC presidents to create a Division IV classification in the NCAA only for academically elite schools, which was roundly panned across the Division III membership, NESCAC included, and thus was jettisoned. Likewise included is a summary of a 2011 lawsuit brought by former Middlebury men's hockey player James "Jak" Knelman against head coach Bill Beaney for dismissing Knelman from the team and the ascent of former William men's basketball player Duncan Robinson to the NBA—both examples of a significant shift in the stakeholder perceptions of what the role of NESCAC athletics should be.

Chapter 8 provides an overview of the importance of recruiting activities in acquiring talented prospective student-athletes through a focus on the recruiting experiences of several former and current NESCAC student-athletes. The evolution of recruiting practices reveals a significant shift toward the formalization and professionalization of coaches' recruiting efforts that often negatively impact prospects and their families. The establishment of NESCAC recruiting guidelines is also outlined, including the "banding system," which limits the number and types of academically qualified prospects each school can admit.

Finally, the epilogue examines how the NESCACs will manage significant issues in the ever-evolving intercollegiate athletics environment, specifically: using athletics recruiting to achieve institutional diversity goals at Amherst, reacting to calls for student-athlete compensation, and managing the likely end of football at several member schools where programs have faced years of losing seasons and increasingly difficult recruiting realities.

CHAPTER 1

An Ideal Is Born

The Future NESCACs in the Emerging Intercollegiate Athletics Landscape

The Nineteenth Century

NESCAC documents state that the conference was founded on March 21, 1971. While technically true, the factors that led to the formalization of the assemblage had been brewing for close to two centuries. Nearly a century before the advent of intercollegiate athletics, students formed literary societies and Greek-letter fraternities and organized on-campus intramural contests. When athletics, games, and contests occurred, faculty usually decried them, as evidenced as early as 1787, when Princeton's faculty forbade students to participate in shinny, a form of hockey, because it was "low and unbecoming gentlemen and scholars."[1] Colleges had always "had lists of things forbidden ... refusing a variety of activities thought to be harmful to moral character, learning or safety," including "card playing, drinking, smoking," and sports, and a student at King's College (now Columbia University) was punished for swimming off campus with confinement to his room and the command to translate Latin for a week.[2]

But students persisted, for the most part because, as one Amherst student of the day noted, such physical activities "served to vary the monotony, and relieve the dryness of college duties."[3] Students participated in exercise regimens, a precursor of the gymnasium movement of the 1820s, with colleges formally incorporating such programs by mid-century. Amherst was the first school to add a Department of Hygiene and Physical Education in 1860, in hopes of channeling student activity to these areas. Soon, though, the movement was perceived by students as "so mechanical, so business-like."[4] Some presidents also criticized the movement; Williams president Paul Chadbourne huffed, "I would rather a man spend an hour digging out a stump than in rolling over in a shed and calling it gymnastics."[5]

In response to the disinterest in gymnastics but a continued and growing interest in physical activity, students chose instead to compete in sports such as baseball, crew, track, and football. As sport grew on campus, students began to look beyond their campus boundaries for challenges, and that came in August 1852 in a crew race between boats from Harvard and Yale at Center Harbor on New Hampshire's Lake Winnipesaukee. The offer to sponsor the race came from James Elkins, a superintendent for the Boston, Concord, and Montreal Railroad. Elkins and the railroad company believed that spectators keen on watching such a race would secure passage on the train to the site, so they paid for the travel and week's lodging for the two teams, who saw the junket as a "jolly lark" staged "for the gratification of the townspeople."[6] The company's speculation proved correct, as about a thousand spectators, including future U.S. president (and Bowdoin alumnus) Franklin Pierce, watched the Harvard crew guide its boat, the *Oneida*, to a win in the morning's 1.5-mile practice race. After a respite of lunch, mineral water, ale, brandy, and cigars, the Harvard students won the official two-mile afternoon race as well. For their efforts, the victors took home a handsome pair of silver-tipped black walnut oars.[7] Other crew regattas would follow, as would expansion into intercollegiate events in other sports. By 1870, "athletics had won a recognized place in college life," and by 1900, "a greater portion of the public know[s] a college almost exclusively through its athletic records, for three fourths of the news items concerning student life deal with sport. ... [I]ntercollegiate contests play by far the largest part in the daily life and talk [of undergraduates]."[8] Frederick Rudolph aptly summarized that for the American college student athletics became "necessary for the fullest enjoyment of life. They were the institutions in which the student embedded his values, the values of worldly success. ... [And] at last the American college and university had discovered something that all sorts of people cared about passionately."[9]

The future NESCACs were among the institutions that first established intercollegiate athletic programs. In July 1859, Amherst beat Williams, 73–33, in Pittsfield, Massachusetts, in the nation's first intercollegiate baseball game. As was the practice of the time, students administered and organized the activity, after the Amherst student body voted to challenge Williams.[10] Amherst's captain, John Claflin, acted in the capacity of a present-day coach "and was responsible for Amherst's conspicuous superiority."[11] A chess match between the two schools was enjoined the next day, with the Williams side resigning on the forty-ninth move.[12]

Students at other future NESCACs were quick to follow suit. Bowdoin,

Hamilton, Middlebury, and Trinity all formed baseball teams before the Civil War, and many formed football squads in the 1870s and 1880s. In 1873, Amherst's Otis Benton finished third out of three in the first intercollegiate track meet, a two-mile run held in Springfield, Massachusetts. In 1875, Tufts beat Harvard, 1–0, in the first solely American intercollegiate rugby football contest. In 1883, Trinity founded the Intercollegiate Lawn Tennis Association and hosted Amherst, Brown, Harvard, and Yale in the first intercollegiate tennis tournament. Wesleyan lost to Pennsylvania in the first intercollegiate polo match in 1884, and Amherst, Trinity, and Wesleyan participated in the first intercollegiate gymnastics meet in 1889.[13]

These contests show that the line between big-time and small-time had yet to be drawn, as during that early period the future NESCACs were larger or nearly equal in enrollment to schools that would in time eclipse them athletically. Around 1880, when Yale was the largest school in the country, only twenty-six schools had enrollments surpassing two hundred; Amherst's enrollment equaled those of the University of Virginia and the University of Wisconsin, Williams's was larger than those of Cornell University and the University of Indiana, and Bowdoin's was nearly equal to that of the University of Minnesota.[14]

In the 1860s and 1870s, school administrators would impose their will on athletic programs only when they perceived athletic matters were infringing upon students' academic activities, but by 1881, Princeton formed the first faculty committee to take control of college athletics from students.[15] One of the reasons for the formation of this committee was concern over the injuries and deaths in football (see p. 28), but another was the potential for publicity and the cultivation of off-campus constituencies. Football in particular became popular on campuses, as "it reinforced elite standards within an educational setting ... [and] stood as a means of expressing, or even inculcating, the qualities of strength, endurance, and valor deemed highly honorable by generations of cultural commentators."[16]

To address such competitive concerns, future NESCACs heeded the call by the Harvard faculty athletic committee in 1883 for a meeting to discuss "professionalism," especially professional coaches. This first faculty conference on athletic reform consisted of eight institutions: Harvard, Columbia, Pennsylvania, Princeton, Trinity, Wesleyan, Williams, and Yale. "Among the resolutions passed by the conference were the following: (1) no professional athletes should coach any team, (2) no team should compete against a professional team or non-college team, (3) participation should only be on a college's home grounds, (4) no student should participate more than four years, (5) all colleges should form faculty athletic committees to approve rules and regulations, and (6) colleges should compete only against others who passed the resolutions. Once passed, the resolutions were sent to twenty-one eastern institutions.... Only two faculties [Harvard and Princeton] adopted [these resolutions]."[17] However, in 1906, Wesleyan and Williams agreed to ban from athletic competition those first-year students who were deficient in high school Carnegie units.[18] The future NESCACs were also involved in seeking to align athletics governing bodies, at first with some of the region's more powerful foes, and then with one another. In 1885, Wesleyan joined Harvard, Pennsylvania, Princeton, and Yale as a member of the Intercollegiate Football Association, the inchoate sport's most influential rule-making authority, but resigned in 1893 after injuries had reduced its squad to four players.[19] The next decade, Amherst, Bowdoin, Dartmouth, Williams, and the Massachusetts Institute of Technology entered into a short-lived football league, referred to as the New England Intercollegiate Athletic Association.[20]

The Twentieth Century

Student-run organizations operated athletic programs well into the early twentieth century at many schools, paying for programs through dues-assessing athletic associations, fund-raising drives, alumni donations, and gate receipts. The games on the field were initially run by team captains, but over time student efforts were augmented and eventually supplanted by support and direction from paid or unpaid coaches. The off-field managerial aspects were run by students for a far longer period.

Two college football historians identified developments that contributed to the rise in popularity of the sport. In his study of football in the South, Andrew Bell noted that the modern industrial era's segregation of leisure and work and the emergence of employees with discretionary income created demand for diversionary entertainment.[21] To this end, Michael Oriard, a former University of Notre Dame football player, concluded "that college football games could attract thousands of spectators with no direct connection to the competing universities." However, the consequence was that "football served disparate interests. For many university officials, building a big-time football program meant ... prestige and growth in return for surrendering control of the sport to the demands of popular entertainment."[22]

To reconcile these interests within the framework of higher education, many school presidents extolled the virtues of football in addressing the need to reestablish the virility of American males, perceived to have gone soft because of the prosperity of the Gilded Age. Williams president

Harry Garfield warned, "Here, as generally in American colleges, there is grave danger of departure from the essential idea of a college as distinguished from an institute of physical culture."²³ Others outside academia lauded the qualities of football players. A Boston-area minister preached in 1911 that had Jesus somehow found himself at a college football game, he would have "been glad to find that the players were not all tutti-fruitti, chocolate éclair, champagne Charlie boys. He would have been glad to find they were not the up-all-night-and-in-all-day kind."²⁴

Popular interest in football was a factor for the future NESCACs as well, as were pressures to promote successful grid programs. In 1890, a Williams alumnus quipped, "You do not remember whether Thornwright was a valedictorian or not, but you can never forget that glorious run of his in the football game."²⁵ In 1903, after a 16–0 loss to in-state rival the University of Maine, an unhappy alumnus wrote the college and demanded, "Old Bowdoin must fling wide open her gates and get some—some stock, sir."²⁶ Subsequently, "athletics and alumni relations became a volatile mix" at Wesleyan, as alumni who desired winning teams became "restive," especially after a 40–0 loss to Williams in 1921, and were angered when Wesleyan opted to drop Columbia in football after a series of "crushing defeats."²⁷ Wesleyan AD Edgar Fauver threatened to resign over alumni involvement in the hiring of coaches and a commitment to the operation of intercollegiate athletics "on a sane basis," but he remained in his post after stakeholder support. Later, President Victor Butterfield sought help from alumni in recruiting more "competent athletes," but only those he thought could "compete evenly" in terms of the school's academic demands. However, when the Cardinals went undefeated for twenty-three straight games in the late 1940s, Butterfield needed to "persuade" many that the "gladiatorial success" was not gained by compromising academic standards.²⁸ Nonetheless, as a history of Wesleyan avers, "there was no reason for serious concern about overemphasis on sports at Wesleyan,"²⁹ furthering a perspective that the school and its cohort had cultivated the ideal approach to the enterprise.

At Bowdoin, President Kenneth Sills had to address issues pertaining to recruiting and financial aid for athletic prospects, and as a result he amended the college's traditional policy of refusing to award prematriculation scholarships. Sills "also counted on being informed whenever [a student denied such aid who chose to attend another school] turned out to be a half-back who later wreaked havoc on [Bowdoin's] Whittier Field.... Reluctant as he was to abandon this position, he was ultimately compelled to yield."³⁰ Most likely the source providing the information would be Bowdoin coaches or alumni.

One of the elements of football that proved difficult to control was on-field, in-game violence. At the turn of the twentieth century, such violence seriously threatened the game's existence. Contributing factors were dangerous game tactics (including momentum plays, such as the flying wedge and linemen lining up in the backfield, and mass plays where teammates pushed and pulled a ballcarrier down the field—even picking up and hurling him through the air was legal) and rules that required ballcarriers to verbally call themselves "down," allowing defenders to pile on until the "down" call was made, as well as the inability or unwillingness of the sport's power programs and managers to curb these practices. As a result, severe injuries were frequent and fatalities common (in 1905, at least three men died and eighty-eight were seriously injured playing college football, although some contemporary press reports put the death toll at twenty-five). President Theodore Roosevelt, a Harvard grad and parent of a son who suffered a broken nose during a frosh game at his alma mater that year, was an unabashed supporter of the sport. "I would rather see my boys play it than see them play any other," said Roosevelt. "The rough play, if confined within manly and honorable limits, is an advantage."[31] Roosevelt had been lauded by Bowdoin president William Hyde as one who "has wrought in the world what he was taught in college and shown the power for good a college man can be." Even though Roosevelt was "at heart a college man," Harvard president Charles Eliot remarked, "it does not seem to me that a university would be an appropriate monument to Theodore Roosevelt,"[32] diminishing the import of his own institution. Indeed, when Roosevelt spoke at the 1905 Williams commencement, the campus student paper reported that a large majority of faculty and administrators had voted for him in the previous fall's presidential election. After the ceremony, the school awarded Roosevelt with its highest honorary degree.[33] Another U.S. president was a booster of college football, the future NESCACs in particular. When a professor at Wesleyan, Woodrow Wilson arranged coaching sessions for players, attended practices, and occasionally traveled with the team on road trips.[34]

In response to the controversy over violence, Roosevelt summoned coaches from Harvard, Princeton, and Yale to the White House in October 1905, just four months after his commencement visit to Williams, to lobby these leading programs to reform the sport. Notwithstanding Roosevelt's efforts (he ultimately had no power to compel changes in the game), the death of Harold Moore (a player at future founding NESCAC school Union College, which left the conference after conflicts over the operations of its men's ice hockey program—see Chapter 5) by cerebral hemorrhage after making a tackle in a game the next month against New York University would prove to be a seminal occurrence in efforts to reform the governance of intercollegiate athletics. Eventually, rules changes were instituted in hopes of making the game safer, including the forward pass—the first of which was credited to Wesleyan's Sammy Moore to teammate Van Tassell in a 21–0 loss to Yale in 1906[35] (although former Wesleyan sports information director [SID] Brian Katten indicated the school couldn't provide absolute evidence of the event, with some reports noting a pass thrown in a University of Chicago game the same day)—a neutral zone at the line of scrimmage with a minimum of seven men required on the line, and the elimination of mass and momentum plays. These alterations helped to create a more exciting game and to usher in decades of growing popularity for college football.

Big-Time for a Short Time

As the American academic and athletic landscapes shifted because of various factors, the future NESCACs found competition against big-time foundational opponents increasingly difficult. The historic eastern powers had not declined in emphasis or ability, but "talent had become distributed nationwide," since the number of degree-granting colleges grew from 25 in 1800, to 52 in 1820, to 241 by 1860 (not including another 40 that had started then ceased operation).[36] In response, school leaders at the future NESCACs sought to build on their shared identity and entered into other formalized agreements to protect their competitive interests, albeit tentatively. This was very much in keeping with the American model of administrative control, where an external oversight board "vested the office of the college president with administrative authority," an innovation in structure and accountability that would have "enduring consequences," one of which was the constant need to raise funds, which meant that presidents would need to be entrepreneurs "in the broadest and best sense of the word."[37]

At a March 1922 meeting of presidents from twelve New England and New York schools (including Amherst, Bowdoin, Wesleyan, and Williams) to discuss athletics problems, some were "convinced that no improvement in control of athletics could come without united action." At another meeting the next month in Springfield, Massachusetts, Bowdoin president Sills helped draw up a resolution in which the heads of eleven New England colleges agreed to urge their trustees and faculties, beginning in the fall of 1923, "to appoint all coaches in the same way as are members of the Faculty and other officers of the institution."[38] These constituted the earliest inklings of coordinated actions among schools that would eventually participate in the Pentagonal Agreement. Additionally, there were cooperative efforts among future Pentagonal students that promoted student-athlete freedom, as in 1908, when students from Amherst, Williams, and Wesleyan voted overwhelmingly to oppose the curtailing of summer baseball, where players could play for pay.[39] Nearly a century later, students would again coordinate efforts to agitate for their participatory rights around opportunities for postseason play (see Chapter 6).

Nonetheless, the management of these issues led to conflicts among the future NESCACs and a "corrosive effect on intercollegiate relations," as evidenced in 1897, when the Amherst student newspaper decried alleged collusion between game officials and Williams players that precipitated a football loss for Amherst. The Williams paper responded that "a certain amount of discourtesy" from Amherst was always expected and that the allegation was an "absolute falsification."[40] In 1915, after Trinity expanded eligibility rules to allow first-year students immediate athletic eligibility, Wesleyan's athletic council opted to suspend play with the local rival. Once resumed, relations between the two schools soured again in 1920, when Wesleyan fans accused Trinity's football team of "rough tactics" and "dirty play," with both schools deciding to sever athletic relations, which would not be resumed until 1925.[41]

The Carnegie Report: Corruption of Just the Big-Time?

Immediately following World War I, "a burst of sporting activity ... most notably in intercollegiate athletics,"[42] led to an acceleration of some of the trends impacting the enterprise, including the 1925 transition by University of Illinois running back Harold "Red" Grange from amateur hero to cold-eyed professional. As soon as his last game of his senior season was over, Grange told reporters he was dropping out of school to play professionally. Illinois head coach Bob Zuppke tried to talk Grange out of it, saying, "Keep away from professionalism.... Football isn't a game to play for money." Grange replied that Zuppke made a living out of teaching and coaching football, "so what's the difference if I make a living playing football?"[43] As for the coaches of the day, none exemplified the commercialization of the position more than University of Notre Dame head football coach Knute Rockne, who enlisted popular sportswriter Christy Walsh to serve as his agent and representative to negotiate lucrative deals for Rockne for ghostwritten syndicated newspaper columns, speaking engagements, and endorsements for coaching clinics and sporting goods. Walsh also helped Rockne use job offers from schools such as Columbia University, Loyola Marymount University, and the University of Southern California to leverage substantial salary raises and football facility construction and improvements from Notre Dame. At the height of Rockne's career before his death in a plane crash in 1931 en route to California to make a film of his life story (for which he was to be paid $50,000), Walsh helped Rockne earn $75,000 a year, a sum that would not be reached by another coach until the 1970s.[44]

These issues and others contributed to the creation of the study *American College Athletics*, commonly referred to as the "Carnegie Report," the third such inquiry devoted to athletics authorized by the Carnegie Foundation for the Advancement of Teaching. The report was written by Dr. Howard Savage, a former teacher at Bryn Mawr College and a member of the Carnegie Foundation staff. The study was initiated in 1926 in response to a 1925 article written by Dr. Henry Apple, president of Franklin and Marshall College, where he suggested "that an investigation might establish that some universities deliberately offer scholarships and other inducements as a reward for athletic ability."[45] As a result, a proposal to study the entire enterprise was submitted to and accepted by the Carnegie Foundation.

The 350-page report was compiled after visits by Savage and others to 112 U.S. colleges and universities and interviews with presidents, administrators, and other personnel, with visits initially lasting as many as six days (later limited to three). Areas of focus included amateurism, administrative control, recruiting, values in athletics, the role of coaches, and the role of the press. Savage found that "whatever the reason, it is certain that the seriousness with which college athletics are nowadays taken has driven certain well-recognized abuses under cover, but at the same time has propagated and intensified them." Of the 112 schools included in its study, the report exonerated twenty-eight from "any such taint of professionalism," including Bates, Bowdoin, Trinity, Tufts, Wesleyan, and Williams.[46] However, noted intercollegiate athletics historian Ronald Smith points out two major shortcomings in the report: that "institutions that were honest in their answers were lampooned in the final document, while those that either lied or concealed data were let off generally unscathed," and that at least twenty-eight institutions inaccurately reported to have no subsidization of student-athletes.[47] Was this directly correlated with the twenty-eight Savage identified, and if so, did that mean the future NESCACs also lacked clean hands? According to Smith:

> If the study found that of the 112 institutions studied, 84 provided subsidies to athletes, it is likely that a number of the New England smaller colleges were subsidizing, either by students at the institutions or by alumni or friends. I know that some of the smaller colleges, like Trinity, had players who were not amateurs and were playing baseball in the summers for money. My guess is that other small colleges were involved in allowing professionalism for their athletes if they could find the resources to do it.[48]

In the "Administrative Control" section of the report, Savage found that "very few [schools] appear to operate upon a consistent or complete educational policy that includes athletics," and "that many university or college presidents have left the shaping of athletic policies to conferences, committees, or specialists in physical education." The problem with this, according to Savage, was that the power then lay with those "who represent not so much the welfare of the institution and its undergraduates as special interests of one sort or another, all of which apparently feel that material prosperity, their own prestige, or professional standing must be served before other ends can be considered."[49]

As evidence, Savage cited numerous cases at schools such as the University of Alabama, Boston College, the University of Iowa, and Stanford University, where presidents, trustees, and alumni intervened to press for the admittance of unqualified student-athletes. Also uncovered were cases where athletes were allowed to pass examinations "under circumstances that were, to say the least, unusual." However, in a review of the academic records of 2,787 student-athletes at fifty-two institutions, Savage concluded, "It cannot be said that in general athletes are greater idlers than non-athletes ... grades of athletes seem to average slightly lower than those of non-athletes."[50] Savage fixed the blame for much of these developments on college presidents, because "often, the shaping of [athletic] policy has depended upon satisfying as many special claims as possible without due regard to the best interests of the undergraduates,"[51] and school presidents, he believed, could best affect reform. This would be a concept that bolstered the ideal image of NESCAC decades later.

While the findings of the report proved to be an invaluable resource for data on the state of intercollegiate athletics at a specific point in time, it ultimately did little to affect reform. The report "triggered refutations and denials by college presidents, ... [and] one ritual was for a college official to endorse the Carnegie study in principle, with the specific disclaimer that its charges did not describe the athletic program at his own campus."[52] Interviews of students on campuses at the time found little concern with the report, while many periodicals questioned its objectivity. However, the general reaction was typified by the comments of Fordham University football coach Frank Cavanaugh: "Why get excited? The report only tells what everyone already knew." The release of the report coincided directly with the 1929 Wall Street stock market crash, leading to precious little media or public interest.[53]

After its publication, the Carnegie Foundation asked Savage to document any reforms instituted in response to the report; he found limited evidence of such measures. A follow-up study was released in 1931, which stated that interest in college football was on the decline.[54] The report recommended that control of intercollegiate athletics be returned to students, to be run by and for students, as if the issues plaguing the enterprise had emerged only since paid coaches and institutional personnel had taken over management duties. Savage later responded that no critic was able to refute the conditions the initial report described, but he acknowledged the report's recommendations were both nostalgic and naive[55] and likely was viewed as no more realistic then as it would be today.

Even a specific effort to involve Savage and the Carnegie Foundation in nuts-and-bolts athletic reform failed, as presidents from Amherst, Wesleyan, and Williams (as well as Lehigh University, New York University, and the future Ivies) approached Savage about the appointment of a board of review for interinstitutional auditing of athletic eligibility of privately endowed eastern colleges. Harvard president James Conant believed that only an outside group like Carnegie could get the schools to come together. But the issue died when Yale and others fought the move, as it was seen as a surrendering of institutional autonomy.[56] While such a move would have bolstered the reputation of the future NESCACs in terms of managerial transparency and connection to the more prominent Ivies, institutional self-interests, and possible concerns over what such audits might find, doomed the proposal. A similar reaction to outside review would occur in the mid–1960s following the NCAA's passage of academic eligibility legislation, known as the 1.6 Rule (see Chapter 3), and again after the publication of two books examining athletics at elite private schools, coauthored by former Princeton president William Bowen and Mellon Foundation researcher James Shulman (see Chapter 7).

Whether fully accurate or not, the Carnegie Report is commonly acknowledged as a landmark moment in the investigation of how the management of intercollegiate athletics, in the approximately half decade since the Harvard-Yale boat races of 1852, became viewed as corrupt and exploitative. But is the study a fair and accurate assessment of the entire enterprise? Ronald Smith gives the Carnegie Report "a poor grade for integrity and honesty. A true scientific study would have looked at what was good about college athletics as well as what was not good." As for the perceived ideal image of the future NESCACs, Smith opined, "My guess, and it is a guess, is that Bates, Bowdoin, Williams, and Amherst were officially (or more likely unofficially) giving aid to athletes. Much of this aid likely came from alumni, who very much enjoyed having a winning team in sports they considered important."[57]

Almost forty years after the report, Frederick Rudolph wrote that the "United States is a nation of small colleges.... These little colleges in the country—or what was once the country—are important enough to the American educational pattern to distinguish it from those other nations of the modern world." To Rudolph, "the Williams pattern, not the Yale or Harvard pattern, was a more typical manifestation of American education."[58] The subsequent decades would show that while the future NESCACs were practicing some of the ills connected to intercollegiate athletics identified in the Carnegie Report, these machinations couldn't be solely attributed to a Williams/future NESCACs pattern. However, these activities were no doubt typically manifested throughout American education, at least in the manner of organizing and maintaining athletics programs. What would occur in the subsequent decades was that the future NESCACs would prove to be unwilling and/or unable to match the degrees of activities practices by the emerging big-time programs, and the eventual acceleration of competitive disparity would demand and lead to the creation of an alternate athletics universe. The big-time period was over, and the small-time period was well under way.

CHAPTER 2

Establishing the Pentagonal Agreement
The Challenges of Formalization and Self-Interest

The Athletics Demarcations Widen Postwar

The developments that led to the emergence of the small-time had been gathering force for decades, but the issues crystalized in the years immediately following World War II, when institutions restarted their intercollegiate athletic programs after virtually all sports had been suspended during the war.[1] Prior to the conflict, athletics programs at nearly every school in the country were curtailed significantly for a period during the Great Depression, as the concomitant fiscal difficulties and turmoil of the period challenged the legitimacy and methods of American higher education institutions. While public universities poised to take advantage of federal New Deal programs had, by the late 1930s, restored much of athletics spending,[2] this was far less the case with small, private colleges. School and conference officials sought to support such expenditures through the argument that intercollegiate athletics, "characterized by unforgiving rules and fair competition, could teach young men playing and watching the contests how to survive and thrive in the modern capitalist world," an administrative defense that was "an interlocking structure of justifications, rationalizations, and accommodations, all of which worked together to buttress the institutions of intercollegiate athletics."[3] Such justifications further bolstered the liberal arts/small-time ideal, especially for those who supported the findings of the 1929 Carnegie Report and criticized the growing commercialization of programs. These programs didn't need to refute the charges of rampant commercialism to which their big-time brethren were susceptible.

Postwar programmatic resumptions served as another substantial transformation point in American intercollegiate athletics, especially among the schools that sought to compete in football, by far the sport with the greatest popular interest on the part of fans and stakeholder groups. In addition to the advent of television and the national postwar economic expansion, changes to game rules contributed to competitive stratification and led many programs across the country to realize the commercial opportunities and increased stakeholder interests associated with football. As in college football's "prosperity decade" of the 1920s,[4] these changes served to delineate further the demarcation between the big-time football programs and the rest, or as one college administrator said at the time, small institutions were facing two choices: "(1) Drop the sport entirely, or (2) Discontinue traditional competition and schedule other de-emphasized schools."[5] Well-known postwar scandals such as point-shaving in men's basketball and academic cheating by student-athletes at the U.S. Military Academy hastened the perception of big-time programs as ethically tainted.

While the Ivies would continue to play with the big-time in football for a few more years, and would, even with their academic profiles, occasionally be competitive in a manner coined as "scrappy integrity,"[6] the future NESCACs' last brushes with the big-time included Williams's one-point loss in football to Army in 1940 and involvement in the nascent March Madness, the NCAA's men's college basketball postseason tournament (Tufts lost to New York University, 59–44, in 1945, and Williams lost to Canisius College, 73–60, in 1955). In 1950, Tufts advanced to the College World Series in Omaha, Nebraska, losing to Washington State University, defeating Bradley University, then being eliminated by eventual champion the University of Texas. In spite of the separation of competitive spheres, the future NESCACs would continue to play the Ivies and larger regional universities in certain sports through the 1980s and into the early 1990s.

One example of the growing disparity in football competitiveness among members of the NCAA—and the fact that the big-time schools were beginning to bristle at the equal power the small-time programs still wielded during this "one school, one vote" legislative era—was a 1951 letter from Bowdoin president Kenneth Sills to Victor Schmidt, commissioner of the Pacific Coast Intercollegiate Athletic Conference (the progenitor of today's Pac-12 Conference). Schmidt had written to Sills, lobbying him to vote for free substitution in football and out-of-season practice. Replied Sills: "I shall instruct our delegates at the 1952 conference … to vote in favor of abolishing out of season practice, but <u>not</u> in favor of the free substitution rules,"[7] as such a measure was seen to damage Bowdoin's competitive fortunes.

Because of the expanding environment of intercollegiate athletics, both in terms of the number of schools competing and the variance in the levels of competitiveness, "the leaders and members of the NCAA experienced this growing discrepancy firsthand, and understood its implications," so in 1954 the association created the position of vice president at large on the NCAA Council, a position designed specifically to speak on behalf of the smaller colleges and universities within the NCAA membership.[8] Also, since the actual number of smaller institutions within the NCAA was growing, in 1957 the NCAA leadership launched the first championship events designed specifically for smaller institutions with the inaugural College Division Championships in basketball and cross-country. "Although the difference between 'small' and 'large' institutions was never formally defined," wrote Matthew Katz and Chad Seifried, "the creation of the College Division marks an important step on the NCAA's long journey towards their modern three-division alignment."[9] Similar championships followed for football and individual sports by the mid–1960s.

Such moves formalized the organizational separation between the realms, and the demand for postseason play would prove tempting for NESCACs as well (see Chapter 6). Bowdoin AD Malcolm "Mal" Morrell, a Bowdoin alumnus (Class of 1924 and captain of the football team his senior year) who would log fifty-two years of service in the athletic department prior to his retirement in 1967, noted this development: "Athletics have become more and more important in the American way of life, and deserve a more and more important place in colleges such as Bowdoin, even though the athletic program can never be as important as some other phases of the college work."

"A proper recognition of the athletic interests is essential to good morale," he stated, as "our undergraduates demand successful teams, as do our alumni. The general public, rightly or wrongly, judges the college in part, at least, by the way the athletic teams perform. Included in what we call the general public are the sub-freshmen, the boys who are going to some college, and even the ones who will never be athletes themselves are interested in successful teams."[10]

Conferences and the Construction of an Idealized Reality

Once individual schools made decisions regarding the operations and management of intercollegiate athletics programs—mostly in response to the changes in the greater intercollegiate athletics landscape that had occurred over the first half of the twentieth century—the need arose for schools to coalesce in pursuit of those ends. Such alliances would begin as loose confederations, which were little more than scheduling agreements, and for the future NESCACs, it would, by the end of the twentieth century, come to mean a highly formalized set of guidelines that influenced every facet of the management of the entire membership's intercollegiate athletics enterprise.

William Bowen and Sarah Levin, whose work would exert substantial impact on NESCAC athletics management (see Chapter 7), describe intercollegiate athletic conferences as "orbits of competition."[11] Such "orbits" developed primarily for the formulation and enforcement of rules governing student-athlete eligibility, ease and convenience of travel and scheduling, and "lifting some of the political burden away from the individual member institutions."[12] Intercollegiate athletics became the avenue through which the early adopters of such programs experienced their "first and main source of recurring contact," and the conference became "the crucial unit in shaping and regulating intercollegiate athletics because it can have more impact on shaping athletic policies than the NCAA." Conferences therefore became "the locus where a small group of institutions in voluntary association agree to work together, to compete while showing some sign of mutual respect and comparable academic standards."[13] Such alliances also provided a sense of a shared organizational identity, where "like-minded management can reinforce the expectations which are extant in the organization ... with rules which operationalize their common philosophy and put their athletes and coaches in social circumstances where they will be dealing with people and similar expectations and constraints and will therefore be less tempted to take the ethical shortcut to win." To this end, "the Ivy League is the classic example, but more recent examples of such alliances [include] the New England Small College Athletic Conference."[14]

But conferences—these so-called competitive orbits that operated between the like-minded for the betterment of all members—also demonstrated that participating schools must simultaneously cooperate and compete. Member schools not only came together and cooperated in the ways described above, but they also competed against each other for media attention, for prospective student-athletes and coaching personnel, and for revenues and resources to run their programs and their institutions. It is this competition that can be a potential source of conflict between schools. Michael Oriard noted that schools that sought to institute rules and regulations on their own campuses put themselves at risk, because of the "short-term advantage it could give the most direct institutional rivals in recruitment of students," and that any meaningful regulatory efforts depended on schools identifying their true competitive "peers" and trusting them to conduct programs in a like manner.[15] These organizations had "meaning that extends beyond the playing field. Institutions generally desire to compete against others that are similar in profile, including their approach to athletics," and given similarities in mission and geographic proximity, "institutions within conferences typically compete in areas outside athletics, whether in recruiting students, hiring and retaining faculty, or attracting research funding." These commonalities "create a peer group useful in benchmarking, [and] one that might even heighten competition between and among members."[16]

The 1895 Chicago Conference, attended by faculty representatives from the seven schools that later founded what would become the Big Ten Conference, was one such successful early effort to control and regulate the eligibility of student-athletes, as was the 1898 Brown Conference, attended by students, faculty, and alumni from nearly all the schools of the present-day Ivy League. The latter conclave in part sought to "'weed out' a 'student who has entered the university for athletic purposes only.'"[17] By World War I, Ronald Smith found that "a number of athletic conferences, usually on a regional basis, had been established, where legislation could be successful in directing individual colleges to follow collective rules and regulations.... Conferences were the locus of reform if it were to be successful, setting standards of amateurism, freshman ineligibility, one-year residency rules, limits on training tables, length of seasons, and a variety of eligibility standards."[18]

In the years prior to World War II, formalized relationships for conferences were by no means the rule. In 1937, the future Ivy League schools rejected the concept of full conference affiliation because of issues with round-robin scheduling, which would have meant that traditional powers (Harvard, Yale, and Princeton) would have to play half of their games on the road, which they were loath to do.[19] This was another failed step toward cooperation, similar to the proposed Carnegie Foundation board of review for interinstitutional auditing of athletic eligibility of privately endowed eastern colleges (see Chapter 1).

The Pentagonal Agreement and the Formalization of an Ideal Realm

The future NESCACs, which had been directly involved in a formative period of intercollegiate athletics in the late nineteenth century, found it difficult to compete with much of the rest of the founding group not far into the twentieth century, not to mention the emerging programs at large, state-funded public schools outside the region. As a result, Amherst,

Bowdoin, Dartmouth, Wesleyan, and Williams needed to establish a competitive realm that could accommodate its athletics ambitions while contributing to the cultivation of its ideal image. As discussed earlier, some limited steps to achieve these ends had occurred since the schools first established their programs. But formalized relations and operations would allow them to set up a competitive realm that was conceptually different from that of the professionalized and commercialized big-time.

In 1951, the five schools—each of which was one of the prototypical "hilltop colleges"—began a limited collaboration on a few issues pertaining to intercollegiate athletic policy. Five years later, Dartmouth departed to join the Ivy League, which had been to that date a loose affiliation around the management and operation of their respective football programs and had become a more formalized conference for all athletic programs, complete with eligibility rules and full round-robin scheduling agreements. It was then that the four remaining schools reaffirmed their agreement in a manner similar to that crafted by the Ivy League, identified in memoranda as the "Agreement between Amherst, Bowdoin, Wesleyan and Williams concerning athletic policies," but nearly always referred to as the Pentagonal Agreement.

The Roots of the Pentagonal Agreement

In 1945, the minutes of what was described as the ninth annual meeting of the representatives of self-described liberal arts colleges—held in Columbus, Ohio, just before the NCAA's annual convention there—noted the attendance of ADs from three future Pentagonals (Morrell of Bowdoin [secretary of the committee], J.E. Bullock of Williams, and Allison W. "Eli" Marsh of Amherst), along with ADs mostly from Midwestern schools. The minutes noted that there was a "discussion of ways of getting college presidents to take more responsibility for the proper conduct of intercollegiate sports—the desirability of more direct institutional control of athletics."[20] Morrell had referenced this group as early as 1939, when he wrote to Bowdoin president Sills about the group's fourth meeting in New York (which Morrell did not attend, though he had attended the previous three meetings). "I think we can subscribe to everything except doing away with gate receipts," reported Morrell of the group's recommendations. "The gates are an evil in the large colleges and universities because they lead to all kinds of commercialism," he rationalized, "but the argument does not hold at all in the small colleges where receipts go to the Bursar's office and the athletic programs are largely supported by appropriations made by the Governing Boards of the College." Morrell ended the assessment by acknowledging a definite distinction between the athletic operations of the two realms. "The well known general criticisms of football programs as conducted by the majority of large institutions are true," he concluded, "and part of the obligation of the small colleges is to point out that most of these evils do not apply to them."[21]

So what did an alliance mean for the athletics image of the signatories? Once the agreement was formalized—a gradual process—it was from the outset challenged by competitive interests from within, on the part of signatories, and from without, owing to continuing changes in the general intercollegiate athletic environment. While presidential control would become part of the NESCAC ideal, in terms of athletics management, Pentagonal school presidents had varying degrees of familiarity, interest, and ability in issues and practices related to intercollegiate athletic management, but nonetheless they attempted to maintain the operation of a loose confederation in the pursuit of practicality (meaning: the less time dedicated to close oversight, the better for them, they thought). However, presidential actions were often met with objections from athletic directors, coaches, student-athletes, and external stakeholders such as alumni.

The agreement, while a significant step in the cultivation of an intercollegiate athletics brand for the signatories, would not be able to address adequately the thornier issues endemic to the enterprise (namely, accusations of recruiting violations volleyed between the signatories almost from day one). Membership in the grouping was especially significant to Bowdoin, as the school had always experienced a bifurcation in its athletics relations. On one hand, Bowdoin had its Pentagonal cadre, while on the other it fostered relations with Maine schools (Bates, Colby, and the University of Maine) in the State Series. But because of changes in the intercollegiate athletic landscape following World War II, Maine's programs came to dominate State Series play, and Maine's football relations with the other three would end by 1965.

Bowdoin's relationship with the Maine schools was only one example of the varied alliances in the early Pentagonal years, as for decades Amherst, Wesleyan, and Williams had maintained a collective known as the "Little Three." Given their geographic proximity, Amherst and Williams had long-standing athletic relations, which, as noted earlier, included the nation's first intercollegiate baseball game in 1859. Wesleyan sought to gain closer associations with the two Massachusetts schools. Even though the schools had competed against one another for decades, to be seen as a "first-rate member" of the elite New England men's colleges meant Wesleyan deciding to discontinue admissions for women in 1909.[22] Soon thereafter, competitions among the schools led to some informal agreements and scheduling accords based on little more than mutual trust and a public perception of their affiliation, as verified by references to the Little Three as such in the newspapers of the day. The grouping's moniker "little" was itself seen as an idealized realm concept, meant to serve as a counterpoint to the commercialized realm of the big-time and the "Big Three" appellation for Harvard, Princeton, and Yale during their dominance of football's early days. As for the reason to connect with Wesleyan, David Potts notes that Amherst and Williams "needed worthy opponents within reasonable proximity," and while Bowdoin was "a respected collegiate colleague ... travel for athletic contests involved a hard ride of approximately 250 miles on rails or road ... [Wesleyan] was less than half that distance for teams from Williams and quarter that distance for those from Amherst. And with its new identity as a respectable New England college, Wesleyan became the more desired competitor."[23] On the enduring strength of the tripartite affiliation, former Williams student-athlete (Class of 1975) and later AD Harry Sheehy said that during his playing days "it was all about the Little Three. If I could beat Amherst twice and Wesleyan twice, that was going to be a good season." However, Sheehy added that because of the switch in focus to winning NESCAC championships, "those days are long gone now. The Little Three is important, but it doesn't have anywhere near the kind of profile it did when I was in school."

In the late 1950s, *Holiday* magazine reported that the Little Three forwarded the notion of "being distinct from any other group of colleges in the East, or, for that matter, the world."[24] What is intriguing is how references to the Little Three weren't dismissed as a diminution in the way that "Little Ivies" often was (see Chapter 4). According to Williams AD Lisa Melendy, "Little Three is not a problem because that is the actual name of the original athletic conference. It is its own strong brand," even though it was likely based on the Harvard-Princeton-Yale alliance of yore. It is also likely that Amherst, Wesleyan, and Williams were comfortable in their collective self-perception, which allowed a sense of separateness from the rest of NESCAC and bolstered their brands further. It was an attitude not lost on others in the conference, bringing to mind the mien captured in the oft-cited 1910 toast made by Dr. John Collins Bossidy:

> And this is good old Boston,
> The home of the bean and the cod,
> Where the Lowells talk to the Cabots,
> And the Cabots talk only to God.

Substitute "NESCAC" for "Boston" and Williams and Amherst for the famed Boston Brahmin families, and the amended analogy for many rings true. One former NESCAC AD said that for many years certain schools' status in NESCAC was diminished, as "there are occasions when we are reminded by the Little Three that we were guests at the party initially. The conference, in the minds of some, was founded on the backs of their elite Amherst-Williams connection, and Wesleyan to a lesser degree."

Coordination and Conflict Among the Future Pentagonals

The earliest record of specific athletic policy coordination among the group occurred in 1951, when Amherst's Charles Cole (an alumnus of the school who taught at Columbia before becoming his undergraduate alma mater's youngest president ever at age thirty-nine and who later become ambassador to Chile under the John F. Kennedy administration), Williams's James Phinney Baxter III (an alumnus of the school, a former "stentorian-voiced" Harvard professor,[25] a Pulitzer Prize–winning historian, and a scion of a Maine family of significant political and philanthropic note), Bowdoin's Kenneth Sills (a Canadian-born Latin scholar and Bowdoin alumnus whose tenure [1918–52] spanned both world wars), and Wesleyan's Victor Butterfield (whose father had been a president at several colleges and who studied at Cornell and Harvard, then came up through the administrative ranks at Wesleyan to become the longest-serving president in school history) used the conclave for a first-ever collaborative effort on a joint athletics policy. That year, the Eastern College Athletic Conference (ECAC)—a regional governing body that had been founded in the late 1930s for the purposes of assigning and evaluating game officials but would evolve to organize regional postseason championships in several sports—voted to permit first-year student participation in varsity competitions in response to enrollment pressures due to the Korean War.

In this first evidence of coordination, Amherst's Cole wrote to Bowdoin's Sills to marshal the Pentagonal schools to vote against the ECAC measure.[26] Baxter responded to Cole, saying, "Certainly our prospective enrollments would not raise the question of departure from principles we all think sound."[27] Wesleyan's Butterfield was less definite, writing to Cole, "I don't think we will move [from not allowing frosh to participate in varsity sports] unless one of the Little Four does. I haven't checked with Trinity or Middlebury on this, but I would be all for the four of us sticking by it regardless of what the others do."[28] Sills agreed as well but wished for a waiver for Bowdoin frosh who had attended the school's summer session to be eligible for the spring varsity, to which Cole agreed.[29] Butterfield's "Little Four" reference is one of the few recorded uses of the amended term, meant to allow for Bowdoin's inclusion.

Also that year, Cole wrote to Sills that Baxter had decided to abolish spring football practice at Williams and that Baxter hoped to do the same for out-of-season practice for other sports. Cole, who hoped to follow Baxter's lead, reached out to the other presidents to "inquire their attitude on the matter."[30] Cole was hoping that the other three would do the same, but as with any cooperative action, even one as voluntary as proposed by Cole, the devil was in the details. Cole anticipated this when he wrote about the need for clarification on six specific points, such as how to define what activities were allowable, when they could begin, and whether individual (not team) sports would be impacted.[31]

The best of intentions and sharing of information often did little to deter the questioning of operations among members, especially since the eventual Pentagonal Agreement would lack any formal mechanisms to ensure rules compliance beyond the avowals of the signatories, a factor that would soon complicate matters, as it would later in NESCAC (see Chapter 5). Morrell's response to Sills in regard to Cole's letter demonstrates the devilish details: "I have read his letter and can approve his purpose, but it seems to me there are a great many things involved that need really careful thought and discussion."[32] Specific issues brought up by Morrell included out-of-season practice for spring sports, as Bowdoin had to consider the rules governing its more local rivals. "Wouldn't it be a pity," Morrell wrote Sills, "to say to our track and baseball men, up here in Maine where we have such a long indoor season because of our climate, that they can't practice in the cage we built for that purpose because we are afraid of over-emphasis?" Morrell added:

> The suggested rule would mean that Bowdoin baseball candidates would not be allowed to begin baseball practice until about three weeks after Amherst, Wesleyan and Williams because our season has to start later because of the weather.... I think I can see the possibility for suspicion and subterfuge if we adopt some of the suggestions.... In general, I still believe in the policy you laid down for me twenty-five years ago when I was about to attend my first New England College Conference on Athletics. At the time you said you were opposed to having a written constitution with powers of enforcement for the Conference. You said that we would keep our house clean and, in so far as possible, compete with institutions that do the same.[33]

This statement was the first of many by Morrell plainly expressing his ambivalence toward the Pentagonal Agreement, as Morrell saw the agreement not as a vehicle to boost Bowdoin's athletics brand, but rather as one that hampered its ability to compete successfully against the other signatories.

The Revised Agreement and Recruiting Conflicts

Following Dartmouth's 1956 departure for the Ivy League, the four remaining schools reaffirmed their association in the "Agreement between

Chapter 2. Establishing the Pentagonal Agreement

Amherst, Bowdoin, Wesleyan and Williams concerning athletic policies." The reaffirmed agreement, modeled closely on the Ivies,' outlined specific protocols for recruiting and admission of prospective athletes, as well as the recognition that athletic staff members were to be viewed as regular faculty members, with "responsibilities and duties ... commensurate with their dignity as members of the faculty and with the dignity of the institution they represent." The memo announcing this accord refers to "previous agreements" that had been "reviewed, confirmed and clarified," and "the primary points ... rest not with the specific phrasing thereof, but rather with the underlying spirit and philosophy upon which the agreement is based."[34]

But as the Pentagonal presidents sought to create a perceived level playing field among members on certain issues, they were often loath to cede any local managerial authority. On the ever-recurring issue of recruiting, James Stacy Coles, the son of a Pennsylvania newspaper publisher who studied chemistry at Columbia and taught and served as an administrator at Brown before assuming the Bowdoin presidency in 1952, wrote his three colleagues in 1956 to ask "if we could exchange views on such present practices of the individual colleges as may be determined in answering these questions, on desired practices for the group, and on practices to which we could all uniformly subscribe." In doing so, Coles reasoned, "I believe that the position of each college would be stronger. While no college in the group should have its practices or standards dictated by others, at the same time, in this particular area, an accepted code would enable practices to be followed which would, in the end, be best for the colleges (budgetarily [sic] and otherwise). ... [T]he uniformity of a code accepted by all could be most helpful."[35] The Pentagonal presidents, who were asserting their role as the final arbiters for athletic policies on their campuses somewhat by default, were not averse to sharing information for the purposes of managing athletics, to some extent hoping to shift some of the burden of imposing potentially unpopular regulations on their own campuses. Such sharing of information would over time become another formalized aspect of conference operations.

The recruiting of prized athletic prospects would prove to be the primary focus of interactions between and among Pentagonal presidents and athletic directors, often in a negative context. Today, the recruiting process is the culmination of years of effort on the part of prospects and their families as they participate in school and youth sports, chasing the dream of receiving athletically related aid to subsidize a college education. But it is hardly a new endeavor. As early as 1903, Williams had shown a proclivity to offer inducements to football prospects, as evidenced in the landmark intercollegiate athletics study penned by Henry Beach Needham for the popular national magazine *McClure's*. Needham was told by a top recruit that a letter the recruit received from the Williams football captain read that if he were "in need of financial aid, there are plenty of scholarships here to be had for the asking. There are good jobs about town, and no money matters will worry anybody." Needham indicated that the prospect had also been contacted by letter by Bowdoin.[36]

The earliest documented conflicts within the group related to the recruitment of qualified athletic prospects. In 1954, Bowdoin AD Morrell briefed his new president about the history surrounding the issue of restricting recruiting visits off campus. "I am sending you a copy of the letter President Cole of Amherst wrote to President Sills in November of 1951," wrote Morrell. "We have lived up to the terms of this agreement since this time.... I remember that I told you of this policy in one of our first talks and, as I remember it, I asked you if you wished us to continue it and you said that you did. It seems to me that it would be interesting to know if the colleges on our schedules believe in these things."[37]

This missive followed word that Amherst's Cole had sent a memo to his athletic staff in March 1954, stating that the Pentagonals had agreed the previous month that "no member of the Physical Education and Intercollegiate Athletics Department should visit a secondary school, whether public or private, save on a specific invitation from an appropriate authority at that school, and for the purpose of being present at or speaking at a banquet, an assembly to present awards, or some similar scheduled function." "This," concluded Cole, "will henceforth be the policy at Amherst. Bowdoin, Wesleyan and Williams reported that they were already 100% in conformity with this policy."[38]

But concerns over recruiting issues among the Pentagonals would not be settled by a simple presidential decree, as demonstrated by letters between Butterfield and Cole in 1955. In a reply to Butterfield, who raised questions as to Amherst's recruiting practices, Cole "reaffirmed the previously made agreement concerning off-campus activities of members of the athletics staffs." Cole stated staff "would not approach prospective students in their homes or elsewhere unless that student had already applied for admission through the normal channels." "The coach at no time can offer scholarships or promise work jobs," Cole continued, and "we are prepared to continue to our adherence to the agreement on out-of-season practices. Bowdoin has already made its position clear and this letter is intended to do the same for Amherst."[39] Butterfield responded with some concern: "I am not sure it is a healthy practice for coaches to visit boys on an individual basis except on the home campus."[40] Butterfield was hardly an acolyte of the big-time intercollegiate athletics enterprise, as he had argued at a 1951 meeting of the American Council on Education (a professional association for school presidents) focused on reforming intercollegiate athletics that the group should prepare a statement "that would move all colleges, on a long-term basis ... toward intramural sports for all, with intercollegiate contests strictly limited to those growing naturally from the intramural program."[41]

Cole's letter quickly sparked concern from Morrell, whose response to his president revealed a distinct level of mistrust of peer schools and concern about potential recruiting disadvantages Bowdoin might face. "I am not sure, after reading the letters from President Cole and President Butterfield," Morrell wrote to his president, "exactly what they plan to have their athletic staffs do this year.... It would be my guess that Wesleyan might plan to live up to the suggested plan and that Amherst does not—at least until it has been discussed further and adopted." Morrell identified that Wesleyan, "with their well organized alumni group, may feel that they do not need the help of the athletics staff and so will favor keeping them absolutely on the campus as far as prospective students are concerned." Morrell also noted, "I am fairly sure that Williams and Amherst have been following the practice of allowing athletic staff members to approach prospective students who have 'indicated their interest in the college in writing to the admissions office.'" Morrell then encapsulated two key issues that challenged all such cooperative agreements: stakeholder interest and the limitations of enforcing compliance with common rules. "You told me yesterday, and I am sure that it is true, that the athletic problem causes the President more trouble than all of the other departments of the College," he wrote. "I suppose one reason that this is true is because in this field of experience the College is in open competition and the results are known to the public. I believe, however, that the troubles we speak of would be considerably less if all the colleges, or colleges on our schedule, had conducted their programs on as high a plane as Bowdoin."[42] Morrell finished his polemic thusly, framing the ideal image issue in moral and academic terms:

> Long ago I made up my mind that if I could help it Bowdoin was not going to cheat in athletics. I believed then and I believe now that a good college can have respectable teams, at least, if it employs really topflight coaches and then uses all of its resources to do, within the very spirit of the code, what many colleges are doing in a completely dishonest way—namely to attract the very best boys. The instructor in English or history likes to have bright boys in his class. How much more would he feel that way if his class competed each Saturday with similar classes in a program open to the public?[43]

Morrell's response indicates a level of frustration with Coles, who as late as 1966—his last full year in office—described himself to a presidential colleague as "a babe in the woods with respect to athletics,"[44] even though he had served as Brown's representative to the Ivy League Eligibility Committee while acting dean of the college prior to coming to Bowdoin. As indicated throughout much of their correspondences, their working relationship pertaining to athletics was characterized by Coles seeking to clarify elements he either didn't understand or didn't agree with, or responding to prodding from Morrell to have Pentagonal rules and regulations more fully enforced to Bowdoin's competitive benefit.

Recruiting Issues Come Home to Roost

The issue of recruiting came to a head in 1959, thanks in part to an item from the February 6 edition of the Williams College student paper, the *Record*. Over the next year, letters between Amherst's Cole and Bowdoin's Coles regarding clarifications of issues pertaining to coaches' visiting prospective students showed the depth and the breadth of the importance and complexity of the issue, the pursuit of institutional self-interest and self-determination, as well as a marked level of distrust among signatories.

The *Record* reported that "to obtain both the highest caliber athlete and the best student possible, the Williams admissions and coaching staffs have been hard at work speaking and interviewing at high schools and prep schools." The paper noted Williams head football coach Len Watters's "many visits" to small towns such as Netcong, New Jersey, and Saugerties, New York, and cities such as Chicago and Philadelphia. The purpose of these trips, continued the paper, was not only to interview prospective students, "but also to create a self-perpetuating interest in Williams." According to Watters, this was achieved through a series of "Father and Son" dinners. "In this way," wrote the paper, "Williams representatives have been able to address groups of up to 200 people, usually including eight to ten prospective freshmen. Films of the Amherst or Tufts football games are usually shown."[45]

Upon receipt of the article, Coles would write to the Amherst president about its content, stating, "I do not think that [the Pentagonal Agreement] prohibits Watters from talking to and recruiting sub-freshmen through the mechanism of dinners organized by the alumni ... [but prohibited] also is the visiting of sub-freshmen in their homes by coaches for the purpose of recruiting." Coles closed the letter this way with a cloak-and-dagger air, one that belied a sense of mistrust among signatories: "I am addressing this letter to you personally and am not circulating copies to Phinney or Vic."[46] Cole responded, "I do not think you are correct in saying that the visiting of sub-freshmen in their homes or other places than at the schools is prohibited by the agreement.... My own view is that we can go along with the present agreement, even though I think it is clear that Watters has been doing a lot of active recruiting within the letter of the agreement."⁴⁷

A month later Coles, presumably using a bit of Old English for gravitas, contacted the Amherst president with the accusation that "anent the Pentagonal Agreement, [Amherst football assistant coach] Dick ['Red'] Gowen has been quoted recently as saying that he has visited schools to recruit athletes, paying his own expenses.... He had no qualms about visiting these schools, even though he knew it was not in accordance with the Pentagonal Agreement." Coles also indicated that Gowen said that the Amherst upperclassmen ran spring football drills three times a week. "I have no idea how nearly these statements attributed to Gowen represent the actual situation. If there is some basis for them in fact, it is unfortunate." Coles ended the letter by proposing a summit of the presidents "to try and thrash the whole thing out," with possible attendance of school ADs.⁴⁸

Cole responded on April 11: "As far as I know, Red Gowen did not visit any schools. If he did so it was without my knowledge and approval." Cole gave a qualified denial regarding spring practices as well. "Of course there might have been. In any case, Gowen is now coaching at Brown ... and I have given the new head coach, Jim Ostendarp, the strictest instructions on living up to both the letter and the spirit of the Pentagonal Agreement."⁴⁹ Cole then agreed that at the next meeting of presidents the issue should be discussed.

Later that year, Cole turned the tables and claimed Bowdoin head football coach C. Nels Corey had committed recruiting violations. "I hear from pretty authoritatively [*sic*] that your coach Corey has been recruiting vigorously, particularly in Marblehead [Massachusetts]. I guess this is within our agreement, if he does not visit schools and the College does not pay his expenses on such trips."⁵⁰ Coles wrote back, alluding to his expanded role as an enforcer of agreement bylaws. "I have checked into the report," Coles replied, "and personally reviewed all vouchers for expenses submitted by him. So far as I can determine, there has been no violation of the Pentagonal Agreement." Corey, Coles explained, had been active in speaking to Rotary Clubs, at sports banquets, and at alumni meetings. "He has not visited schools, but I would be surprised if, in the course of his trips, he has not had boys introduced to him, and has not talked with them, just as anyone would." "The Bowdoin alumni have, for reasons which you can well appreciate, been very unhappy with the varsity sports picture at Bowdoin," Coles offered, referring to a measure of stakeholder interest and dissatisfaction. "This has resulted in a very marked degree of interest on the part of the alumni."⁵¹

In reviewing Coles's letter to the Amherst president, Morrell wrote Coles:

> I can assure you that members of our staff have not visited prospective students in their homes since the agreement was first approved.... Before the agreement was made, we did visit schools but never on any such scale as most colleges, including Amherst, did it. And we were never in a position to promise admission, scholarships or even jobs, and this cannot be said of Amherst.... I personally wish the whole thing could be abandoned by all of the four colleges and I am sure that would not mean that any of the colleges would really carry on to excess in this field.[52]

As noted, Morrell's take on the agreement was never positive, as he knew that any rules were impossible to police and enforce, and that if his president expected Bowdoin's coaches to follow the guidelines while others did not, the agreement served to hamstring Bowdoin's ability to compete for recruits.

Cole responded to his Bowdoin counterpart in a somewhat exasperated tone: "Your reply on football recruiting was what I expected, but it seems to me a little ridiculous to have a rule that coaches cannot go to schools and yet to let them travel around to meetings, large and small, where promising athletes are brought in for recruiting purposes. I presume that coaches visit prospects in their homes as well." In referencing the Williams/Watters issue, Cole said, "It seems a more backhanded and round about method than going right to the schools and seeing the candidates. I would think if we were going to recruit, it would be better to recruit openly, firmly, and frankly rather than covertly, sub rosa and by other devious methods."[53]

Clearly, the Bowdoin and Amherst presidents were unable to resolve the discord, which led to the possibility that Bowdoin would withdraw from the agreement—a move Morrell likely would have favored and one with significant ramifications for Bowdoin's athletics ideal image. In response to a March 24, 1960, letter from Butterfield (who had sent a similar letter to Baxter) asking about coaches visiting prospective students, Coles sent a copy of the agreement. (He also sent one to the soon-to-retire Baxter. In receiving the document, Baxter apologized to Coles: "I am sorry that my copy has been mislaid in my files."[54])

"Bowdoin coaches do not visit schools or visit students in their homes," Coles wrote. "They do feel free to visit the homes of alumni, as do any members of the Bowdoin faculty. I asked Charles if he wanted to bring this up at the Pentagonal meeting at Amherst when we were there in February, and he said he thought everything was working out all right."[55] The Bowdoin president seemed to be painting Cole as either negligent or obstructionist, leading to discussions that Bowdoin may want out of the agreement, either because it wanted to recruit more aggressively or because the others were recruiting improperly. In a letter from Cole to Baxter, in light of the fact that Amherst and Wesleyan were hosting "sub-freshman" days on and off campus, Cole stated that Bowdoin "should be released from the agreement if it wished to be and that the status quo should be continued for the Little Three."[56]

In response, Coles wrote to his three colleagues:

> Bowdoin College has given consideration to the acquiescence of Amherst, Williams and Wesleyan, to the suggestion of President Cole that Bowdoin be relieved from the Pentagonal agreement with respect to recruiting by coaches. Subsequent to the conclusion of the meeting at Dartmouth we at Bowdoin have given this careful consideration, and I report to you that so long as the present agreement is in effect at the other three colleges, Bowdoin wishes to be a full partner to it and will set its policies accordingly.[57]

The next day, Cole responded: "I am glad you are staying in. I hope we can get the other colleges to live up to the spirit as well as the letter."[58] Bowdoin, or at least Coles, had blinked, based on the sense that Bowdoin's athletics identity would be damaged more by leaving the agreement than by struggling within it. By maintaining membership, Coles was clearly not acting to uphold some exalted concept of academic primacy or to honor the spirit of agreements. Ultimately, Coles chose to stay with the group at the likely cost of competitive success for Bowdoin, and he always harbored reservations about how Bowdoin might be able to survive athletically as a Pentagonal signatory. In 1967, in a letter to a Bowdoin board of trustees member, Coles admitted that "in spite of the many questions and misgivings which there are about the agreement and its effect, there was a general consensus that we were better off with it than we would be without it." Coles's concern was that "wide-open competitive" recruiting would be won by the "college with the most resources." That spelled trouble for Bowdoin, Coles wrote, because "in the four college competition, Bowdoin College is low on the totem pole with respect to its resources. For a college in that position, restrictions limiting the amount of activity of all sister colleges are more advantageous than a contest in which the college with the most money is going to win."[59]

Coles then went on to refer to Bowdoin AD Morrell as part of the problem, commenting, "Actually, I think that Mal Morrell has leaned over backward and has placed extremely narrow interpretations upon this agreement—much narrower than the agreement calls for. In other words, I think we can be much more aggressive within the terms of the agreement than we have in the past."[60] Given Coles's willingness to ascribe blame to his AD, one wonders whether the reference to limited resources was a veiled message about insufficient annual fund contributions from trustees, alumni, and other stakeholders.

"Let Us Keep It Simple!" Recruiting Conflicts Recur in the Early 1960s

At the advent of the 1960s, Pentagonal presidents continued to evince little interest in investing significant levels of time and energy in managing and supervising intercollegiate athletic policy issues, even while they sought to maintain their ultimate hold on decision-making authority relating to athletics. But the period would demand that presidents respond to significant shifts in the social landscape, including antiwar protests and ever-expanding cultural changes, calls for increased racial diversity in the admissions processes, as well the transformative move to coeducation.

Allegations of football recruiting irregularities at Amherst again raised objections in 1964, when Wesleyan AD Hugh McCurdy alerted his president of a "specific case of [an] Amherst football coach transporting a prospective student from his home to campus." The matter was discussed by the Pentagonal ADs, and the "feeling was that more details in written agreement would tighten things up better. ... [V]isiting prospective students in home or going there for the purpose of transporting him to visit your college—all except Amherst feel that this violated the spirit of the rule."[61] Amherst had also requested the ability to begin fall practice earlier because of earlier opening of school.[62]

The presidents, possibly concerned over damaging their collective ideal image, were worried about public scrutiny when reviewing these proposals at a meeting scheduled for October 14 of that year. New Williams president John Sawyer (a Williams alum [Class of '39] and a former history professor at Harvard and Yale) sent a letter to Butterfield stating, "I hope it can be handled, however, in a way that avoids any prior publicity that might build up any expectations of changes in our separate campuses or lead to renewal of pressures that we would then have to cope with once again." Next, Sawyer set the tone regarding his stance on athletics: "To keep the quality and great virtues of our present athletic program requires restraint and a constant readiness to hold the line at important points. I hope we would give very careful thought before making any change that might begin the escalation that has caught and distorted athletics at so many institutions."[63]

Butterfield replied,

> I agree that we ought to avoid prior publicity that might build up expectations of changes. I suggest we do not take the initiative in announcing that we are

Chapter 2. Establishing the Pentagonal Agreement   53

reviewing this agreement and suggest that we ask our departmental chairmen not to mention the fact. If we are asked, however, I think we have got to say that we do intend to review the agreements as a matter of periodic practice but that there are no special proposals before us. If you and the others feel that this is o.k. we can let the matter ride at that."[64]

Prior to the meeting, there were questions as to whether ADs should be included. Amherst's new president, Calvin Plimpton (an Amherst alum [Class of '39] who had served in Europe in World War II, studied at Harvard and Columbia to become a physician specializing in metabolic diseases, and come to Amherst from an assistant dean's post at Columbia), wrote to Butterfield: "Spike [Coles] and Jack [Sawyer] were not disposed to meet with our Athletic Directors.... From my own point of view, I would like very much to have the Athletic Directors there, since I feel a little timid making decisions on policies which will affect them, without having the benefit of their opinions. I will go along with what the rest of you wish, but I would enter a plea that we have them there."[65] New to the position and likely in defense of his school's programs, Plimpton sought the elements of political cover supplied via the conference membership's ability to diffuse responsibility for potentially unpopular decisions.

At the meeting—sans ADs—the presidents chose to amend the agreement so that "coaches and other members of the Physical Education Department may not visit prospective students in their homes," but, as noted by Butterfield, "that whatever the spirit of the rule this phrasing does not technically prevent a coach from meeting a prospective student in a hotel or even at his school, perhaps to the inconvenience or annoyance of school officials or coaches." Butterfield then suggested wording that was later adopted in the revised agreement dated December 2, 1964,[66] but Plimpton demurred, preferring the initial proposal: "I am most reluctant to add all kinds of additions which might plug up some theoretical loop holes. This agreement depends upon our mutual understanding and cooperation much more than on any legality. If, in the future, we find abuses arising, we certainly can take steps. As a matter of fact, there has not even been a real abuse, but only one isolated incident. Let us keep it simple!"[67]

One wonders whether Plimpton sought simplicity in order to take a laissez-faire approach toward Amherst's coaches' recruiting business or whether, as a new president, he was moved to inaction because of an unwillingness and/or unfamiliarity to deal with the details necessary to strictly monitor recruiting. Either would explain multiple presidential actions and inactions for decades to come. The managerial actions, motivations, and implications regarding the creation and maintenance of the Pentagonal Agreement in the years from 1951 to 1964 reflect a gradual formalization of athletic relations among the Pentagonals. The presidents, as a group, seemed to want it both ways, to have ultimate control of athletic policy management and to invest little of the effort necessary to maintain a workable affiliation. The group's lamentations that athletic problems caused "more trouble than all of the other departments," about being an athletic policy "babe in the woods," struggling to find misplaced files relating to athletics, spending time reviewing and verifying coaches' travel receipts, and claiming that few if any rule violations were even occurring, account in large part for the various conflicts regarding the adherence to even the very basic rules and guidelines outlined in the agreement. These conflicts were also exacerbated by a significant degree of distrust of and displeasure with presidents by ADs, coaches, and other stakeholder groups, both their own and those on other campuses.

While Plimpton pined for a simple agreement, any such model would prove to be ultimately unworkable and would lead the group toward a greater degree of formalization and affiliation through the creation of NESCAC in 1971. As noted previously, all conferences, these so-called competitive orbits that operate for the betterment of all like-minded members, require that participating schools simultaneously cooperate and compete, for wins in games and, most definitely, for the prospective student-athletes to run their programs successfully. In these moments, when push came to shove, schools wanted to do what they could to win, either within the rules or outside them. However, this approach would be called out by the NCAA in the case of Bowdoin track athlete Alex Schulten through the NCAA's passage of academic eligibility requirements.

CHAPTER 3

Alex Schulten, the 1.6 Rule, and the Artifice of the Ideal Image Exposed

A significant aspect of NESCAC's ideal image was the notion that this cadre of elite liberal arts schools promoted and upheld the notion that its student-athletes were academically proficient and that the institutions were dedicated to the preservation of high academic standards. This ideal image had been additionally burnished, like all of Division III, by eschewing the awarding of athletically related financial aid to its student-athletes. These two elements were part of the foundational tenets that helped foster first the Pentagonal and then NESCAC ideal, but in the mid–1960s, actions taken to enforce a national academic eligibility standard by the NCAA forced the future NESCACs and their more prominent confreres in the Ivy League to address admission and aid policies that contradicted their idealized public stances on these issues.

Academic Eligibility Standards: An Overview

For the first century or so of American intercollegiate athletics competition, most institutions maintained a separate admissions standard for athletes, choosing to admit any athlete without abiding by the school's stated admissions policies. Since the formal inception in 1905 of what would become the NCAA—the first national governing body for the enterprise—a constant struggle ensued to come to grips with the thorny issue of academic eligibility. This was waged through the NCAA's legislative mechanisms, which raised the ire of various stakeholders, including member institutions, coaches, athletes, school presidents, politicians, and social critics. The twin goals of this arduous process can be defined as:

1. What factors would determine the appropriate level of academic achievement required of prospective student-athletes, and

2. How and when to assess these factors in the admissions process and then again once students were enrolled.

These dual factors would eventually become known as initial (pre-enrollment) and continuing (post-enrollment) eligibility. The constant friction over what constitutes acceptable benchmarks by which student-athletes are to be deemed eligible has led to an ever-evolving set of evaluative criteria, with an ever-changing corresponding degree of effectiveness in assuring that the young men and women who participate in athletics are not merely athletes but also truly students. While this actual tethering in the big-time would be called into question continually, the small-time and the future NESCACs seldom had to answer such queries.

Initial Eligibility

Initial eligibility refers to the determination of the appropriate level of academic achievement for incoming prospects. As noted in Chapter 1, the future NESCACs took part in agreements that sought to codify academic eligibility of student-athletes. By the early 1920s, most major conferences had adopted a freshman ineligibility policy, meaning that all first-year students were ineligible to compete with and against upperclassmen, leaving them to compete on frosh-only squads. Many dismantled these limit rules in conjunction with the manpower shortages that accompanied World War II and the Korean War, but some reestablished them soon thereafter. Even though frosh were ineligible at certain schools, they were still eligible to receive athletically related aid. The freshman eligibility issue endured until 1972, just after the formation of NESCAC, when the NCAA approved first-year participation in all sports (four years earlier it had been allowed in all sports except football and basketball, although Bowdoin and other future NESCACs has allowed first-year students to play football as early as 1967, since the schools did not permit NCAA postseason participation).[1] The NCAA's decision was due in part to "deep financial pressures among athletic departments."[2] This financial issue would impact the simultaneous addition and expansion of women's programs in NESCAC (see Chapter 5).

The Sanity Code

In 1939, the NCAA inched toward the creation of an association-wide standard through the establishment of eligibility rules for National

Collegiate championships. These rules were made more specific in 1946, stating that only those student-athletes admitted to their schools under the same admissions standards as all others would be eligible, and at the time of participation all student-athletes must be enrolled in a full course of study as defined by their school.[3] As with all NCAA rules, however, these were not backed with any enforcement mechanisms, hence their impact was negligible.

The NCAA's first step in coupling rules with an enforcement mechanism occurred soon after the 1946 National Championship rules clarification. At a "conference of conferences" in Chicago that year, school presidents and faculty members crafted a set of principles to deal with what they perceived as an acceleration of unsavory recruiting practices and athletic subsidies. These recommendations were then sent to the NCAA membership for consideration.[4] These principles came to be known as the "Sanity Code," owing to a belief by its supporters that "adherence to such principles [was] necessary to restore sanity to the conduct of intercollegiate athletics."[5] The creation of the code was an effort by these established conferences to stem the rising tide of competition for recruited athletes. Its name was a revised version of the original "Purity Code" title, which was dismissed as sanctimonious by scornful media members.[6]

Whatever the moniker, the terms of the code required that student-athletes be admitted under the same admission standards as all students and possess similar academic credentials as the rest of the student body once enrolled. The principles were brought to the membership for approval at the 1947 convention, including the requirement that student-athletes receive only need-based financial aid. The principles were approved by the membership, as was a proposal that the executive committee "appoint a special committee to study and propose amendments to or revisions of the constitution for consideration at the 1948 Convention."[7]

At the 1948 convention, the membership approved into its bylaws amended versions of the code. Section 4 of the code, "Principles Governing Financial Aid to Athletes," sought to address and reconcile the NCAA's academic and athletic dichotomy. Section 4(b) read that financial aid ("scholarships, fellowships or otherwise") would be permitted "if approved and awarded on the basis of qualifications in which high scholarship on the part of the recipient is the major factor."[8]

To be a scholarship athlete, the NCAA and the Sanity Code's backers now stated, you had to be, at the very least, a student capable of admittance regardless of athletic ability. The code dictated neither what players a school could admit nor which frosh student-athletes could be eligible to compete, but it did take an unprecedented step in the next most influential area: how schools could spend their athletic financial aid dollars.

The adoption of the Sanity Code also represented the NCAA's first attempt to couple the rules on amateurism, financial aid, and eligibility with an enforcement mechanism. To uphold the code, a three-member Constitutional Compliance Committee was created to hear cases and make rulings on infractions, as well as committees to investigate complaints. However, the only penalty the NCAA could impose was expulsion from the association, an extreme measure indeed.

The code met with significant opposition before adoption, as it would until its removal. Southern schools felt that traditionally stronger academic and athletic programs in the North would gain competitive advantages, and several schools, including the University of Virginia, flatly refused to comply. Virginia president Colgate Darden, Jr., believed athletes should be paid enough to allow them sufficient time both to study and to participate, because holding a job to pay for college while participating in athletics meant "sacrificing" an academic career.[9] Virginia and six other schools (Boston College, the University of Maryland, the Citadel, Villanova University, Virginia Military Institute, and Virginia Polytechnic Institute), referred to by some as the "sinful seven," were cited for violations of the code and actually expelled by the Constitutional Compliance Committee, but they were retained after a vote before the whole membership failed to secure the necessary two-thirds majority.[10]

The Constitutional Compliance Committee continued its investigations through 1950, finding Clemson University, the University of South Carolina, and four others in violation. The schools vowed noncompliance, which led to a battle over the merits of the code at the 1951 convention. Large northern schools and schools from the South lobbied successfully, by a vote of 130–60, to eviscerate the code through the adoption of Amendment D, which deleted Section 4.[11] The Sanity Code ultimately failed for lack of enforcement, and in its place the NCAA convention substituted a constitutional provision requiring that student-athletes make "nominal progress" toward a degree.[12] This elastic standard, subject to local interpretation with limited impact, was something to which all members could subscribe.

The 1.6 Rule

On the heels of the demise of the Sanity Code followed the establishment of formal athletic scholarships, as well as point-shaving scandals in basketball programs across the country and cheating on tests by football players at the U.S. Military Academy. These events renewed the concern about the role of athletics within higher education. To this point, "with an athletic scholarship system in place, it became absolutely imperative for the NCAA to establish a minimum academic level for awarding scholarships. To not do so would have fueled public cynicism that already surrounded professionalized college sports."[13] Big-time stakeholders who demanded exciting and well-played games also sought the preservation of the idealized notion of the student-athlete, where participants in games were also fully integrated in and engaged with the pursuit of a degree. The bulk of NCAA legislation over the next decade dealt with recruiting and athletic aid issues, and it was left again to conferences to create and enforce academic standards, although in 1959 the NCAA did strengthen academic eligibility standards for its championship competitions, requiring that student-athletes be enrolled in a full course of study of no fewer than twelve semester or quarter hours.[14]

As a result, the membership of the NCAA approved a national standard in 1965, set to take effect on January 1, 1966, that required an incoming college athlete to achieve a predicted first-year college GPA of at least 1.6 (on a 4.0 scale) before the prospect could receive athletically related aid, based on a computation of a prospect's class rank and standardized test score on either the Scholastic Aptitude Test (SAT) or the American College Testing (ACT) test. The 1.6 Rule was the association's first-ever minimum academic standard for the awarding of athletically related financial aid. The prospect's standardized test scores were also utilized in determining eligibility, which, according to former NCAA executive director Walter Byers, "provided an essential national comparative standard."[15]

Bowdoin: The Primary Opposition to 1.6

Opposition to the 1.6 Rule was not surprising, for, much like with the avowals of noncompliance expressed in response to the Sanity Code, many schools saw the rule as a threat to the acquisition of prized athletic prospects. Indeed, Ronald Smith noted that the rule passed with "a great deal of soul searching and rancor."[16] But criticism and defiance came from unexpected sources as well, namely the members of the Ivy League and the future NESCACs. These schools, which enjoyed public recognition and prestige as engaging in the idealized version of intercollegiate athletics, stated that they were unwilling to submit to NCAA control over their admissions processes and academic autonomy and chose to denounce the measure. Furthermore, the Ivies felt that since their student-athletes were competing in their classes against high-achieving students, their athletes might have GPAs well below the 1.6 mark, even though they were good students compared to student-athletes at other schools.[17]

Bowdoin would become more active and more public than any other school in fighting the 1.6 Rule. When the rule passed and became effective as Article 4, Section 6-(b) of the NCAA's bylaws, Bowdoin issued a press release stating, "it will continue to determine its admissions policies and financial aid programs to best serve the interests of Bowdoin students, and this cannot comply with the new rule." Said James Coles: "Bowdoin College does not differentiate between 'student-athletes' and other students. Financial aid determined on the basis of need is available to all students making normal progress toward graduation."[18]

The press release also stated that in a letter to NCAA president Everett D. "Eppy" Barnes, Coles wrote:

> So far as we can understand, this applies to "student-athletes," their admission to college and the matter of scholarships. Bowdoin College does not differentiate between "student-athletes" and other students and consequently believes that the [required certification] form involved has no application to us. All our students are admitted by our own policies and procedures and the awards of scholarship aid are determined by us on the basis of need and performance. We have no intention of altering this procedure.[19]

Interestingly, Bowdoin neither identified nor made public concerns similar to those of the Ivies, which had expressed the sense that the 1.6 Rule penalized those prospects the Ivies categorized as "late bloomers," students from "slum schools," and the "disadvantaged."[20] This referred to issues of the changing admissions activities of elite schools, which, at the time, had begun to seek students from outside their traditional private school and affluent suburban bailiwicks, since research was emerging that standardized testing was unfavorable to less privileged groups.

The Bowdoin press release then stated that based on the action, Bowdoin would be barred from sending athletes to NCAA-sanctioned track and swimming championships (the terms of the Pentagonal Agreement did not permit only *team* sports to participate in NCAA postseason events). This meant that Bowdoin's Alex Schulten would be precluded from participating in the hammer throw in the upcoming NCAA indoor track-and-field championships, an event he had won at the outdoor championships in 1964.[21] Schulten was the top seed in the association's indoor meet scheduled for Detroit in mid–March.[22] Of Bowdoin's decision, Edward Born (Bowdoin Class of 1957) attempted a numerically themed lampooning of the NCAA in the college's alumni magazine:

> If the NCAA were serious about restoring sanity to intercollegiate athletics (assuming there ever was any among the big-time powers), it would seek to eliminate all vestiges of commercialism instead of passing rules in areas outside its competence. Why not start by limiting the seating capacities of

stadiums in which college football games are played to 16,000 and the amount received for television rights to these games to $1.60?[23]

Alex Schulten: The Direct Victim

Frederick Alexis "Alex" Schulten was born in 1944 in New York City and grew up in Woolwich, Maine. He was the son of T. Tarpy Schulten, president of a local bank and a former Republican state senator who also maintained a turkey and sheep farm. As a sophomore in 1964, Alex Schulten won the NCAA championship in the outdoor hammer throw with a toss of 191 feet, 6 inches, to earn Amateur Athletic Union (AAU) All-American recognition in both the collegiate and university divisions. Later that summer, Schulten was a finalist at the U.S. Olympic Trials, just missing out on an Olympic berth for the 1964 Tokyo Summer Games (an event that Bowdoin's Frederic Tootell won at the 1924 Paris Summer Games). As a junior, Schulten continued to excel, going undefeated in the thirty-five-pound weight throw and capturing the 1965 Indoor College Championship. He was again undefeated in the hammer throw outdoors, earning AAU All-American honors and notching the top collegiate throw of the year with a school-record 202 feet, 11 inches—a mark that still stands. When he graduated, Schulten held every school record in the hammer throw and thirty-five-pound indoor weight throw (which also still stands).[24] Schulten also embodied the ideal image of the collegiate scholar-athlete and Renaissance man. He was an English major who earned dean's list honors, the president of his fraternity (Alpha Kappa Sigma), and a tenor in the glee club and the Bowdoin Bachelors, an a cappella singing group.[25]

While Schulten was clearly a world-class athlete, Bowdoin officials appeared less than enthused with supporting his efforts. The college opted not to aid Schulten with his expenses and travel for the several collegiate championship meets and the Olympic trials, a decision met with derision from stakeholders. In a September 1964 op-ed in the Bowdoin student newspaper, the authors wrote (in part with an eye to Schulten's continued Olympic potential):

> One is puzzled when confronted with the Bowdoin College officials' refusal to sponsor our fine hammer thrower Alex Schulten to the NCAA meet in Oregon and the small college meet in California. Could it be that they lacked faith in Alex's ability? Apparently school officials attempted to discourage Alex's trip.... The accolades that were won, as Alex captured two firsts, were won not only for Alex himself but for Bowdoin. He was announced and publicized as Alex Schulten of Bowdoin College.[26]

Nonetheless, the college still sought some measure of connectedness with Schulten's success. Schulten was pictured on the cover of the March 1965 *Bowdoin Alumnus*, having just completed a throw in the school's Hyde Cage in a meet against Boston University.

Opposition to 1.6 Solidifies and Spreads

In early February 1966, a week after the issuance of the press release, Bowdoin's Coles wrote a confidential memo to AD Mal Morrell, telling him that the presidents of the Pentagonal Agreement schools would be discussing 1.6 at a meeting later that month. Coles stated to Morrell that Amherst "has not gone along with this rule" and that Wesleyan "is now in the process of reviewing its position on the rule."[27] Coles may have had conceptual misgivings about the fairness of 1.6 and what it might do to the individual and collective athletics images of the Pentagonals, and he sought to parse out a way to avoid its application. He cited a memo from the NCAA's Barnes dated October 8, 1965, which spelled out that the rule was "'applicable to student-athletes first entering member institutions January 1, 1966 and thereafter.' Thus any men currently enrolled at Bowdoin would not be affected by this rule." Coles ended with the threat that "should the NCAA not change its position,

Standout hammer thrower Alex Schulten was denied the chance to compete in NCAA championships because Bowdoin refused to certify that it did not provide athletically related financial aid. Courtesy George J. Mitchell Department of Special Collections & Archives, Bowdoin College Library, Brunswick, Maine.

Chapter 3. Schulten, the 1.6 Rule, and Artifice Exposed   63

it might be very much worthwhile for the Pentagonal Colleges, along with the Ivy League Colleges, to consider withdrawing from the NCAA, to form their own association with their own championships in individual sports to be run concurrently with the NCAA championships."[28] Likely Bowdoin and the Pentagonals would have welcomed a collective action that would cast their lot with the Ivies, given their personal and ideological connections with the group. The question unanswered in Coles's threat was what benefits would the Ivies gain through turning away from the NCAA to align with Bowdoin and the Pentagonals? Such a move would likely be viewed as athletic diminution on the part of the Ivies by most observers, with potentially damaging impacts to competitiveness and spectator interest. Simply put, joining forces with the Pentagonals was an unpractical branding move for the Ivies, as noted by former Ivy League commissioner Jeff Orleans (see p. 79).

To garner support for his newfound disdain for the NCAA, Coles sent copies of Bowdoin's January 24 press release to colleagues around the Northeast. In response, Bucknell University president Charles Watts told him, "We are contemplating similar action.... I see that Colgate has agreed to it, which surprises me a little bit, as has Lehigh. I will let you know what we decide to do."[29] Colgate president Vincent Barnett, Jr., wrote Coles and noted, "Williams, Wesleyan and Trinity ... have indicated their adherence to the rule. It seems to me there is room for some difference of opinion here, and I hope the matter can be ironed out in some way that avoids an open split."[30]

But a split seemed to be in the offing, and Gordon S. White, Jr., of the *New York Times* wrote on February 18, 1966, that the NCAA was looking to head it off by giving Bowdoin and fifty-six other member schools (including the Ivies, Amherst, Hamilton, Middlebury, and MIT) a one-week extension to prove compliance with 1.6 (Middlebury, like Bowdoin, had also refused to comply). The NCAA's Wiles Hallock stated that the extensions were granted "because [the schools] have had correspondences with the NCAA office on the problem and in some cases it is a matter of technical difficulties."[31] But White noted that the Ivy League "has insisted all along it will not fill out the required form of compliance and has even threatened to resign from the NCAA over the issue."[32]

Two days later, the NCAA reported that 410 of its 571 member schools were in compliance.[33] Two days after that, the Ivies indicated compliance, even though the schools never filled out the proper forms[34]—likely to preserve the league's slot in the upcoming NCAA men's basketball tournament. Princeton president Robert Goheen said in a statement that the Ivies were unwilling to submit the certification forms, but that each institution would be willing to send a letter to the NCAA outlining its academic standards. "We have discussed the matter several times," said Barnes. "There is a meeting of the minds between myself and President Goheen. No form is necessary. The letter will suffice."[35]

Nevertheless, a week later the Ivies were banned from all NCAA postseason events after Pennsylvania and Yale were deemed ineligible because the schools refused to comply.[36] After Pennsylvania informed the NCAA it would not comply, NCAA executive director Walter Byers ruled that "on the basis of Pennsylvania's statement, it is ineligible for NCAA events. The NCAA Council is the governing authority in this case and any decision to change the present situation is a matter for the council."[37] The actions of the Ivies would seem to have bolstered Bowdoin's position on 1.6, as the institution would have been seen favorably by some to be acting like the Ivies. The *New York Times* article also mentioned that Williams would not comply, furthering its fellow Pentagonal's stance.[38]

In late February 1966, NCAA president Barnes wrote to *Sports Illustrated* after the magazine wrote critically of 1.6. Barnes reiterated that "the legislation simply states that if a college intends to compete with its sister institutions for national championship honors, it should require a minimum 1.6 average of students who are receiving financial assistance based in any part on athletic ability before they may engage in intercollegiate activity."[39] Coles responded to Barnes soon thereafter, writing to him that "scholarships [at Bowdoin] are granted only on the basis of [students'] academic promise ... [and] are granted only on the basis of determined financial need and academic ability.... No distinction is made with respect to participation or non-participation in intercollegiate athletics." Coles then summarized that Bowdoin recognizes that these policies "would be in conformity with the standards of academic progress and performance expected by the NCAA of men participating in intercollegiate athletics, and accordingly, the students of Bowdoin College can participate in NCAA sponsored championships for which they may qualify."[40] The nature of Coles's response would seem to have put the issue to rest; he was stating flatly that Bowdoin gave no athletic aid, therefore compliance with 1.6 should have been a simple matter. But what Bowdoin said and what it actually did in relation to athletic aid would prove to be unaligned.

Schulten's NCAA Fate

On March 10, Nathaniel Kendrick, Bowdoin's dean of the college, spoke at the annual winter sports awards banquet, and he said, "Bowdoin could not justifiably turn over to the National Collegiate Athletic Association its authority to rule on admission, eligibility, or scholarship awards to students." Kendrick then predicted, with a possible pun

Chapter 3. Schulten, the 1.6 Rule, and Artifice Exposed 65

on Schulten's event, "I don't think this controversy is finished by a long shot."[41] A reporter at the event noted that Kendrick added, "Alex Schulten never got a scholarship from Bowdoin."[42] What is intriguing about Kendrick's remarks is if he was responding to questions from the audience or a reporter, it would indicate that there was interest in the issue. It is also equally intriguing that Kendrick made specific reference to Schulten in offering a denial that he received a scholarship. Aside from the fact that Kendrick was making public private personal information on Schulten's academic and financial status, it would seem to indicate that the concept of athletic aid was the crux of the fight with 1.6.

Other stakeholders also demonstrated interest in the issue. In June 1966, Bowdoin track coach Frank Sabasteanski forwarded to Coles a letter Sabasteanski received from a former Bowdoin student track manager, James Bradner, Jr., who was attending law school at Ohio State University. The letter Bradner sent was supportive of the college's stand against 1.6, opining,

> Perhaps it is inevitable that the scholastically oriented smaller colleges will have to withdraw from the NCAA and form their own athletic association.... What I think I am trying to say is that I hope Bowdoin will stick firmly to its present policy regarding the NCAA 1.6 rule.... I wanted the Athletic Department to know that at least one individual enthusiastically supports their conception of athletics and its place in the collegiate atmosphere.[43]

Bradner's passion is clearly expressed, including in the degree that it lobbies for Bowdoin to separate from schools like Ohio State and form a new type of association. While this suggestion, as others like it, would never come to pass, it does presage by several years the movement within the NCAA to create the current three-division classification system, which, by establishing specific missions and visions for each of the three tiers, would help keep a growing and increasingly disparate association from splintering.

However, other alumni were less than enthused with Bowdoin's tack on the issue, as evidenced by a letter published in the college alumni magazine from Joseph Tiede (Class of 1952), who wrote, "It seems to me that Bowdoin and the other protesting colleges are skirting the issue and thereby punishing their own athletes for no compelling reason.... Is Bowdoin in the habit of admitting athletes, or any students, who cannot meet the minimum NCAA requirements? That is doubtful. Then why should it object to an effort that would raise the standards that need raising? ... This attitude, in my opinion, is selfish, short-sighted, and sanctimonious."[44] Tiede's letter raises some intriguing points, especially in its ability to capture a sense of confusion as to why Bowdoin would choose to fight 1.6 and deny athletes like Schulten a chance at athletic success for what he called "no compelling reason." Like the letter from Bradner, Tiede agreed that an institution like Bowdoin, with its academic and athletic directions, should not be impeded with the dictates of 1.6. But the actions that Tiede interpreted as "selfish, short-sighted, and sanctimonious" would turn out to be focused on covering up practices that were more problematic.

The NCAA Offers a Loophole

The next February, just prior to that year's NCAA men's basketball tournament, the Ivies and the NCAA reconciled after "personal conversations" between Yale president Kingman Brewster and NCAA president Marcus Plant, which "emphasized how the Ivy Group admissions policies are such that they do not admit any students, athletes or not, who would fall below the 1.6 prediction."[45] Following this, Bowdoin's Coles wrote to Plant seeking "a copy of the agreement which the NCAA has reached with the institutions in the Ivy Group. Would this same agreement be available to Bowdoin College ... should we find it not inconsistent with basic institutional policy?"[46] Plant wrote back that Bowdoin needed to submit a statement that Bowdoin "does not accept any student, athlete or not, who would fall below the 1.6 prediction" and "confirm that for the continuing student, beginning in his sophomore year, he must earn a grade point average of at least 1.6 on a 4.0 scale if he is to be eligible for intercollegiate athletic practice or competition or if he is to receive financial aid in which athletic ability is considered in any degree in making the award."[47]

Coles replied two days later (after feedback in a memo from AD Morrell), indicating he still did not fully embrace the waiver Plant offered. "It is with respect to our inability to confirm Point 2 that Bowdoin College has been unable to indicate its practice to be in conformity with the NCAA 1.6 Rule," responded Coles, adding, "I hope that it may be possible for the NCAA to resolve this problem in such a fashion that all of its member institutions may have full and equal participation in all NCAA-sponsored championships."[48] Coles was still holding out against the NCAA's membership-approved interpretations of the 1.6 Rule in stating that the college would allow any student-athlete to compete regardless of his GPA. He was, however, being disingenuous in claiming that he hoped "that all of its member institutions may have full and equal participation in all NCAA-sponsored championships," since the Pentagonal Agreement did not permit any team sport to participate in any postseason competitions whatsoever, including NCAA championships. This postseason team sport ban had been formally approved by the signatory schools in 1961, with a substantial amount of debate concerning the ban occurring up to the point it had been approved, much of it in the form of complaints from students, coaches, and athletic directors.

While the 1.6 Rule was in theory a separate issue from that of postseason competition, the banning of Schulten because of it did add fuel to the fire surrounding the team sport ban. Initially, some of the flak was related to the perceived double standard that individual sport athletes could compete in postseason contests while team sport athletes could not. While the issue would not have been of much significance previously, the fact that the NCAA was beginning to hold college division championships meant that Bowdoin teams now had a more realistic shot at postseason qualification. This would become more problematic when the formal Division III classification was created in 1973, and it would be an issue that would continue to cause trouble for Bowdoin and its NESCAC members (see Chapter 6).

Athletic Aid: The Key Factor in the 1.6 Fight

It was noteworthy that Bowdoin officials failed to note the references to the athletic aid issue outlined by the NCAA's Barnes in his *Sports Illustrated* letter and later reinforced by the NCAA's Plant in March 1967. In the letter, Barnes stated clearly that the rule required "a minimum 1.6 average of students who are receiving financial assistance based in any part on athletic ability."[49] A year later, Plant told Coles that Bowdoin needed to "confirm that for the continuing student, beginning in his sophomore year, he must earn a grade point average of at least 1.6 on a 4.0 scale if he is to be eligible for intercollegiate athletic practice or competition or if he is to receive financial aid in which athletic ability is considered in any degree in making the award."[50] Bowdoin (as well as the Ivies and the other Pentagonals) had said all along that no such athletic financial awards were being made. So was aid going to some student-athletes based on athletic ability after all? It seems like much of the wrangling over the issue could have been avoided if the recalcitrant schools simply certified that no such aid awards were being issued. This issue was highlighted in part by a letter from Yale president Kingman Brewster to Williams president John Sawyer written in September 1967. "As you undoubtedly know," wrote Brewster, "Marcus Plant and the Secretary of the Ivy Group have been engaged in informal conversations and correspondence to see whether the Association [NCAA] and the Ivy League might resolve their remaining differences with respect to the 1.6 legislation." Brewster then admitted, "I am sorry to say that on the basis of existing interpretations this does not seem possible, especially with respect to [the section] of that legislation covering financial aid and athletic eligibility for students already enrolled," and stated, "Yale University is not able to comply with the legislation as currently interpreted ... and therefore will not expect its teams or athletes to be eligible for Association contests."[51]

The issue to which Brewster referred—financial aid and athletic eligibility for students already enrolled—would prove to be the same issue for Bowdoin as well, as evidenced by the creation and maintenance of the Arthur D. and Francis J. Welch Scholarship. Established in 1966 concurrently with the emergence of the 1.6 issue, the Welch Scholarship was given by Mr. and Mrs. Edward Morgan and Mr. and Mrs. Vincent Welch (Bowdoin Class of 1938) to honor fellow Bowdoin alumni Arthur D. Welch (Vincent's father) and Francis J. Welch (Vincent's uncle). It was anticipated that the fund would provide a $1,200 scholarship beginning in '67, with an additional $1,200 scholarship added each year until further notice. The fund was endowed with $54,000 in 1967 and funded through the deed of forty-two oceanfront lots in Ocean Beach, Maryland. Subsequent funds were added in the following years: $101,500 in '68; $125,750 in '69; $213,075 in '70; $219,890 in '72; $223,306 in '73; $228,153 in '74; $226,455 in '75. The qualifications of the Welch Scholarship were first listed in the 1967–68 *Bowdoin College Bulletin*, a college publication that served notice of courses offered, admissions policies, as well as other pertinent college information, noting the restriction: "Preference to students athletically adept and from outside New England."[52] This was not the only scholarship intended for Bowdoin student-athletes, as the 1967 bulletin lists one other grant with restrictions that recipients be athletically adept: the Class of 1940 Memorial scholarship, established in 1965, based on a fund totaling over $15,000.[53]

At the time the Welch Scholarship was established, Coles sent a memorandum to the director of admissions Richard Moll and the director of student aid Walter Moulton outlining Vincent Welch's perspective on the fund. Welch wanted the men who held Welch Scholarships to be "athletically adept and who will contribute significantly throughout a major portion of the school year to the College through athletic competition, as well as in other ways, to the extent of their ability."[54] This memo leaves no doubt that Coles was aware that Bowdoin was giving athletically related aid and that the creation of 1.6 forced the school to recognize it wasn't holding true to its stated policy denouncing such aid.

In response to this problem, the language outlining the provisions of the Welch Scholarship was amended in 1968 to "Preference to academically talented students of high character, with leadership potential and athletic proficiency, and from outside New England."[55] While it could still be argued that the Welch Scholarship was still athletically related aid, this charged was leavened with additional nonathletic requirements.

Chapter 3. Schulten, the 1.6 Rule, and Artifice Exposed 69

Interestingly, the restriction language for the other award targeting the athletically adept, the Class of 1940 Memorial scholarship, remained unchanged.

There was no doubt, however, in the mind of Welch as to what purpose his gift was intended. In 1970, he wrote to Moulton (with copies sent to new president Roger Howell, Jr., and new AD Daniel Stuckey, a Princeton hockey alumnus who came to Bowdoin after teaching and coaching at St. Paul's School in New Hampshire) expressing dismay on the qualifications of recipients. "Only one student [Ray Chouinard] has been selected who has met the athletic objective, and he's from Massachusetts," while noting that another, Allen Auerr, "has given up football in favor of tennis, which is not a sport contemplated by the scholarship, and he is also from Massachusetts." Welch also listed a third Welch scholar, freshman John D. Curtiss, who "apparently went out for football, but I haven't seen his name mentioned even once in any description of any freshman football game. It should also be observed with respect to Curtiss that the Welch Scholarship wasn't used to attract him to the college but rather was given to him after he was already admitted, which likewise does not meet the objective of the scholarship."[56] Welch's letter makes it clear that his gift was meant to attract athletically proficient prospects, and he felt the college had not met his expectations in leveraging the gift. It could be argued that since Bowdoin's public stance was that it did not provide any financial aid based on athletic ability, the college was unwilling to publicize or promote actively the scholarship, although information on the grant was available to the public through its catalog of courses, published annually and disseminated widely. However, if Bowdoin were uncomfortable with the notion of using the money to attract athletically proficient prospects, one wonders why the grant was accepted at all.

College personnel were quick to address Welch's concerns, furthering the evidence of its full knowledge of the existence of athletic aid. Director of Student Aid Moulton wrote to Welch about Allen Auerr, whom Welch addressed in his letter, explaining that it was "an old and rather familiar story. Allen lost some of his enthusiasm for football and decided not to go out for the team this year. He will continue to play tennis and will undoubtedly compete on the varsity level in this sport." Moulton noted that Allen's reasons for not playing were "rather vague: a general restlessness and some concern for his academic work which I would lump together under the term sophomoritis." "I suspect this will happen to a Welch Scholar now and then," Moulton advised, "but I hope we can pick them well enough in the future to avoid this kind of thing."[57] AD Stuckey and other administrators were also well aware of the award, as Stuckey wrote about Auerr to Director of Admissions Moll (with copies send to Moulton, new president Howell, and A. LeRoy Greason, Jr., dean of the college and future Bowdoin president). Stuckey noted that Auerr "was a fine football player as a freshman but he did not come out for the team this year and the boys were counting on him. He still holds the scholarship which may be good for another six years." Stuckey then advised his colleagues, "We don't want to get to the point where people either play or they lose their scholarships, [but] on the other hand, it is frustrating to see this situation wherein the very generous scholarship is not rewarding the kind of person that Vinnie really wants to reward.... I really think Vinnie would be disturbed to think that the scholarship was being used this way."[58]

After this, Moulton wrote to Welch to further assuage his concerns, saying the college would "review the bidding on procedures for selecting the Welch Scholars in the future," while adding, "I will select ten to fifteen (or more) of the best looking prospects from the candidate pool. After consultation with Dick Moll and Dan Stuckey, I will invite the students to participate in a competition for the Welch Scholarship. We will continue to offer Welch Scholarships only to top flight student athletes from outside New England." The goal would be "to increase our yield against Harvard, Yale, Princeton, et al, and to give greater meaningful publicity to the scholarship."[59]

Moulton's comments indicate that Bowdoin was not prepared to give publicity to the degree that Welch desired, keeping the scholarship somewhat under wraps by contacting potential recipients only after they had become part of the applicant pool. However, the word on the scholarship did leak out. Dick Whitmore, a basketball student-athlete at Bowdoin (Class of 1965) and later head men's basketball coach and AD at Colby, said, "You got four years at Bowdoin plus graduate school. It took care of several guys, I'll tell you that. In the end they had to stop that because of [1.6]." According to Whitmore, there was "very little supervisory elements that looked at financial aid that schools were doing.... I'm sure there [were] a lot of things happening at Colby at the time, same thing happened at Williams, same thing happened at Amherst." Whitmore's reference to Williams is borne out by a scholarship initiated in 1968 by the Williams Sideline Quarterback Club in the memory of a former member, to be awarded to a resident of Berkshire County who "has shown an active interest in football or other sports."[60] A week after receiving the letter, a Williams press release announced the creation of the scholarship.

A Compromise Is Reached

Toward the end of 1967, the NCAA's Plant sent out a notice to all member schools announcing proposed amendments to 1.6 would be voted on at the association's 1968 annual meeting that January. While defending 1.6 as "one of the most constructive pieces of legislation in the history of the Association," Plant allowed that "both the Committee on Academic Testing and Requirements and the Association's Council now believe that an adjustment should be made ... to accommodate the legitimate concerns expressed by a number of member institutions which follow selective admissions procedures."[61] The amendment stated that the continuing eligibility portion of 1.6

> shall not apply to institutions that use the Association's national experience tables or more demanding institutional or conference predictive formulae in [the initial admissions process] ... Such institutions shall be limited only by the official institutional regulations governing normal progress toward a degree for all students as well as any other applicable institutional eligibility rules.[62]

While Bowdoin's administrators had been making efforts to prompt the NCAA for exceptions, based on the proposed amendments it was clear that Bowdoin was not alone. The NCAA would be sued several times in conjunction with efforts to overturn 1.6, although unsuccessfully. The passage of the measure, however, resulted in the academic caliber of student-athletes improving considerably nationally. Nonetheless, attempts to weaken 1.6 had to be defeated at almost every convention until 1973.[63]

After the association's 1968 meeting, Bowdoin AD Stuckey reported to Athern Daggett, the former dean now serving as Bowdoin's acting president (Coles had retired effective December 31, 1967, a somewhat curious midyear departure): "Without considering the parliamentary jousting that went on, the result was that the amendment proposed by the NCAA Council will be in effect ... which passed by a vote of 232 to 92. ... Bowdoin can set its own policy in regard to financial aid and athletic eligibility, since its prediction tables are more demanding than the national tables."[64]

Bowdoin's Greason was now responsible for matters pertaining to 1.6 and duly supplied to the NCAA the college's predictive formula for first-year students via telegram on March 7. Greason reported that students were admitted to the college on the basis of five factors: performance in College Board tests (the SAT and three achievement tests), school records and statement, letters of reference, personal characteristics, and (usually) interviews. "The emphasis may vary as the Faculty Committee passes on each case, but no student is admitted for whom passing work is not expected."[65] The formula noted statistics for the 258 students most recently admitted (the Class of 1971, which at that time was still all male): 190 came from public schools, of whom 61.6 percent were in the top 10 percent of their class, and 68 came from private schools, of whom 64.2 percent were in the top third. The SAT verbal median was 605, and the math median was 632.[66]

In terms of continuing eligibility, the formula noted Bowdoin's unique grading system—high honors, honors, pass, fail—rather than the traditional A, B, C, D, F letter system. In this system, "pass" was defined as "satisfactory performance consistent with standards for graduation." Grades were not averaged because they had no numerical equivalents, "but a student who receives a failing grade is usually ineligible for scholarship assistance. Without numerical equivalents, comparison is difficult, but it may be assumed that a student permitted to continue in college on scholarship is achieving a 1.6 minimum."[67] It is interesting to note that Greason's formula referred to scholarship aid and the fact that any student receiving it was "achieving a 1.6 minimum." This stipulation could be interpreted as Bowdoin covertly indicating that if the college did provide athletically related aid, the recipient would qualify under 1.6 guidelines, but just the previous year Coles had written that he had an issue with the rule taking away aid from a student who did not achieve a 1.6 minimum. This doesn't seem to jibe with Greason's point that any student still in school by definition had a 1.6 and therefore wouldn't be relieved of aid.

A week after Greason's telegram and letter were received, the NCAA's Byers wrote back to Greason to notify him that, based on the information provided, "I am pleased to confirm that Bowdoin College's policies and procedures satisfy the requirements of NCAA Bylaw 4–6-(b) and your institution is eligible immediately for NCAA events insofar as this legislation is concerned."[68] Thus individual athletes were now free to resume championship participation. However, because of the Pentagonal Agreement, team sport athletes were still banned. The ultimate impact of the short-lived 1.6 Rule was Bowdoin continued to offer athletically related aid, while eventually submitting documentation that showed all its students met the rule's criteria. When 1.6 was replaced with 2.0, the case for academic certification became all the easier. Even though NCAA strictures did not restrict Bowdoin from giving athletic aid, the college's stated philosophy and image, made in part with the alliance with the other Pentagonal schools, meant that the NCAA's expansion of oversight forced college officials to respond to 1.6 in one of two ways: stop the aid or stonewall. They chose the latter.

There is a final irony to the Alex Schulten saga. In July 1972, fifty-three members of the U.S. Olympic track and field team—including five-thousand-meter runner Steve Prefontaine—took part in a ten-day training session at Bowdoin's Whittier Field on the John Joseph Magee Memorial Track in preparation for the ill-fated Summer Olympic Games in Munich, Germany. According to Bowdoin's alumni magazine, "What brought America's top amateur male athletes to Bowdoin was the Magee Track, considered one of the finest outdoor running surfaces in the country. ...

Chapter 3. Schulten, the 1.6 Rule, and Artifice Exposed   73

[T]he athletes charmed hundreds of spectators at their two-a-day workouts in an intimate fashion no track fan at Munich ever could experience."[69] Six years after 1.6 and one year into NESCAC, Bowdoin seemed to embrace elite track-and-field athletes in a way it never did with Schulten. It is not known if Schulten, then a track coach at Colby, was one of the hundreds of spectators who were charmed by the likes of Prefontaine and others. Schulten died unexpectedly in 1986 at the age of forty-two, and he was named posthumously to the Bowdoin College Athletic Hall of Honor in 2009.[70] One of the factors that may have led to Schulten's death, as well as some disputes within his family, was his faith: he was a Christian Scientist and did not believe in the application of traditional medical treatment. Colby coaching colleague Waldo Covell recounted an exchange with Schulten in the early 1970s in which Schulten disputed Covell's opinion that penicillin was the greatest scientific discovery of the twentieth century, while Dick Whitmore indicated that Schulten's wife once sought medical treatment for their child against her husband's wishes.

CHAPTER 4

The "Potted Ivy" Conference
From the Pentagonal Agreement to NESCAC

The formation and maintenance of the Pentagonal Agreement was from the outset challenged by competitive interests from within and from without. Pentagonal school presidents, who possessed varying degrees of familiarity and interest in issues and practices related to intercollegiate athletic management, attempted to maintain the operation of this loose confederation, often over the objections of their athletic directors, coaches, and student-athletes. Over the course of the 1960s, they cobbled together an expanded and more formalized configuration, NESCAC, adding seven more schools to the fold (Bates, Colby, Hamilton, Middlebury, Trinity, Tufts, and Union). Not all were prototypical New England "hilltop colleges," and in keeping with the less-than-accurate naming practices that characterized the Pentagonal Agreement, two members were universities (Tufts and Wesleyan), albeit small ones, and two others were located not in New England but in New York (Hamilton and Union). Additionally, the conference acronym, decried by a former member president as sounding "like something one takes to induce vomiting," was the same as that of a preexisting group, the New England State College Athletic Conference, an imposition that evinced little concern from the usurpers.

In June 1969, in the midst of the expansion discussion, Wesleyan AD and head football coach Don Russell penned a succinct rationale for expanding the Pentagonal grouping, citing first that "events of recent years … have made it quite evident that the control of intercollegiate athletics has passed into the hands of institutions whose philosophies differ…. If our minority role seems to be a permanent one, it would appear that this by itself would be reason enough to form a conference of some sort. A united effort could aid in protecting the interests of our type of program."[1] Russell went on to identify "recruiting and finances" as "major problems in intercollegiate athletics today": "there are schools on all of our schedules today who appear to be willing to risk strong moves into recruiting in the field and athletic scholarship programs. It is grossly unfair to the student athlete to put him into competition with recruited scholarship opponents." Russell continued:

> The spirit behind the forming of this conference today is undoubtedly similar to that which prevailed when the Little Three and the Pentagonal came into being. If the Presidents of the Pentagonal Colleges involved in the athletic agreement feel that it has been a worthwhile experience it would appear that the natural course of action would be to welcome schools of a like nature who wish to formally join in the agreement. The diffusion of pressure from alumni and student groups would be greater in a larger conference than in the present Pentagonal.

Russell's clear and cogent summation of the factors driving the Pentagonal expansion process included the need to bolster the logistical and administrative power in the implementation of athletics policy through conference membership and the ideal concept the Pentagonals enjoyed by expanding it to a larger cohort. The actual result of the process was the preservation of a substantial level of autonomy among members—for instance, there would be no requirement of round-robin scheduling—and the continued delegation of presidential control over the operations of intercollegiate athletics to a level unmatched in any other such intercollegiate athletic conference or national governing body. The tenets of the Pentagonal/NESCAC assemblage presaged many of those formally delineated by NCAA when the organization established its three-tiered competitive and governance model in 1973, yet, ironically, would not serve to influence the NCAA's process at all,[2] further evidence of the uniqueness and apartness that characterized the thinking of the decision makers during the initial formation and ultimate evolution of the conference.

The Desirability of Pentagonal Expansion from Internal and External Sources

As the Pentagonals were developing closer ties in the early 1950s, other schools both regionally and nationally sought to establish connections with the assemblage to further their own athletic purposes. In 1954, Tufts president Nils Wessell wrote to Bowdoin president James Coles about issues pertaining to recruiting and spring football practice (Tufts was Bowdoin's oldest football rival, with the first competition between the schools dating back to 1889), as well as a "recent memorandum from President [Carter] Davidson of Union College suggesting the formation of a conference of liberal arts colleges in the northeastern part of the country."

Wessell stated that such a grouping "is of real interest to us at Tufts. I hope personally that something can be done in the very near future to make this proposal a reality."[3]

Wessell's motivation came from complaints from Tufts students regarding the performance of teams and discussion on the types of schools against which Tufts competed, even though the school had just moved to university status. The school's athletics administrators, coaches, students, and student-athletes debated the issue for subsequent years, leading to the 1970 *Report of the State of Athletics at Tufts University*, presented to new president Burton Hallowell (formerly executive vice president at Wesleyan) and AD Harry Arlanson. The report criticized the conditions of athletics facilities, the lack of financing afforded teams, and the program in general and recommended athletics be completely overhauled or abolished.[4] While Tufts had been dogged by financial issues for decades as it sought to improve its admissions selectivity for its undergraduate programs,[5] the impact of the report likely influenced Hallowell's approach to improve the quality of the undergraduate experiences at Tufts, part of which no doubt meant improving the quality of the intercollegiate athletics experience. Becoming part of any Pentagonal expansion would assist in meeting this charge.

In response to Wessell, Coles wrote that "the formation of an athletic conference such as that suggested by President Davidson would be unwise for it would foster more undesirable emphasis and more undesirable rivalry among the colleges concerned." Coles then indicated that Bowdoin was "not prepared to enter any such formal or informal conference," but claimed he "would be pleased to meet with any group of similar colleges for the purposes of discussing common problems of athletic or other origin."[6] Coles promptly shared his response to Wessell with Amherst president Charles Cole.[7] From Wessell's letter it is clear that other schools in the region were seeking the benefits of becoming part of an expanded grouping that included the Pentagonals, but the current membership, to that point, doubted whether any such expansion would benefit them.

That same year, indications of interest in an expanded Pentagonal Agreement emerged from other external stakeholder groups. In what is possibly the earliest of the many cross-references between the media, the Union College student newspaper concocted a plan to form what it called a "Little Ivy League," to comprise the Pentagonals; the future NESCACs Hamilton, Middlebury, Trinity, Tufts, and Union; and Haverford College, Hobart College, the University of Rochester, and Swarthmore College. The editorial board of the paper filed a brief general report with the Associated Press wire service and reported that renowned *New York Times* sportswriter Arthur Daley pledged to promote the idea. The Union paper

Chapter 4. The "Potted Ivy" Conference

cited football as the sport behind the conference concept but felt it could be extended to all sports, while noting the major impediments to such a league: specifically, that most of the teams suggested for the league played several, if not more, games with teams outside the league; that four of the schools mentioned were already grouped (the Pentagonals) and would have to elect to break up or to add members; and that a daunting amount of rescheduling and organizational work was necessary for the group's formation. When the Bowdoin student newspaper picked up on the story, it supported the idea in concept but observed that "with so many teams in the league the situation seems to call for a splitting of the teams geographically into two divisions, or else cutting down the number of teams in the league."[8] Another famed sportswriter, Red Smith of the *New York Herald Tribune*, dubbed the concept "the Potted Ivy League."[9] To promote the idea, the editors of the Union student paper took a rare ivy plant, the African *Hedera helix*, obtained in Liberia by a Union college biology professor, and presented it to the Amherst student body as a reward for winning the theoretical conference football championship. According to Union College historian Wayne Somers, the paper awarded the "potted ivys" the subsequent two years, but after no progress on the league was made, the promotion was dropped.[10]

Several years later, an op-ed piece in the Bowdoin student newspaper wrote in strong support of the conference expansion issue in response to an article published in the *New Haven (CT) Register*. A significant factor in this shift was the emerging sense of the inability to compete with certain schools Bowdoin now scheduled, especially in football, as Bowdoin's program was in the midst of a dismal stretch, posting a record of 2–31–1 from 1954 to 1958. The piece called for "the formation of a 'Little Ivy League,' to include the 'Little Three,' and approximately five other colleges of similar enrollment and make-up, to be officially formalized as the Ivy League was three years ago. ... [The] proposed list of members now includes eight schools: Bowdoin, Williams, Amherst, Wesleyan, Trinity, Middlebury, Colby, and Union." The paper believed that such a league "would indeed make for greater student interest, if the college were competing with more colleges that resemble Bowdoin more closely than some of the schools with which we now attempt to compete, with the scores of certain football games during the past five years or so."[11]

The notion of equating an expanded grouping and connecting it to the established Ivies was a compelling one for some, but for others it would become problematic. To many, the Ivy League was a bastion of the most elite and academically selective institutions in America, if not the world, and when discussing NESCAC, many would describe it, without intent to deride, as the "Little Ivies." As noted, the Pentagonal Agreement was modeled closely on that crafted by the Ivies. But NESCAC's image was harmed by this perceived little sibling status, for, as one current NESCAC SID put it, "nobody likes to be known as somebody's little brother." When asked about NESCAC's relationship to the Ivies, current Williams AD Lisa Melendy responded, "I think the 'Little Ivies' title is problematic because it makes us seem like Ivy knockoffs or less than, rather than our own very strong brand. It does not feel like a favorable comparison when no comparison is necessary."

However, the Ivies had served as an incubator of Pentagonal/NESCAC presidents, as an overwhelming majority had attended and/or previously worked at an Ivy institution, most commonly Harvard. In 2020, all but one sitting NESCAC president (Trinity's Joanne Berger-Sweeney) listed Ivy degrees or work experience (or both) on their résumés. Hamilton's David Wippman demonstrated a trifecta of sorts, with a bachelor's degree from Princeton, a master's and law degree from Yale, and administrative work at Cornell. Interestingly, Middlebury president Laurie Patton's official biography on the school's website makes no reference to her undergraduate degree from Harvard. The biggest departure in presidential backgrounds over the decades has been the decline of undergraduate study at NESCAC schools. Of the first Pentagonal cadre, two of the four (Baxter and Cole) were leading schools they attended as undergrads, while in 2020, only three of eleven had a NESCAC undergrad degree: Connecticut College's Katherine Bergeron (Wesleyan), Bates's Clayton Spencer (Williams), and Wesleyan's Michael Roth (the only president and alumnus). At the AD level, in 2020 only three had Ivy ties (Trinity's Drew Galbraith, a former athletic administrator at Dartmouth; Amherst's Don Faulstick, a former assistant football coach at Princeton; Wesleyan's Mike Whalen, a former assistant football coach at Pennsylvania).

It could be argued that the Ivy comparison enhances the NESCAC ideal, since the Ivies compete at the Division I level, which, like it or not, brings the Ivies a level of guilt by association with the perceived ills that many assign to the athletics doings there. Bill Cleary, a former longtime hockey coach and AD at Harvard and a frequent critic of Division I's embracing of commercialism, captured this notion in the mid-1990s: "We're restrictive. They're a little more restrictive. Maybe they're right and we're wrong. They certainly keep it where college athletics were meant to be."[12] Former Dartmouth AD Harry Sheehy, former head basketball coach and AD at Williams, remarked, like Cleary, "I hope that underlying philosophies are similar," and that "there are more similarities than there are differences. But [Williams president] Jack Sawyer specifically didn't want to name [NESCAC] the Little Ivy League. He felt like we were going to be a different animal." Sheehy allowed that "there's a natural

Chapter 4. The "Potted Ivy" Conference

tendency to want to align yourself with something that you think is good" and "there are tons of similarities.... Dartmouth is Wesleyan on steroids. The Ivy's physical plants are bigger, the budgets are bigger, but I think that a lot of the same caring about the student-athlete experience is present at both places."

A letter to the editor of the *Hartford Courant* in 1983 also highlighted the issue of image, when the writer advocated that NESCAC change from its "presently unwieldy six-word" name. "A metaphor like the 'Little Ivies' may be all that's needed to give NESCAC focus and even more spirited competition," stated the letter.[13] An alumnus sent Trinity president James English a clipping of the letter. To the alumnus English responded cordially, promising to bring the issue up to his presidential colleagues at their next meeting, but he admitted ambivalence, stating, "Somehow I hate to use the word 'Ivy' in our name ... even though it would be nice if that became our informally accepted designation."[14] While it is not clear if English ever raised the issue, the conference's name remained. Such was the challenge of aligning with an organization with a well-established and identifiable image, while admitting that yours was a lesser version of it.

Interestingly, NESCAC's existence may have put pressure on the Ivies to differentiate themselves from NESCAC. Former Ivy League commissioner Jeff Orleans had this response when one of the Ivy presidents confided in him that the school's faculty was agitating to move to Division III. Orleans replied that moving to Division III would put more pressure on the Ivies, because "it's one thing for your team to lose in the first round of the NCAA basketball tournament to Michigan. But it's another to lose to Williams."[15] And wouldn't Bates, Hamilton, and Trinity love the chance to take down Harvard, Princeton, and Yale? This would come to pass when Trinity built a dominant men's squash program in the late 1990s (see Chapter 5).

Whether positive or not, a perceived evolution of the NESCAC brand by current conference ADs has led to an expression of degrees of détente with the "Little Ivy" comparison. A current NESCAC athletics administrator concluded, "I don't have a problem with it. We have more similarities with Ivy schools than differences," and averred that the tag may strike a false chord with some because "some NESCAC institutions (both purple [meaning Amherst and Williams]) think of themselves as better than the Ivies." According to Middlebury AD (and former Panther student-athlete) Erin Quinn, "It seems to me that the term 'Little Ivies' has lost some favor over the years. I remember when I was a student and recent grad, it seemed as if 'Little Ivies' was an oft-used and appropriate shorthand for NESCAC institutions." "I hear it a lot less nowadays," said Quinn, speculating that "perhaps with the rise in prestige for many NESCAC institutions, they prefer to stand on their own two feet?"

Whatever the real or perceived connection to the Ivies, by the early 1960s, some schools were clearly intrigued with the Pentagonal model. In 1962, Robert Livingston, president of Oregon College of Education, had contacted Bowdoin's James Coles and other school presidents about the possibility of the "formation of an entirely new organization of institutions subscribing to complete amateurism in intercollegiate athletics." In reply, ironically presaging the Welch Scholarship issue to come, Coles wrote that Bowdoin "does subscribe to complete amateurism. It has no athletic scholarships, and adheres strictly to all amateur codes." "However," he concluded, "we do not think there is much to be gained by working outside the NCAA. Our policy has been determined by the belief that colleges like Bowdoin could have more influence within the NCAA, particularly if they could work together within that group so as to wield their influence more effectively."[16] The 1.6 issue would cast doubt on the high-minded ethos Coles espoused.

In late 1964, Coles questioned the appropriateness of Pentagonal expansion in response to a query sent to each Pentagonal president by Norwich University president Major General E.N. Harmon. "I cannot see any particular advantage to Bowdoin College by the organization of a conference such as the one you suggest. It could alter our schedule significantly," Coles wrote Harmon.[17] Coles later sent a memo to the Pentagonal presidents stating that no one should indicate to Harmon that this issue would even be discussed by them: "If we told him we were going to discuss this ... he might consider this to be encouraging, which for Bowdoin would not be intended."[18]

That same week, Amherst's Calvin Plimpton responded to a letter from Middlebury president James Armstrong, stating, "I think your proposal for uniting with the Pentagonal on athletics is something we should properly consider at the next Pentagonal Meeting this winter. We will put it on the agenda. I am reluctant to become involved with General Harmon [and] his program at Norwich,"[19] which, given its Vermont location, was a longtime athletic rival of Middlebury's. Plimpton wrote to Harmon directly the next day formally declining the offer Harmon made to Coles. "I think we are pretty close to where we would like to be," stated Plimpton. "One way of keeping this kind of participation in proper perspective is not to have it enlarged.... Hence, while I would be delighted to cooperate with you on a personal basis, I must decline your invitation to join a larger group of institutions."[20] Wesleyan's Victor Butterfield also wrote back to Harmon that week, echoing Plimpton and Coles.[21]

While Norwich, possibly because of its military school profile, was not attractive to the Pentagonal presidents, other schools like Middlebury were. Butterfield wrote to Armstrong about this same time, noting, "I feel quite different about you and your concern; and if the Pentagonal group can find a way of extending agreements somewhat further among a smaller group in ways that would help us all to keep things in balance, I would like the idea in principle and would be glad to discuss it."[22] Armstrong wrote back to Butterfield in early 1965, stating that at his school, "I believe I will find complete support for all sections of the Pentagonal agreement with one possible exception. I refer to the permissiveness toward individual participation in NCAA meets or tournaments,"[23] which was also a contentious issue on Pentagonal campuses. Armstrong also promised to supply budget information.

1967–68: The Pentagonal Door Is Ajar

As expansion overtures were being made and rebuffed and formalization concepts were being posited, Bowdoin's Coles broached with his Pentagonal colleagues that the agreement itself was no longer an adequate governing document. In 1967, Coles wrote to his associates that "more and more there seems to be criticism of the agreement, and particularly in the uniformity of the strictness in which it is enforced at one institution or another. All of us hear tales told by our coaches of infractions of one sort or another by any institution other than our own." Coles then recounted the recurring recriminations among schools, where "a coach at Institution X is alleged to have told a coach at Institution Y that he was never instructed with respect to the rules governing recruiting by coaches, and that he has made a point of not inquiring about those rules, so that he can be free to recruit as he desires."[24]

Coles then posited, without evidence, that "the Ivy League seems to have developed an athletic agreement which apparently is operating satisfactorily and which is somewhat more liberal than the restrictive agreements to which our four colleges are signatory."[25] At that same time, Coles sent a letter to a former colleague, Brown University dean Robert Schulze, to request a copy of the current Ivy League agreement on athletics, "together with copies of any eligibility cards, memoranda distributed to Athletic Directors, athletes, and others, and such other data as might be illuminating." "The Pentagonal Agreement," wrote Coles, "seems to be creaking in spots, and may need some revising. It occurs to me that the Ivy League agreement has worked pretty well, and might be useful as a model in any revision we might be making of the Pentagonal Agreement."[26] This contact is further evidence of Ivy influence on Pentagonal/NESCAC athletics management.

But two weeks later, Williams's Sawyer responded: "We feel that departures from the basic sanity of our present athletic program should be considered with the greatest care, lest we slide into the progressive escalation that could very much alter the kind of athletics we engage in and the distinctive institutional reputation and policies in which we have long taken pride." Sawyer also was wary that changes "could also alarmingly increase the cost of our athletic programs if we had to release coaches from their duties in other seasons to scout the country for talent for a particular sport the way the big-time teams do." Sawyer warned that "if the Ivy League has slipped into the wrong direction here, I'm not at all sure we should follow them." He concluded, "I think there is an optimistic side to our policies.... As the professional development takes over bigger-name places—for instance, Cornell's all-Canadian hockey team this year—it seems quite possible that ordinary American college students who enjoy sports will find our kinds of programs increasingly attractive."[27] While the all-Canadian issue at Cornell, as instituted by Head Coach Ned Harkness, would eventually become an issue for NESCAC (see Chapter 5), Sawyer's response was supported by Bowdoin dean A. LeRoy Greason, Jr., who, when asked by Coles to review the Ivy agreement, determined, "The [Ivy] rules governing Eligibility seem far more detailed than necessary for our purposes."[28] Through these words and subsequent actions, Sawyer, who replaced James Baxter in 1961, was beginning to assume the role of "the architect of NESCAC," as described by historian Stephen Hardy. Sawyer had been a student of Baxter's during his undergrad days at Williams and was heavily involved with college life (glee club member, fraternity brother, editor of the campus newspaper), and in true NESCAC administrative fashion he earned a master's at Harvard and taught economics at Harvard and Yale. Interestingly, Sawyer never completed his doctoral work at Harvard after leaving to serve in the navy during World War II. Sawyer, possibly because Williams teams had enjoyed more success under the agreement, wrote, "I have talked over some of these questions with several of our Trustees at our mid–Winter Meetings just concluded and find deep-rooted and emphatic support for the merits of the athletic program we have collectively shared and followed."[29]

The push toward greater formalization, with the likely goal of lessening competitive differences among schools, accelerated at a June 1967 Pentagonal presidents' meeting. At that time, the group opted to exchange more information regarding athletics, specifically in the areas of the academic performance of football players receiving aid as compared with all other aid recipients, and decided:

> No student shall be eligible who has received financial support from any sources except (i) from personal or family resources; (ii) in return for services

(other than that of an athletic character) rendered through employment at normal wages; (iii) from financial aid awarded by or with the specific approval of the regular academic authority of the institution in which the player is a student; (iv) from Government grants to war service veterans or regularly enrolled members of ROTC units.

The presidents also stated that they "shall meet annually and jointly with Admissions officers, Athletic Directors, and Coaches, to affirm the principles and review the practices of the Four College Agreement, and encourage suggestions and actions for improvement."[30] Such actions clearly indicated that while some presidents were happy with the nature of the agreement in its current form, there was a sense that competitive forces were pushing the group toward a stricter set of standards, which, whether realized or not, would require far greater presidential oversight to maintain.

As the Pentagonal presidents had communicated in encouraging fashion toward Middlebury and in discouraging terms to Norwich, it was now necessary that Pentagonal leadership make clear to its stakeholders why both expansion and greater formalization were beneficial. Acting Bowdoin president Athern Daggett sent a memo to Bowdoin's Governing Boards Committee on Physical Education in July 1968, outlining the expansion issue from Bowdoin's perspective. Wrote Daggett: "Part of the motivation, at least to Bowdoin, was a certain feeling that it would be greatly to our advantage to extend the coverage of the limitations which are placed on us by the four-college agreement." Daggett described these limitations as two-fold: those placed on the use of the athletic staff in connection with admissions, and those prohibiting postseason games. Daggett noted that at Bowdoin and at Williams, "whenever it has looked as if we might qualify for post-seasonal play in hockey or basketball (the latter has concerned Williams more than it has us...) there has been considerable agitation against the limitation on playing post-season games." Daggett closed by commenting, "The feeling has been that by extending the coverage of the prohibitions we would gain in various ways."[31] The concerns over postseason opportunities was not only significant for Bowdoin in relation to its hockey program but also for other non–Pentagonal schools, as with Middlebury in skiing and Colby for baseball (see Chapter 6).

As for other stakeholders and aspirant schools, the Bowdoin student newspaper again highlighted calls for expansion, even citing the comments of Tufts AD Harry Arlanson in the *Tufts Alumni Review*. The Bowdoin op-ed said, "It is interesting to note that Tufts' football problems are very similar to ours," and quoted Arlanson as saying, "One solution to Tufts' scheduling problems would be a Little Six or Little Eight League. It could embrace schools like Tufts, Amherst, Williams, Wesleyan, Trinity,

Bowdoin, Colby, etc." Arlanson continued that "aside from giving every league member a reliable and predictable schedule of opponents year after year despite frequent variances of scores, it would provide a uniform code of ethics in conducting the entire football program—and perhaps other sports, too." "It would enable uniform financial aid assistance for student-athletes," stated Arlanson, along with equalizing logistical matters such as game scouting and film exchange. "A league championship would keep a goal in front of the players all the time," he proposed, where "even the lowest team would stay alive with the ever-present incentive of knocking off the league leader, whereas now one or two early losses usually kill any real objective for a team."[32] Siding with the school's oldest football rival, the article's author, Dick Mersereau—who would later become Bowdoin's women's basketball coach and presidential assistant—put the question to Bowdoin's administration thusly: "I hope that Bowdoin is aware of Tufts' enthusiasm and that we have some of our own. Is Bowdoin going to pursue the idea?"[33]

1968: Whither Bates?

In July 1968, the ADs from the Pentagonal schools, plus those from prospective members Colby, Middlebury, Trinity, and Tufts, met at Amherst and "unanimously reaffirmed our conviction that such a conference operating under the Presidents' Agreement would be advantageous to us all. We therefore respectfully request that our presidents consider this idea at their earliest convenience."[34] Soon thereafter, in a memo to Daggett, incoming Bowdoin president Roger Howell, Jr. (a former dean and history professor at the school), wrote favorably about the possibility of Pentagonal expansion. "My initial reaction," wrote Howell, "is that a conference of teams would be a good thing if there could be established consistent and common aims and practices. How events should be scheduled inside the conference seems to me to be a matter that the various athletic directors concerned can best handle." But Howell addressed the plight of local rival Bates, which had been absent from much of the expansion discussions:

> I am somewhat alarmed by the exclusion of Bates from consideration by the first group of colleges. To isolate them in any way will certainly not aid our relations with them, and if there is to develop real cooperation among the Maine colleges, Bates will have to play a full part. I am also a little worried, in connection with the second group, about the inclusion of the Coast Guard Academy; I am not fully up-to-date on the athletic records of New England colleges, but I suspect that in most sports they are rather out of our class.[35]

Chapter 4. The "Potted Ivy" Conference 85

Howell and Wesleyan's Edwin Etherington, who replaced the long-serving Butterfield in 1967, came into the Pentagonal athletics management cadre together. Both were alumni of their schools, but Etherington, a six-foot-two "young John F. Kennedy–like figure" with "movie star good looks," had returned to Wesleyan after earning a law degree at Yale and serving as president of the American Stock Exchange, and he would leave after only three years to pursue (unsuccessfully) the Connecticut Republican Party's nomination to run for the U.S. Senate.[36] Howell's background was more in keeping with that of a NESCAC president, having served as professor and administrator at Bowdoin after earning a Rhodes Scholarship and a subsequent D.Phil in British history at Oxford. Howell would leave the presidency in 1978 to return to teaching at Bowdoin and died in 1989 at the age of 53.

At the request of Howell, Daggett then wrote to Amherst's Plimpton, noting that in addition to Colby, Middlebury, Trinity, and Tufts, "we feel very strongly that in any proposed new association ... we would oppose leaving Bates out unless that was Bates' own wish. In this case, I understand they want to be included."[37] Soon after the July 1968 AD vote, new Bates president Thomas Hedley Reynolds wrote Daggett and stated, "This whole matter is of tremendous importance to Bates in many ways and I appreciate your helping hand.... I have been given to understand that there is no feeling among [the eight ADs] that Bates should be excluded."[38] The next day, Reynolds—a Williams alumnus who earned advanced degrees at Columbia and taught and served as dean at Middlebury prior to coming to Bates—sent a more formalized request to Daggett, admitting to

> feeling a little bit like a bride who doesn't really know whether the bridegroom is going to show up or not. If we at Bates are not permitted to join with you, we feel we would be isolated and eventually it would become difficult to play the kind of colleges we think we should be playing. Perhaps more important, there would be academic implications, again separating us from the only colleges in New England with which we are closely associated in size, spirit, and aspiration.[39]

Clearly, Reynolds was worried about Bates's closest rivals acting in consort and Bates being left on the outside looking in, and he contacted other Pentagonal figures as well, including Wesleyan's Etherington, who wrote back with less than encouraging news. "It seems evident to me, however, that it would be impossible to form a small league (e.g., eight colleges) without excluding some that ought logically to be included. For that reason, I have been toying with the possibility of a larger group which might work out a shared commitment concerning the place of athletics and within which multiple scheduling opportunities would be available."[40] Etherington responded in a similar fashion to Union president Harold

Martin, who had also written to seek inclusion ("It is always possible that some different approach—perhaps involving more institutions, a wider geographic area and greater flexibility of scheduling—will be opened up for consideration"[41]), and told Colby president Robert Strider, "It may be, however, that the best course would be to leave things as they are and just strive for better communications and understanding among all similarly situated institutions in this part of the country."[42] To Bowdoin's Daggett, Etherington confided, "Without meaning to sound un-energetic, I have to say that I think all of us have probably got higher priorities than the athletic league matter if we consider the fact that a lot of thinking, negotiating, corresponding and probably grieving would almost surely be involved." Etherington then advocated delay, stating, "I hope we may consider putting the matter on the back of a stove without necessarily disconnecting the gas pipe."[43] In response, Daggett agreed that "the matter certainly seems to be getting somewhat complex," while commenting how wonderful the summer weather has been: "We had fourteen days on the water with only one of fog."[44] Higher priorities indeed.

Soon thereafter, however, Daggett was working with Colby's Strider to get Bates included, and he lobbied Amherst's Plimpton to that end. In August 1968, Bowdoin AD Daniel Stuckey warned Daggett, "I am not at all sure that the Little 3 would continue negotiations on this subject if too many extra parties were brought in. If, however, Bowdoin's position is that it would not join such a conference unless Bates were included, I will make such a statement."[45] Daggett wrote back to Stuckey the next week: "I recognize your apprehension regarding the attitude of the Little Three. I think it may be difficult to get past the obstacle. However, I do myself feel, and this feeling is supported by the two Deans [Greason and Howell], that we should not join such a conference unless Bates were included." "This is, of course, our own opinion," Daggett clarified, since the matter had not been discussed by the college's Faculty Committee on Athletics or by the Governing Boards Committee on Physical Education. "Consequently, we cannot speak officially for the College," he wrote, "but I think you can say that the Bowdoin administration feels strongly on the matter."[46]

However, Daggett had sent a memo to the Governing Boards Committee on Physical Education a month earlier outlining the issue. Wrote Daggett: "It has been the feeling of those of us who have discussed the matter here that we should strongly support the inclusion of Bates in this group. To leave Bates out would isolate her very definitely. She would be just about the only small liberal arts college in New England not included. Our long association with her seems to me to indicate we should support her inclusion."[47]

Daggett pursued this line further in a staff meeting in late August, when

Chapter 4. The "Potted Ivy" Conference

the group took the time to evaluate the 1968 football schedules of the eight proposed members. Daggett noted that Bates was scheduled to play four of the proposed members (Bowdoin, Colby, Middlebury, and Trinity), while Hamilton, another possible member, played only two (Middlebury and Wesleyan). Daggett wrote, "Discussion, in general, confirmed our opinion that Bates was discriminated against by the eight-college arrangement. The [schedules] seem to strengthen our position in assisting that Bates be included."[48]

Former Bates men's basketball coach and Williams AD Bob Peck indicated that Bowdoin wanted Bates in "for good reasons, but there was kind of a 'looking down' on Bates from the rest of the group. But internal politics got taken care of." The reasons for inclusion, said Peck, "were obvious. Nice, very convenient scheduling. [Bates] wasn't that strong in a lot of things and was [a] respectable [institution]—much more now than it was then—but it was a respectable place, and it was the convenience of playing a neighbor school, eighteen miles of traveling, and not that strong [athletically]." As for the perception of Bates's status, Peck noted that Bates president Reynolds "was a Williams guy." "And it's so funny," recalled Peck, "[what an] old [Williams] professor, Dick Newhall, said to me one day about Reynolds becoming president at Bates: 'You know, it's interesting that a young man who really didn't have much talent could make something out of himself.'" Left-handed compliments aside, Reynolds's Williams and Middlebury connections, along with the support of Bowdoin and Colby, would serve to secure Bates's inclusion.

1968: Conference or League?

In mid-September 1968, Williams's Sawyer sent a memo to his Pentagonal colleagues that Middlebury president Armstrong had inquired "on where things stood re the July 1st recommendation" on expansion from the eight ADs. In response, Sawyer reported, "Those of us who were parties to the Pentagonal Presidents Agreement had planned to meet early this fall and give the question a thorough review." Sawyer noted that interest from Bates, Hamilton, and Union "posed serious complications of where any line on numbers could be drawn" and led to questions "of the feasibility and desirability of organizing a conference in view of the very different schedules our teams played in different sports, problems of travel distance, and other considerations."[49] Sawyer then added that he had raised the question with Armstrong of whether Middlebury's interest in skiing and soccer success "might not find the [Pentagonal] Agreement difficult to live with." Armstrong had responded that Middlebury would be "fully willing to accept its terms, which are eased for Middlebury by the fact that the Easterns in skiing are a regularly schedule event and that individuals are given latitude for post-season competition anyway."⁵⁰

Sounding a plea first lodged in 1964, Amherst's Plimpton responded that he was seeking to "keep our athletic arrangements fairly simple": "I would go along with making available to the other colleges what our ground rules are and saying if they would like to join in this kind of practice that would be fine with us and make it no more formal than that."⁵¹ While it is clear that Middlebury and Armstrong were angling for Pentagonal inclusion, there was also the sense that Middlebury wanted to protect its involvement in postseason skiing championships.

In October 1968, Bowdoin AD Stuckey wrote to Daggett that Colby AD (and head baseball coach) John Winkin was continuing to work with ADs at Middlebury, Tufts, and Wesleyan "to continue the league idea.... I suggested to him that he carry the ball on this new venture since I had done my part with the Little 3, and since I was not sure what position Bowdoin would take on such a new alignment."⁵² Later that month, Wesleyan's Etherington wrote to his Pentagonal colleagues following up on their request that he pen a summary of their perspectives on the issue. Etherington concluded that the existing agreement "could form the basis of an agreement (as opposed to a league), or some modification of an agreement could also prove to be an acceptable basis for a less formal understanding within a larger group of institutions." To Etherington, a "league" was something more official and involved, and he indicated that it "has at least some superficial appeal, and appears to have some support among some of our athletic directors." But to him, it was not "a practical or wise approach for at least two reasons: (a) It would be impossible to form a small league (e.g., eight colleges) without excluding some that ought logically to be included. (b) The formation of a league might be interpreted as a new point of emphasis on intercollegiate athletics, especially football, in spite of the fact that the true purpose would be to keep football and other sports in proper perspective." His solution was "to form a larger 'conference' which might work out a shared commitment concerning the place of athletics and within which multiple scheduling opportunities would be available for each participant."⁵³

Etherington's conference versus league discussion may have seemed to be focused on clarifying a distinction without a difference, but it was clear that whatever future grouping might be, he was reflecting the view that Pentagonal presidents wanted fewer operational ties binding members' fortunes and actions. Etherington went on to reiterate that "each of us ... probably have higher priorities than the athletic league or conference matter," and then he proposed that "we might ask our athletic department representatives to consider ... the possibility of forming a conference. They would then advise us as to the possible makeup of such a group, give us a list of the affirmative reasons as well as a statement of any negative considerations, and a recommendation."[54] Here, Etherington was the first to suggest a rational and formalized review process for expansion, the lack of which would often serve to hamper presidential decision-making, most notably in the process to vet potential applicants for addition in the early 1980s (see Chapter 5).

Bowdoin's Daggett circulated Etherington's memo to Howell, who responded that it raised "some real problems about how to proceed." To Howell, "the crucial problem is whether we should continue to discuss it in terms of eight colleges or whether the four colleges to whom this memo has been addressed should consult together and reach a common ground first." For Bowdoin, wrote Howell, it was "of the greatest importance to us to maintain close contact with the Pentagonal group. We certainly want to avoid antagonizing them." Howell found that having the ADs draw up a statement about the possibility of forming a conference was acceptable, but he warned that "great care should be taken that the invitation to them to do so should not be construed as an invitation to go ahead with planning the conference, but should appear to be simply an invitation to consider the possibility of forming such a group."[55] Evident in the response were Howell's sense of apartness from the Little Three and his concerns to keep close ties with them, as he was wary of crossing the group should Bowdoin be seen as pushing too hard for the inclusion of Bates and Colby.

In response to Etherington's October 1968 memo, Daggett wrote back to him two weeks later, agreeing that "we all have higher priorities than the Athletic League or Athletic Conference matter" and "to have the Athletic Directors draw up a statement about the possibility of forming a conference," but he echoed Howell's proviso that "such an invitation would not be an invitation to go ahead with planning the Conference."[56] Indeed, Daggett later took pains to correct the language in one of Etherington's communiqués that stated that Bowdoin, Colby, and Tufts were the driving forces behind the new league concept: "The Athletic Directors of Trinity, Middlebury, Colby and Tufts approached the four representatives of the Presidents' Agreement colleges," he amended, "and asked that the eight of them meet together to discuss matters of mutual interest. Thus the four of them approached the four of us. Bowdoin, as I understand it, had no part of initiating the meeting. The fact that the meeting was here on our grounds led to the designation of Dan Stuckey as corresponding secretary for the whole group of eight."[57]

Concurrently, Sawyer wrote Etherington and agreed with the "laying at rest the idea of forming a league, while ... encouraging others to adopt the philosophy and athletic policies outlined in our Presidents' Agreement."[58] Sawyer also related that he had shared the memo's content with Middlebury's Armstrong, who "indicated that [Middlebury] would be glad to adhere to such a statement and that in time other responses might thus separate the sheep from the goats. This would move things toward a more consistent set of athletic relationships, even without the formation of any athletic league having tight scheduling requirements and the added pressures which competitive league standings would tend to generate." This response indicates the ground that Sawyer was staking out, wanting his cake and to eat it, too—that is, to control the administrative operations of other signatory schools but not formally agree to align with them. Such a stance allowed the original Pentagonals to maintain a position of primacy without deigning to fully embrace the newcomers with logistical concessions such as full round-robin scheduling, which would have necessitated Amherst and Williams to travel to games at Bates and Colby on a regular basis.

In mid–December 1968, Etherington sent the summary to all Pentagonal presidents and the presidents at Bates, Colby, Hamilton, Tufts, Trinity, and Union. Soon thereafter, Sawyer sent a memo to the Pentagonal presidents that reflected his efforts "to set down as simply as possible my understanding of the areas of possible agreement that emerged from our discussions." To Sawyer, "there appears to be substantially greater readiness to enter into a larger and more informal conference of like-minded institutions which would not disrupt long-standing associations and might remain open to other members of similar standards and objectives." This was, he wrote, "in contrast to the evident resistance in forming a tight little league which would exclude traditional friends and, it was felt, might send out the wrong signal about our objectives." Sawyer then offered a parenthetical that "perhaps it will help clarify our discussions if we could use 'conference' and 'league' with these approximate meanings."[59]

Sawyer went on to outline five points for a "possible basis" of a conference "that might remain flexible on number of member institutions." First, the existing Pentagonal Agreement would be the "basis of policy." Second, each institution would "retain full freedom of scheduling with no obligation to play given teams in any sport, recognizing the existing diversity of arrangements and traditional associations." Here he noted that football would play no more than eight games, "with no obligation to play more than five (or six?) of the other members and with no championship or other systematic rankings envisaged here or elsewhere." Third, Sawyer expected "a confidential full disclosure of information from Admissions or Financial Aid Officers to be exchanged among the Presidents regarding all scholarship or other financial aid given to students on Freshmen or Varsity football teams, in recognition of the focus of pressure on this sport." Fourth, ADs would meet "at least annually to work out any difficulties or misunderstandings, with any unresolved issues to be referred to the Presidents." Fifth, any subsequent change of the agreement would "require a ¾ vote of the Presidents and to follow a full year's deliberation unless made by unanimous agreement."[60] With this proclamation, built on the previous efforts of Etherington, Sawyer the architect was on record with a definition and blessing of the managing ethos of any new expanded amalgam.

1969: The Final Lineup Is Settled

In January 1969, in response to Sawyer's bull, Howell responded (using the royal "we" with abandon, a practice for which he could perhaps be excused as a prominent scholar of British history) that it was "a thoroughly satisfactory statement and we would gladly concur with it." Howell noted that "we agree that the word 'conference' is preferable to the word 'league,' but we have the feeling that even 'conference' might suggest to the press that we are forming a competitive league." Howell instead suggested "that perhaps the best thing would be to call this a small conference athletic agreement rather than to term it a conference." "Finally," he wrote, "we would like to stress that at Bowdoin we regard this as a matter of very low priority. Since early this fall we have all been attempting to put this matter on the back burner. We would like to urge that it finally be placed there."[61] Howell's addendum that the conference issue was "a matter of very low priority" was likely to keep his Pentagonal colleague assured that Bowdoin was ultimately one of them and not pushing the issue too hard. His concern may also have been that a newly formalized assemblage would likely demand more attention from signatory presidents, something which none would ever relish.

Soon thereafter, Bowdoin AD Stuckey wrote to Howell with a reference to the proposed group as "the infamous 8 plus Bates." He chided Howell for not sending him a copy of his letter when his peers had seen it. "I knew nothing about this letter," Stuckey complained. "It seems to me that I should either stay out of these discussions if I do not know what is going on, or else I should get copies of what comes and goes between Bowdoin and the others."[62] Howell apologized, stating, "I agree with you that there seems to have been some breakdown in communications," citing as the reason the "juggling [of] administrative offices back and forth" during his transition to president.[63]

In March 1969, Colby president Robert Strider—a West Virginia native and the recipient of three Harvard degrees, who had been at his post for nine years after three as Colby's dean of faculty—penned a letter to the Pentagonal presidents plus his contemporaries at Bates, Middlebury, Trinity, and Tufts, seeking to move the expansion issue forward. While echoing the now-familiar refrain that "it is unlikely that the athletic program represents the highest priority for any of us," Strider wrote, "It seems wise to several of us that we should, if we can, get together and talk the matter out. If it seems possible then to move forward in this area we can get things moving. If it does not, we can turn our attention to other things."[64] Sawyer wrote back, indicating that "at our Fall discussions there was a clear resistance to the idea of any tight little athletic league that would exclude old friends with which various of us have had long associations, such as Hamilton and Union in our case. We'd accordingly be reluctant to explore such an idea without their inclusion."[65] Later that year, Colby AD John Winkin told the Colby student newspaper that the possibility of the initiation of such a conference was far from assured, as some of the college presidents involved seemed skeptical. Winkin also stated that for Colby teams to be qualified to compete in the proposed conference, the level of what he called the "major" sports (football, baseball, and basketball) had to be improved.[66]

Sawyer's comments were the first evidence of his stumping actively for Hamilton and Union, quite likely for many of the same reasons Bowdoin sought inclusion of Bates and Colby. However, there were other factors at play for Sawyer and Williams. Then-Hamilton president John Chandler—a former Williams administrator, the native North Carolinian would later become Williams president—noted, "When I was at Hamilton, I was on the Williams Board, so Jack [Sawyer] and I talked a lot about NESCAC. Jack and I were friends, and that was part of his thinking. If I hadn't been at Hamilton, probably Hamilton wouldn't have been considered." Former Williams AD Bob Peck underscored the fact that while the Maine schools were not geographically attractive to Williams for travel, both Hamilton and Union were, "especially with Union. Hamilton was three hours [away], like Boston, which was better than Maine, which was tough to travel." Chandler concurred, noting that "Union is closer to New England than Hamilton is. [That's why] Union was part of the original group." These comments echoed the logistical concerns that had been expressed by the Little Three decades earlier regarding their involvement with Bowdoin.

Howell responded positively to Strider, sending five possible meeting dates from mid-March to early April for a gathering in Boston, as suggested by Strider.[67] Plimpton responded to Strider that Amherst was "once more under pressure to allow and encourage post season games.

Chapter 4. The "Potted Ivy" Conference

John Chandler (left) and John Sawyer. While president of Hamilton, Chandler's connections with Williams and Sawyer, "the architect of NESCAC," assured Hamilton's place in the expanded configuration. Courtesy Williams College Archives and Special Collections.

Our Athletic Directors and our students, however, want us to take a new look at the problem." Plimpton felt that Howell was in favor of the move, Etherington and Sawyer were opposed. "I feel a little bit that we would like to maintain our current system," said Plimpton, and added, "It would be delightful to have others join with us in our athletic arrangements but the difficulties of trying to arrange a meeting are so gigantic that I hesitate in making it a formal commitment."[68]

In expressing agitation at the logistics of even scheduling a meeting with all interested parties, Plimpton, like Howell earlier, was anticipating the increased demands of presidents that an expanded association would bring. Bowdoin AD Stuckey wrote to Howell indicating that Williams AD Frank Thoms had sent him a letter, also sent to the ADs of the ten other potential members, which stated that the Pentagonal presidents "have indicated that any discussions of a conference must begin with a general agreement on policy." Enclosing Etherington's summary of the existing agreement, Thoms requested "each of you to send me in writing your response to this agreement as well as your ideas on the objectives of such a conference." "Apparently there is heat under this thing even on the back of the stove," opined Stuckey, adding, "I am not sure what has rekindled the interest in this but the fact that Williams College is heading it might mean something."[69] Stuckey's point signaled that any final decision on the process would land with Sawyer and that all roads leading to a realized expansion ultimately ran through Williamstown.

In December 1969, Etherington responded, with more than a hint of ennui, to Williams AD Thoms of the drafting committee with what he termed "some minor substantive changes," noting that he had sent both the ADs' draft and his response to Howell, Plimpton, and Sawyer and that Wesleyan AD Don Russell had reviewed the draft. Said Etherington: "I have made the point that I cannot get up too much enthusiasm for the conference idea except to the extent that it appears to be important to many of the athletic directors and to a number of institutions not now party to the agreement. I have also asked that the initiative, from this point forward, be taken by someone who has a greater substantive interest in the project than I have."[70] In a concomitant letter to the Pentagonal presidents, Etherington furthered this notion: "As demonstrated by the fact that I have been slow to complete this minor task, I simply cannot get excited about the conference idea. I do not see much if anything wrong with it, but I also do not see the move as one having any relative priority in these times." However, Etherington did opine that "I would still be opposed to anything which sounds like a 'league.'"[71]

"Happy to Live with the Confusion"

In the draft's introduction, Etherington took the first stab at naming the group, describing it as "an informal Conference to be known as The Northeastern Conference," and that its basis was the Pentagonal Agreement. The introduction specifically cited that a continued "freedom of scheduling both inside and outside the Conference" would be maintained, and members would "exchange information on scholarship and physical education budgets." Etherington's draft renamed the "Preamble" as "Basic Principles," moved Item IV into the introduction, and reordered the other elements. Point I was now "the emphasis on intercollegiate athletics is to be kept in harmony with the essential educational purposes of the institution." Point II was "competing players are to be representative of the student body." Point III was "the academic authority in each college is to control intercollegiate athletic policy."[72]

Under the "Policies" section, Etherington adopted language suggested by Sawyer and changed scheduling (II. A.) to read, "Each institution is to retain full freedom of scheduling, with no obligation to play given teams in any sport, in view of the diversity of arrangements and traditional associations," and added under II. B. (also from Sawyer), "While the member institutions are encouraged to compete with one another, there are to be no championships or other systematic intraconference rankings in any sport." The ADs' language on postseason play was unchanged, as was the recruiting and aid sections and the concluding statement. However, under an added Section VIII, Etherington included Sawyer's notion that the ADs would meet regularly "to review current practices. They are to submit in writing a common report to the Presidents concerning issues discussed, with particular emphasis on any unsolved problems," and a Section IX that said "any revision or amendment of this agreement shall be by three-fourths vote of the Presidents."[73] While he and his presidential brethren may have decried the time and effort required of athletic administration, Sections VIII and IX specified that presidents—like it or not—were to wield absolute control over intercollegiate athletics policy issues, reaffirming the ideal image of athletic policies run by institutional CEOs rather than ADs.

Early the next month, Howell (again with the royal "we") responded to Etherington: "Our position here is still to be in opposition to any sort of a league. We are moderately in favor of the conference scheme."[74] As to the actual naming of the assemblage, Sawyer responded, "First, to use a more modest name than 'Northeastern,' which might logically be presumed open to a large number of much more high-powered athletic enterprises." Sawyer instead suggested "the New England Small College Athletic Conference, with the thought that Hamilton and Union would find it no serious problem to accept this and that it much more accurately defines the nature of the group, which will probably be known in the press as the Potted Ivy Conference anyhow."[75] While possibly aware of sportswriter Red Smith's assessment of the idea a decade previous, Sawyer's aside is yet another allusion to the similarities between the two groupings and a concern over the likelihood of NESCAC's perceived lesser relative status.

However, in 1972, after the group formally coalesced, it learned that another "NESCAC" had already existed for a decade. The original NESCAC was the New England State College Athletic Conference, comprising state colleges in Massachusetts, Maine, and New Hampshire. This league originated in 1934 as the New England State Teachers College Conference, with the name changed in 1962.[76] The league reconfigured soon thereafter when the Massachusetts schools left to form the Massachusetts State College Athletic Conference, while others formed what would become the Little

East Conference. When alerted of this by Howell, Sawyer sent a handwritten note back, indicating that "this had led to a proposal that ours be called the 'Colonials' but John Chandler and I thought this snobbishly pretentious so better to live with the confusion till a better idea. Have you another alternative?"[77] In response, Howell wrote, "I have no other suggestions and am happy to live with the confusion."[78] However, in October 1972, Sawyer received a letter from Richard Costello, AD at the University of Maine at Portland-Gorham (now the University of Southern Maine), who was serving as president of *his* NESCAC. Costello wrote "to indicate some problems resulting from the fact that our Conference's initials are the same as the New England Small College Athletic Conference." Costello cited potential confusion in media coverage and in posting meetings when at ECAC and NCAA conventions. Costello ended his letter with "the membership of NESCAC would appreciate your consideration of the problem and any action that you might deem appropriate."[79] Sawyer wrote back a week later, acknowledging that the presidents were aware of the issue. As to the possibility of press confusion: "I should indicate in all candor, does not particularly bother us, our Conference having from the beginning made it a deliberate policy not to maintain or publicize league standings or take any action that would build up the pressures on competitive results." "At the very least," offered Sawyer, "we could both request use enough of the name to identify each group (N.E. State College Conf. and N.E. Small College Conf.)."[80]

The Deal Is Done

In April 1970, a more formalized conference draft was circulated, and it included a detailed membership list of schools—Amherst, Bates, Bowdoin, Colby, Hamilton, Middlebury, Trinity, Tufts, Union, Wesleyan, and Williams—and was specifically referred to as "New England Small College Athletic Conference." The postseason section, Section V, now reflected a more formalized procedure regarding exceptions, stating:

> Authorization (for teams or individuals) to enter specific post-season competitions must be approved in principle and in advance by a ¾ vote of the Presidents after recommendations by a designated Committee on Post-Season Competitions. This committee will recommend by September 10 each year which tournaments or championships are judged consistent with the terms and spirit of this agreement. Team participation is expected to be the exception and not the norm.[81]

The draft furthered that "each institution naturally retains full autonomy with respect to not participating in post-season play if its

Chapter 4. The "Potted Ivy" Conference

administration or faculty so decides even when a given competition has been approved," and it continued:

> Assuming approval of the competition under the procedures indicated above, the following conditions will govern once a post-season bid is received:
>
> 1. The coach and team members vote on their accepting or not accepting the bid.
> 2. If the vote is to accept, the coach and team captain(s) present their case to the institution's Committee on Athletics.
> 3. The final decision to accept or reject the bid is made by the institution's Committee on Athletics in consultation with the Administration and Faculty as each institution shall determine.[82]

While the draft attempted to codify the intricacies likely to follow regarding the desirousness of postseason play, the proviso that such competitions were expected to be "the exception and not the norm" was in no small measure mistaken.

At this point, Middlebury's Armstrong wrote to Bowdoin's Howell, "The time has come for us to determine whether or not we wish to establish a small college athletic conference. I have strong reason to believe that there is among us a genuine desire to form such a conference among institutions with common goals, generally similar in educational standards and in size." It is unclear why Armstrong—who grew up in Princeton, New Jersey, received undergrad and graduate degrees from his hometown institution, and was a professor and dean there prior to assuming the presidency at Middlebury in 1963—was, as the head of a non–Pentagonal school, calling the question with Howell and Bowdoin. "I now write to you to inquire whether your institution is willing to subscribe to the enclosed Agreement," he wrote to Howell. "More important than the particular provisions of the Agreement is the spirit which underlines the whole—a spirit of full commitment to the basic principles of the Agreement, of cooperation and trust. No rule will achieve in themselves what the Conference aims to achieve unless there is an unqualified endorsement by each institution."[83]

Once again Bowdoin was questioning the benefits of the association, and Armstrong was alluding to the impression that Bowdoin was waffling on the decision and as such Bowdoin may be left out of the emerging assemblage. "Your institution will need to proceed internally to reach a decision about membership," wrote Armstrong to Howell. "If there are serious reservations about any of the provisions in the Agreement, I believe you should decide not to accept membership."[84]

On the same day he wrote Howell, Armstrong pushed the issue further by preparing a press release, dated May 7, that stated:

> After long discussions and careful consultation, eleven New England liberal arts colleges are seriously considering the formal adoption of an agreement on athletic policy as the basis for a New England small college athletic conference.... After review through appropriate institutional channels, each college will indicate whether it is prepared to enter into Conference membership.... It is hoped that all eleven colleges will be able to reach institutional decisions by the fall of 1970.[85]

The timing of the issue is important to note, as Howell and Bowdoin were weathering a campus strike (supported by students and faculty and derided by many alumni and board members) in response to the Kent State University student deaths, and as such the conference issue was likely not foremost on Howell's mind.

Nonetheless, on May 8, Bowdoin's Faculty Committee on Athletics (comprising Stuckey, Greason, three students, and five faculty members) unanimously recommended "that the Faculty ratify the Athletic Conference Agreement for the proposed New England Small College Athletic Conference."[86] The next month Howell sent a brief missive to Armstrong. "I want to let you know that the necessary formalities have been completed here," Howell wrote, "and Bowdoin will join in the New England Small College Athletic Conference."[87] Like a decade prior, Bowdoin once again decided being on the inside was better than the alternative.

By August 1970, perhaps in a show of power over the group, all but Amherst and Williams had endorsed the agreement (according to Armstrong, the two "did not have time last spring to complete formal institutional approval"[88]), and a meeting for later in the year was requested before a formal declaration be made. The NESCAC presidents did meet in Hanover, New Hampshire, on November 12, even though Amherst had yet to endorse the move. At that meeting, convened and chaired by Armstrong (Plimpton of Amherst was not present but said to be represented by Sawyer; Colby's Strider was also not present but signaled approval after being briefed by Bates's Reynolds[89]), "all presidents endorsed the Agreement for their institutions and agreed to enter the conference. The conference is therefore in existence and the policies, procedures and spirit of the Agreement are in force." Also, "the Presidents confirmed their profound conviction that the Conference can only work if the Presidents themselves are actively involved and take a firm hand in support of the Conference Agreement."[90]

Soon thereafter, Sawyer wrote to Armstrong that he had spoken with Plimpton about the issue. "I told him of our clear consensus on the spirit, purpose and priorities of the whole and it is now my understanding that he will proceed to get formal approval of Amherst's entry and hence that the New England Small College Athletic Conference can become operative as planned."[91] Sawyer then offered to serve as the first chairman of a four-man executive committee. Sawyer would indeed become the chair; also on the committee were Howell, Hamilton's Chandler, and Tufts's Hallowell, with the proviso that Howell "would take charge of whatever is needed on the post-season review for selective authorizations"[92] To this, Howell responded to Sawyer, "I will be glad (?) to take on the post-season review. What am I supposed to do and when?"[93]

Sawyer responded in a handwritten note: "I'd judge to 1. recommend that the Div. II ECAC hockey, if that is your judgment again, and 2. Ponder any others you'd like the Comm. and then the Presidents to consider prior to next Sept 10, or whatever date and procedures the Agreement provides. Does this seem right?"[94] In a note to Howell, Bowdoin's Greason indicated he asked AD Stuckey "to prepare a list of acceptable post-season events for us to look at."[95]

1971: The Realities of Formalization

Documents list the founding date of NESCAC to be March 21, 1971, but the first joint meeting of ADs and a larger executive committee (Sawyer, Reynolds, Chandler, Hallowell, Plimpton, and Amherst president-elect John Ward) didn't occur until the following May at Williams. In this home court setting, Sawyer's remarks had a foreboding and admonishing tone. "I come here today with full knowledge that I have been viewed by some as the 'heavy' on certain questions—and I probably won't disappoint on this score," Sawyer began. "In setting our course and facing specific problems, we should recognize that there can be divergence between a coach's competitive drives or career ambitions and the well-being of his students and the program as a whole. Unless we sustain the latter on healthy lines, we could find ourselves in a situation where both intercollegiate athletics and the jobs that go with it are seriously cut back."[96] The minutes of the meeting then summarized Sawyer's three main points pertaining to "the survival of intercollegiate athletics": that they will not be "1. Dependent on won-loss records. 2. Helped by concentrating upon certain sports. 3. Aided by the aspirations of over-aggressive coaches."[97] For the first time on record, NESCAC's godfather indicated that coaches were the main problem in the challenges to managing athletics within NESCAC.

As for the other invitees, NESCAC would have a significant impact. Tufts's ability to join NESCAC "defines Tufts athletics to this day,"[98] while former Hamilton president Eugene Tobin noted that "we joke internally that Hamilton was the westernmost of the New England colleges." "To be able to say that this institution was competing with Williams and Amherst and Tufts," said Tobin, "certainly helped to a certain degree with admissions at a time when Hamilton was changing its academic reputation and becoming stronger and more rigorous and raising its profile in terms of selectivity." Tobin added that being a part of NESCAC "was an important factor certainly for coaches ... [and] for alumni, many of whom competed with their colleagues, and for feeling good about their alma mater. It was valuable to be a member of NESCAC."

However, some stakeholders at Union were less than sanguine about joining. In 1969, Union head football coach George Flood expressed concern about the pending expansion, stating, "My objective of a conference would be as a controlling organization that would have as its goals improvement of competition among the schools and the production of a competitive drive toward championships."[99] Ironically, Flood's objective, "the competitive drive toward championships," was exactly what would occur at Union, as the school, under an administrative leadership and booster involvement that did not support or pursue NESCAC membership, would invest in the development of a nationally prominent men's ice hockey program. This would put the school's goals at odds with the initial version of NESCAC's ideal image and would test the nascent collective's ability to enforce its image and identity. Ultimately, NESCAC coalesced because "an organization of this kind was necessary to protect their interests—*to advance their values.*"[100] But how these interests and values would be advanced by both NESCAC and Union would come to mean a parting of the ways.

Chapter 5

The New Conference Faces Immediate Challenges

Cultural Changes and the Impact on NESCAC Athletics

In the fall of 1969, just weeks after the Woodstock music festival, the three-day gathering of an estimated five hundred thousand music fans and/or recreational drug users in Bethel, New York—perceived by many as the signature American countercultural event of the 1960s—Bowdoin ice hockey co-captains Stephen and Erland Hardy performed what they termed "shuttle diplomacy" between sophomore goaltender John Bradley, who sported shoulder-length hair, and head coach Sid Watson. The personal grooming trend Bradley featured was anathema to certain elements of the American population, including most sport coaches. "It was hilarious," recounted Steve. "We finally got the two of them to compromise on hair length. Then John taped the peace sign on his blocker. Those were the days." This conflict occurred a year after an op-ed piece in the Bowdoin student newspaper described the impact of hair length in sport. The paper's sports editor wrote, "Long hair has been deemed unbecoming an athlete and has been cause for suspension until altered. It's an amusing situation when a coach has to exclude a player from competition due to personal appearance and an even more amusing one when the player is willing to sacrifice the experience of competition to a principle as inane as coiffeur."[1] A similar conflict occurred at Tufts that year between head men's soccer coach Herb Erickson and player John Melling. This one was settled through a best-of-three handball showdown, with Erickson winning two games to none, forcing Melling to shave his Van Dyke beard. "I knew I could take him," said Erickson as he watched Melling shave. "I've got too much know-how and experience for him." Melling was gracious in defeat, stating, "I can't complain. It was simply a case of having a relevant discussion on the issues," but admitted, "I underestimated Coach Erickson's handball ability."[2]

Conflicts around hair grooming between players and coaches were a very real part of all levels of the American sport and educational landscape during this period; in 1969, a federal judge in Illinois ruled that a high school could expel a male student simply for having long hair.[3] These disputes were part of a broader range of conflicts throughout American society that highlighted an emerging youth culture at odds with established perspectives on appropriate social behavior. In Hardy's recounting of the coach-player conflict at Bowdoin, his use of the phrase "those were the days" alludes to a time in which such disputes were commonplace on college campuses across America and were interpreted by many as important cultural statements.

Meanwhile, conflicts related to civil rights, the Vietnam War, and academic freedom were also arising on college campuses across the country, marking the period as the most contentious and violent for institutions and stakeholders to that point, exemplified most dramatically by the student riots and building occupations at the University of California at Berkeley and Columbia University and the killing of four students during a campus uprising by National Guard troops at Kent State University in 1970. Incidents were not limited to these activist hotbeds: 84 acts of arson, bombings, or attempted bombings were counted at colleges and universities across the country during the 1968–69 academic year. In a 1969 survey of students from forty colleges and universities by *Fortune* magazine, 12.8 percent of respondents identified themselves as "revolutionary" or "radically dissident."[4] An official at the U.S. Office of Education summed up the campus management challenges of the times succinctly: "I feel sorry for the poor bastards who've got to run the colleges this year."[5]

In his annual report to the trustees and overseers of the college, penned soon after a campus strike following the Kent State shootings, Bowdoin president Roger Howell, Jr., informed the group that the faculty had voted to request the Governing Boards to make extensive changes in the nature of graduation requirements, including institutional interest in coeducation. "There is no question," wrote Howell, "about the general desire of students and faculty to see Bowdoin become a coeducational institution. Although an all-male college has been a pleasant experience for many people, it has seemed to others to have become increasingly an anachronism of a day of complex social needs."[6] The arrival of coeducation was the most radical of proposed changes, because Bowdoin was a place that had always "valued 'manliness' (though its definition was reconstructed with each generation of students)."[7] This reconstruction was evident in 1970, as the all-male student body approved of the addition of women; in fact, coeducation received "a greater consensus" than the opinion that the hockey team be allowed to participate in postseason play (a corresponding poll indicated that 725 of 950 students favored such participation).[8]

However, coeducation was not universally embraced across the country, and while undergrads might have welcomed the chance to connect socially more readily with women, some chafed that the women in class were "just too damned aggressive and conscientious," and some alumni were angered by the change.[9] Other future NESCACs were moving this way as well. Trinity opted for coeducation in 1969, Williams and Wesleyan in 1970, and Amherst in 1975. Hamilton had founded a women's adjunct, Kirkland College, in 1965, but opted to dissolve it and subsume its students and faculty in 1978.[10] While these decisions were not made in response to the passage of Title IX of the Education Amendments of 1972, the landmark federal law that addressed sex discrimination in higher education, the moves did benefit women through an expanded access to elite institutions, even if the initial motivation on the part of most all-male schools was to continue to attract and retain desirable male students who were increasingly seeking greater access to and connection with females.[11] In the case of Trinity, the decision to coeducate was a financial imperative, with a college strategic plan stating flatly that "co-education had become a matter of Trinity's survival."[12] This approach was far removed from earlier in the century, when Wesleyan's decision to disavow coeducation in 1909 allowed the school to be seen as a "college for males" and helped move the school from a "'backward status' amongst prestigious New England colleges," with a subsequent bolstering of the school's football program. Additionally, publicity about the program's success "reinforced Wesleyan's male image in New York and Boston newspapers."[13] Tufts, with its all-women

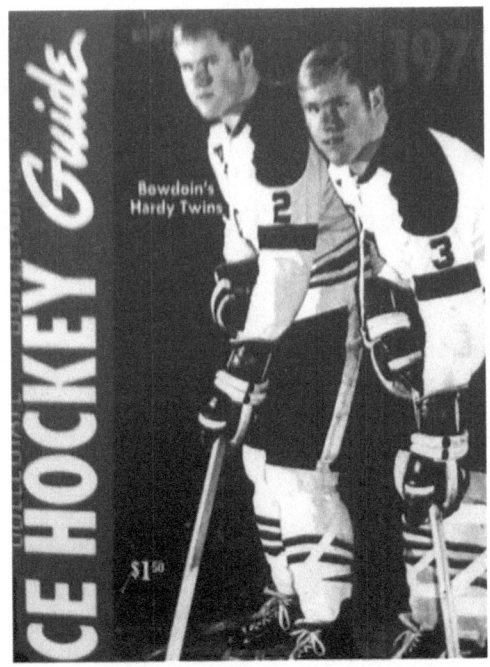

Twin brothers Stephen and Erl Hardy served to settle a hairy dispute between Bowdoin goalie John Bradley and head coach Sid Watson. Courtesy George J. Mitchell Department of Special Collections & Archives, Bowdoin College Library, Brunswick, Maine.

adjunct Jackson College (which it integrated into its College of Arts and Sciences in 1980), also battled a sense that a school that offered education to women was less attractive to males and, at the urging of trustees, sought to develop stronger athletic programs in response.[14]

The Impact of Title IX

The eventual growth of women's intercollegiate athletics programs was aided in large part by the passage of Title IX, which sought to increase equity for women in federally funded educational programs. One of the initial impacts of the Title IX federal legislation was an increase in the number of females participating in collegiate athletics. In the 1971-72 academic year, before the passage of Title IX, the number of female athletes participating in college athletics totaled 29,977, compared with 170,384 male athletes (and only about 1 percent of the average college or university athletic budget was expended on women's programs[15]).

Although signed into law in 1972, the enforcement of and compliance to this legislation was not a straightforward affair. With the initial passage of this legislation came much debate as to whether Title IX applied to intercollegiate athletic departments. Language within the legislation was not specific, only referring to application within education programs or activities receiving federal financial assistance. Various groups and individuals, such as the NCAA and U.S. senator John Tower (R-TX), used different approaches arguing against Title IX's applicability to intercollegiate athletics. As a result, when Title IX was passed, numerous ADs and college presidents did not feel athletics was included within the law and therefore did not comply with the legislation.

The early decades of intercollegiate athletics were mostly the preserve of comparatively affluent white men at the Ivies and future NESCACs— hardly surprising, given the fact that well into the twentieth century only 5 percent of American men went to college. By 1920, however, nearly half of all college students were women, but while the number of women on campuses was significant, their opportunities to participate in intercollegiate athletics were far fewer and usually quite restricted. The entrée of women into the previously masculine sphere of physical activity was seen as threatening by many males (especially since football was considered an "antidote" to an encroaching effeminacy hastened by the lack of physical challenges available the modern world).[16] It was this mind-set that averred that a woman's role in athletics was to serve as a supporter to brothers, sons, and boyfriends.

Women's sports were also stymied by the notion that strenuous physical activity was severely detrimental to the supposed delicate constitutions of women and could cause debilitating injuries to them, thereby rendering them unable to bear and raise children, which many thought women were foremost put on this earth to do. As a result of these and other concerns, women's programs were kept "low key," because female teacher-coaches "wanted to preserve young women's modesty and accommodate their perceived daintiness" and because of "a general suspicion of competition, particularly as it was being practiced in men's sports."[17]

In spite of these restrictions, many women, like their male counterparts decades before, sought to play, and the sport of basketball became a popular activity for collegiate women, forming what was deemed to be "a central part of student life at many women's institutions."[18] Initially the sport was seen by males to be less physical and therefore less threatening to them if women had chosen to play it. At Smith College in Northampton, Massachusetts, physical educator Senda Berenson devised a version of the game where movement was more limited than in men's basketball (the floor was divided into three sections, with players not allowed to move into the other two and no player allowed to dribble more than once). To many, however, the idea of young women running, jumping, sweating, and yelling in a public forum was highly distasteful and borderline immoral (this during a time when a woman's sexual reputation was called into question if her skirts failed to touch the ground), so much so that men were barred entry from many of these early contests lest the passions of the moment cause all parties irreparable harm.

Apparel options were, in the words of former Jackson College student-athlete Dorothea "Dorie" Ellis, "nothing short of WOW!" Basketball uniforms were "voluminous blue serge bloomers, white middy blouses and black ties, long black cotton stockings.... [T]he field hockey team wore brown serge tunics (just above the knees), white long sleeve blouses, long black stockings.... My daughter, Faith—Class of 1954—wore the same brown tunic that I sported in 1929–1931. Evidently the budget for women's equipment was very limited."[19] By the 1960s, Jackson College athletics were a mix of varsity, dorm, and sorority teams, with intercollegiate contests versus Pembroke College (Brown University's women's adjunct), Radcliffe College, Simmons College, and the University of New Hampshire in archery, badminton, basketball, bowling, fencing, field hockey, riding, softball, swimming, and tennis.[20]

When final regulations concerning the applicability of Title IX were released in 1975, revenue-producing sports were not excluded and institutions were provided with guidelines to follow to determine whether equal athletic opportunities for members of both sexes were being provided. Although these 1975 regulations helped lay the groundwork in terms of how intercollegiate athletic departments should implement the law, there was still much confusion among athletic administrators in terms of what they were required to do to maintain compliance with Title IX. Intercollegiate athletic administrators moved slowly, if at all, in making changes to accommodate more fully female student-athletes. As a result, in 1979 the Department of Health, Education, and Welfare released Title IX policy interpretations to explain how the law should be applied within college athletics. These policy interpretations addressed three areas: the provision of athletic scholarships, the effective accommodation of student athletic interests and abilities (i.e., sport participation), and the benefits and opportunities provided to each sex (i.e., equipment, facilities, schedule, etc.). The interpretations are still in place today and have guided the enforcement efforts surrounding Title IX compliance.

The act of adding women's programs were more straightforward at coed NESCAC schools like Colby and Tufts. And while there were challenges in delivering programs, some of which were based on delays in interpretations of the law's requirements, NESCACs were generally ahead of other schools in offering women's programs that, over time, were supported on equitable levels with men's. This was in stark contrast to Division I schools like Brown and Colgate, where female athletes brought lawsuits either to hasten the addition of or to halt the elimination of women's programs. However, one former NESCAC AD stated that gender also had a delaying impact, noting that NESCAC then "was led by a group of men who had come from a football background." "It was true of nearly every institution after Title IX and some of the implementations of Title IX had occurred," said the AD. "That's the way departments were structured. Men who ran football programs who had administrative abilities were moved fairly successfully into leadership roles." At Amherst, this disconnect impacted logistics. Heather Schwemm, a lacrosse player, found that "activities supposedly designed for women students were modelled on the men's activities," and she was "appalled that we all had to take 'gang showers' just like the guys. ... [T]he truth is, many women don't care to parade naked around the locker room 'just like the guys.'"[21] There were also cultural issues at Amherst, as cited by former basketball player Sherry Boschert, who indicated that the "all male" athletics staff "basically drummed out" one of the team's coaches after "she advocated for the women's program, and because she [was] a lesbian." However, Boschert noted also that the team's head coach broke up an affair between the coach and a player, "engendering the wrath of the players."[22]

Nonetheless, NESCAC schools opted for early, though gradual, expansion of women's athletics programs, with little if any coordination or conflict among member schools. At the end of the 1976–77 academic year,

Chapter 5. The New Conference Faces Immediate Challenges

Bowdoin field hockey coach Sally LaPointe provided her president a "state of women's athletics" update, in which she reported that "interest is still strong and as the number of women increase on campus [up to five hundred that year] so does participation in athletics." LaPointe recorded that sixty-three women came out for field hockey, which necessitated the addition of a part-time assistant, but that women's squash was "limited by the number of teams willing to travel to Maine," a fact that impacted the men's team as well, as the NESCAC agreement did not then require round-robin scheduling. "All in all it was a busy year but a fine one," LaPointe summarized, "but I have never felt the need for increasing the help for women as I have this year," with twelve women's teams and two full-time coaches, as compared with twenty-one men's teams and nine full-time coaches.[23] One former Bowdoin female student-athlete from this period offered this perspective on the resource issue: "It was kind of an interesting balance between having a group of women who you really loved and loved you, and having virtually no recognition by the College ... to be that tight and to work that hard, but not have the College see you as a serious athlete. But we had a good time."[24] Former head basketball coach Dick Mersereau summarized the college's approach in financial terms: "As far as they [the administration] were concerned, if a group of women wanted to do basketball, well, the good news was, we would respond, we would have a team. The less good news was ... get by as cheaply and as easily as they possibly could."[25]

While this mind-set was interpreted as slighting women's programs, as the 1970s dawned, historian John Thelin described the enterprise of American higher education as a "troubled giant" on the brink of a "new depression," hastened by economic factors "over which they had little control," such as inflation, declining productivity, and increased energy costs. In response, many presidents sought first to cut costs through deferred maintenance and budgetary reductions. Mid-decade, these issues were exacerbated by enrollment declines and the expansion of academic and social support services.[26] While Bowdoin's allocation of resources seemed meager, in 1974 expenditures on women's sports nationally represented only 2 percent of that spent on men's sports. Within NESCAC, Tufts was spending 10 percent of its athletics budget on women's programs. However, Mary Sturtevant, the school's women's lacrosse coach, stated that the issue was not solely about expenditures. "The problems of women's intercollegiate athletics often get completely obscured when you start talking about dollars and cents," said Sturtevant. "What we are talking about is a student's whole sense of what intercollegiate athletics should be and what we are going to provide for him or her to achieve that.... I'm concerned more about equity than equality of dollars and cents."[27] To this end, Tufts, which benefited from the fact that it was essentially a coeducational institution, moved toward parity by scheduling more intercollegiate competitions, hiring more coaches, adding programs, and affording greater access to facilities. Other coed NESCAC schools addressed these issues quickly as well. Colby added intercollegiate women's ice hockey in 1972, while Bowdoin, a school with its own campus rink and extensive success in men's ice hockey, didn't add a women's intercollegiate hockey program until 1984 and Williams not until 1993, a delay that is in part explainable by the lack of women playing the sport at the high school level until that time.

One former NESCAC AD described the financial challenges at his school during the time in terms of meeting equity goals. While NESCAC, along with the Ivies, were among the first conferences to add women's programs, "we added a whole women's athletic department out of pretty much the same money we had for the men's program. So for us to add women's lacrosse, we had to cut JV men's lacrosse, and to have women's soccer, we had to cut JV men's soccer. And budgets were tough then with double-digit inflation." This AD also explained, "We weren't really influenced by Title IX [to add women's programs]," adding, "I mean Title IX was there, but it wasn't really impacting schools until the 1980s." That was because until various lawsuits and administrative interpretations were settled, the legal imperative of applying the statute to athletics was minimal. It is fair to wonder if the reluctant old guard and willing administrators of the 1960s would have embraced coeducation had they been able to foresee the law's long-ranging impact on campuses.

John Cullen, former head women's soccer coach at Bowdoin, described the process of how the formerly all-male school handled the addition of women's soccer. In 1978, Cullen was a part-time assistant for Sid Watson's men's ice hockey program, and as the demand for a women's program increased, Watson gave Cullen more coaching and administrative duties. In 1979, head men's basketball coach Ray Bicknell was assigned the head coaching duties for the new women's soccer program, and the next year, when forty women showed up for preseason practice, Bicknell asked whether Cullen could coach a JV team. In a few years, Cullen assumed the head coaching position for women's soccer, was a women's hockey assistant when that program began, and also helped as an assistant for softball for several years.

The end of his time at Bowdoin had been when, in Cullen's words, "there was a coach for every sport." NESCACs would be influenced by the growing specialization in youth sports, where kids were opting, often at the urging of private club team coaches, to eschew participating in multiple sports to focus on one so that they might be better positioned to claim a coveted intercollegiate athletics scholarship (see Chapter 8).

Union: "They Were Kicked Out for Cheating at Hockey"

The one full-blown athletic scandal that has ever hit NESCAC involved recruiting. But unlike other conferences, in which schools go on and off probation, NESCAC promptly parted ways with Union College when the school was accused of off-campus recruiting in its quest for hockey players in 1977. Union athletic director Richard Sakala insists the school withdrew from the league and that the issue was Union's desire to play Division I hockey, but Wesleyan [AD] Donald Russell issues a sharp rebuke: "They were kicked out for cheating at hockey."[28]

So did Union elect to leave on its own to chart a course different from that allowed by NESCAC, or was it forced to pursue this track as a result of a NESCAC banishment? That Union left the fold a mere six years after pressing for inclusion was surprising, given that Union had actively solicited membership under the presidencies of Carter Davidson and Harold Martin and Williams, the western outpost of the Pentagonal assemblage that played Union regularly in many sports, had lobbied for Union's inclusion as a partner for Hamilton, whose president John Chandler's well-established ties to Williams had secured Hamilton's expansion slot.

In spite of these factors, there were immediate indications that Union was an ill fit for NESCAC. In 1972, a scant year after official formation, NESCAC's executive committee (Chandler, Hallowell, Howell, and Sawyer) rejected Union's request that its men's basketball team participate in the NCAA College Division tournament. Howell wrote to Martin, "It is the feeling of the committee that this tournament goes beyond the NESCAC guidelines and I must tell you that the ruling is that competition in the tournament is not appropriate."[29] The request was a curious one, since the next year Martin wrote that postseason play "not only emphasizes the competitive aspect of sports, but makes serious inroads on the time and energy of players."[30]

Martin's stance may have been in part why soon thereafter he was replaced by Thomas Bonner, who came to Union from the presidency at the University of New Hampshire (UNH). Appointed to succeed Martin in March 1974, Bonner was not a party to the school's efforts to join the new expanded confederation. Some cite Bonner's exposure to big-time hockey at UNH as explanation of his inclination to use hockey for similar purposes at Union. The college's self-published history opined that Bonner was "perhaps influenced by the high-profile Division I hockey program at the University of New Hampshire (with which he had found it politically useful to be identified), but also reflecting his belief in the general importance of athletics as a factor in the public recognition of an academic institution, the president looked for a well-known and highly successfully coach."[31] Noted hockey historian (and former UNH professor) Stephen Hardy curtly summarized Bonner's time in Durham: "He was at UNH for only three years. It's hard to see that he made any mark here." The move from a state-funded, comprehensive university to a small, private liberal arts college was also a surprising one, and the apparent disconnect would impact Bonner's later challenges at Union.

On Martin's last day as president, the school and trustees announced the acceptance of a gift from H. Laurence Achilles, former Union chaplain, religion professor, and hockey coach, for the construction of a new rink and curling sheets. The $1.5 million facility would be completed in time for the 1975–76 season. Because the gift was made on short notice, "before realistic estimates of the ice facility's cost could be prepared, it proved necessary to consume Achilles's maintenance endowment in the building's construction."[32] This also led to a natural predicament to develop revenue from hockey to pay for the related expenses.

While Bonner may have inherited the commitment to hockey—or may have been hired with knowledge of it and brought in because of his experiences with hockey at UNH—in his first report to the board of trustees in January 1975, he cited plans to improve morale, which would include "competitive athletic teams," specifically football.[33] To that end, Bonner hired Tom Cahill, who had been fired as Army head football coach in 1973 after his team failed to win a game and lost to Navy, 51–0, the worst loss in the history of that storied rivalry. Cahill lasted only four years at Union and left with a record of 11–20–1.

Bonner was also looking to make changes in the administrative and operational structures at Union, proposing to faculty in 1976 that Union become a "comprehensive college in a university setting" and to expand the school "beyond its primary full-time undergraduate orientation," which meant enlarging Union's limited graduate and continuing education programs,[34] thus shifting Union away from its small, liberal arts foundations and away from the identity and image of its newly established NESCAC connections.

To address these challenges of improving and expanding Union's position through a relaunched men's hockey program, Bonner hired Nevin "Ned" Harkness, who had Ivy imprimatur from his success at building the program at Cornell (winning national titles in '67 and '70—the '70 team went 29–0, becoming the only undefeated, untied team in NCAA history). Harkness had also won a national championship at nearby Rensselaer Polytechnic Institute (RPI) in 1954. After the landmark 1970 season, Harkness left Cornell for the head coach post with the National Hockey League's Detroit Red Wings, becoming the first coach to jump from the collegiate ranks to an NHL head coaching position.[35] Stephen Hardy, who was ECAC Hockey Supervisor from 1976 to 1979, noted that Harkness's "collegiate approach did not work with grizzled pros" and recalled a story about Harkness's first day of preseason training with the Red Wings: "Number one mistake by Ned—he goes in the locker room. Supposedly, with such a veteran team, you don't just waltz in on the players. And Alex Delvecchio's got a cigar going, and somebody else's got a cigarette going." "And Ned goes near-ballistic," said Hardy. "'There's no smoking, this is training camp! You're professional hockey players!' And Delvecchio takes a long drag on the cigar and blows smoke toward Ned and says, 'Yeah, sure, Coach.'"

Following his short-lived NHL tenure, Harkness came to Union in 1975, prior to the completion of the new rink, with the charge to resurrect the Union program, which had been dormant since 1949. "Well, sir," Harkness allegedly growled (Harkness was renowned for his rumbling idiolect) to Bonner when offered the Union job. "Under the circumstances I don't think I can promise you a national championship the first year. But if you can wait a few years … when do I start?"[36] The move to Union was prompted, according to Stephen Hardy, because Harkness had been reaching out to colleges to inquire as to their interest in bringing him in as head coach. When Hardy was an assistant hockey coach at Amherst, head coach and AD Ben McCabe came to practice one day and said to Hardy, "Guess who was just on the phone with me? Ned Harkness."

"What's Ned want?" Hardy replied.

"Well," responded McCabe, "he's looking to see if I'm looking to hire a new hockey coach."

"Ned got canned by the Norris family," surmised Hardy. "They moved him upstairs, and he basically didn't have anything to do. Ned was angling for jobs and who knows who else he called." Hardy recalled that McCabe rebuffed Harkness by saying, "'Thanks, Ned, but we're all set,' knowing exactly what Ned would do with Amherst hockey, which was the last thing Ben wanted."

Since Harkness was trolling for positions, it is intriguing to speculate, given his connections to Union through his father (who had coached there in the 1930s), his ability to schmooze with boosters, and his dedicated efforts to promote college hockey in general, that Harkness may have laid significant groundwork with those in positions of power at Union to take the post before Bonner took the helm. To secure a job, according to Hardy, Harkness "would have enlisted a group of very rich and influential alums, like Achilles, who had a lot of influence over the institution. Ned would have cultivated them like nobody's business."

Union's vision to achieve hockey prominence was not far-fetched, as schools such as Clarkson, RPI, and St. Lawrence were (and still are) competing at the Division I level even as they maintained Division III status in other sports. Plus, for Bonner's vision, competing against the Ivies (much like with Trinity's men's squash program twenty years later—see Chapter 7) would have seemed more fulfilling than playing the likes of Norwich, Salem State, and even Williams.

Internal Conflicts: Issues with Harkness, Issues with Culture

Much to Bonner's likely approval, the popular sporting press soon took notice. An article by Pat Putnam in the February 7, 1977, edition of *Sports Illustrated* was a rare take by the magazine to focus on the college game, or to focus on a NESCAC program of any kind. Titled "No Heels in the Achilles," a rather painfully stretched pun based on the donor-named rink, the two-page piece featured a photo of a well-dressed Harkness following game action intently from the Union bench.

It is important to remember the importance of *SI* in the image-making of American culture in the latter half of the twentieth century. In his history of the magazine, author Michael MacCambridge wrote that *SI* at its peak was "the cultural centerpiece of the rapidly expanding universe of sports." The magazine had "a breadth of vision that no other sports magazine had ever possessed" and would emerge as "the blueprint for modern American sports journalism, and the quintessential middle-class magazine of the postwar era." "*SI* gave the American sports fan a sense of himself and his community, of how pervasive the pull of sports had become," wrote MacCambridge, and "made an art out of in-depth reporting on those games, and thereby made the games themselves more important to Americans."[37]

SI had previously delved into the Pentagonal realm in 1958, when the magazine published a black-and-white fish-eye panoramic photo of the Amherst-Wesleyan football game. The photo of the 19–0 Amherst win on a cloudy October day in Middletown features the school's chapel and academic buildings more prominently than the game action. The magazine later rated the shot as one of its top 150 college football photos of all time.

SI returned to the Pentagonal scene in 1960 with its feature "Guys and Dolls among the Ivy," a seven-page pictorial spread focusing on the festivities and games during the "Fall Houseparties Weekend" at Williams. The article's eight photographs capture football game action (a 10–9 Tufts victory, described in the caption as one narrow enough to leave "partisans of

Chapter 5. The New Conference Faces Immediate Challenges 113

both teams happy," highlighting the idealized notion that wins and losses at this level were not matters of life and death). Also included is a photo of "burly Tufts fullback" Duncan MacDonald in a sideline embrace with his concerned mother, along with another shot featuring exhausted Williams cross-country runners at the end of their meet.[38]

But the majority of the spread is dedicated to capturing idealized images of a "football weekend at a men's college," described as "a thoroughly tested, thoroughly proved combination of minor athletic events (cross-country), the Big Game, imported dates [a reported seven hundred women made the trek to the 'leafy campus' in Williamstown], dances in the student union, candlelight dinners, campus walks, and, importantly and inevitably, a good deal of snuggling and guzzling at fraternity houses."[39] The rest of the accompanying captions continue to reflect the dominant cultural perspectives of the day, targeted toward *SI*'s predominantly male readership. "All alone (but not for long) at a fraternity house window," reads one caption, "Sue Kunzelmann, who is still a schoolgirl at Connecticut's Westover, contemplates the new and wonderful world of college men." Another caption says, "Two by two, Williams men and their dates paired off at odd moments during the weekend, some to play pool in Baxter Hall [named for its then president], some to dance at the Alpha Delta Phi–Kappa Alpha fraternity party and still others (albeit few) to seek intellectual stimulation in the Nixon-Kennedy debate on television."[40] And in all the photos, students don the era's de facto autumnal preppy uniform: crewneck sweaters and button-down shirts, woolen skirts and overcoats. If there were ever a pictorial capturing of an idealized moment, this was it.

As for the 1977 *SI* piece on Union, Putnam described the campus as "picturesque," employing the oft-used thematic trope common to national media coverage that served to bolster the idyllic idealized image of NESCAC schools. Putnam portrayed Union's athletics scene as a "bastion of athletic dormancy," into which came Harkness, "a broken-nosed warrior invading an ancient world of wisdom." The critique of Union's "athletic dormancy" sets a tone far different from the one *SI* writer Douglas Looney would convey nearly two decades later; he looked at NESCACs approach to athletics and saw an enterprise decidedly preferable to the excesses and commercialization of the big-time.

Putnam also mentioned that Harkness came to Union with a rep, for he was once labeled "the Poison Ivy of the Ivy League." This was in reference to the title of a 1967 *SI* piece on Harkness penned during the season when Cornell would win its first NCAA championship. Author Mark Mulvoy found that Harkness's "methods and manner may be anathema to the button-down-collar crowd."[41] Mulvoy, who was Boston Irish Catholic and

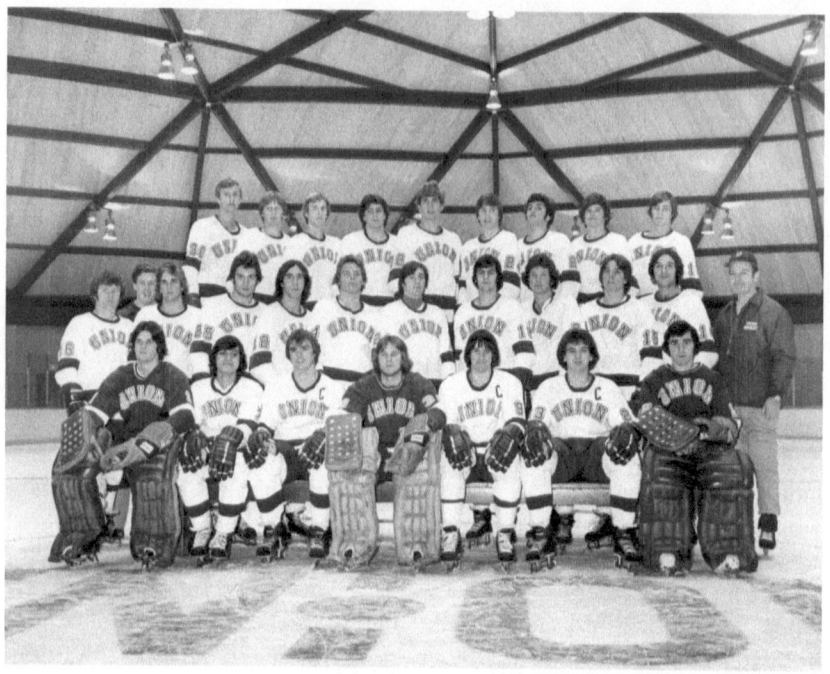

The 1976–77 Union men's hockey team. Infamous head coach Ned Harkness is second row, far right. Courtesy Special Collections, Schaffer Library, Union College.

attended Boston College, was clearly sympathetic to Harkness's approach that tweaked college hockey's tweedier elements at places like Dartmouth, Harvard, and Yale. Stephen Hardy supported this notion, saying, "Ned wasn't liked because in the Ivy League that was still the era of the old gentleman-coach, like [Ralph] 'Cooney' Wieland at Harvard. And Ned comes in and it's a different dynamic." According to Hardy, Harkness "was part of a transition period with younger coaches coming in who would be fighting over recruits. When he went to Cornell, they weren't very good, so he upset the apple cart. Before then it had been Harvard and Dartmouth who were strong. And all of a sudden Cornell gets good with upwards to 100 percent Canadian players."

Mulvoy also highlighted this bone of contention within the collegiate hockey community concerning the recruiting of Canadian players, who were viewed as quasi-professional mercenaries compared with their American counterparts. Mulvoy's take was a far cry from what *SI* had published in 1955, when the magazine attributed the growth of college hockey's respectability to the "annual invasion by hundreds of Canadian students ... who swap their talent for a scholarship."[42]

There was also the perception that these Canadian hockey Hessians were also academically suspect. As evidence of this, Stephen Hardy notes that Cornell had the only agricultural school (Cornell Agricultural College, which began as the state-funded New York State Agriculture Experiment Station and became part of Cornell in 1923) in the Ivy League. "And for whatever reason," Hardy said, "many hockey players tended to be in the aggie school. And by '67, most of them were Canadian." Hardy also recalled attending a Cornell-Harvard game in Cambridge in 1967, when pregame the Harvard students unfurled a banner that stretched from blue line to blue line near the Cornell bench. The banner read: "Welcome, Future Farmers of Canada." Cornell won the game, 9–0. "And I remember talking to one of the Cornell players about that later," said Hardy, "and he got really pissed. He said, 'Who's to say for these kids from Ontario or Saskatchewan, who are probably going to go back to work there, that this is bad?' The aggie school also housed its highly ranked school of nutrition," Hardy pointed out, "but the pushback was Cornell was all Canadian, Ned's hiding them in the aggie school, and that he was going to do that at Union."

Hardy also clarified that Harkness's approach wasn't new, as Jack Kelley had recruited Canadians at Colby during the 1950s and 1960s, but for Union, a charter member of NESCAC, "this was going to be a problem." Roster data from when Harkness was at Union, while incomplete, shows that Union teams were approximately 50 percent Canadian players, primarily from Ontario, while teams at Bowdoin, Colby, Middlebury, and Williams each had four or fewer Canadian players, generally from Ontario or Quebec. But some in NESCAC saw the recruiting trend as contrary to the conference's ethos, as evidenced by the comments of Williams president John Sawyer. "As the professional development takes over bigger-name places—for instance, Cornell's all-Canadian hockey team this year," stated Sawyer, "it seems quite possible that ordinary American college students who enjoy sports will find our kinds of programs increasingly attractive."[43]

Mulvoy's 1967 piece also highlighted multiple examples of Harkness's coaching gamesmanship, such as turning out arena lights and claiming power outages to suspend play when his teams were tired. Hardy corroborated this: "One of the stories when he was at RPI was that if he got ahead, he'd turn the heat up in the visiting locker room, or he would lower the brine amounts in the ice so it would get soft. So there were all these stories about Ned and how he ran his program. And the word was 'He's gonna do it again at Union.'"

Once ensconced in Schenectady, Harkness supervised the rink's completion and courted local businessmen into "sponsoring such necessities as

3,000 seats, a scoreboard, a carpeted and stereoed locker room that would be welcome in the NHL."[44] "If you can't go first class," said Harkness, "don't make the trip."[45] This quote alone was a likely harbinger of the friction to come, but Putnam allowed that "Harkness hopes to be playing in Division I soon, and that is where this gifted team belongs, but for the moment he has run into strong opposition on the Union campus. There are fears that a big-time athletic team would give Union the reputation of being a jock school." The qualifier "for the moment" would prove to be wrong, and while there were already indications that Harkness's Union tenure wouldn't end well, Putnam made no mention of concurrent and burgeoning NESCAC dissatisfaction.

As to the academic proclivities of the players, Putnam noted that the team finished with a 2.61 cumulative GPA, with nine players making the dean's list, adding that "athletes can't hide at Union. There are no crip courses, no basket-weaving majors." Harkness likely wanted this information included by Putnam to counter the developing storm over the academic profiles and performance of his players. "I know a lot of people at the school were afraid I had imported a bunch of goons," Harkness told Putnam. "At first they looked at them like they expected to see horns growing out of their heads. Never has any team had so much pressure."[46]

The program quickly emerged as one of the nation's strongest and answered Bonner's call to generate stakeholder excitement. A standing-room-only crowd of 3,400 braved a blizzard and subzero temperatures to see the game against Division I UNH (Bonner's former employer), "and it was never close. In one of the most shocking upsets since RPI's win in the 1954 NCAA Championship, Union stunned UNH 8–4."[47] One imagines it likely that Bonner was there to witness the havoc his creation wreaked on the charges from his former school. There would be more havoc to come, and it would ultimately claim Bonner as victim.

Conflicts on Campus and with NESCAC

While some Union stakeholders were enthused with the on-ice efforts of the Flying Dutchmen, many in collegiate hockey circles were wary of Harkness's return. NESCAC hockey opponents were part of the disenchanted, as illustrated in a 1976 letter to Bonner from new Middlebury president Olin Robison, who had replaced James Armstrong the previous fall. In it, Robison, a former Baptist pastor from Texas with degrees from Baylor University and Oxford who previously served in administration roles in the Peace Corps, in the U.S. State Department, and at Bowdoin, wrote to complain about "the atmosphere" and "style of play" encountered

Chapter 5. The New Conference Faces Immediate Challenges 117

by the Middlebury team—a future Division III hockey power two decades later (see Chapter 7)—at Achilles on January 16, an 11-4 Union win. Wrote Robison:

> It struck me and many of the other Middlebury fans there that evening that Union has chosen to reenter college hockey with a style and aggressiveness which we found unacceptable. Since it is our feeling that Union has made a decision to play a style of hockey that is incompatible with the way we think the sport ought to be played by a liberal arts college like Middlebury, we have decided to cancel next year's game with Union and not to reschedule Union in hockey into the foreseeable future. ... [W]e are not attempting to sit on judgment on your program. I assume you have good reasons for pursuing the sport in this way.[48]

Robison could make this move—after just one game between the two schools in the very first season of the Union program's reboot—since NESCAC bylaws did not require round-robin scheduling.

In preparing his response to Robison, Bonner asked Thomas Kershner, the chair of Union's Athletic Committee and chair of the economics department, to gather information on the events of the game in question, where Union scored three goals in the game's first two minutes. Kershner found that none of the writers from the four local papers described any untoward crowd incidents or commented negatively on Union's "style of play." Seventeen penalties were called during the game, nine against Union (all minors), while two Middlebury players were given major misconduct penalties. While the game officials made no adverse game report to supervisors, they did note that Robison came to their dressing room immediately after the game to ask them why the game was not stopped when the Middlebury goalie lost his mask. Kershner also marked that no one in the Union athletic department had received any communication from anyone in the Middlebury athletic department on any matter since the game and wrote that he was confused by this: "I understand that athletic concerns normally emanate from appropriate campus groups as well as the athletic department" and are "normally pursued through the offices of the respective athletic directors." Kershner closed by saying that he and his wife had attended the game themselves, and he was "struck by the enthusiasm and cheering on the part of fans for both schools," and though he acknowledged that "an above average number of penalties were called, it was our sense (widely shared) that any roughness—as with the penalties—was about evenly divided between the two teams." Kershner concluded that Robison's displeasure likely resulted from sour grapes: "They were disappointed by the outcome of the game—the more so because they expected, with some reason, to win."[49]

Thusly informed, Bonner immediately wrote to Robison and enclosed a copy of Kershner's report, requesting that Robison "reconsider the actions you have taken, now made public through copies of your letter, and join me in arranging for a further review."[50] In a letter dated March 5, Robison replied curtly that, after discussing the matter with Middlebury administrators and athletic department personnel, "we must stand by our decision."[51] Regardless of Union's internal fact-finding, the on-ice actions were now on record to be alienating the NESCACs.

Concurrently, as presaged in Putnam's *SI* piece, "pressure was already developing, encouraged by Coach Harkness and certainly not opposed by President Bonner, to 'move up' to Division I—a prospect which some students and many faculty members viewed as inconsistent with Union's values and reputation." Such a move, the Union historian Wayne Somers observed, "was clearly incompatible with Union's continued membership [in NESCAC]."[52]

At the same time, Bonner announced his intention to appoint a Task Force on Athletics, as "so emotional has this subject become that I want the responsibility for decision-making widely shared by all those affected."[53] The task force was charged with examining the pros and cons of NESCAC membership. In late October 1976, the school's student newspaper published an early draft of the report that suggested that Union might move to Division I hockey and withdraw from NESCAC. Angered at the paper for publishing the piece, Bonner demanded an apology in an open memo to the college community. The paper refused, citing that it had listed the draft-only status of the report. Ironically, the final report, released in December, recommended withdrawal from NESCAC, as nearly all Union coaches disagreed with the conference policy that banned team sport postseason participation. In this sense, Union coaches were like the vast majority of their colleagues across the conference, as the ban was never embraced by coaches or ADs and had served to be an irritation until its removal in the mid–1990s (see Chapter 6). But Somers found "most of the faculty, many of the students, and at least some of the alumni were opposed to leaving what they perceived as an academically prestigious association consistent with Union's history and aspirations."[54]

In March 1977, as Union men's hockey was completing a 20–2–1 campaign, a letter from Williams president John Chandler, who had returned to Williamstown in 1973 to replace John Sawyer, brought to light evidence that during the previous year Harkness had violated NESCAC recruiting rules and lied about the matter when confronted by Bonner. Chandler and former Williams AD Bob Peck recalled the process:

> **PECK:** You remember that, John, what we did. You and me. We nailed Ned Harkness for cheating.

Chapter 5. The New Conference Faces Immediate Challenges 119

My hockey coach, Bill McCormick, kept coming to me and bitching about Ned, "He's doing this, he's doing that." And I said, "OK, get the thing and we'll nail his ass."

So my hockey coach came to me and he said, "You know, Ned is going in kids' homes," and so forth. And I said, "OK, let's get him." And he said, "Well, I don't know...." And I said, "Then shut up. I don't want to hear it."

So very shortly after that, Bill was recruiting a kid from Michigan, and Ned was recruiting him also, and Michigan State was recruiting him. So he ended up going to Michigan State. And Bill, through his conversation with the hockey coach at Michigan State—which might have even been his hockey coach, I don't know—we got this information. So I said, "Let's document it."

So they set up a call with the [Michigan State] hockey coach and the kid, and me and McCormick. So we wrote it all down, and we gave it to John [Chandler]. And John sent it to [Bonner], who was kind of weak. Originally [Harkness] denied it, and the president stood behind him. Then we got the evidence, and I think he suspended him for one game.

CHANDLER: And Bob and I did not mean to bring public embarrassment. We wanted—and expected—the president to handle it quietly and to do a thorough job of cleaning up. Instead, he stupidly went to the newspapers [*laughter*] and blew himself up. Bob and I both were appalled.

Press accounts of the day confirmed these recollections. The Associate Press reported in March 1977 that Peck had informed Bonner of Harkness's recruiting violations. "Yes, I know who blew the whistle," replied Harkness in the article. "It was Williams College. Williams spent a year putting this thing together." Peck acknowledged the reporting, arguing that the actions were justified because conference rules were instituted "to reverse the very bad trend of recruiting and commercialism in college sports." Harkness, who had indeed lied to Bonner about committing the violation, admitted he "did something wrong, but it wasn't murder. I'll pay the price. But everything I have ever done since coming to Union two years ago was for Union. I lied, but I lied to save my hockey program." Harkness felt the recruiting issue was "blown out of proportion. The boy I talked to in his home was a Canadian lad. He had already been accepted at Union, but he needed financial aid. So I went to his home. Now, I know it's against [NESCAC] recruiting rules. At the time it didn't even dawn on me."[55] Harkness also admitted to the *New York Times*, "I lied, but I lied to protect my hockey program," but rationalized, "I guess if you win, you pay for it down the line."[56] After the issue became public, Bonner immediately suspended Harkness and offered his own resignation to the board of trustees, who refused the resignation, opted to reinstate Harkness, and voted 12–8 to terminate membership in NESCAC in March 1977.[57]

Dissatisfaction was percolating on the Union campus as well.

According to an understated college-sponsored analysis, the hockey crisis led to an academic one, where "standards of admission can sometimes be overwhelmed by non-academic considerations"—that is, the "irregular recruitment of some athletes handier on the ice than in class. Scandals in the manner of admissions and financial aid disturbed the campus and called for correction.... The issue also drove the director of admissions (Jay Shulpe) from office."[58] To this point, Stephen Hardy offered, "I bet you Ned's kids at Cornell and Union performed well academically, but no one wanted to hear that." The data provided in Putnam's *SI* piece notwithstanding, Union faculty were already questioning the academic profiles of hockey participants, leading to a faculty committee investigation regarding the entering credentials of hockey recruits. One review of admission data showed that two hockey matriculants had combined SAT scores of 620 and 790, when Union "seldom accepted students with combined scores below 1000," although several prospects rejected by Union eventually ended up at Ivy League schools.[59]

After the end of the fall term in 1977, several hockey players were ruled ineligible because of their academic performance, after which Harkness resigned, and a few days later, the team stated it would not play without him. Harkness left with a record of 45–8–2, and when the team returned to finish the season, it lost all thirteen games, usually by lopsided scores. Harkness's full-time replacement was Charlie Morrison, who immediately disclaimed any interest in playing Division I and who was described by the college's history of the event in verbiage reminiscent of NESCAC's foundational mission, as "a first-rate coach who was thoroughly committed to the traditional view of the proper place of athletics in a small college."[60] Bonner's time in Schenectady was over as well, as he resigned in June 1978 to assume the presidency of Wayne State University in Detroit. According to Bob Peck, who may have been emboldened to call out Union at the time because he was in the process of being named AD at Harvard (a position from which he withdrew after student and alumni complaints regarding the vetting process[61]), "I was told that nobody from Wayne State called Union to ask about his resignation," but Bonner took the post, stating, "I look forward to returning to a major public university that is committed to both high quality and wide access." He resigned the presidency there in 1982 to return to teaching.[62]

In 1991, Union did realize its goal to move to Division I in hockey and won the championship in 2014 (with nine Canadian players). While Bonner was priming for a departure from NESCAC as early as 1976, probably the simplest explanation of the split can be offered by former Amherst AD Peter Gooding, an émigré from England by way of Canada who began coaching men's soccer in 1968 and was named AD the year the Union

Chapter 5. The New Conference Faces Immediate Challenges 121

scandal broke. "Union was, in terms of our regulations, cheating, particularly with their hockey recruiting," recalled Gooding. "And when they were called on it, we said, 'You can't do this, otherwise you'll get booted.'" To that, Gooding said, Union's response was "'Look, hockey's too important to us. And so we're out.' And it all happened basically at the same meeting. So one side could say they were booted out, and the other could say they were leaving."

Much like in the case of the NCAA's Sanity Code in the late 1940s (see p. 58), NESCAC, because of its loosely organized managerial structure, lacked any sanctioning power, and because it had no enforcement apparatus, expulsion was the only option. Over time the NCAA would develop a more formalized enforcement structure—much to the chagrin of many intercollegiate athletics stakeholders, NESCAC included—and essentially usurp the enforcement roles of conferences.

This idealized notion of purity and simplicity, sought for years by Pentagonal-era presidents, was challenged during the Union scandal. Ultimately NESCAC and Union established ground on which both could operate their programs within their stated goals and missions. In 1984, at the start of the college football season, the *New York Times* reported, in a nearly full-page article with two photographs, of football success at Union, as the program was coming off its appearance in the Stagg Bowl (the NCAA's Division III championship game) the previous season. The piece (found in the archival files of Trinity president James English, sent to him by a trustee with the handwritten note: "I thought you'd be interested in this") avers that "the foundation for the building [of the football program's success] was the school's decision to leave [NESCAC]." "That conference," stated AD Richard Sakala, "is a much more rigid conference than NCAA rules allowed." Sakala also claimed that Union's profile within the conference was of a diminished tier, which explains in large part why the NESCAC fit was problematic. "Naturally, if a student was looking at Union and Williams or Union and Amherst, in most cases the student did not choose us." Sakala also cited the inability to pursue postseason opportunities as an issue. "The argument was that it took away from academics," said Sakala, adding, "Leaving the conference was a very important step for us." The separation from NESCAC allowed Sakala "to send his coaches looking for promising players."[63]

It is likely that Sakala made his statements fully aware that many readers would have known of the institutional fallout from the Bonner regime, and he was taking pains to note that a different approach was under way on campus. But whatever the comments he made in 1984, ten years later Sakala admitted that there were recruiting irregularities under Harkness, "but says it all worked out because Union is now happily playing Division

I hockey." "Still," wrote Looney, Sakala told him "wistfully" that "NES-CAC represents the true spirit of college athletics."[64] This appreciation was shared by Roger Hull, president at Union from 1990 to 2005. According to Eugene Tobin, a Rutgers and Brandeis alumnus who was president at Hamilton from 1993 to 2003, Union sought to rejoin the conference, but "the problem of course was the Division I hockey program. It was too complicated." And as a result it never happened.

"Membership Would Bring Some Very Substantial Benefits to Us": The Anti-Union Joins NESCAC

Union's exit meant NESCAC's membership dropped from an asymmetrical eleven to a more logistically reasonable ten, at least in terms of managing policies and operations like scheduling. But the departure left Hamilton even more of a geographic outlier than before. In 1974, before Union's departure, the University of Rochester had sought inclusion, which would have bumped the roster to an even dozen and would have aided with the issues of proximity. Rochester president Robert Sproull wrote to Wesleyan president Colin Campbell, who replaced Edwin Etherington in 1970, to push his case. Sproull noted that his AD "informs me that your conference is governed by the Presidents of its member institutions, and that membership would allow us flexibility in scheduling but would restrict such items as off-campus recruiting of students." "I doubt if any of these regulations would change our practices," Sproull wrote, "but insofar as they did we should agree to follow out your precepts." While admitting that Rochester was "somewhat removed from the center of gravity of your institutions," Sproull suggested, "To offset this, you and your fellow institutions have many alumni in the Rochester area, and the Syracuse and Buffalo alumni groups would find it easy to come to games in Rochester."[65]

Documents reveal that NESCAC at least considered the move, which would have given its westernmost members another geographic rival. In January 1975, Rochester AD Dave Ocorr met with NESCAC ADs to discuss potential membership. Williams AD Bob Peck outlined the discussion this way: "I think it is fair to summarize that there are serious reservations about extending the Conference geographically as far as Rochester, although the two New York Colleges in our conference were favorably disposed to Rochester being included as it would help their travel arrangements with another conference school."[66] As a result, Rochester remained on the outside.

Instead, in a move that seems difficult to rationalize, the conference

Chapter 5. The New Conference Faces Immediate Challenges 123

opted to invite into the fold Connecticut College (or "Conn," as it is referred to in NESCAC circles), a formerly all-women school located in New London. Conn historian Paul Marthers argued that the single biggest factor that resulted in the founding of what was then the Connecticut College for Women in 1911 was the fact that Wesleyan had decided to stop enrolling women in 1909 (making it, like nearby Trinity and Yale, single sex), which brought about a movement to provide educational opportunities for women in the state. Wesleyan officials and alumni directed funds and support to aid the newly established all-women school. As previously noted, Wesleyan had made the move to be seen as a "college for males" and to help move the school from a "'backward status' amongst prestigious New England colleges." The subsequent bolstering and success of the school's football program garnered publicity and "reinforced Wesleyan's male image in New York and Boston newspapers."[67]

Conn—along with the women's schools Mount Holyoke College, Smith College, and Wellesley College and soon-to-be coed Vassar College and Wheaton College—had established connections with some NESCACs through its participation in the Twelve-College Exchange, where students from these current and former women's schools and from Amherst, Bowdoin, Dartmouth, Trinity, Wesleyan, and Williams could spend a semester or a year at one of the other campuses. There were other tangential connections was well; for example Colby president Robert Strider, who would step down in 1979, had taught English at Conn from 1946 to 1957.

After the move to coeducation, Conn's new president, Oakes Ames, a Harvard undergrad alum and former Princeton faculty member, opted to expand the school's athletics programs to attract male students and hired Charles "Charlie" Luce from Boston University to serve as the men's basketball coach and Conn's first AD. Luce led the college facilities upgrade process with the addition of an ice arena and a new indoor athletic center.[68]

In July 1981, Ames contacted Tufts president Jean Mayer, alerting him that Ames had written to Colin Campbell and John Chandler to express Conn's interest in joining NESCAC. "I understand that the possibility of our membership is under discussion in the Conference," Ames said, making a formal request to join for the 1982–83 academic year, "or as soon thereafter as possible."[69] Ames went on to state Conn's case, noting that the school had "launched an effort to develop our intercollegiate and athletic programs" and that "our philosophy now, as then, is in complete agreement with that of NESCAC": "members of our athletics staff and the deans have studied and discussed the NESCAC Conference Agreement. They strongly concur with the Conferences' point of view about the role of athletics in a college." Perhaps indicating his own ignorance, Ames neglected to outline specifically the elements of this philosophy or the stated role of athletics. Ames also sought to draw further connections between Conn and NESCAC, writing, "The interests and goals of our students are exactly like those of the students in your group," again failing to explain what these interests and goals might be and how he had learned of the similarities.

In September 1981, NESCAC ADs discussed Conn's application, and according to the minutes of the meeting supplied to Tufts president Jean Mayer, a French scientist who came to the school in 1976 by way of the Harvard School of Public Health, by his AD Rocky Carzo, since the group had "not been officially 'charged' by the Presidents to assess [Conn's application]," it felt "uncomfortable making any recommendations." Carzo then offered several options if charged, including whether NESCAC should "consider or reconsider those schools who have formally requested consideration as well as those who have inquired informally, i.e., Norwich, Rochester, WPI, Skidmore, Vassar, Connecticut College, etc."[70] As noted, both Norwich and Rochester had formally inquired as to possible membership and had been rebuffed. Carzo also cited an August 1981 letter from Mayer to Ames discussing the expansion issue and said the ADs would be happy to take it up in its upcoming December meeting.

That same month, prior to the ADs meeting, Carzo was contacted via letter by Conn director of admission Jeanette Hersey, who, at the urging of Conn AD Luce, outlined Conn's admissions procedures. Hersey indicated that "students who possess ... personal qualities, such as leadership [and] athletic ability" were important factors in Conn's admissions decisions, with the result that "students participate equally, to the extent of their interest and commitments, in all aspects of community life," adding that "the profile of the Connecticut College athlete is comparable to that of all other students."[71]

In January 1982, just prior to when NESCAC was slated to take up the expansion issue, Ames wrote to new Trinity president James English seeking support for Conn's entrée. After reminding English that Ames had contacted Tufts's Mayer (who also served as NESCAC chair) the previous summer regarding Conn's interest in joining the conference, Ames restated his case: "Over the past seven to eight years, the College has developed its intramural and intercollegiate programs to the point where about two-thirds of the students are involved in athletics." Ames also stated that Conn was "competing successfully with many of the NESCAC members in a wide range of sports, and its philosophy seems well-matched to that of the Conference" (again with no indication of what this philosophy might be), and that "membership would bring some very substantial benefits to us, and we hope that our involvement would also be valuable to the group and its members."[72] A review of Conn's sports schedules that year provided

Chapter 5. The New Conference Faces Immediate Challenges   125

to English verified the connections with NESCACs and the overall competitiveness of its teams. Conn played local NESCACs Trinity and Wesleyan in nearly every sport, along with Middlebury in men's soccer (the team's final record that year: 10–5); Tufts in field hockey (5–8–2); Amherst in men's ice hockey (12–11); Amherst, Bates, Middlebury, and Williams in men's basketball (16–8); Amherst in women's basketball (8–7); Amherst, Bates, and Colby in men's lacrosse (9–3); and Amherst, Bates, and Tufts in women's lacrosse (2–10). English responded that few were "as much a part of her family as I," indicating previous contacts with Conn, and he admitted that "the evil and vicious" would see "the grossest of conflicts of interest" in his supporting Conn's candidacy, but "somehow I have managed to cope with these in the past and suspect that I can do the same at least one more time!"[73]

At a full NESCAC meeting in April 1982, new Colby president Bill Cotter, with undergrad and law degrees from Harvard and work experience with the Ford Foundation, indicated that the rationale for accepting Conn was because of a factor described as "presidential interest." What is unclear is whether this meant interest on the part of NESCAC presidents or on the part of Ames. Additional factors included that Conn was a coeducational liberal arts school currently competing with NESCACs and it had "actively sought admission to the conference." Bates AD Bob Hatch noted that the ADs expressed concern as to whether the presidents were considering further expansion, and the minutes reflect that "MIT surfaced as the center of this discussion." Mayer indicated he would inquire as to the possible interest on the part of Tufts's Boston-area neighbor in joining the fold,[74] although why Tufts would want to allow a nearby competitor to gain equal status with it by conference inclusion is questionable. Of the MIT candidacy, Amherst's Peter Gooding agreed that the "obvious" expansion choice was MIT, "because many NESCAC schools competed with them in many sports. And MIT was one of the few schools that would bring additional status to NESCAC." "So we made a couple of informal inquiries," said Gooding, but the move "was out of the question because they did have some Division I programs, and they were incredibly independent in the way they ran their programs."

Ames's lobbying (and English's stated conflicts) aside, Luce was the essential figure in the expansion process for Conn because of his personal connections with NESCAC decision makers, which, according to Gooding, was the sole reason Conn was included: "Charlie was a nice man, and he was very close friends with people like [Williams AD] Bob Peck and others in the conference." "They were good friends, they visited, had beers, and that sort of stuff," recalled Gooding, "and it was truthfully as absolutely trivial as that." Gooding also recalled that "Charlie knew it would make an enormous difference to Conn College [to join NESCAC]. If Conn College has one person to thank it was Charlie Luce, because he single-handedly got them in." Former Colby AD and head men's basketball coach Dick Whitmore agreed, pointing out that Luce had many friends at the AD level, including former Colby AD and head football coach Dick McGee.

Gooding elaborated on the NESCAC meeting where the decision was made, explaining that the process was "typical of the half-assed way we did things. There was no systematic attempt to research institutions, to invite institutions to join us. It was personal friendships and allegiances. Completely unscientific." He continued: "And at that meeting one of the presidents said something like, 'Isn't this sort of unscientific? If we're going to expand, shouldn't we at least be looking at schools we might like to invite?' But everything we did was informal." Of the general deliberative process: "We use to meet once a year, and we'd meet with the presidents' executive committee, and by the way usually only one of them showed up. That showed you the degree of interest on their part."

After acceptance, NESCAC membership would come to serve as Conn's "aspirational peers and competitors," but this peer system "has been both a blessing and a curse" for the school, says Conn historian Paul Marthers.[75] Conn "has always been able to define, or at least legitimize, its institutional quality" through this association, and Conn "officials and alumni are quite content to claim the NESCAC 'brand' that stands for high quality academics and athletics."[76] But the "lack of institutional wealth" puts the school at a "competitive disadvantage"

Charlie Luce's friendships with his peers among NESCAC athletic directors secured Conn's spot in the conference. Courtesy Linda Lear Center for Special Collections and Archives, Shain Library, Connecticut College.

Chapter 5. The New Conference Faces Immediate Challenges 127

within NESCAC. Conn currently has the second-smallest endowment and continues to be the "poor cousin" of the group, since the school is "too tuition dependent for comfort" and is below the NESCAC median in the areas of faculty salaries and the ability to offer need-blind admission (the school enrolls as many full-pay students as most NESCACs). Conn's dilemma, Marthers concludes, is that the school will always be seeking "more resources to keep pace with its well-heeled and more prestigious" NESCAC peers, but the move in part has aided its "remarkably rapid ascent into the upper ranks of national liberal arts colleges."[77]

After Conn's addition, there continued to be inquiries by other schools, as recalled by former Hamilton president Eugene Tobin. "We were constantly being solicited by other colleges who wanted to join," said Tobin, "so it was clearly apparent that NESCAC had a reputation that was very important to both preserve and sustain, and that being a member of NESCAC was clearly seen as being attractive to colleges. As a group, during my time we never seriously considered expansion. There were votes and there were conversations, but there was a comfort level to keeping it at eleven."

Despite the fact that the bonhomie between Luce and NESCAC ADs was identified as the critical factor in Conn's move to NESCAC, Conn's "good fortune" to get an invitation occurred, according to former Vassar College provost and former Conn president Norman Fainstein, "when Vassar's president turned the league down—a decision some at Vassar still regret."[78] Vassar, located in Poughkeepsie, New York, made sense in terms of providing a proximate geographical partner to Hamilton, but no records exist in Vassar's administrative files that such a formal offer to join NESCAC was either made or entertained. Gooding could not recall the proffering of any such invitation, but "the idea of Vassar was likely promoted by Hamilton. And there was an unspoken resentment toward Hamilton anyway because most of us felt they shouldn't be in the conference."

The minutes of the September 1981 NESCAC AD meeting do refer to Vassar as one of a number of schools that had either formally or informally inquired as to possible inclusion or had possibly been contacted by a NESCAC school, so any such inquiry would have been decidedly informal. In terms of intercollegiate athletics, formerly all-female Vassar not only had to add programs for its men but also had to add competitive sports for its women as well. The addition of men's programs was in part a response to the perception that the school was "inhospitable to men," not because of hostility but because the school was suffused with a strong "aura of feminism." Director of Admission Richard Stephenson observed, "Unless Vassar's essential character changes, I doubt we will ever have great appeal to the upper-middle class, 'all-around guy' typified in my mind by the stereotype of the Dartmouth, Amherst, or Williams man."[79]

According to Marthers, Conn's move to NESCAC, described as "the Ivy League of Division III sports," "made a big difference.... To Oakes Ames, the most tangible symbol of Connecticut's success at coeducation was the invitation to join NESCAC and compete head-to-head with the region's top formerly all-male liberal arts colleges ... as well as against long coeducational [schools]."[80] As a result, by 1985, Conn was enrolling men at equal rates as women. Gooding agreed that "the status of schools like Connecticut College, Bates, and Colby rose measurably because they were immediately associated with schools like Williams, Amherst, and Wesleyan. It sounds elitist of me but it's true." Another former NESCAC AD concurred: "Conn College, I'm sorry to say, wouldn't have the stature it has now if it hadn't affiliated itself with NESCAC back in 1982. It helped Conn a lot."

So the benefits of NESCAC membership for Conn were clear and several, but what did Conn bring to NESCAC? According to Gooding, not much. "I was ambivalent about the whole thing," he recalled. "Conn didn't have football, and in the back of my mind I thought, 'Great, that suits us down to the ground,' because a lot of the bullshit we spent our time on was usually something to do with football. Someone cheating or someone doing something so they could win two games. And bringing Conn into the mix without football would ease those tensions a bit." Another former NESCAC AD commented, "There are a lot of questions on why the other ten, after Union dropped out, should be involved with Conn College. They didn't have football, they didn't have baseball and softball [one former Conn AD stated, 'We probably never will'], they didn't have great facilities." Colby's Dick Whitmore added, "The voting process was not publicized, nor the impact of a non-football school adequately discussed," leading to "four decades of a mostly albatross situation." But even after nearly four decades in the fold, former Williams AD Harry Sheehy offered the perspective that "half the kids at Conn College wanted to be somewhere else in NESCAC." Given the views expressed above, the marriage of Conn and NESCAC proved to be hardly a match made in heaven for either party.

"Too Perfect": An End-of-an-Era Homage

In its first decade, NESCAC had parted ways with a school that was ill fitted to its mission and added another, whether rationally or not, that seemed to. A managerial structure not based on a rule book chock-full of

Chapter 5. The New Conference Faces Immediate Challenges 129

operational minutiae, while ideal in the abstract, had led to shortcomings in the expansion decision-making process.

Nonetheless, NESCAC marched on into the last decade of the century buoyed by acclamatory exposure in the national sporting press. The 1994 "Pure and Simple" *Sports Illustrated* article would serve as a landmark homage and ideal image touchstone for NESCAC stakeholders at a watershed moment for the conference. Up to that point, the NESCACs, especially the programs at the conference's better-known schools, received sporadic coverage in the national media, much of it—the 1977 *SI* Union hockey piece excepted—often bolstering the conference's ideal image. One post-Union example was a piece in the *Wall Street Journal* that outlined the 1985 decision of Amherst head football coach Jim Ostendarp to deny rising cable giant ESPN the right to broadcast the school's one hundredth game versus Williams. "We're in education, we aren't in the entertainment business," said Ostendarp, adding, with a straight face apparently, "I'm against having Budweiser paying for it when we don't allow drinking on campus." While Williams head coach Bob Odell expressed disappointment regarding the decision, stating, "I think it was a great opportunity for our young men to play on TV and for people to see the kind of football we play," new Amherst president Peter Pouncey, an Englishman with degrees from Oxford and Columbia (he also served as a faculty member and dean at the latter institution), deferred to Ostendarp, or "the Darp" as he was universally known. "I don't see it as a mortal sin to appear on a television screen," said Pouncey, "but I certainly wouldn't have crowded him on his decision. We spend half our time pointing to the Darp as a model of what our coaches should be, a coach with his arm around an athlete's shoulder saying, 'Do you like Beethoven?'"[81]

The notion of a coach whose game-day attire featured a three-piece blue serge suit, a narrow striped tie, and a brown fedora—a reincarnation of the mentor-coach of football's leather helmet era, who upheld the tenets of a liberal arts education and whom his president declined to pull rank on—bolstered Amherst's ideal image bona fides. However, the game, which both schools promoted as "The Biggest Little Game in America," was televised nonetheless—over closed circuit to alumni gatherings in twenty-nine cities. "That's great," said Ostendarp, "because they know what it's all about," even though one stakeholder, the president of the Williams Alumni Association, carped, "My regret is that 34 million households won't have the chance to watch Williams trounce Amherst."[82] Amherst won, 35–20. Twenty-two years later (fifteen years after Ostendarp retired), the live broadcast of ESPN's *College GameDay* program originated from Williamstown prior to that year's game, a 20–0 Williams victory.

Whatever the motives of Amherst and Williams, the decision to eschew national TV coverage was not unprecedented. Three years prior, both Bowdoin and Wesleyan denied overtures from CBS to broadcast games from their campuses when the network was seeking programming to fill the void during the 1982 NFL players' strike. CBS executive and Amherst grad Thomas Wyman wanted to show Bowdoin's home game versus Amherst, but Bowdoin was unwilling to move the game from Saturday to Sunday because of its Parents' Weekend schedule of events. Tufts at Wesleyan was the network's second choice, and Tufts AD Rocky Carzo was in favor of the broadcast, as was CBS commentator John Madden, who liked the idea of showing a Division III game. "Maybe this will show there's still some purity in athletics," said Madden. But Wesleyan president Colin Campbell nixed the proposal, stating that such a broadcast would be inconsistent with the underlying spirit of NESCAC. Rebuffed, CBS instead showed Baldwin Wallace at Wittenburg. Leigh Montville of the *Boston Globe* applauded the declination and its alignment with the conference's ideal image. "So Tufts will play Wesleyan on Saturday, and Amherst plays at Bowdoin," he wrote, "and TV will be at none of them. So the outside world will look and say that all this is crazy, that no one rejects the chance to be on television." Montville saluted the move as one that preserved a realm that is "friendly, intimate, real," maintained by NESCAC, whom he described as the "spinster aunts who have lived for so many years in the big, rambling Victorian house at the corner of the big-time athletics scene. ... [S]omehow the old girls never looked better than they do right now."[83]

Following the publication of Looney's piece, *SI* ran excerpts from five letters from readers applauding the coverage. One from Chicago found it "refreshing to know that some still play for the love of the game," but two others took the time to point out that there were two NESCAC alumni—Hamilton's Guy Hebert (a goaltender with the NHL's Anaheim Ducks) and Wesleyan's Jeff Wilner (a tight end with the NFL's Green Bay Packers)—who were playing professionally. The letter referencing Wilner was sent by Richard Beal, a Wesleyan assistant football coach, who noted that Wilner had also been a double major in economics and government. The fact that the coach wanted *SI*'s readers to know of his former charge's professional success smacks of a coach seeking to gain a recruiting advantage by promoting a pathway to the pros that ran through Middletown. The magazine also included photos of both Hebert and Wilner in their pro gear. Also published was an excerpt from a letter from Williams SID Dick Quinn, correcting Looney's assertion that no NESCAC team had ever won a national championship, for the Williams women's swimming team had won Division III titles in 1982 and 1983.[84] One former NESCAC AD hoped the article would, in time, be used "as a marketing tool that says, 'You can come here and make that kind of choice and graduate with an amazing degree and play at the highest level.'"

These comments reveal a sense that a new NESCAC ideal was real and growing, an ideal that valued something more than the pure and simple ethos portrayed by Looney. In short order, this new ideal would reach full flower with the decision to rescind the ban on NCAA postseason play in 1993. The decision would lead to a complete transformation of NESCAC's ideal image, from the version that began and evolved throughout the twentieth century and ended with the decision to embrace the postseason, to a second version that continues to today.

CHAPTER 6

"When All Hell Broke Loose"
The Realities of Postseason Play

Of all the measures governing intercollegiate athletics management included in the Pentagonal and NESCAC agreements, the postseason ban for team sports was far and away the most nettlesome. In Looney's *Sports Illustrated* article, he noted this when he wrote, "But even NESCAC has its hint of controversy, and here it is: In a break with tradition, NESCAC teams are now being allowed to compete in NCAA Division III postseason championships."[1] Looney recognized the potential for this decision to affect the image of the conference, reporting (erroneously, as pointed out by Williams athletics personnel, since Williams women's swimming had won titles in the early 1980s) that "no NESCAC team has ever won an NCAA title, but last season 18 teams from eight NESCAC schools qualified for Division III postseason play."[2] Looney also provided a harbinger of discord when he cited that the men's tennis and golf teams at Williams qualified for NCAA postseason play but were not allowed to compete because of conflicts with final exams. "But once in a while," Looney highlighted presciently, "even in NESCAC, the competitive spirit gets the upper hand: Last year Wesleyan's baseball team missed graduation to play in the NCAA tournament,"[3] advancing to the Division III national championship game and losing to the University of Wisconsin–Oshkosh, 6–2, in Battle Creek, Michigan.

The allowance of postseason team play would soon lead to calls from stakeholder groups to field championship-quality teams and to a concomitant escalation of recruiting and program intensity. To one former NESCAC president, "things were in some ways simpler in 1971, because [we] were on an island. Now we're one set of definitions juxtaposed to another on a spectrum." "The NESCAC founders didn't want to be Michigan State, [and] they didn't want to be Ithaca College," said this president, adding that the key dynamics were the invention of Division III, which acted as a "boundary world that keeps luring you into its standards, which are less

Chapter 6. "When All Hell Broke Loose"

restrictive than yours but so tantalizingly close." The creation of this "tantalizingly close" realm energized many coaches of NESCAC team sports to advocate for the chance to play in NCAA championships, most actively in the late '80s and early '90s, citing that such participation would aid recruiting and enhance "the total athletic/academic experience of the student-athlete and significantly promote NESCAC standards throughout the country."[4]

The ultimate trigger to rescind the ban was a 1990 dispute that underscored the perceived inequities between the treatment of individual sport athletes and coaches, who since the time of Alex Schulten (see Chapter 3) were permitted to compete in NCAA championships, and team sport athletes and coaches, who were not permitted. That year, five Williams women's cross-country runners qualified for the NCAA championship, and under NCAA rules, five runners constituted a team. NESCAC rules defined a team as seven members, and NCAA officials reprimanded NESCAC for ignoring their rule.[5]

NESCAC stakeholders were well versed in the contradictory nature of the ban, and Trinity president James English tried to clarify the disconnect in 1984, when a parent of a female Trinity swimmer opined that not allowing team participation did not afford the school "to benefit from national recognition on a par with other Division III colleges."[6] This was after Williams women's swimming had won Division III championships in 1982 and 1983 by qualifying in the same manner as its women's cross-country team in 1990, which finished third nationally. "The question of where you draw the line," admitted English to the parent, "turns out to be a very complicated one, with no very satisfactory answer. Part of the rationale is that individual athletes may make the decision whether or not to go without being subject to peer pressure by teammates."[7] This refrain was one often rejected by postseason supporters such as hockey historian and Bowdoin alumnus Stephen Hardy. "The presidents argued that the third-stringer might not want to go because they weren't going to play or get any of the benefits, which really misses the point of the whole concept of being part of a team," noted Hardy. "And missing time from school? Give me a break."

"So that is where it rests," summarized English in 1984, but he closed the letter with an offering of sorts: "The NESCAC presidents do revisit these things every few years, and this one could well change. On the other hand, we are trying to dig in our heels wherever we can to slow down the onslaught of 'big athletics.'"[8] English was prescient in terms of predicting a change. NESCAC presidents did indeed address the decades-long dissatisfaction with the postseason policy, and in 1993, the agreement was amended by the Presidents' Executive Committee to permit participation for all sports except football in NCAA postseason championships for a three-year experimental period beginning that fall. The committee chair, Wesleyan's William Chace, stated, "We aim to treat all our student athletes and their teams consistently and equitably. We also want to preserve our traditional emphasis on athletics as part of our total academic program. This decision serves both goals."[9] The move was justified by Wesleyan AD John Biddiscombe to show that NESCACs "can sponsor nationally competitive athletic programs without sacrificing academic standards." He continued that the "primary emphasis would remain on in-season competition rather than postseason tournaments. We will continue to stress the harmony of academics and athletics. In the future, when a NESCAC team is selected for an NCAA Championship, it will give our conference an opportunity to demonstrate how well the two can be integrated."[10] The decision to participate would be left to each school president, which was easier said than done.

While all other teams would now be permitted to play in NCAA postseason events, football would not. Williams football co-captain Bobby Walker told *SI*'s Looney that excluding football was "very unfair to us, but I know they are concerned football will grow into what they fear most."[11] Perhaps NESCAC presidents were following the lead of the Ivies in another attempt to link the conferences' ideal images, but Paul Sweeney, the long-time director of athletic communications at Tufts, noted that the "fear" Walker identified was the concern "that the marquee college sport of football could subvert the NESCAC ideal of the scholar-athlete with the lure of big gate receipts and pressure from alumni to field championship-contending teams." Sweeney went on to state that the seventy-five-player "requirement" of football rosters led to worries "that the recruiting of that many players might lead to lower admissions standards and an escalation of recruiting and program intensity."[12] Sweeney's premise that football is the marquee sport in American intercollegiate athletics is accurate, but it is less clear how the NESCAC ideal would be threatened by the lure of gate receipts, given the well-established Division III ethos under which Tufts and NESCAC operated, where crowd sizes for football seldom surpassed a thousand. In addition, it was not a NESCAC requirement to field football squads of seventy-five, but rather squad sizes were capped at that number.

In stating that the recruiting of "that many" football players might "lead to lower admissions standards," Sweeney reiterated a commonly held view within NESCAC, as on many other campuses, that football players were often less academically qualified than other student-athletes, not to mention the non-student-athlete population. This belief created a significant degree of conflict on NESCAC campuses, especially following the

Chapter 6. "When All Hell Broke Loose" 135

publication of two books on sports in higher education coauthored by former Princeton president William Bowen (see Chapter 7) and led to other forms of conflicts on NESCAC campuses.

Former Amherst AD Peter Gooding agreed with Sweeney. "Thank God football wasn't part of [postseason play]," said Gooding, "because football in many respects is the main problem in small colleges in terms of how it distorts admissions." Gooding also identified a cultural issue at play that impacted the decision: bias against football players. "I often feel really badly for them," Gooding commented. "There's a subtle and negative bias against them. I was the dean of the freshman class for a couple of years, and I was shocked at the kind of comments that faculty would write on these youngsters' papers. One faculty member [was] an absolute prick. At the top of a kid's paper he wrote, 'You must be a football player.'" Another former NESCAC AD revealed that this perception was often transferred onto all student-athletes, not just football players, because "they are such easy targets, because they are always out in front and in the media's eye. It's easy to dispense negatives. Some of that comes from jealousy, some of it comes from ignorance, some of it comes from just not caring. Some [faculty] live in their own worlds, so the only thing important to them is what they do. They don't see the importance of athletics." In addition, a study at Williams in the early 2000s indicated that nearly half of varsity athletes claimed to experience levels of discrimination in class from faculty. The report also cited friction among students on this point, noting that "athletics is resented by many of our top students."[13]

Football notwithstanding, the policy shift showed that NESCAC decision makers were discomfited with the stakeholder perceptions of inequity between individual and team sports, but Biddiscombe's view foreshadowed how NESCAC's ideal image could and would be altered by the change, despite averring that by participating in postseason play against the rest of Division III, the NESCACs could showcase their efforts as the embodiment of the true intercollegiate athletics ideal. But that ideal would only be realized if NESCAC teams could compete successfully.

What is intriguing to consider is whether the presidents ever considered pulling back from NCAA postseason play entirely and extending the ban to include individual sports. However, a presidential proposal to limit postseason play for teams several years later would be met with significant pushback, so any similar move at this time could likely have elicited similar responses. But it could be argued that if the presidents really desired to maintain the ideal conference image, no postseason for anyone, team or individual, would have been the move to make. According to Colby's Dick Whitmore, there was "significant discussion regarding pulling back" from postseason play entirely. "This was where true conference championships models were developed, and after going through the budgetary and philosophical impacts, there was a significant presentation by Middlebury (development people as I recall) as to the value of national team [postseason] participation. This was ultimately the most impactful in the final decision." According to Peter Gooding, the presidents didn't suggest dropping the individual sport option because they recognized such a move would be "more trouble than it was worth, and [individual participation] involved so few student-athletes either missing classes or extending their season." The fact that staff from Middlebury presented the argument in favor of postseason play is interesting, given that Middlebury athletics was about to embrace fully and eagerly such participation (see Chapter 7).

While Eugene Tobin didn't recall any discussion about pulling back from postseason play, he agreed that discussions "were really about whether we were putting ourselves at a disadvantage in admissions as well as in recruiting athletes if we were not allowing for postseason opportunities. That was one of the more fraught questions that emerged because it forced institutions to look seriously at the degree of balance they were comfortable with in terms of postseason opportunity." On the individual sport versus team sport double standard, Tobin also agreed that the issue of fairness "was always brought front and center in terms of any conversation, the lack of equity and fairness. The coaches of those sports that did not have postseason opportunities would argue vociferously. And it was hard to argue against it." Tobin continued that the response at the time from those who were "either indecisive or opposed to it was that those were individual athletes, and these were not teams, therefore the numbers of students who would be away from campus for any length of time would be modest compared to a basketball or hockey team."

The potential positive impact of the expansion of postseason opportunities would have significant ramifications for not only the management of NESCAC athletics policy but also the perception of the conference's image. The presidents sought equity for image purposes, as well as to continue to compete for valued athletics prospects. For decades, the Pentagonals and NESCACs had rejected the athletic overemphasis on wins and losses. But this Before Postseason (BP) era, of which Looney's article served as a de facto valedictory address, would quickly give way to the reality that NESCAC schools could compete for and win Division III national championships. This was the birth of the After Postseason (AP) era. The transition point in 1993 was described by John Cullen, a former Bowdoin women's soccer coach, as "when all hell broke loose." "At first I was all for it," said Cullen, who at the time had worked at Bowdoin for fifteen years in various coaching and administrative capacities. "I wanted our athletes to have the chance to compete at the highest level, but then it became an environment where you had one coach for every sport, and we had to start canvassing the world for recruits." Cullen observed that when he started at Bowdoin, coaches "had faculty status and we were expected to teach. Now they are staff, and that took away any real connection with academics." In the end, Cullen "struggled with asking a junior for a commitment to come to Bowdoin. But that was the way NESCAC was going. If you didn't do that, you couldn't compete." Athletic stakeholders like Cullen had lobbied for years to allow postseason play. Their ultimate success would change the nature of NESCAC's ideal image forever, and it would also become clear that once the AP era began, there would be no going back.

The Evolution of Conflicts over Postseason Play

Given the importance of the postseason issue in the cultivation of NESCAC's image, it is worthwhile to track its evolution from its Pentagonal roots. It is also noteworthy to mention that the mere fact that the grouping even opted to turn down postseason invitations helped to burnish its collective ideal image. As noted in Chapter 2, the earliest conflicts among the Pentagonals involved recruiting issues, and, as Looney pointed out, the "one full-blown athletic scandal that has ever hit NESCAC involved recruiting," with Union's men's ice hockey program. But the postseason issue, which began with the creation of the NCAA's College Division championships and was exacerbated in 1973 with the implementation of the association's three-tiered classification system, would prove to be the defining issue in the history of the conference.

There were several examples of future NESCACs participating in the early years of NCAA postseason play: Tufts (1945) and Williams (1955) competed in the early men's basketball tournament; Tufts (1950) and Trinity (1953, 1958) competed in baseball. However, conflicts over postseason participation at certain peer schools soon emerged. In January 1957, Colby president J. Seelye Bixler wrote to NCAA president Clarence "Pop" Houston, a former AD at Tufts, about an issue pertaining to NCAA baseball postseason play from the previous season. Because of conflicts with spring final exams, Bixler asked NCAA officials to name a representative to the College World Series instead of via a playoff. "So far as I can see, any play-off is extremely likely to conflict with the final examination schedule of one or more colleges," Bixler explained, "and if other college faculties feel about the matter as our faculty does, there is very little chance of excusing a team during such periods. The result is, of course, great disappointment on the part of the boys and many friends of the College." Bixler said, "I feel confident that our faculty would not object to a post-season game even if it should involve the absence of some of the seniors from graduation exercises but, on the matter of final examinations, their position is adamant," and he surmised that if the "authorities by looking at the record would name the representatives, it would certainly be a great help to us and I believe also to others."[14]

Bixler sent copies of the letter to Bowdoin president James Coles and Bates president Charles Phillips, writing, "You may recall our unhappy time last spring. Naturally, I should like to avoid it again if possible."[15] Afterward, Bowdoin AD Mal Morrell briefed Coles on the issue. "I served for two years as a member of the District I NCAA Baseball Selection Committee," Morrell wrote, "and I know that many colleges find it impossible to compete in the play-offs because of conflicts with exams. I know, too, that it would be very difficult to select the best team in New England on the basis of its record and statistics on batting, fielding and pitching performance." In a signal of the coming expansion of NCAA postseason play, Morrell also alerted Coles that "the College Division of the NCAA is now holding championships. One was held in basketball last year and again this year. Others will be held in track, cross country and tennis this year. The plan calls for a championship in baseball next year. Perhaps the best opportunity for Colby to use influence in affecting the type of play-off and championship would be in the College Division."[16]

Bates's Phillips replied to Bixler, "We doubt very much if our faculty would approve taking time off either from Commencement or from a final examination schedule. Moreover, the likelihood of Bates having a baseball team which would be invited to compete in national competition is not great."[17] Meanwhile, Coles wrote to Bixler that the no-playoff suggestion was "a good one," but "with Commencement coming as late as it does, for us the present system is better." "As you know," Coles continued, "the NCAA communicates with each college sometime in the early spring, asking whether or not it can be considered for participation in the NCAA championship. Since the dates of the play-offs have always conflicted with our final examination period, Bowdoin almost invariably answers this inquiry in the negative." Coles concluded by insisting, "Should Bowdoin ever by chance have a team which might be named for the NCAA play-offs, it would be most embarrassing for us to be named by the NCAA if it did conflict with other necessary appointments of players on the team at the College. We therefore believe it would be better to maintain more institutional control."[18]

Bixler, an Amherst undergraduate alumnus with a doctorate from Yale and the acting director of the Harvard Divinity School prior to coming to Colby in 1942, was seeking greater outside help and political cover, such as a formal conference agreement, to deal with a local issue, but Coles

Chapter 6. "When All Hell Broke Loose"

and Bowdoin were not willing to cede control to Bates or Colby on this issue, possibly because the two Maine schools were not part of the Pentagonal Agreement. Perhaps Bowdoin would have acted differently if the request had come from a Pentagonal cohort. Nevertheless Coles did support Colby in its request to change the playoff rule.[19] In 1958, Colby accepted a bid to the NCAA postseason tournament in baseball, and the team, under the direction of head coach and later AD John Winkin, lost to the College of the Holy Cross. The next season, the team again qualified for the NCAA postseason playoffs, but Bixler, nearing the end of his presidential tenure, said no: "The game would conflict with final exams. Students were furious. Winkin gritted his teeth, and the team stayed home."[20]

As indicated by Morrell, in response to the growing divergence in size and mission among the ranks of its ever-increasing membership, NCAA leadership decided to launch the first competitive events designed specifically for smaller institutions. Although the difference between "small" and "large" institutions was never formally defined, the creation of the College Division marks an important step on the NCAA's long journey toward the current three-division alignment. In 1957, the NCAA hosted the first College Division championships, both in basketball and cross-country, with the intention of adding sports if the inaugural events were deemed a success. The first College Division basketball tournament was an "incredible success," with a reported five thousand fans packing the gym at Evansville University to watch Wheaton College of Illinois defeated Kentucky Wesleyan in the championship game. An estimated thirteen thousand fans watched the tournament action in the Indiana city.[21]

In 1961, Bates and Williams participated in the fifth annual College Division men's basketball Northeast Regional at Springfield College in Massachusetts on March 10 and 11. Bates, under head coach and future Williams AD Bob Peck, defeated host Springfield, 75–63, in the first round, while Williams edged the University of Rochester, 74–72. Williams then bested Bates, 75–68, in the regional final to advance to the Elite Eight the next week in Evansville, where Williams lost to eventual champion Wittenberg in the opening round, 64–51. Former Williams AD Harry Sheehy highlighted the impact of this event: "It actually petrified the campus [administrators] because the kids were so excited about it. And the presidents looked at it and said, 'What is this, what's going on?' because it's hard for a president who has never been an athlete to make sense of that world. And they're hearing from their faculty all the time. There's just a natural distrust between athletics and academics." Reports from the event support this notion. A *Sports Illustrated* article from 1993 announcing NESCAC's return to NCAA postseason play explained that part of the rationale for the decision was that Williams administrators had "watched in dismay" as Wittenberg students celebrated the win, "appalled" by their demonstrative behavior.[22]

That year, concurrent with the College Division championship expansion, Bowdoin's Coles wrote to Wesleyan president Victor Butterfield on the issue of the Pentagonal postseason ban. In 1961, as Williams's James Baxter and Amherst's Charles Cole were set to retire, Coles sought a renewed opportunity to address the issue. Coles wrote to push Butterfield, as the "senior president," to call a meeting of the presidents involved, together with the ADs and directors of admission, "if you think it wise ... for the purpose of reviewing the entire Pentagonal Agreement on Athletics.... To use an appropriate metaphor, the ball is in your hands!"[23] While the appropriateness of his metaphor is questionable (did he mean "the ball is in your court"?), Butterfield agreed and a meeting was set for the following October. Coles pushed for ADs and admissions personnel to attend as well, but Butterfield first wanted to get feedback and permission from incoming Amherst president Cal Plimpton and new Williams president John Sawyer before eventually extending the broader invitation.

ADs and admissions personnel were eventually invited, and all attended. The meeting minutes reflect that several revisions to the agreement were proposed by Bowdoin and Williams, with the following motions approved: coaches could visit schools only by invitation for banquets, etc.; out-of-season practices were banned; season start dates were firmly set (fall, September 1; winter, November 1; spring, February 1); an agreement was made to exchange scholarship information; postseason play for teams (NCAAs, etc.) was banned but allowed for individual sport athletes; and form letters to schools by coaches "constituted a poor practice and should not be continued."[24]

"With reference to the Pentagonal agreement recently reaffirmed and extended (as well as in other ways liberalized)," wrote Coles to Butterfield after the meeting, "there has been student concern expressed about the limitation on post-season team participation. This we expected." "Essentially, if the stand we took was proper in October [1961]," Coles reasoned, "and unless there are new facts which were not available to us at that time, it is a proper stand now. If the Faculty of the Ohio State University bans post-season bowl participation for its football team, there would seem some incongruity were colleges like Wesleyan to permit post-season competition. The arguments which you have received and forwarded supporting a different policy do not impress me."[25] Coles was referring to a decision by Ohio State school administrators to decline invitation to play in the 1962 Rose Bowl because of a fear that "football was becoming too big and was detracting from the school's academic mission."[26] Ohio State students protested the decision, a reaction that would be echoed on NESCAC

Chapter 6. "When All Hell Broke Loose"   141

campuses decades later after a similar administrative move to limit post-season play.

But there were concerns on the part of others about how the revised rules would be received, especially following Williams's run in the 1961 College Division basketball tournament, as evidenced by a letter from Williams AD Frank Thoms to the other Pentagonal ADs. Thoms wrote, "Word has gotten around at Williams, from sources unknown, and perhaps on your campuses too, concerning decisions reached at the meeting." Thoms was seeking to set a common release date for the information, because "our students have already acquired misunderstandings through the rumor mill, and we would like to prevent these from becoming larger."[27]

Thoms's concern was well founded. Prior to a February 1962 meeting of Pentagonal presidents, the Bowdoin student newspaper wrote that Butterfield's "recent listing of an 'over-emphasis of athletics' and 'team pressure' as his reasons for the exclusion of Wesleyan from post-season team competition in NCAA-sponsored tournaments has aroused a flock of criticisms from various officials." The paper cited the comments of Scott Lowden, chairman of Wesleyan's Student Senate Athletic Committee, that "the rule binds the discretion of the four colleges to a policy against a situation which is not and could not be acute so long as admissions and recruiting agreements remain the same." Furthermore, wrote the paper, the Wesleyan chair "stated that to forbid any possible opportunity of 'team competition in post-season NCAA competition is to de-emphasize enthusiasm, not athletics.' Such are the views of many people on this restriction."[28]

The paper continued: "Officials from the four colleges think that the regulation will disallow the kind of athletic competition which would lead to a disproportion between athletics and more intellectual fields. Actually, athletic experience and the chance to compete have never indicated a preoccupation with athletics. ... [T]he competition that these four colleges have prohibited never created anything worse than high morale and a fine sense of loyalty." The paper concluded in terms that would frame this discussion for years: "If this rule continues to exist, it can definitely not improve the moral strength of the four colleges involved. ... [A] deterioration of each school's unity could easily appear. Therefore, it is thought that the officials responsible should reconsider their ruling and decide whether or not a natural interest in athletic competition is so detrimental to the character of a college."[29]

Despite these strongly voiced concerns, the Bowdoin student newspaper printed the following front-page headline in March 1962: "Pentagonal Conference Upholds Post-Season Rule." "Reflecting student disapproval at the respective colleges," wrote the paper, "the delegates also reconsidered their agreement not to send athletic teams to any post-season tournaments." Reasons listed in initiating and maintaining the ban included "the detrimental absence from classes which preparation for and participation in post-season tournaments would supposedly have on team members," yet "individuals may still compete in these tournaments."[30] The paper then opined, "Once again, the delegates of the Pentagonal Conference gleefully ignored strongly organized student opposition on all five [sic] campuses to the post-season agreement." The paper commented that President Coles went along with the decision, which was an example of "manifested collective indifference to the wishes of students in a peculiarly student-oriented area" and directly opposite to the stated preferences passed by Bowdoin's student council, which echoed a resolution passed prior by Wesleyan's student government. "Naturally, nobody cared," the Bowdoin paper complained.

In June 1964, the four Pentagonal ADs met at Bowdoin, and minutes of the meeting reflect that, like a clear majority of students, all the coaches of the four schools wanted the team ban rule reviewed and changed. ADs Mal Morrell and Red Richardson also wanted it changed, but Hugh McCurdy and Frank Thoms wanted it retained.[31] That meeting precipitated another presidents' meeting, scheduled for the following October, prior to which the presidents expressed worry about public scrutiny and stakeholder concerns in reviewing these proposals. Sawyer sent a letter to Butterfield reading, "I hope it can be handled, however, in a way that avoids any prior publicity that might build up any expectations of changes in our separate campuses or lead to renewal of pressures that we would then have to cope with once again."[32]

Sawyer then tipped his hand in how he would review the ADs' requests. "To keep the quality and great virtues of our present athletic program requires restraint and a constant readiness to hold the line at important points," he wrote Butterfield. "I hope we would give very careful thought before making any change that might begin the escalation that has caught and distorted athletics at so many institutions."[33] Butterfield replied that he agreed to avoid publicity that might build up expectations of potential changes. "I suggest we do not take the initiative in announcing that we are reviewing this agreement," he responded, and suggested that ADs not mention it either. "If we are asked," he continued, "I think we have got to say that we do intend to review the agreements as a matter of periodic practice but that there are no special proposals before us. If you and the others feel that this is o.k. we can let the matter ride at that."[34]

At that subsequent October 1964 presidents' meeting, the postseason team ban was retained, but in May 1966, at another Pentagonal ADs

Chapter 6. "When All Hell Broke Loose"

meeting, the group discussed a request by Bowdoin and Williams to participate in the ECAC College Division hockey tournament that had been denied by the presidents: "This has been a bone of contention with students and coaches since it has been in effect.... Mal [Morrell] also wished that the post season ban be abandoned and that each college should be allowed to make its own decisions about accepting an invitation to take part."[35] Morrell was likely seeking to promote and to defend his school's strong hockey program.

In response, in early 1967 (at the same time he was playing things out with the NCAA over Alex Schulten and the 1.6 Rule—see Chapter 3), Coles wrote to the other Pentagonal presidents: "We still have complaints from our coaches and undergraduates with respect to post-season championships. One might wonder whether or not the pain this causes is worth the possible gains from this particular rule."[36] Sawyer, who had also chosen not to comply with 1.6 certification, deflected Coles's query, saying, "We feel that the post-season teams issue has come to be accepted and has a great deal in its favor as a general policy of agreement among the four of us, in contrast to the build-up of pressures that comes on any one institution at the time a winning team builds up steam for a post-season trip—a trip that may take students who can ill afford it away from the campus for an extended period beyond their regular schedule." "While there is minor grumbling from time to time," Sawyer concluded, "we have weathered the major storm on this question and I, for one, am not eager to invite it annually."[37]

As referenced in Chapter 4, in the final stages of Pentagonal expansion, team postseason play was a major element of discussion. During deliberations in 1969, Calvin Plimpton admitted that Amherst was "at the moment, once more under pressure to allow and encourage post season games. Roger Howell at Bowdoin, I know, would like to take a fresh look at this. I think Jack Sawyer, Ted Etherington and I feel a little bit that we would like to maintain our current system," allowed Plimpton, but "our Athletic Directors and our students, however, want us to take a new look at the problem."[38] Plimpton was feeling some heat from campus stakeholders regarding access to postseason play and was likely looking to ease the political burden by broadening support of the ban among the Pentagonals. Indeed, Amherst AD Red Richardson would send a letter to the other Pentagonal ADs that April stating that "the department of Physical Education and Athletics at Amherst is strongly interested in changing the Pentagonal ban on post-season tournaments. We have drawn up a statement which we expect to present to the President and the Amherst Athletic Committee for consideration."[39]

Plimpton's perspective on Bowdoin was accurate, since Bowdoin AD

Dan Stuckey received a letter dated May 7, 1969 (with a copy sent to Howell) from the entire Bowdoin coaching and training staff, reading, "We would appreciate it if you would advise the members of the Pentagonal Agreement that our department would like to have the ban on post-season team competition revised to allow member colleges to participate if the individual school so wishes. We feel the rule is not beneficial to all concerned, and that this change should be made." "It is our understanding here," offered the letter, "that the athletic departments of the other member colleges are in agreement with us."[40]

Later that year, Etherington opined he was not so set against the postseason play issue. "It was my position [last June]," he wrote, "that we might permit post-season contests in connection with NCAA-sponsored events. The arguments against are strong, and I have continued to weigh them. I still feel, however, that we may be unwisely rigid on this at a time when sound sports programs seem especially necessary at institutions like ours where student morale represents a serious problem." "I feel strongly enough about this to suggest that our four institutions arrange a conference involving an academic officer, the athletic director, and an interested student from each of the campuses," Etherington advised. "That group of twelve could then formulate a recommendation to us, and we could reconsider the ban—or at least the comprehensiveness of the ban—if it is recommended that we do so."[41]

Etherington's reference to student morale is worth noting. While the Pentagonal schools had not yet experienced campus upheaval, by the end of the academic year they would, in the form of strikes on nearly all the future NESCAC campuses following the Kent State University shootings in May 1970. Given the social and political climate of the era, Wesleyan's president, who was always less solid on the postseason ban, was open to a broader degree of stakeholder involvement in the conference process as a way to defuse tensions and promote morale on campus.

During the 1969–70 academic year, as Bowdoin experienced notable institutional challenges and transformations, the hockey program embarked on its most successful campaign ever. But because Pentagonal signatories were not allowed to compete in any postseason tournaments, the Polar Bears could not accept an invitation to the ECAC Division II hockey championship. To show support for the program, Roger Howell worked to lift the postseason ban by seeking a waiver from his Pentagonal colleagues for Bowdoin to participate, if invited, in the tournament. "I have, in all conscience," Howell reasoned to his fellow presidents, "reviewed the conditions under which this particular event takes place, and they seem designed to assure that the dangers the Pentagonal Agreement is intended to guard against will not occur." "There may be some inconveniences," he allowed, but he saw "a boost to student morale in this venture of positive value."[42]

Despite some misgivings expressed by his fellow presidents, Howell's lobbying efforts paid off, and Bowdoin was allowed to play after Howell agreed to the following points: that the participation be approved by the college's Faculty Committee on Athletics, that all games would be played on the home rink of one of the teams involved, that Bowdoin would not be involved in more than two games, and that the tournament would not overlap with the beginning of the spring sports season. Bowdoin's student newspaper confirmed that the team would appear in the ECAC Division II tournament, which would be played in Brunswick if the team garnered the top seed. "If the Bears should win the remainder of their matches or the tournament," crowed the paper, "a school holiday should be declared before it is demanded. Or at least before it is observed."[43] The Polar Bears routed Merrimack College, 9–1, in the semifinals but fell to the University of Vermont in the finals, 4–1.

The successful hockey program had become something around which Bowdoin stakeholders of all stripes could coalesce positively. Postseason play was a popular notion with students, and Howell, a Bowdoin alumnus, was a strong believer in the model of amateur athletics practiced by the college and well aware of how athletic success could impact the institution. Given this, it is unlikely that Howell turned Machiavellian and used hockey strictly to mollify stakeholders, but the fact remains that Howell worked hard to promote the hockey program and the successes Sid Watson's teams were earning.

In August 1971, following the formal announcement of the conference's formation, a list of NESCAC "operational policies" were circulated, outlining that "post-season competition for the individual performer is approved" and that "participation in regional tournaments during the academic year be limited to events played on college campuses which do not lead to further competition or conflict with examination schedules, provided they do not extend the season more than 7 calendar days beyond the Saturday of the final week of scheduled competition is approved."[44] The issue was discussed at a joint meeting between the executive committee and conference ADs at Wesleyan in May 1972. According to the minutes of the meeting, Sawyer "indicated general approval of the old E.C.A.C. four-team Division II Hockey format but emphasized he could not, at this point, speak for all Conference presidents." Tufts's Burton Hallowell "expressed some reservations about any kind of team post-season tournaments with the possible exception of soccer." Howell restated his rationale for supporting participation in ECAC Division II hockey, as did Hamilton's Chandler, but the latter "was concerned about financial escalation which might result from post-season competition."⁴⁵ Interestingly, Trinity AD Karl Kurth suggested the creation of conference end-of-season play-offs in soccer, basketball, hockey, lacrosse, and baseball.⁴⁶ While ahead of its time but contrary to the precepts of the agreement, this would eventually be adopted by the conference following further conflicts.

The continuation of the Pentagonal postseason ban into NESCAC was also received negatively by schools new to the fold, such as in 1972, when NESCAC's executive committee rejected Union's request that its men's basketball team participate in the NCAA College Division tournament. At Tufts, head men's basketball coach Tom Penders, who would go on to success at Columbia, the University of Rhode Island, and the University of Texas, left the school in 1974 over the restriction (his Jumbos teams went 54–18 during his time), and strong women's lacrosse teams in the 1980s also chafed at the ban.⁴⁷ As late as 1986, NESCAC coaches were still seeking to amend or omit the ban, as evidenced by a discussion at a conference presidents' meeting on whether qualifying basketball teams could be permitted to participate in NCAA postseason play. According to meeting minutes, "there was no wish expressed to move away" from the ban policy,⁴⁸ even though the Williams women's swimming team had been awarded NCAA Division III team championships in 1982 and 1983 based on the performance of team members who had qualified as individuals.

Managerial Realities of the AP Era

Following the 1993 decision to rescind the NCAA team sport ban, participation in such postseason play quickly led to unprecedented levels of national success for NESCAC teams. While some ADs, presidents, and stakeholders were comfortable with this newfound degree of athletic prominence and emphasis, some were not. Other issues that prompted conflict were at play as well. Conference members had dealt with contentious issues before, including disputes between schools over admissions standards and practices, increased administrative demands to appropriately address conference business, and the lack of commitment on the part of some members to schedule other member schools in certain sports because of traditional rivalries. But now, as Colby's Bixler had done four decades before, presidents were again having to decide on allowing their teams to compete in postseason play. And like Bixler, those who opted to decline invitations because of logistical and philosophical conflicts were pilloried by stakeholders.

The most noteworthy example of this was the decision by Williams president Harry "Hank" Payne—who like John Chandler had come to

Williams after a brief stint as president at Hamilton, prior to which Payne, a Massachusetts native, had earned degrees from Yale, taught at Colgate, and served as provost at Haverford—to keep the school's women's lacrosse team out of NCAA championship play in 1996 because the games conflicted with spring final exams; two of Williams's men's teams had been denied permission to participate in 1994 for the very same reason. In justifying the move, Payne told one member of the team, "[I] do not think such a process would be healthy for the relationship of athletics and academics here."⁴⁹ Soon thereafter, the parent of a team member emailed Payne with an encapsulation of stakeholder concerns: "What will the lasting memories, especially of the seniors on this exceptional team, be of Williams? Many of these women have actually shed blood for the Purple and the White. What will the motivations be for the underclass members next season?"⁵⁰ In addition, the bid Payne rejected was then awarded to Amherst, which readily accepted. Payne also said he "could not and would not require faculty" to make special arrangements to allow teams to take part in NCAA competitions, but a Williams student newspaper op-ed stated that this argument fell apart when the ten faculty members whose exams conflicted with the tournament "said they had no problem allowing the team to take the exams a few days early and strongly supported the women in their quest to compete at the highest level."⁵¹

Bowdoin president Roger Howell sought waivers for his men's hockey team to participate in postseason play; he is pictured here with team mascot (early 1970s). Courtesy George J. Mitchell Department of Special Collections & Archives, Bowdoin College Library, Brunswick, Maine.

The Williams student newspaper also noted that the team's coach, Chris Mason, had met with Payne in January to raise concerns about a possible ban but that Payne was unmoved. He told the paper, "There may come a time when the rule will change, or our calendar will"—however, until such a time, "this limitation will remain in force, and is sensible to all concerned." Payne also stated that "this rule was designed to protect student athletes from the pressures and distractions of competition during this period and from the inevitable pressures to go along with the team regardless of academic consequences." The paper bristled at this, calling Payne out for his "condescending" tone. "The fact is," wrote the paper, "those who are being 'protected' neither need nor want such protection," and it decried the "lack of faith in these students' abilities to juggle academics and athletics (a talent that most likely helped many of them get into Williams in the first place)."[52] This final point was both true and highly indicative of what the consequences were for Payne, Williams, and the rest of NESCAC when giving importance to athletic proficiency in the admissions process, while simultaneously seeking to mitigate the impact of these athletic proclivities once students arrived on campus.

But Payne brought the condemnation upon himself when he ignored one of what Dr. Jerome Quarterman, a researcher in contemporary sport management, deems the basic elements of conference formation—that is, when institutions face managerial conundrums, schools in a conference work together to lift some of the political burden away from the individual members.[53] As a result, Payne's move to disallow the women's lacrosse team's postseason berth, whatever the reason, was doomed as soon as Amherst snapped up the bid he declined. Eugene Tobin, who had worked with Payne during their time together at Hamilton, despaired for Payne over the reaction to the issue. "I remember him getting hammered at the time," recalled Tobin. "Williams takes so much pride in its academic quality and its athletic prowess that the alumni reaction was so vociferous that it would have taken the wind out of you as a leader, even though you were making a decision that you thought was in the best interest of the institution." "I'm sure he was prepared for it intellectually," Tobin surmised, "but you're never quite prepared for the visceral reaction. And this was before social media."

In September 1998, perhaps to create cover for his decision and to assuage alumni, faculty, and athletics staff, Payne convened a group of these stakeholders as part of a "Commission of Post-Season Athletic Competition." The charge of the group was

> to develop knowledge and perspective about the history and philosophy that have guided the College's participation in intercollegiate athletics and specifically post-season competition; to lead a discussion within the broad College community of the issues surrounding postseason play; and to offer specific and on-going advice to the President regarding imminent decisions on these issues.[54]

The commission's findings questioned "the wisdom of creating a format where only the champion of the conference will be allowed to go to NCAA

Chapter 6. "When All Hell Broke Loose"

postseason championship competition.... We hope the presidents will, therefore, discuss the fairness and wisdom of rules that could allow more flexibility and opportunity to compete at the national level."[55] The presidents would indeed review the issue, but their next steps would generate further angst rather than assuage stakeholder concerns.

Nevertheless, Payne resigned from the presidency in the fall of 1999, citing his intention to pursue other interests. At the time, he was the highest-paid college president in the country, with nearly $900,000 in salary and benefits as part of the package related to his departure.[56] As one former NESCAC AD put it: "Payne got into trouble by trying to micromanage with women's lacrosse when they were number one and not letting them go to NCAAs. The poor guy. But in retrospect I look at the errors that Payne made, [Colby president] Bill Cotter would never have made. Never ever have made them. Colby's lacrosse team would have gone, whatever the faculty was going to say. [Cotter] was three steps ahead of all the other presidents. Cotter was a very aggressive, very shrewd guy." According to another NESCAC AD, Williams trustees "run the place.... It's a very fine academic school, and the strongest Division III athletics school in the country, in terms of size and budget, number of staff. And that only happens because of widespread support from trustees."

Other issues were problematic for Payne, including managing donations for building projects, such as $30 million for a dance theater that many on the campus saw as unnecessary. As one Williams administrator said, "It probably got the president fired because he accepted the gift. We didn't need it. It's disruptive. It caused problems in the community." The dispute over postseason play and the resulting compromise decision were considered by many to have contributed significantly to the trustees nudging Payne out of office.

Williams president Harry Payne ran afoul of stakeholders when he denied permission for Williams's women's lacrosse team to participate in the 1996 NCAA tournament. Amherst's team went instead, and Payne resigned in 1999. Courtesy Williams College Archives and Special Collections.

So the end for Payne at Williams was less a storming of the barricades and more of a classic palace coup. After Williams, Payne became the head of Woodward Academy, a private preparatory school in Atlanta, Georgia. In 2008, at the age of sixty, he committed suicide by jumping from an eighth-floor window of an Atlanta hotel.[57]

The Presidents Float the One-School-Per-Sport Postseason Participation Model

As the second three-year experimental period of team NCAA postseason play was drawing to a close, the climate of conflict highlighted in the Payne-Williams case precipitated presidential reconsideration of the policy. The presidents had been scheduled to act on the measure to consider the discontinuation of participation in NCAA postseason championships at a league meeting in December 1997, but they delayed their decision until their next meeting in April 1998.

After the December 1997 meeting, the presidents issued a statement that read, "We considered the appropriateness of post-season play and affirmed it. Continued team and individual competition in NCAA championships is still under active consideration."[58] The group also established four task forces to review other pressing conference issues, including the mission and "collaborative spirit" of NESCAC, a "modest" conference administrative structure (including a possible conference commissioner, to "collect and analyze data, provide reports and surveys," among other tasks), postseason play, and "to consider boundaries and balances between academic programs and athletics, so as to minimize conflicts between classes and examinations and athletic travel, practices, competitions and post-season play."[59] While neither a new nor recent practice, some of the sharing of information included the academic and financial aid profiles of student-athletes. One president said the sharing was "actually quite reassuring.... There were the predictable stretches in terms of averages, but the stretches were about comparable school to school. If [a school's average combined] SATs were 1400, your football team was 1300. If the [average was] 1300, your football team was 1200." "Those differentials were not really out of line," said the president, "nor were the percentage of student-athletes on financial aid or the size of their grants, nor any of the other things that might have been red flags."

Student-athletes in particular were quite vocal in expressing their support for maintaining the opportunity to participate in NCAA championships. Said Bowdoin student-athlete Ryan Buckley: "Cutting short an athlete's potential is certainly a travesty. It is a travesty because athletic

Chapter 6. "When All Hell Broke Loose"   151

and academic potential and achievement are one in the same.... By cutting short bids for NCAA play, we are also cutting short certain invaluable lessons that can be taught nowhere else. After all, do we cut short a student's potential for cum laude? Certainly not."[60] Buckley's comments indicate that to him and peer stakeholders, academic and athletic achievement should be given equal status, for these were to student-athletes of approximately equal importance. A student-athlete at Hamilton added that NESCAC's new AP-era image—one of athletics success in a highly selective academic environment—would suffer under the plan. "We are deluding ourselves if we think we will be able to attract these same quality individuals be creating our organization outside the parameters of mainstream competition," stated the student. "The reality is these individuals will no longer choose NESCAC schools. Because of their records of success, both academically and athletically, they will have plenty of alternatives allowing them to fully develop and challenge themselves in both realms. Ultimately, they will become better 'educated' in a broader sense, by avoiding the NESCAC."[61]

Even some members of the region's sports media, who usually ignored NESCAC athletics in favor of covering higher-profile Division I activities, also questioned the proposed policy change. "Why do the presidents ... want to ban New England Small College Athletic Conference teams from NCAA tournaments? I don't know. They say they espouse excellence, so I can't understand why they would restrict qualified teams from competing against the best," Mike Szostak of the *Providence (RI) Journal* wrote. "Students should be encouraged to go as far as their talents will take them, even if they develop those talents on playing fields in addition to classrooms."[62]

The presidents had misread their stakeholders and were caught off guard by the public furor, and as a result they delayed their decision. As one president later put it, "We sort of punted." Former Williams AD Harry Sheehy added the perspective that before going to the postseason, NESCAC schools didn't really know how good they were, "and then we found out that we were really good, and this caught the presidents by surprise." Tom Parker, a former director of admission at Williams and then dean of admission at Amherst, concurred. While he stated that no NESCAC admissions personnel were consulted in the decision to opt for postseason play, Parker thought the move "was a real big mistake. But I honestly believed that we would get out of NESCAC and get the crap beaten out of us.... I thought we'd get killed.... And lo and behold, we [did] a lot better."[63] Former Amherst AD Peter Gooding disputes this, saying, "Tom Parker was being strategic. He knew the presidents would not support the proposal if they knew they were opening Pandora's box and our athletes would be all over the country, extending the length of seasons, missing classes, changing recruiting practices." "I knew the NCAA tournaments would radically change the culture in our departments," said Gooding, "because we would become immediately competitive in most of our sports." *Sports Illustrated* seemed to know as much as well; its 1993 college basketball preview ranked the Williams men's team eighth in its Division III preseason poll.[64]

While ADs viewed some of the proposed policy changes favorably, they also expressed the opinion that presidential power and influence had in general negative implications for the conference. ADs noted that actions policies were impacted greatly as presidents changed. One AD's comment demonstrated the unease with this arrangement: "Presidents and deans come and go and make silly decisions with regards to sport within the academy. They're often driven by internal political issues that have no long-term relationship to anything. It's just that you have a committee that happens to be particularly powerful at a given time, and the president's running for cover." "Or the opposite occurs," said the AD, when a president "is seeking favor with a [fund-raising] campaign looming." The practical applications of presidential control and actions were often viewed as detrimental because presidential authority was perceived as erratically subjective and/or greatly uniformed.

After the next presidents' meeting in April 1998, the group acted on several important motions and chose to evolve into a qualified playing conference—football excepted, meaning schedules would remain at eight games—and to "create appropriate mechanisms to determine a conference champion in all sports where it is practical." As for postseason play, it would "allow only the conference champion to pursue post-season competition on one venue deemed appropriate—normally NCAA Division III," read the statement, as "these changes will lessen conflicts with academic schedules."[65]

The decision to evolve into a "playing conference" would mean that all NESCAC schools would finally be required to play the others in each sport, a factor that had been a source of conflict since the founding of the conference, as the Maine schools struggled to fill schedules, the Connecticut and Massachusetts contingents were loath to make regular forced marches northward, and nearly every school save for Williams dreaded trips to Hamilton. The presidents had agreed in 1984 that "schools should work to achieve greater interaction in all sports,"[66] but the statement was a hope rather than a requirement. In 1988, Colby president William Cotter stated that "he was not content with the progress made on the matter, especially in women's sports."[67] If NESCAC were to send only its champion, then a method to determine a champion had to be devised. Round-robin scheduling would be the result, and thus a win for Bates, Bowdoin, and

Colby, but it would be at an additional cost, meaning multi-hour trips from Maine (446 miles for Colby) to Clinton, New York, to face Hamilton.

Sheehy said that full scheduling "was both good and bad. There were a lot of years where Williams was the only NESCAC team playing Hamilton. Then Hamilton added Middlebury, and then [Middlebury AD and head men's basketball coach] Russ Reilly and Murph [Hamilton AD and head men's basketball coach Tom Murphy] got into some sort of tiff and that ended." Sheehy listed another logistical challenge: the use of travel partners "got screwed up. It meant that we were going to have an open Saturday in the fall. We were trying not to play midweek games, and then we have an open Saturday of all things. It really impacted things." Sheehy then recounted when he suggested the scheduling issue was going to be a problem. Hamilton president Joan Stewart replied, "Look, we just want to be part of the club." "It was a challenge," recalled Sheehy, "but once the presidents decided, it's like anything: once you've lived with it for a while, it becomes what you do." Nevertheless, it would be another decade until Hamilton teams were fully integrated into NESCAC, with basketball, field hockey, soccer, and lacrosse programs finally entering into the full scheduling agreements for the 2011–12 seasons. Full conference scheduling with every team playing every other would mean expanding the football schedule from eight to nine games, but that did not occur until the 2017 season.

The new one-team-per-sport postseason plan was set to take effect for the 2000–2001 academic year and was the result of a compromise among the presidents, some of whom had lobbied for a complete retreat from postseason play. One president at the time revealed that the conference was at risk of dissolution over the issue: "I've supported these reforms, including the latest ones, because I felt we were about to split up over this championship issue, and I myself compromised. I'm a purist, I'm a 'no-championship' type in my personal attitude, but I felt the compromise was a sensible one to say some championships, but limited championship play, when the Maine schools were advocating that, and Wesleyan, Amherst, and Connecticut College, the purists, went along." "And then all the other schools … went along compromising too," noted the president, "so it saved us."

In support of this decision, and to reinforce its ideal image in the face of its near demise, the group unanimously adopted a mission statement that said, "Members are committed first and foremost to academic excellence and believe that athletic excellence supports our educational mission … [and are] committed to establishing common boundaries to keep athletics strong but in proportion to the overall academic mission of the member institutions." The mission statement affirmed the organization's founding ethos of academic primacy and the reliance on "mutual trust," and it encouraged members "to compete with one another." Student-athletes were to be "representative of the overall student body" and "admitted with the expectation of their full participation in the life of the college."[68] The mission statement essentially reaffirmed the conference's stated policies and procedures as outlined in the current conference agreement. The presidents also approved the establishment of a "conference office" and the appointment of a "conference coordinator for record-keeping, research, public information, and organization of special studies," to be named as soon as the fall of 1998. The position of conference coordinator was ultimately filled in May 1999 by Andrea Savage, a former Amherst student-athlete and coach who had been an assistant AD at Yale.

The creation of the conference coordinator position was the final realization that the ideal model of presidential control and a laissez-faire administrative structure based on little more than commonly espoused philosophical tenets was no longer tenable. Under the guise of ultimate control, Pentagonal and NESCAC presidents were often ill-equipped and/or uninterested in investing the time and energy required to managing their collective athletic endeavors. According to one former NESCAC president, "Even though virtually all of the final decision-making rests in the hands of the presidents, it is a fond belief that we can gather three hours once a year in January and make all the athletic policies we need to make. Now who in their right mind would argue that? Well, NESCAC tries to."

"The reality has come up against the illusion," said the president at the time. "The president who chairs NESCAC meetings simultaneously keeps the minutes of that meeting. Think about that. We would never run our institutions that way. We would not run our own staff that way. But that's what we do, and periodically express our horror when something we don't know about transpires."

Another NESCAC president explained that "presidents are very busy people. Athletics is a part of their responsibility, but it doesn't loom as large for them as it does for the ADs and the coaches, where it's their lives. And student-athletes, who are much more numerous than they were." This president also noted, "Not only do [presidents] not have the kind of time and expertise that our athletic departments have, but the leadership of NESCAC changes year to year. So there's no continuity as to what did we decide two years ago. Finding the minutes is sometimes difficult. In the eleven schools, the average [presidential] term is seven, eight years. You're likely to have a new president every year."

A third president echoed these sentiments and expressed a sense of surprise and lack of preparation to deal with athletics issues: "When I came here, frankly, it was a much bigger deal than I expected it to be.

Competition was greater. The levels of seriousness a great deal more intrusive. Alumni concerns much stronger."

But another president portrayed the moves relating to the conference and postseason as an effort "to take the conference back." The presidents had "always been the titular leaders ... [but] in the old days they were really controlling it and keeping all these lids on." This president also conceded that certain moves "were sort of artificial, like the 'no standings' rule," where the conference released league standings not by won-loss record but in alphabetical order. "That's quite silly," said the president. "Everybody knows what the records are anyway, whether you write it down or not. Listing the NESCAC schools in alphabetical order and saying next to them what their won-loss record is really seems to me quite precious."

But the move to formalization, and its resultant strictures, was not universally embraced by athletics administrators, according to Peter Gooding: "I still believe it was strategically the worst decision for Amherst to support NESCAC as a playing conference. We would have been a terrific independent."

Stakeholder Response to the One-Team Postseason Plan

Stakeholders, specifically student-athletes, voiced a considerable amount of concern in response to the presidents' postseason compromise and the self-proclaimed efforts to reclaim control. In the fall of 1998, the College Council at Williams sponsored a forum on the postseason issue, attended by interested council members, student-athletes, and coaches. The attendees put forth that the new policy "actually increases pressure on student-athletes since it is harder to make it to nationals. Friendly NESCAC competition becomes fierce. Losing early games defeats morale for the rest of the season and makes the remaining NESCAC games all the more stressful."[69]

The forum also purported that the policy "unfairly limits coaches' opportunity to succeed on a national level," that postseason participation had produced "no evidence [of reduced] academic achievement," and, echoing one of the driving forces cited in the deliberations around permitting team participation in 1993, that the restrictions could cost Williams "crucial exposure by participating in fewer national contests" and drive academically capable student-athletes to schools that could compete more freely in postseason play.[70]

Later that fall, a coalition of NESCAC student representatives organized to discuss the issue. Students held a meeting at Amherst that November to review the presidential proposal, with student government presidents and athletes from ten of the NESCAC schools in attendance. The members present agreed to establish the forum as a permanent body, christened the "NESCAC Student Forum." Those present agreed with the presidents' conference play and commissioner concepts but were vehemently opposed to the one-school NCAA championship limit.[71] The members then declared their intention to work with their respective ADs to "establish an official statement on the [postseason] issue. Student leaders hope that this effort will complement the attempts of individual schools to rally their respective communities around the issue."[72] The interested students continued to confer during the early months of 1999.

Athletics administrators also expressed disfavor with the proposed plan and its limiting of postseason opportunities. Said Peter Gooding in a feature article in the *Chronicle of Higher Education*, as NESCAC gained more national media coverage, but this time less favorable: "It means there'll inevitably be three or four or even five very good teams in the NESCAC each year in various sports that won't be able to participate. In the first round you will see a lot of very weak [teams] from various conferences getting absolutely shelled."[73] Of the move, Harry Sheehy said that sending one team "was like being a little bit pregnant. Either you're in or you're not. I told [Hank Payne] that either you believe the experience is positive and you send your teams or you don't."

Wesleyan SID Brian Katten offered a similarly negative view of the proposal at the time, saying, "I don't think there is an SID among us who does not think the intended NESCAC restriction on postseason play is a farce." Katten then listed the ten fall and winter sports during the 1998–99 academic year with NCAA tournaments and counted fifty-four NESCAC teams that qualified. "That would only be ten under this ridiculous new proposal, meaning forty-four teams staying home," concluded Katten. "Last year, it was seventy-seven teams in seventeen sports, meaning only seventeen would go and sixty stay home. Really worthwhile."[74]

"It Just Sort of Faded Away": The One-Team Plan Never Takes Effect

The presidents' decision to evolve into a playing conference benefited those schools looking for increased conference scheduling commitments. This revision, along with the preservation of limited NCAA postseason play, seemed to have a significant impact on the future of the conference, as some members who wished to continue their association with NCAA championships were rumored to have considered leaving NESCAC

Chapter 6. "When All Hell Broke Loose"

had the presidents voted to end the postseason allowance, while others were rumored to also have considered leaving if greater conference playing commitments were not forthcoming. The presidents seemed to have struck a compromise while striving to reaffirm the primacy of academic goals.

But because of the negative response from stakeholders, the proposed one-team-per-sport plan never took effect. When the plan was released, one AD said presciently, "I'm not sure that ten bright men and one woman are going to continue to think this makes sense, because it just doesn't make any sense at all." According to Harry Sheehy, "I never remember the presidents making a formal statement on it. It just sort of faded away," while Colby's Dick Whitmore noted that the "'one team' discussion came after the cow had left the barn, when team play was approved and NESCAC teams were selected in multiples." Another former NESCAC AD said the plan was never implemented because it "certainly would have put the presidents in a difficult position. Every time a team would have been selected, it would bring up the argument again." "Also," the AD continued, "Williams was so dominant, many schools feared that at-large selections were their only hope. Plus, individual sports like swimming, track, and tennis had been sending many students for years." Peter Gooding added that presidents "never really 'hung in' with the option because they only occupied the chair for one year, at most two meetings, and they were quite happy to leave it to the next president because it was so controversial on various campuses."

In addition, as the NCAA began to offer automatic qualifiers (AQs) to other conference champions, the number of spots for at-large bids decreased. For example, in 1995, the second year of NESCAC postseason eligibility, Colby, Hamilton, Trinity, Tufts, and Williams received bids to the men's basketball tournament. While four NESCAC teams (Bowdoin, Conn, Hamilton, and Trinity) received bids to the 1999 men's basketball tournament, two got bids in 2000 (Amherst and Hamilton) and only one in 2001 (Amherst). Had the presidents waited, the expansion of AQs would likely have defused the issue on its own until the NCAA expanded tournament fields. When that occurred, NESCACs returned to regular multiples bids, but by then the presidents couldn't enforce the dictum that many stakeholders opposed so stridently. Conference executive director Andrea Savage reinforced the timing with the Division III AQ issue: "The number of at-large teams that could be selected dropped significantly, and that had the same effect as the proposal. After that happened, there was a comfort level with saying, in effect, it's been the same outcome."

But some stakeholders were less than enthused about the realities of the AP era. Former Bowdoin head women's basketball coach Stephanie Pemper, who was the architect of the perennially strong women's basketball program there before becoming head coach at the U.S. Naval Academy, identified the one change as a motivator for her to move from Brunswick to Annapolis: "I had two [recruiting] horror stories at Bowdoin ... very educated, wealthy families, and just ugly stuff. On the front end, the unrealistic feelings about the daughter and her skill set, lying about what other coaches felt about the daughter. And the daughter getting to school and [the parents'] overreactions to what was happening with her playing time. And then they started picking at other things I was doing, all a reflection of frustration. And then, ultimately, the daughter choosing not to play. It's part of why I left Bowdoin. I feel like there was a community I was immersed in over thirteen years ... of people who think that everyone cares about what they think."

Pemper, who compiled a record of 235–48 at Bowdoin (with nine NCAA tournament appearances) and was the Women Basketball Coaches Association NCAA Division III National Coach of the Year in 2004, was not alone in her observations. "My last five years as an AD," said Peter Gooding, "I grew tired of meeting with parents and athletes who wanted a coach fired because the team didn't make the NCAAs. Many active coaches in NESCAC would happily go back to the old model."

One former NESCAC AD provided the most succinct summary of the change and what it meant: "Once they opened that door, everybody wants to win a national championship. I mean, that's what the competitor does. You want to be the best there is in the country." The AD continued,

> Around the time the postseason ban was lifted, I went to lunch with Mike Walsh, AD at Washington and Lee University, and his comment to me was "What's wrong with you people in NESCAC?" And I looked at him and said, "What do you mean what's wrong with NESCAC?" And he said, "Why have you decided to go to NCAA postseason play? Don't you understand that to the rest of the country you were a model, you were different?"
>
> Then he said, "Within a matter of three or four years, you're going to be just like the rest of us." And how prophetic his words were.

Chapter 7

No Longer So Pure and Simple
Managing the AP-Era Ideal

National Media Love for the AP-Era Image

While Looney had expressed deep affection for NESCAC's BP-era image of the elite, academically inclined, small liberal arts schools nestled in picturesque New England locales pursuing the treasures associated with the "sweatiest of the liberal arts," *Sports Illustrated* found AP-era NESCAC to be an even more intriguing concept, a mélange that combined Looney's characterization with a newly established ability to achieve national athletic success. Over the next few years, the magazine mined the topic on several occasions, contributing to the new AP-era ideal image of the conference with highly favorable coverage. In October 2002, *SI* featured NESCAC plaudits in the magazine's cover story focused on America's best sports colleges. The piece sought to determine the top such schools in the country based on such factors as winning percentages of all teams, student-athlete graduation rates, Directors' Cup standings, and financial support for all programs. While Stanford and Texas were deemed the top two in NCAA Division I, the article also volunteered choices for the top programs in Divisions II and III, giving the D-III nod to Williams. "These are heady days in Williamstown," wrote Scott Cacciola, "where the tiny school with the sterling academic reputation has been busy cultivating a Division III dynasty." The article went on to note that in 2000–2001, the Ephs notched three NCAA titles, thirty-one teams went a combined 595–50–1, two athletes were national players of the year, and the school won its sixth Directors' Cup in seven years. Of its two thousand students, 38 percent participated in an intercollegiate sport and another 25 percent played on one of eighteen club teams. Cacciola also reported on one of the school's quaint traditions, where President Morton Schapiro (identified in the piece as the "No. 1 Ephs fan"—an appellation the former University of Southern California dean of arts and sciences likely encouraged, given what had contributed to the end of Hank Payne's presidency) "will look outside his window one morning this fall and declare Mountain Day," when classes are canceled and students and faculty hike up a nearby mountain. "As usual at Williams," the author joked, "they will end up on top."[1]

At least one other NESCAC AD admitted that Williams was a benchmark for the rest of the league. "Williams sets the standards for excellence," said Hamilton AD Tom Murphy. "Because of its success our league has become much stronger. Now it's up to some of us to step up."[2] But other NESCAC stakeholders were motivated to challenge the anointing of Williams. Eric Bergofsky of Exeter, New Hampshire, wrote to *SI*: "If you measure success by national championships, nobody comes close [to Middlebury]." Bergofsky listed seventeen titles won in men's and women's lacrosse, men's and women's ice hockey, women's cross-country, and women's field hockey. Bergofsky also pointed out his daughter Julia, a Middlebury women's lacrosse player, who won the award for the top NCAA Division III women's athlete in 2001.[3] Parental pride aside, the letter was a clear indicator that stakeholders were now viewing national championships as part of the collective image of NESCAC athletics.

Middlebury women's lacrosse standout Julia Bergofsky served as an example of what stakeholders now valued in NESCAC athletics competition. Courtesy Middlebury College Athletics.

Trinity: Athletic Success and Institutional Advancement

As Union had with men's ice hockey two decades prior, Trinity's push to create a nationally strong men's squash program was very much in the

Chapter 7. No Longer So Pure and Simple

tradition of higher education leaders using athletics as a means to further institutional athletic ends. In 1995, Trinity president Evan Dobelle hired Paul Assaiante (pronounced *ah-see-ON-tay*) and charged the new coach to build a squash program good enough to take on the then dominant programs at Harvard, Princeton, and Yale. Assaiante recalled the meeting with Dobelle when this goal was made clear, telling him,

> Coach, here's the deal, I noticed the squash team plays the highest caliber of institutions in competition. You play Dartmouth and Pennsylvania and Yale, whereas your tennis team plays Williams and Middlebury and Bowdoin—and that's all great. But I need to be able to walk into boardrooms and raise money and get people excited, because I'm trying to give this school a facelift and a morale boost. And the fact that you're competing with these schools is very important to me.

Dobelle then asked, "How do we take it to the next level in this pond? Because if the tennis team wins the Division III national championship, that's great and we can promote it. But if the squash team wins the national championship against a Princeton or Harvard or a Yale, that's *very* compelling."[4]

The needs Dobelle sought to address through a potential squash power were several. When James English, a former bank chairman and vice president of finance at the school, became president in 1981, Trinity was facing a decline in student interest because of facilities issues and an endowment that lagged far behind many NESCAC rivals. At the time, the college received about 3,000 applications for 450 places in the freshman class, yet it had to admit more than 1,200 to get the 450 because most of those to whom Trinity offered admission went to other colleges.[5]

Nearing the turn of the century, these issues persisted, in large part because Trinity was never physically a prototypical New England hilltop college, owing to its location in the Frog Hollow neighborhood of Hartford, described as "crime-ridden" and "blighted." As a result, applications for admission were down, "with Trinity losing out to colleges of comparable status, like Williams and Amherst, in more idyllic surroundings. Parents were understandably reluctant to spend $27,000 a year to send their children to a school only blocks from the scene of a drive-by shooting," with some students, faculty, and staff "nervous about venturing off campus."[6] Indeed, Dobelle himself stated in his inaugural address that "only a few feet from our campus ... the sole tutor to these children too often is the harsh reality of the streets."[7] Currently, one of the school's salient physical landmarks is a substation of the Hartford Police Department situated on the border of campus.

Dobelle sought to reshape the area through a partnership between public and private entities to the tune of $225 million.[8] According to a laudatory profile in the University of Massachusetts alumni magazine (Dobelle received several degrees from the school), the site was deemed a "Learning Corridor" and was to include a Montessori elementary school, a middle school, and a high school program with a math, science, and technology orientation and numerous enrichments, along with a job-training center and the aforementioned police substation. According to the magazine, "It seems universally recognized that it couldn't have happened without Dobelle. He drove the planning, talked it up, raised money for it, generally revved its engine. ... [F]ormer HUD secretary Henry Cisneros is quoted as saying, 'Dobelle understands the stakes better and is doing it better than anyone.'"[9] To realize these and other initiatives, donor fundraising was the key, and a prominent squash program was promoted as a way to help cultivate donors and facilitate giving.

As Dobelle alluded in his charge to Assaiante, squash was managed and governed very differently from the vast majority of American intercollegiate sports. The NCAA does not hold postseason championships for squash (those are organized by U.S. Squash), and many intercollegiate programs are sponsored by the Ivies. Given these factors, Dobelle had identified squash as a sport in which his school could compete against the Ivies and potentially share and steal some of the Ivies' ideal brand equity.

Assaiante, who grew up in the South Bronx section of New York City and didn't pick up a squash racquet until age twenty-seven, was able to create a squash juggernaut by recruiting international players. When named coach at Trinity (having worked previously at the U.S. Military Academy and Williams), he expected to coach "white toast, Main Line, Greenwich, Brookline, prep school–type kids." When Dobelle indicated his goals for the program, Assaiante informed the president what it was going to take to be successful. "The best squash is not being played in this country," he told Dobell. "I coached the U.S. team in Cairo. We had our best finish in a decade. We finished seventeenth. So you've gotta let us begin looking in different ponds."[10]

This approach was hardly new, as American intercollegiate squash had been dominated by foreign-born players for years, but when Trinity started to do the same, many of the established powers cried foul. The reaction of the squash establishment, Assaiante said in a 2004 *SI* profile (another example of the magazine's interest in NESCAC), was "Trinity? How the hell could it be Trinity? How dare you?"[11] Yale coach Dave Talbott questioned the academic qualifications of Trinity's recruits, even though Assaiante claimed the new international players were stronger academically than the domestic players Trinity used to attract.[12] One former

Chapter 7. No Longer So Pure and Simple

Trinity president Evan Dobelle encouraged head coach Paul Assaiante to build a men's squash power to best Ivy League programs and cultivate stakeholder interest. Courtesy Trinity College Photograph Collection, Watkinson Library and College Archives, Hartford, Connecticut.

NESCAC president said Trinity would try to game the system, noting that one of its athletic recruits was exempt from the conference's banding system (used to assess the academic qualities of prospects—see Chapter 8), "and we found out that they were defining 'underrepresented' in crazy ways. They were recruiting kids from California and deeming them as 'underrepresented' because they had so few students from California. And they did the same with their international squash kids." Slots in the "underrepresented" category, intended to be used for racial minorities, were exempt from the same academic requirements as other recruits.

Trinity's ascent was also a reaction to the hegemony of Amherst, Middlebury, and Williams in the early days of the AP era, when, as one former NESCAC president commented, the conference was experiencing "a kind of divergence between the successful and the less successful. There are two or three schools now, particularly one, that are in a state of dominance. In fact, they have quite possibly set out to achieve a state of dominance. And there are some that are middlingly successful, and then there are others that are extraordinarily unsuccessful." The president then listed several reactions. "The league in the main has become more competitive," the president stated, with "people recruiting more vigorously, and the recruiting practices are more disputed and are subject to greater argument and accusation and counteraccusation. In other words, if you are a school that is losing a great deal, you pick a couple of sports and make sure you have something to be proud of."

So Dobelle chose squash, and Trinity was able to improve in part because it could admit prospects whom competitor programs did not, as Trinity's admissions acceptance rate was 65 percent, compared with 20 percent for Amherst and Williams. *New York Times Magazine* writer Paul Wachter found that Trinity enjoyed another significant recruiting advantage: lower admission standards. "The kids that play squash for Trinity could not get into Williams (and Harvard, Yale and Princeton)," said Zafi Levy, head coach at Williams, who played for Assaiante at Trinity. Wachter also reported, "Trinity's admissions office, with support from the president, is able to give more slots to squash players than its competitors do." Yale's Talbott claimed that "at Yale, where sports aren't the emphasis, the president isn't going to put that much focus on any sport." Furthermore, Wachter noted that Trinity's admissions office allotted seventy-one spots to athletics prospects who would otherwise not be able to gain admission.[13]

The breakthrough occurred in 1996, when Trinity landed English prospect Marcus Cowie, its first significant international recruit, because Cowie had been denied admission to Harvard. Bill Doyle, Harvard's then head coach and a Trinity alumnus, put Cowie in touch with Assaiante. "Trinity made a tremendous pitch," said Cowie, who met with Dobelle and was courted by Luke Terry, a Trinity graduate employed in Credit Suisse's London offices.[14] Trinity attracted good international squash players because Dobelle encouraged and supported international recruiting trips by coaches, and he pushed squash prospects with demonstrated financial need to the top of the school's financial aid priority list. In addition to their travels, coaches worked to include both alumni contacts and Dobelle in the recruiting process. Dobelle himself convinced Cowie to come to Trinity with this pitch: "You know, Marcus, we don't really want to lose to Harvard anymore. You could be a big part of that." Upon arriving at Trinity, Cowie led the Bantams to a 6–3 win over the Crimson, the first-ever win for Trinity over Harvard. Soon thereafter, the word was out about Trinity; according to another English player, "It's sort of known in England that if you wanted to play squash [in America], you go to Trinity."[15] Assaiante, who claimed to have no recruiting budget, worked the phones and email to open the pipeline for players from India, Malaysia, Mexico, Pakistan, Sweden, and Zimbabwe.

According to Trinity's women's squash coach Wendy Bartlett, who also built a successful program, Dobelle made promoting squash part of his personal mission, an approach similar to that of Thomas Bonner with men's ice hockey at Union two decades before. "He made it clear he was not an academician. He came in as a visionary and a businessman and a politician.... People may not have liked the way he went about it, but he got an awful lot done. He was super at fundraising, ... [and] he loved winning." "Dobelle was right," said Assaiante, commenting that winning promoted good feelings with alumni: "When I walk into their office and they take me down the hallway to meet the partner who was a soccer player at Princeton, and they grind on each other for a few minutes."[16]

As a result, Trinity became the dominant squash program in the country. In 2011, the Bantams notched their thirteenth straight undefeated season (244 straight match wins) and captured their thirteenth straight national championship. The school's website claimed it was the longest winning streak in the history of intercollegiate varsity sports.[17]

Trinity began the 2011–12 season ranked number one, with the team's top players hailing from India, Malaysia, Mexico, South Africa, and Sweden. In 2012, the Bantams fell to Yale, 5–4, ending its dual match unbeaten streak at 225. The Yale win was hardly an upset, as the Elis had lost 5–4 to Trinity in the national championship the previous season, and Trinity had lost its top four players to graduation. Prior to the defeat Assaiante had commented that "there's a lot more parity, and four or five schools have a shot at the championship this year."[18] Yale and others caught the Bantams by copying them—that is, by recruiting foreign players, as Yale head coach Talbott noted that of the eighteen players in their match with Trinity, only four were American (three for Yale).

The school's perspective on the era, as describe on the school's website, was that the team's unprecedented winning streak "captivated Trinity and beyond—followed by major media outlets across the globe and the nation, including *Sports Illustrated*, ESPN, the *New York Times*, and the *Hartford Courant*. The history of the team will forever remain a legendary piece of history at Trinity College, where squash has been enthusiastically embraced. The team remains one of the most feared in college sports."[19] Assaiante offered a less sanguine synopsis on Trinity's impact. "Soon it will turn, and soon the dominance will come back to the Ivy League," he predicted. "The thing that cracks me up is in two, three years, when we're four or five in the league again, I'll be Coach Assaiante, great guy, and we'll be Trinity College, cool school."[20] Nevertheless, in 2018, Trinity won its seventeenth national championship.

While squash garnered much of the athletics spotlight, Trinity also improved greatly in other sports. The football program won thirty straight games from 2002 to 2006, defeated Bowdoin and Wesleyan by a combined 104–0 in 2003, allowed only 36 points in 2005, and compiled a record of 122–16 from 2002 to 2018. Baseball won an NCAA Division III title in 2008 with a record of 45–1, the best ever winning percentage in NCAA history, as well as advanced to the NCAA national final rounds in 2005 and 2009.

Men's hockey won the Division III national championship in 2015 and advanced to the NCAA Division III finals in 2017. To support these efforts, in 2016 the school spent $6.2 million to construct new baseball, softball, and soccer fields, projects funded entirely through donations from Trinity stakeholders. "I couldn't be happier with the new stadium," said Trinity head baseball coach Bryan Adamski. "The facility has created excitement amongst our players and alumni.... The turf will allow us to get outside earlier in the year and better develop our student-athletes."[21]

Dobelle After Trinity

Dobelle's tenure at Trinity was brief, and as Wendy Bartlett observed, "[Dobelle] spent a heck of a lot of money ... on all kinds of things," and his replacement "was sort of cleaning up after all of the money Evan spent."[22] Trinity went through three presidents in three years until James Jones, a Georgian with a PhD from Columbia, came to Hartford from the presidency at Kalamazoo College and served from 2004 to 2014. Dobelle departed in 2001 for the University of Hawaii, but he left there in 2004 as part of a settlement after questions about his personal spending (an initial firing for cause was rescinded as part of the settlement). He was president at Westfield State University in Massachusetts (at a salary of nearly $250,000 a year) from 2008 until his resignation in 2013. While claiming he made Westfield State "the hottest college in New England" and launching a $170 million building scheme,[23] Dobelle was forced to pay the Commonwealth of Massachusetts $185,000 in damages, fees, and costs to settle allegations that he used school credit cards to pay for personal expenses. In addition, Dobelle was banned from any future employment at Massachusetts state schools, and his name was removed from the library at Middlesex Community College, where he had served as president from 1987 to 1990.[24]

The Game of Life and Reclaiming the Game Challenge the Ideal Image

In 2001, as NESCAC programs ascended to the top of NCAA Division III in numerous sports and the Trinity squash juggernaut was rounding into form, *The Game of Life: College Sports and Educational Values* offered a critical view of these developments and made a significant impact on NESCAC campuses. The book, coauthored by former Princeton president William Bowen and Mellon Foundation researcher James

Shulman, provided an analysis of the resources and energies devoted to the maintenance of intercollegiate athletic programs at academically selective American colleges and universities. The authors sought to present data on what they identified as the "myths that permeate college sports,"[25] such as that sport builds character and that athletic programs make money. Data were collected from ninety thousand individual admissions records and survey responses from students and graduates at thirty "selective" schools, including Hamilton, Tufts, Wesleyan, and Williams. In addition, three sitting NESCAC presidents—Campbell of Wesleyan, Payne of Williams, and Bob Edwards of Bowdoin—were credited by the authors for contributing "telling comments and revealing stories."[26] Janet Lavin Rapelye and Tom Parker, both with extensive NESCAC admissions experience, were also acknowledged as contributing information and perspectives.

At the behest of NESCAC presidents, William Bowen, a former Princeton president, was the lead author in studies that impugned the impacts of athletics on NESCAC campuses. Courtesy Princeton University Special Collections.

Said Bowen after the book's publication: "A key question for any selective college is how do you ration the small number of valuable places in the class."[27] The authors concluded that athletes are given significant preferences in the admissions process, athletes perform at a lower level academically and are more limited in their professional career focuses than the general student population, and athletics expenditures can be justified only if the programs support the core educational mission of the school.

Underscoring the level of investment of NESCAC parents, such as the previously mentioned *SI* letter writer Eric Bergofsky, Harvard Law School professor Hal Scott—a parent of two daughters who were Williams student-athletes—published a highly critical response to *The Game of Life* in the *Journal of College and University Law*. Scott also denounced Shulman personally and professionally in November 2002 while both participated in a Harvard University symposium dedicated to examining the impact of the book. Scott may have been exercised in part because, in the book's prelude, the authors chose to feature the 1996 Williams women's lacrosse postseason controversy. The authors even titled that section "Pure and Simple," recalling Looney's 1994 *SI* article, and referenced the piece when stating that "simplicity proved elusive," noting that a western Massachusetts paper reported that the team's dreams of being the top team in the country had turned into a "nightmare."[28]

Scott's article began as a benign critique, saying, "The fundamental problem with this book is the failure to articulate and defend a clear vision of what the goals of colleges and universities should be. The proper role of athletics in educational institutions can only be judged in that context." After that, Scott's assessment was far more pointed. "This is not to say the authors do not have such a vision—it is there, but only between the lines," Scott wrote. "In the authors' view, the sole aim of every college and university should be to 'educate' their students in academic disciplines."[29] Using an economic defense, Scott argued that "the marketplace rejects" Shulman and Bowen's academic vision[30] and the "anti-market bias of the authors clearly emerges at the end of the book when they acknowledge that athletics cannot be de-emphasized unless the schools 'act in consort' ... That raises serious antitrust issues and would damage our rather free education markets."[31]

Scott then staked out a cultural defense, claiming the book "has a distinct liberal bias" and the authors "fail to recognize that there is a need for a conservative point of view on campus, often represented by athletes, to counterbalance the overwhelming liberalism that emanates from most faculty and students." "The liberal bias is abundantly clear," Scott charged, "in the failure of the authors to justify cutting back on athletic admissions while continuing to justify affirmative action for minorities."[32]

The heart of Scott's disagreement with the authors, however, was that he thought Shulman and Bowen "clearly believe that 'jock' culture has a negative effect on the educational experience. The authors refer to this culture throughout the book but never really define it."[33] Scott did not deny the existence of "cheating, falsifying of academic records, point shaving, gambling, violence, and other blatant abuses" the authors identified, but he responded (without evidence), "But are they problems at Princeton? At Williams? At Stanford? I doubt it."[34] The passage of time would—at least in the case of Stanford as well as Yale, with the "Varsity Blues" criminal case brought by the Federal Bureau of Investigations in 2019 identifying incidents of academic fraud and bribery in these school's admissions

Chapter 7. No Longer So Pure and Simple

processes—provide evidence to contradict Scott's assumption of the upright management of selective school athletics.

Shulman allowed that "underneath it all [Scott] had some legitimate points about selections and preselections, but it was the worst scholarship I've ever seen in my entire life. He kept writing things and putting them in quotation marks for things that we didn't write, like a 'jock culture.' You can say jock culture, but we didn't say 'jock culture.' You can say we implied it, or you interpreted that, but you can't say we wrote it."

Immediately after the contentious 2002 Harvard Business School event, Shulman had an encounter with Scott. "I said, 'Professor Scott, I'm glad we had a chance to air our differences, but I just have to say, you shouldn't put quotes around something that someone didn't write. I don't think that's good practice,'" Shulman recounted. "And he said, 'Put it on the record! Put it on the record!' And I said, 'I will. We're going to write a response, but you shouldn't say somebody wrote something they didn't write. It's not a good way of arguing something.' And again he said, 'Put it on the record! Put it on the record!' And he was up in my face like he was going to punch me. And I'm thinking, 'I can't believe this. Maybe I'm dreaming this because I'm in this foggy parking lot outside of the building, and this man is going to hit me!' And that was the last I saw of Hal Scott."

One line of inquiry Scott could have pursued—as others had—was Bowen's complicity in what the book identified as negative trends relating to intercollegiate athletics, since these snowballed during Bowen's tenure at Princeton (1972–88), as well as research methods and assumptions. Nonetheless, the book's findings and claims prompted significant levels of debate concerning the role of athletics on NESCAC campuses. In response, NESCAC presidents asked Bowen and other collaborators to perform a similar study of their schools, even though Bates and Trinity had recently completed similar studies on their own campuses. The 2003 book *Reclaiming the Game: College Sports and Educational Values* (curiously sharing the same subtitle as the preceding book) contained additional research that concluded that NESCAC athletes had a significant advantage in the admissions process and graduated at a higher rate, but most earned lower grades than the majority of their classmates, "bunched" in certain majors, and practiced social self-segregation that distinguished recruited athletes from students at large. These developments, stated the authors, showed evidence of a significant "athletic divide" present on NESCAC campuses. The book offered multiple reform recommendations, including limiting recruitment activities, reducing the number of admitted recruited athletes, adjusting admissions criteria, and, since the issue had proved to be so problematic within NESCAC, a national ban on NCAA postseason play, quite possibly to take the heat off NESCAC after the aborted one-team-per-sport postseason proposal.

That schools cooperated with the authors on data collection and shared information gave many the sense that Bowen had been enlisted by NESCAC presidents to take on the issue of the role of athletics in their stead and that the book would help the presidents confront problematic issues on their campuses. When the Carnegie Report failed to generate a follow-up study (see Chapter 1), this sharing of information among presidents and athletics managers occurred periodically over the course of their athletics relations, often when presidents were struggling to manage administrative crises and sought to collect data both to make informed decisions as well as to seek shared political cover.

Shulman agreed with the sense that Bowen was taking up the mantle for NESCAC presidents. In a prior Bowen book, *The Shape of the River: Long-Term Consequences of Considering Race in College and University Admissions* (coauthored with former Harvard president Derek Bok), Shulman noted that "everyone wanted something to be done about that issue. For comparison, because I was a collaborator on *The Shape of the River*, I must have given a hundred talks on that book, from dean's offices [to] Dupont Circle—groups of all kinds.... Of course they wanted Bill or Derek first, but they could only do so much." Shulman continued that presidents "wanted backup on affirmative action because they knew they wanted to do it, they knew it was the right thing to do, they cared about it, they knew there were constituencies for it and constituencies against it." "And on athletics," Shulman went on, "they may have felt there were trade-offs they didn't like, or complications that they didn't like, even with the collective arguments about pluses and minuses. It's just recognizing that decisions have trade-offs, and you have to figure out where your values are and what's important."

"It is a use of [presidents' political] capital, to get involved in anything," reasoned Shulman. "Same thing with fraternities. When they got rid of fraternities on campus, it took a while, and it was incredibly hard, and [there was] a lot of anger from a small constituency, a one-issue constituency, with a lot of letters saying, 'I'll never give a goddamn dollar to the school again,' and a lot of angry people when you go to the clubs." "But you can't do that all the time," concluded Shulman.

As for stakeholder perspectives regarding athletics, Shulman indicated that "the data were so clear. Forty percent of alums from these three different points of time thought that schools had just the right emphasis on athletics, and 40 percent wanted less emphasis on athletics, and that 20 percent wanted more." "So what that meant was when those first four questions for the president from the Bowdoin Club of Tampa, Florida,

Chapter 7. No Longer So Pure and Simple   171

were about the hockey team, it doesn't mean that those people aren't real or they don't care," said Shulman, "it just means that represented one out of five alums. But it doesn't look that way because those were the first four questions."

Eugene Tobin, a coauthor with Bowen on *Equity and Excellence in American Higher Education*, offered his takeaway from the books: "The 'opportunity costs' of having to turn away high-achieving students because as many as 25 percent or more of the places at some colleges had been claimed by recruited athletes seemed both unfair and too high a price to pay," Tobin concluded, noting that the authors also cited the "signaling effects" of such admission practices on secondary schools, prospective students, and their families (see Chapter 8 for the impacts of this).

Middlebury professor Timothy Spears said the debate over the two books was "heated." "On some campuses, mine included," he wrote, "the faculty formed committees to investigate whether intercollegiate athletics, and athletes, were problems. Meanwhile, coaches, athletes, parents, and alums looked for ways to fend off what felt to them like a personal attack." Spears, a former football player at Yale whose brother played football at Bowdoin, allowed that "the pressure was really on the NESCAC presidents to make changes, and what changes they did make were slight modifications on the admissions formula for recruited athletes." Spears also allowed that since the NESCACs fielded a higher percentage of varsity teams than big-time schools, "the culture of athletics, as Bowen defined it, was potentially more corrosive."[35]

Tobin recalled discussing the book with members of the athletic department, "where of course there was skepticism among many coaches, which I think is understandable." So to address this, Tobin ordered copies, "which we discussed at length with our athletic director and a number of coaches. These were not easy conversations, nor did they produce a consensus about policy changes, but they did introduce greater awareness, especially around studying recruited athletes' academic performance and the college's priorities in terms of admissions and financial aid."

Nonetheless, one former NESCAC AD bristled at the conclusions in the Bowen books. "To be honest, I've tired of people taking shots at NESCAC athletes and suggesting they 'don't belong,'" commented this AD, adding, "I thought Bill Bowen was corrupt. For example, one of his points was that the acceptance rate for recruited athletes was significantly higher than other populations. Of course it was. Supported recruits were prequalified [meaning they had been vetted by admissions offices and weren't advanced unless their credentials merited acceptance]! He absolutely understood this. It is just one example of how he manipulated data."

Division IV: The Lost Cause in Defense of the BP Era

As part of its many suggested reforms, *Reclaiming the Game* advanced consideration of the creation of a separate grouping of schools across the country, referred to in the book as "Division X" (it's unclear whether this X stood for the letter of the alphabet or the Roman numeral). The authors argued that this could address the fact that the vast majority of Division III institutions did not share the same academic profiles as NESCAC. The Division X concept meant that schools that joined would agree to roll back many of the expansions that had occurred at Division III schools over the prior three decades to a point more representative of the original tenets of the classification codified in 1973, and closer to those of the NESCACs.

The concept, which looked to extend what Pentagonal expansion did in the late 1960s, was supported by some NESCAC presidents, including one NESCAC president whose teams had participated extensively in NCAA postseason play, who said, "[Another NESCAC president] nailed it. He said we have to go out to Nebraska and play Nebraska Wesleyan for [a championship]. Who benefits from that? Our students going to Nebraska? Our alumni and students who can't see the game? Or the players who have to take an extra day of travel to play in the postseason. That doesn't make any sense." "There's nothing wrong with Nebraska Wesleyan," offered the president, "[but] I know some of the other presidents are very interested in the notion of either Division IIIA or Division IV, where there are very clear criteria that have to do with the selectivity of the student body." This president envisioned a grouping that included the NESCACs, Pomona, Carleton, Colorado College, Davidson, Washington and Lee, and Kenyon, "a group of schools that really are like us. And then we think about a national championship within that universe. That would be exciting. I would hope we would evolve in that direction."

But as it turned out, save a handful of presidents, very few within NESCAC and Division III overall shared this excitement, even though by 2007, some presidents were speaking publicly on the issue, including Middlebury's Ronald Liebowitz. Hired from within to succeed John McCardell in 2004, Liebowitz, a New York City native with a PhD from Columbia, offered this blunt appraisal to the *New York Times*: "The status quo in Division III is not a workable option. We must have fundamental change in the structure of the division."[36]

Liebowitz sought to employ a basic advantage of conferences—that is, seeking to shift and to share the political burden for hard decisions regarding Middlebury's athletics programs, which had grown dominant under the leadership of his predecessor. Concurrent with the rise of the Trinity men's squash juggernaut, multiple programs at Middlebury achieved unprecedented levels of success, chronicled in yet another laudatory *SI* piece, a full-page article published in November 1998 titled "Green Mountain Giant: Tiny Middlebury Produces Teams to Match Its Impressive Facilities," with a photograph of two-sport (field hockey and lacrosse) athlete Heidi Howard. Staff writer L. Jon Wertheim outlined how "this highly-regarded liberal arts school ... this unremittingly preppy school—best known for its language departments and the summer immersion program ... is a wellspring for athletic success at the Division III level."[37]

While Wertheim, like many before, was quick to set an idealized scene ("one would be hard-pressed to label Middlebury College a bona fide jock school. Not so long as the varsity athletes pump iron in the same weight room as the rest of the student body, there are no athletic scholarships, and the football coach won't cut any student who wants to be on his team"), he went on to evoke a comparison with the 1927 New York Yankees in listing the "Murderers' Row" of recent Panther team successes: women's field hockey was 1998 NCAA champions; women's cross-country placed seventh in the NCAAs; men's soccer, undefeated in the regular season, lost in the first round of the NCAAs; women's ice hockey hadn't lost to a conference opponent in fifty-two games; women's lacrosse had been in the NCAA semifinals five seasons straight and was 1997 NCAA champs; men's hockey had won four straight NCAA titles; the ski team—like Trinity squash, competing against Division I schools—perennially finished with a top ten national ranking. "Success breeds success," AD Russ Reilly said to Wertheim with a shrug.[38]

But was Reilly's succinct summation the whole story? Wertheim indicated as much when he wondered how Middlebury had "transformed itself from a modest member of.... NESCAC into a sports powerhouse." One explanation was that Middlebury had adopted a Division I "build it and they will come" philosophy toward recruiting through significant facility upgrades, an approach Trinity used as well. Since the beginning of the decade, the school had constructed a track-and-field complex, a football field with stands, "a swanky natatorium (read: wildly expensive pool)," and what Wertheim called "the crown jewel," a $17.5 million hockey rink funded largely by donations, the biggest from alumnus and former hockey player Chip Kenyon. "I'm not sure kids are going to come here just because we have a great new building," said Bill Beaney, the men's ice hockey coach who also oversaw the golf program. "But appearances matter, and we hope they'll see this and realize the commitment it stands for."[39]

Middlebury's building spate was the first salvo fired in what would become NESCAC's facilities arms race. The shabby locker rooms at Williams, which *SI*'s Looney identified four years prior as a symbol of

NESCAC's rightly focused priorities concerning athletics, were about to go the way of leather helmets and using nails in locker room walls to hang clothes. While a few venerable facilities, such as Bates's Alumni Gym (built in 1926), remained in use for their initial purposes, every NESCAC school has upgraded or built new athletics facilities in the last two decades. Prior to its field improvements, Trinity built its first on-campus hockey facility in 2006, and in 2009, Bowdoin replaced its Dayton Arena, which opened as only the third indoor rink in Maine in 1956, with Watson Arena, named in honor of its longtime head men's ice hockey coach and AD. That same year, Conn opened a new ten-thousand-square-foot fitness and athlete training facility.

Other more recent examples include Bates's christening a $2.5 million rowing boathouse (funded entirely by donations) in 2016 and Hamilton building an indoor practice facility for all teams in 2018. In 2020, Colby finished construction on an entirely new set of indoor athletics facilities, including an aquatics center, fitness facilities, a gymnasium, squash courts, tennis courts, a track, and an ice arena, at a cost of $150 million, part of a number of expenditures by President David Greene that led one former NESCAC development officer to remark that Greene was "spending money like a drunken sailor."

Now, every NESCAC campus had multiple all-weather artificial turf fields, most of them lighted, allowing some spring sports to move the starts of their seasons into February, which would have been unthinkable logistically a decade ago. In 2020, Bates women's lacrosse hosted its first home contest on February 26, a night game versus Babson College, where the low temperature was 33 degrees. Two weeks later, Bowdoin lost to Colby in baseball, played on Colby's recently renovated and turfed Coombs Field. The high temperature in Waterville that day was 41 degrees. When the new facility had opened for the 2016 season, head baseball coach Dale Plummer remarked on March 30, "We've had approximately ten practices on the field. It's key for our infielders and outfielders to see some real fly balls before the spring trip.... This playing surface is one of the finest in the country." Colby softball coach Lisa-Ann Wallace, whose facility was also upgraded at the time, said on March 29, "Since February 18th we've been outside. I've had only three practices indoors. Huge [positive] impact."[40]

As for Middlebury's athletics boom, Wertheim alerted readers of concerns about the athletics emphasis. "Not that all this warmth and Patagonia fuzziness for sports has met with unqualified applause," he wrote. "A number of students and professors worry that the school has made a Mephistophelian bargain and the unseemly appurtenances that attend big-time athletics are lurking around the corner. Perhaps a more salient concern is whether the $25 million earmarked for the new pool and

Chapter 7. No Longer So Pure and Simple 175

hockey rink might have been put to better use, say, endowing more professorships or providing more student financial aid." Middlebury's president denied that athletics were exacting an academic price. "We're striving for excellence across the board," John McCardell told Wertheim.[41]

The spending spree did lead Middlebury into some significant financial difficulties that required cost-cutting measures in other areas, contributed to in part by the economic slowdown following the Great Recession. But Wertheim repeated the phrase attributed to Amherst president Tom Gerety in Looney's *SI* piece four years earlier, perhaps to assuage concerns about challenges to the ideal athletic image: "Middlebury athletics ... might simply be the sweatiest of the liberal arts." He reinforced the ideal image notion by reporting that Middlebury games were

> played in front of sparse crowds, ... [and] feature little jaw-dropping athleticism but lots of superannuated virtues such as ample ball and puck passing and plenty of postgame handshakes. What's more, Middlebury is a place where the term "student-athlete" doesn't provoke smirks. A full 100% of the senior varsity athletes graduated last year, including lacrosse captain Brandon Doyle, who nearly missed a crucial game when his French horn recital ran late.[42]

In his view, vestiges of the BP era's ideal image survived but were superseded by the AP version of a level of excellence not previously achieved. This was the fin de siècle version of the NESCAC ideal: a big-time version of the small-time.

In light of these developments, Liebowitz took his case for Division X—now referred to as "Division IV"—directly to Middlebury's stakeholders in a piece in the school's alumni magazine. Liebowitz's reasons for D-IV were strikingly similar to those posited by Bowen and Levin: Division III's rapid growth in membership, with new members having "more lenient rules than NESCAC governing their athletic programs," and future NCAA legislative changes these schools might vote into place, which could "give our competitors on-field advantages that appear unfair." Liebowitz then claimed that "a number of D-III member institutions are encouraging colleges that share our conference's philosophy on the balance between athletics and academics to support the proposal for a Division IV," which would "allow the new division to introduce new and perhaps more stringent rules guiding athletics." He continued that "it didn't seem right to me (or 'fair') that some of our varsity teams compete against programs with student bodies that are two, three, and even five times the size of Middlebury's—programs that begin their seasons weeks ahead of our teams, with many more games/contests under their belts, and with fewer restrictions on their recruiting and admissions." Liebowitz then warned, "What would happen if NESCAC teams began to get beaten and beaten badly in first-round NCAA tournaments as a result? How much pressure would presidents of NESCAC schools begin to feel from student-athletes, coaches, athletic directors, alumni, parents and others if our current success gave way to early tournament departures?"[43]

But the successes of the AP era kept coming for Middlebury, especially in men's hockey. Under Bill Beaney, the program notched a record of 302–46–20 from 1995 to 2007, with twelve consecutive NCAA appearances, including an NCAA record five straight titles from 1995 through 1999. Middlebury put together another string of national titles from 2004 through 2006. This was now the new AP ideal, and whatever misgivings presidents might have, the genie was not going back into the bottle. Liebowitz acknowledged as much when he wrote in the *Middlebury Magazine* article, "My coaches have already told me, 'Forget it, it would be such a negative to be in a sub-division.' Personally, I doubt students would stop choosing Williams, Amherst or Middlebury because we're in Division IV. But I know others feel differently."[44] Clearly Liebowitz and other interested presidents knew they were in no position to impose the restrictions proposed by Division IV alone, as to do so would be to risk succumbing to competitive disadvantages versus peer schools, so any hoped-for changes had to be done in consort with a critical mass of schools, preferably those who could help them maintain the ideal image.

Other D-IV doubters included former Williams AD Harry Sheehy, who said, "We were kind of being forced philosophically to go to Division IV. I fought it like crazy because we had spent twenty-five years branding Division III, and that was a powerful brand at the end. The Division III national championships are really highly regarded. And I felt that if you want to split up, then you go call yourselves Division IV." "We'll stay right here in Division III," said Sheehy, "because there was a natural sense that we were going to be downgraded. And then we were going to have to spend all this time building up a brand? I'm going to be in the grave before that brand got built."

These comments were echoed by Lisa Melendy, named to the AD position at Williams in 2011 after Sheehy left for the AD post at Dartmouth. When she heard of the Division IV proposal at the 2007 NCAA convention, Melendy told the *New York Times*, "When the leadership started telling us about the inevitability of the split, we all looked around and said, 'Who decided we had to split?' ... At the convention there were people walking around saying, 'I'll never join a Division IV.' No one wants to be in Division IV. The name has such a substandard sound. It sounds like you've been demoted."[45] Several years prior, Williams head football coach Dick Farley sounded the same tone when, as *SI*'s Looney related, Farley, "in moments of despair[,] inform[ed] his charges, 'If you can't play here, you can't play, because there is no Division IV.'"[46]

Chapter 7. No Longer So Pure and Simple 177

Initial Division IV models proposed a grouping based on a minimum sport-offering requirement, perhaps as many as eighteen, with restrictions on recruiting, length of playing seasons, and out-of-season practices—issues that were almost identical to those at the heart of the founding agreements of first the Pentagonals and then NESCAC. As noted by one NESCAC president, D-IV likely wouldn't include schools like Nebraska Wesleyan, and this perspective was not lost on others in D-III. Amy Carlton, commissioner of the American Southwest Conference, a grouping of sixteen colleges in Arkansas, Louisiana, Mississippi, and Texas, commented about the exclusive nature of the Division IV proposal. "Don't these more restrictive proposals come down to how deep your pockets are? When you've got 600 students, how are you supposed to pay for the extra sports teams that are required?"[47] John Dzik, AD at Piedmont College, a member of the USA South Athletic Conference, seconded the notion in the *Chronicle of Higher Education*, stating, "If the Division III leadership and the NCAA really want to put their money where their mouths are, they would restructure the division based on comparable resources," noting that the most successful schools in Division III were also the wealthiest in terms of endowments.[48]

In 2008, a working committee of the NCAA sent a seventy-five-question survey to all D-III schools to collect data and opinions on the proposed bifurcation. The survey was organized into sections to ascertain respondent perceptions of the current state of Division III in the areas of recruiting, financial aid, sport sponsorship, academic performance, playing and practice seasons, presidential leadership, national championships, and the consideration of a potential new classification and its components. Ninety-six percent of the Division III membership responded, and 82 percent expressed support or strong support for the maintaining of the current Division III structure, while only 15 percent supported creating a subdivision of D-III or a new divisional classification. Members believed that the current structure worked well, that a compelling case for structural change had not been made, and that urgent claims of philosophical divides among members had been overstated.[49] While D-III vice president Dan Dutcher acknowledged that "the membership seems to be saying pretty clearly that structural change is not the way to go," he also opined, "It's also clear that some pretty significant issues remain that need to be dealt with in some way."[50] Whatever way that would be, it wouldn't include the Pentagonal-like expansion that created NESCAC in 1971. Ultimately, Liebowitz said after moving on from Middlebury to become president of Brandeis University in 2015, the Division IV concept failed because NESCAC was so successful in Division III. "You couldn't make the case that grouping of similarly sized, academically inclined institutions made sense when NESCAC was cleaning up all the championships," he said. "I was torn about that. I did write about it and I did think it had merit, but it was really frustrating to be in a division that had such a disparate array, in terms of size, in terms of composition, in terms of rules and regulations. NESCAC was the strictest in terms of when teams could begin competitions, etc. If you follow the argument you would conclude it was unfair, but when NESCAC was so successful it was hard to make that case."

Middlebury, Knelman, Beaney, and the Litigation of the Right to Play

Concurrent with the start of the NESCAC AP era was the emergence of a significant trend in youth sport specialization in American youth sports. This trend would soon impact deeply NESCAC athletics and school admissions practices. NESCAC ADs and presidents who were in place just prior to the publication of the Bowen books and the push for Division IV declared that the conference was not immune to the growing interest, emphasis, and specialization in youth sport across the country, as expressed particularly by student-athlete and parent stakeholders. The following comment from one president captures the concerns with the stakeholder influence on the ideal image: "[There is] huge, passionate parental involvement, with parents that come hundreds of miles for every game," said the president. "It gives me the image of what I call the 'hothouse generation' of student-athletes. These are kids who have been groomed since they were three years old, and the parents have been on the sidelines so that the parents have been trained just like the kids."

The term "hothouse generation" describes prospects cultivated by coaches and parents into highly proficient, highly specialized athletic prodigies. NESCAC ADs also acknowledged this hothouse generation phenomenon and how it had changed the nature of their programs away from an ideal operational structure, which was likewise impacted by the ever-escalating costs associated with attending NESCAC schools. One AD described the changes that had developed as a result: "The evolution of speciality in all the sports from the earliest ages is now having the greatest impact upon even schools like ours. And where there used to be a predominance of multisport athletes, that predominance of multisport athletes has declined. But it has declined only in part because of the pressures that are involved in the college." "Twenty years ago," said the AD, "it didn't bother the students that they had an assistant from another sport being the head coach of their sport with a limited amount of knowledge. Now, with the cost factor that's involved, there is a demand for excellence, and

Chapter 7. No Longer So Pure and Simple

the demand for excellence crosses the boundaries into the coaching. And at this point, student-athletes will not be satisfied with a coach that their sport is his or her secondary priority. That's a product of [speciality]."

A precipitate of the ratcheting up of demands by the hothouse generation is that NESCACs had to bolster and augment programs and staffing decisions. Another AD described the increased expectations of students and its impact on coaches. "Soccer has become a year-round sport," said the AD. "They play all the time. They come to college, and they expect to play all the time. So their first question to me will be 'What do you do with indoor [soccer]?' 'Well, I can't coach it,' I say. And the response: 'What? Why not?' So it's not like, 'Oh, great, now I'll have time to study!'"

This ratcheting became a concern in NESCAC, not only because of the costs of institutional support for athletics (e.g., upgrades of athletics facilities) but also because of a significant shift in the stakeholder perceptions of what the role of NESCAC athletics should be. The decision to participate in NCAA postseason championships was a contributor to this ratcheting, as identified by another AD, which resulted in "increase in pressure: pressure to get to the national tournament, pressure to win the national championship." "And while people will say no one is under pressure to do that," said the AD, "there certainly is subtle pressure. The students want to get there, their parents want to get there, the alums want to get there because they love the attention."

Looney's 1994 *SI* piece offered a very different BP stakeholder perspective with the observations of a Middlebury football player, who stated, "I played purely for the love of the game. Did I ever long to look up and see 75,000 screaming fans? Not really. To be honest, it was a better feeling to see 3,500 screaming fans and to know they were part of the community and that you belonged to that community and that most of the people up there were your friends." This player considered his football experience "to be a real valuable asset in my life. The discipline, hard work and competitive nature I learned playing at Middlebury is something I'll carry with me the rest of my life."[51]

However, in the AP era, this player's perspective would no longer predominate. National success and achievements, along with the changed stakeholder perceptions of the hothouse generation, were contributing factors leading to a 2011 lawsuit brought by Middlebury student James "Jak" Knelman over the decision of head men's hockey coach Bill Beaney to dismiss Knelman from the team during the 2010–11 season. Knelman, who graduated prior to bringing the suit, sought compensatory damages in excess of $75,000, punitive damages, attorney's fees, and prejudgment interest as permitted by Vermont law.

Lawsuits regarding student-athlete participation were not unprecedented in the history of American intercollegiate athletics, and several, most notably *Waldrep v. Texas Employers Insurance Association*, sought to establish a contractual employee-employer relationship between student-athletes and colleges and universities. Knelman's case sought to show that Middlebury ice hockey was not just an educational and personal development enhancer for life during and after college—not merely the "sweatiest of the liberal arts"—but rather, much like for many Division I participants, a financial investment in a possible future professional hockey career.

Knelman, a native of the youth hockey hotbed of Edina, Minnesota, played two games at Division I Colgate University in 2007–2008, then played junior hockey for the Chicago Steel of the United States Hockey League for a season and a half prior to matriculating at Middlebury for the 2009–10 season.[52] As outlined in court documents, Knelman alleged that his relationship with Middlebury was contractual in nature and that Middlebury breached its alleged promise to provide him with procedural due process before was dismissed from the team. Knelman further alleged that his relationship with Middlebury was fiduciary in nature and Middlebury had a "duty to act in Knelman's best interest and with the highest standards of integrity and good faith in its dealings with Knelman," and he asserted a parallel claim of breach of fiduciary duty against Beaney.[53]

The plaintiff further contended that the manner in which Beaney handled Knelman's dismissal from the team was arbitrary and capricious and subsequently defamed the plaintiff in his chosen prospective career as a professional hockey player. Knelman's defamation claim was based upon Beaney's alleged statements that Knelman was "selfish" and "had problems" on the team the prior year, that Knelman's dismissal was "not an isolated incident," and that Beaney did not think hockey was "a priority" for Knelman. There had been disputes between the two over Beaney's decision to play Knelman on defense rather than at forward, which Knelman had preferred.[54]

On the night of January 15, 2011, after a 4–3 overtime loss to Wesleyan that afternoon—the Cardinals' first win in thirty-six tries against the Panthers—team members were required to attend an athletic department fund-raising banquet honoring the school's 1960–61 men's hockey team. Knelman, however, had planned to have dinner with his parents that night. One week prior to the banquet, he told Beaney about his plans and inquired how long the banquet would last. Knelman attended the banquet but left approximately thirty minutes before the banquet concluded without seeking or obtaining permission to leave early from the coach or the team captains. As a result, Beaney suspended Knelman from the team for the remainder of the season.[55] One wonders whether Knelman would

Chapter 7. No Longer So Pure and Simple 181

have been excused to give a French horn recital, like former Middlebury lacrosse captain Brandon Doyle.

Knelman then filed suit in the U.S. District Court for the District of Vermont, arguing that the Middlebury student handbook and the NCAA manual provided certain due process protections and that suspension from the team constituted a breach of contract and breach of fiduciary duty. At the time of filing, Middlebury chose not to respond and instead issued the following statement: "As with most lawsuits, there's more to the story than has been presented by one side's attorney. Middlebury values its student-athletes, the successes they have achieved in academics and sports, and the coaches who provide their teams with leadership and support."[56]

Soon thereafter, a post on NESCAC Hockey, a website dedicated to the goings-on associated with the conference's men's programs and not affiliated with the actual conference, explained why some NESCAC student-athletes now pursued their sport. In reviewing Middlebury's response to the case, the site, which includes links and tweets on recruiting information from the conference and individual programs, noted that a "strange tactic on Middlebury's part is adamantly denying that a Middlebury hockey career can be a pathway to a professional hockey career." "This is a defense that will be easy to refute," said the site, "as many Middlebury graduates play professional hockey in Europe or in U.S. minor leagues. It is not as though the NHL is the only form of professional hockey."[57]

The website, the existence of which indicates the level of stakeholder interest in the management and outcomes associated with the programs, then identified "large numbers of Middlebury grads in the ranks of professional hockey," including 2004 graduate Kevin Cooper; 2008 graduates Tom Maldonado, Mickey Gilchrist, and Scott Bartlett; 2009 graduates Jamie McKenna and Mason Graddock; and 2010 graduates Charlie Townsend and John Sullivan.

The site then opined on "a lack of grace on the part of Middlebury in its defense. These include denying ... that Knelman was a 'significant contributor' to the Middlebury hockey team ... [and] denying that Knelman was 'a lead scorer' ... (He was tied for fifth leading scorer on the team at the time of his dismissal)." The site also wondered why Middlebury and Beaney "'admit' that 'the hockey team's winning percentage increased after Plaintiff was dismissed from the team.' This insertion is gratuitous as Knelman's complaint did not address this issue or require Middlebury and Beaney to raise it."[58]

Middlebury and Beaney conceded that the decision to dismiss Knelman from the team was Beaney's alone and that "several" players expressed disagreement with his decision and asked him to reverse it.

Beaney "eventually" told the team that Knelman's early departure from the banquet was "not an isolated incident." Middlebury was unable to rebut Knelman's assertion that a key academic administrator expressed support for him in private meetings. Similarly, Middlebury was unable to refute Knelman's claim that the head of the Environmental Studies Department told him she was fed up with Beaney and that Knelman should go to the student newspaper. Another sign that some members of the Middlebury faculty and administration did not support Beaney's defense included Middlebury's inability to respond to Knelman's assertion that several faculty reviewed the draft of his complaint about Beaney.[59]

In 2012, the district court granted summary judgment to the college and coach, dismissing Knelman's claims, and in 2014 the U.S. Court of Appeals for the Second Circuit affirmed the decision. The Second Circuit applied Vermont law for the proposition that the relationship between a student and a college is contractual and that the terms of the contract are contained in the brochures, course-offering bulletins, and other official statements, policies, and publications of the institution. The court, however, rejected the player's argument that the due process protections in the "Judicial Board Procedures" section of the college's student handbook applied to sanctions imposed by a coach on an athlete. The court explained that the student handbook specified certain sanctions for nonacademic conduct infractions and disciplinary offenses, academic dishonesty, and plagiarism, "but it does not include athletic penalties, such as benching an athlete for a certain number of games, suspension from a team, or any other reprimand a coach might mete out." In addition, because the student handbook did not incorporate by specific reference the NCAA manual, the court held that provisions of the NCAA manual were not part of the plaintiff's contract with the college.[60]

In reaching its decision, the court opined that while Beaney's decision to kick Knelman off the team for the remainder of the season was "arguably harsh, there was no breach of contract." In affirming the dismissal of the breach of fiduciary duty claim, the court explained that "while schools, colleges, and educators assume the responsibility of educating their students, the law does not recognize the existence of a special duty for purposes of a fiduciary duty claim." To the ancient legal maxim "the law does not concern itself with trifles," we may now add "the law does not concern itself with second-guessing discretionary coaching decisions."[61]

In the wake of the case, Beaney stepped down after the 2014–15 season. He had a career record of 516–184–51 in twenty-eight seasons at Middlebury, although in the seasons following the Knelman suit his record was 48–44–11, with no NCAA tournament appearances. He remained the school's golf coach. Upon the announcement of his retirement from

Chapter 7. No Longer So Pure and Simple

Coach Bill Beaney led his teams to multiple NCAA men's hockey national titles, but ended up defending his decision to cut Jak Knelman in court. Courtesy Middlebury College Athletics.

coaching hockey, Beaney stated, "A coach is only one part of a successful program. It requires the commitment of the entire institution, from the president to the director of athletics, from the faculty to the entire coaching staff, and of course to the quality and character of the players."[62] And today, one can find no reference to any Middlebury alums playing professional hockey on the school's athletics website.

The Hothouse Generation in Full Flower: Duncan Robinson

In his 1994 *SI* piece, Looney listed a few former NESCAC athletes who had advanced to the professional ranks but declared, "No NESCAC player has made it to the NBA."[63] That changed in 2018, when former Williams men's basketball player Duncan Robinson debuted with the NBA's Miami Heat. Robinson's pre-NESCAC pedigree was fairly common for the league: a New Hampshire kid who, because of a lack of interest from college recruiters, had done a postgraduate year at a time-honored NESCAC favorite, the venerable Phillips Exeter Academy. Robinson became the first player at Williams to score more than 500 points (with a total of 548) in his first season, and the team advanced to the NCAA Division III finals, losing to the University of Wisconsin–Whitewater by 2 points after defeating Amherst by 29 in the semis. Robinson was named the national rookie of the year by D3hoops.com.

But Robinson transferred after only one season when Ephs head coach Mike Maker left for the head coach post at Division I Marist College. Maker assisted Robinson in connecting with University of Michigan head coach John Beilein, as Maker had served as an assistant coach under Beilein at West Virginia University. On Robinson's ability, Beilein said, "Knowing that a kid is averaging 19 points as a freshman and leads his team to the national championship game, you don't have to be that crazy to think this kid can play for us."[64] Robinson was offered a full grant-in-aid to play at Michigan, and as such, he was "believed to be the first NCAA DIII player to go from DIII to DI and receive a full scholarship," according to a Williams athletics website. Robinson played three years at Michigan after sitting out a year per NCAA transfer rules. In his senior year, Robinson was named Big Ten Conference Sixth Man of the Year, earned Academic All-Big Ten honors, and helped the Wolverines advance to the Division I title game. In total, Robinson played in 115 consecutive games at Michigan and scored 1,072 points.[65]

Robinson was not selected in the 2018 NBA Draft. He signed as a free agent with the Heat and spent most of the 2018–19 season in the NBA G League, the league's developmental league, playing for the Sioux Falls Skyforce in South Dakota, but he did appear in fifteen games for the Heat. At the end of the NBA's 2019–20 season, the six-foot-seven, 215-pound Robinson averaged 30 minutes and 13.3 points per game, shooting 44.8 percent on three-pointers as the Heat advanced to the NBA Finals. Of Robinson's emergence, one NBA writer commented, "It was unprecedented for a DIII player to jump up to high-major college basketball and excel. To see that same player now become a vital part of an NBA contender is even more mind-blowing.... Defenses can't let Robinson have an inch of space, otherwise they are likely going to surrender three points."[66] Robinson's own view was measured. "It has been a journey, and I am certainly humbled to be in the position that I am in," Robinson said. "I appreciate everything coming my way, and I just want to keep it rolling and continue to impact winning."[67]

While one can easily argue that Robinson would have never made it to the NBA without going to Michigan, it is also arguable that Robinson would have never had a shot at Michigan without exceling at a program like Williams's, even after only one season there. And at the completion of the COVID-addled 2019–20 NBA season, there were as many former NESCAC players in the NBA as there were former Ivy Leaguers (Miye

Chapter 7. No Longer So Pure and Simple

After one season at Williams, Duncan Robinson transferred to Michigan, then became the first NESCAC alumnus to play in the NBA. Courtesy Williams College Athletics Communications.

Oni [Yale] with the Utah Jazz). While it is true that there are likely to be few if any future Duncan Robinsons, the path to a professional career is one that all NESCAC athletes know is not merely a pipe dream. While Jak Knelman was the first in the AP era to attempt to codify the contractual nature of NESCAC athletics as a pathway for a possible professional career, those who could benefit from the AP era's realities might include former All-NESCAC First Team men's basketball player Austin Hutcherson, who left Wesleyan in 2019 after his sophomore year to transfer to the University of Illinois. After sitting out one season as per NCAA transfer rules, he will have two years of eligibility with the Big Ten program.

CHAPTER 8

Recruiting

The Realities of Athletics Resource Acquisition

> Recruiting is, and will continue to be, a difficult problem. Obviously every coach, just like every professor, wants first-class material, but those who are genuinely first class both in the classroom and on the athletic field are a rare commodity, particularly in the entrance pool of the small college.
> —Roger Howell, Jr., Bowdoin College president (1968)[1]

> Athletic conferences collectively exemplify the recruiting behavior of their membership.
> —John F. Rooney, *The Recruiting Game*[2]

Early Recruiting Dynamics

The NCAA's definition of the term "recruiting" is "any solicitation of a prospective student-athlete or a prospective student-athlete's relatives (or guardian[s]) by an institutional staff member or by a representative of the institution's athletic interests for the purposes of securing the prospective student-athlete's enrollment and ultimate participation in the institution's intercollegiate athletics program."[3]

In a very real sense, recruiting is about resource acquisition for athletics programs. Student-athletes are one of the bedrock resources necessary for the maintenance of winning programs, and recruiting is the process through which programs obtain this vital resource. In fact, former NCAA president Myles Brand verified this concept in a speech before the National Press Club in Washington, D.C., when he told his audience, "The ability to compete successfully is tied to recruiting incoming student-athletes."[4]

Success in recruiting has a direct correlation to how much a team can win, how long a coach can keep his or her job, and how much a coach can earn as a result of his or her success. Many of the rules related to recruiting are in place to limit the extent to which programs and schools might go to procure a prized prospect. And for all the importance placed on recruiting, the most significant challenge for the idealized image of NESCAC is to portray an admissions process where academic primacy is paramount over athletic proclivity. While many view the process as the purview of an immensely powerful cabal whose doings are shrouded in a cloak of mystery, the actual workings of the NESCAC athletics recruiting process, thanks in large part to the actions of presidents and administrators, is, with some exceptions, relatively straightforward. These methods have evolved over time with a well-attuned sense of maintaining ideal perceptions on the part of both internal and external stakeholders.

As outlined in Chapters 2 and 4, conflicts among the Pentagonals were mostly concerned with recruiting issues and the actions of certain coaches to attract prospects who would help them win games, but during the period of the Pentagonal Agreement, actual recruiting processes were usually restrained. While certain hockey coaches (Charlie Holt at Colby, Dave Snyder at Wesleyan, and Sid Watson at Bowdoin) organized on-campus scrimmages among prospects—a form of tryout never specifically permitted under the Pentagonal or NESCAC agreements—the initiative to pursue prospects was usually left to the discretion of individual coaches. "I think most of the hockey coaches had tryouts one way or another," said hockey historian Steve Hardy.

The reflections of student-athletes from the late 1960s and 1970s highlight the oft-informal and laissez-faire nature of the process. Writer Sandy Stott, who played soccer at Amherst after attending Phillips Academy Andover, had a "short list of four schools, which covered the anticipated range of difficulty—Amherst (where my father attended), Dartmouth, Trinity, and Lawrence University. My college counselor and I had acknowledged that I could and would play soccer for whatever school I attended and that the application would reflect that. My test scores and athletics were positives—my spotty academic record, not so much, though I had applied myself enough to get an eighty average in my senior fall, which put me in the middle of my class." Stott highlighted the importance of athletics in his college plans.

Stott's senior season was a good one, he recounted, with a notable game against the Dartmouth freshman team, where he scored twice and got ejected late in the game for arguing with the referee. "The Dartmouth coach found me following the game and inquired about my possible interest in Dartmouth, and I said, 'Yes, I'm interested.' He said someone would be in touch, and shortly after that game, they asked for a written expression of interest and outlined how I would fit in there. I put Dartmouth atop my list of possibles and went back to being a mildly disaffected high school senior."

Stott then visited Dartmouth and Amherst, and at each school he met with someone from the soccer program. "I understood from the admissions dean at each school that I had a good shot at being admitted," he recalled, but when it came to actually applying, which meant filling out the forms, "I went with the easiest form first. That was Amherst's, which asked for no essay, and so was a simple thirty-minute task. Dartmouth's, I recall, wanted not one but two essays." Stott sent in the Amherst application, and a little more than a week later, "as I procrastinated about writing my Dartmouth essays, I got a letter saying I was in at Amherst. Thank you, legacy and athletics and test scores. I shelved the other apps. I was going to Amherst."

Another former Amherst soccer player, Chris Dorrance, a Phillips Exeter alumnus (where he was a central defender and a captain his senior year) recounted that he had contacts who alerted coaches to his interest in Amherst, Middlebury, and Williams. "Most of it was parent-to-friend," he said, "and my own visits, which never included writing or visiting with a coach. In fact, I never thought of myself as a stellar athlete despite being captain of the Exeter team."

Dorrance added that his father had gone to Williams, "and I assumed I would go there," but Middlebury coach Joe Morrone recruited him and had one of his players drive him over from Exeter for a weekend that included frat parties. "Amherst was a trickier proposition," Dorrance allowed, as "I wasn't thinking about it since it was the archrival of my father's alma mater." But the Exeter faculty had a strong Amherst contingent, including soccer coach Don Dunbar (a former Amherst All-American) and Dorrance's history teacher Charles "Chuck" Trout, "in whose class I had more than my usual success."

"In those days, the admissions directors came to Exeter and gave us individual interviews," said Dorrance. "I was basically told I would be admitted to Williams," but late that fall, Dunbar offered a few students a Sunday visit to Amherst, where Dorrance had many close friends. "Afterward, I was told Amherst would take me early," he said. "When I reported that to my father, he—who had no influence as a donor—called someone [at Williams] and they relayed that I could apply early to Williams and be admitted." Rather than accept that offer, Dorrance decided to wait until April to decide. "Had you asked me in March, I would have told you I was going to Williams. Then I woke up one morning in early April and decided that I would go to Amherst. I wasn't conscious of the deliberations internally but accepted my instinct to go there. As you can imagine, my dad was disappointed, but it was my call."

Chapter 8. Recruiting 189

Scott Dunbar (Amherst Class of '77) also came from Exeter, where his dad was a teacher and the soccer coach. "My senior year I visited Bowdoin, having played them in a game there earlier that fall, and talked with their coach, Charlie Butt, who was a friend of my dad," he recalled. "He was the only coach with whom I spoke. We played the Amherst freshmen at home. I don't think I met [Peter] Gooding before I applied. My interview at Amherst was in the summer and he was undoubtedly elsewhere."

Dunbar was a multisport prospect (hockey and soccer) and visited Wesleyan during a holiday break in his senior year, where he participated in a hockey practice with those on campus, but he never ended up applying there. Dunbar recalled that his father and his friend Jack Heath "did most of the 'screening.' They knew most of the coaches and the admissions officers." As for his teammates and recruiting, "I don't remember a lot of talk [about the college process] among players," he recalled. At his first frosh soccer team meeting, Coach Jim McNitt announced that they had six high school All-Americans. "I didn't even know such a thing existed," said Dunbar, noting that the players were from New Trier (Illinois), University School (Ohio), and high schools in Connecticut and Maine.

The impact of the prep school pipeline was evident, as the NESCACs were very content to conclude that academic and athletic success at Andover or Exeter would correlate quite nicely into successful performance in their communities. Coach involvement in the process was limited (at least from Amherst and Williams), although there was a bit of gamesmanship between Amherst and Williams in the case of Dorrance's candidacy. Dorrance, who became a private school educator, provided summarized the process: "There was an alumni and school faculty network in those days who promoted local kids for their alma maters. It wasn't coaches going to all kinds of tournaments or promising a sixteen-year-old a place. I was not a stellar student, but I had the support of teachers and alumni for whatever reason. I don't think it was because I was a superstar; I wasn't." Dorrance also brought up a point often raised by alums of the era pertaining to the advent of coeducation: "We were also fortunate that most schools [we were considering] were single-sex. Would we have been accepted if they weren't?"

A sampling of football players at Colby from this era, collected by Colby football alumnus and former Bowdoin assistant football coach Donald Joseph, reveals variations of the Amherst examples. David Lane (Class of 1974), from Thornton Academy (a public-private high school in Saco, Maine), was an all-state defensive back his junior year and an all-state quarterback as a senior. He was heavily recruited by many schools, receiving multiple mailings, and visited Bates, Bowdoin, Colby, Wesleyan, and several large public universities, including the University of Rhode Island.

Lane was not a product of the traditional NESCAC elite prep school feeder system and navigated the recruiting process mostly on his own. He had two guidance counselors at his high school, "an older gentleman and a younger woman. The younger woman told me, 'Don't apply to Colby. You will never make it.' The older guy said, 'Just keep your nose clean and do the work and you'll be all right.' My SATs were not that good—I didn't test well on those—but my grades were okay."

Unlike the experiences of the Amherst prep school cohort, Lane indicated significant coach involvement in recruiting. "By far [Colby head football coach] Dick ['Max'] McGee was the most attentive and the most personal, and he reached out to me early," recalled Lane. McGee even sought out Lane when he was competing at the state track meet held at Colby during the spring of Lane's junior year to chat about his events during the meet. "For a high school kid that meant a lot to me," said Lane, "because it made me feel important and that I could play at Colby." Lane was also impressed with McGee's sales pitch when the coach told him, "We have not had a lot of success at Colby, but we will be getting better athletes and will be a lot more competitive." "I believed him," said Lane. "I found Max genuine and honest and very personable."

His senior year in high school, Lane visited Colby, driving the family car up Intestate 95 to Waterville. "I arrived late on a Friday and spent the weekend. It was a real eye-opener. Lambda Chi Alpha had a huge party and it was wall-to-wall people with everyone drinking. I didn't drink, but I was definitely excited to be there. At one point one of the defensive tackles grabbed a kid from upstairs who was fighting and dragged him down the stairs and threw him out the door."

A high school football star in Maine, David Lane chose to attend Colby in large part due to the recruiting efforts of head coach Dick McGee. Courtesy Donald Joseph.

Lane's family was blue-collar. "Both my parents

worked. We didn't have a lot of money. But Max said that financial aid will help with college costs." Lane also sensed that Harold Alfond, a Colby alumnus and generous benefactor to all Colby athletics (whose family foundation continues to support many projects at the college, including a $101 million donation in 2020), may have helped in some way. As a result, Lane applied early decision and was accepted. He would go on to be a four-year star at receiver, kick returner, and place kicker, and he still holds the school record for longest kickoff return for a touchdown (101 yards versus St. Lawrence in 1969, Lane's first collegiate game). McGee's promise to Lane about improvement proved true, as Lane's senior year the Mules went 7–1, to date one of the best seasons in program history.

Significant Recruiting Formalization Takes Shape

Conflicts and concerns over recruiting challenged presidential control from the earliest days of the Pentagonal Agreement. Presidential actions leading to increased conference formalization in the late 1990s, combined with the impact of the publication of the Bowen books, led to greater degrees of stakeholder scrutiny around recruiting and admissions issues. In his study of Wesleyan's admissions processes, author Jacques Steinberg referred to admissions at elite, selective schools as "often intuitive and idiosyncratic,"[5] impacted by the predilections and biases of the admissions staff itself (for example, one student earned his way off the school's wait list by embarking on a campaign of sending a postcard each day to admissions officers inscribed with a reason he should be admitted). Wesleyan's admissions processes were also complicated by what Steinberg identified as "competing institutional priorities," which included support for athletic programs, alumni cultivation, preserving relations with feeder schools, academics, support for the performing arts, and racial and geographic diversity. To illustrate these conflicts in terms of support for athletics, Wesleyan admissions director Barbara-Jan Wilson stated, "Academics are always going to drive the decision [to admit a student], but it's hard to put a football team on the field without a quarterback."[6]

NESCAC presidents and ADs were acutely aware of conflicts between schools in the articulation of admissions practices that were "intuitive and idiosyncratic" across the conference. The existence of admissions priorities concerning athletics, and the perception by some stakeholders that certain student-athletes were academically less qualified than their non-athlete classmates, led to an increased effort among presidents to manage conflicts through the sharing of student-athlete academic information.

Initially, specific information shared included standardized test scores, deciles in high school class, and first-year college grade point averages for football, men's ice hockey, women's lacrosse, and women's soccer student-athletes. One president characterized this sharing as a way not only to assure outside stakeholders that member schools were staying true to the conference values, but also to try "to reassure each other, and I think ourselves, that what we're doing is in line with the founders and framers back in the early seventies."

But levels of coordination around recruiting and the awarding of financial aid had been going on periodically among the Pentagonals. At a meeting of presidents in June 1967, "the following issues were strongly reaffirmed":

1. That the proportion of football players on scholarship should be the same as the proportion of all students on scholarship.
2. That the average academic performance of football players receiving scholarships should be the same as the average for all scholarship recipients. (This information and effort disappeared some time ago.)
3. That the academic performance of football players should average the same as students generally.
4. That exchanging and comparing such information would help each of us realize these ideals for ourselves, give us a common front against alumni and other pressures and help us keep fairly and justly in line with one another.
5. The Four Colleges should get open and publicized Board and Faculty support for the above ideas listed in No. 3. The College Presidents should instruct their Admissions officers to abide by these ideas and make policy and practice clear to coaches and alumni.[7]

These actions, however, were never in absolute concord, and at the end of the twentieth century, presidents found their schools competing for many of the same prospective students and that schools would ultimately act in their own best interests in the admissions process. The nature of this competition and institutional self-interest was described by another president, who said, "We're out to cut each other's throats in competition for students. That may be a little overstated, but we're competitors. And so there's this constant balance of altruism and self-interest. It's not all altruism. We're not all there because we're altruists."

The fallout from this battle between self-interest and altruism in NESCAC was the extremely high levels of overall success by Amherst, Middlebury, and Williams in multiple sports and by Trinity in squash and other sports, and it would also come to pass at Tufts in the 2010s (e.g., three national championships in men's lacrosse, four straight Final Fours for women's basketball, three national championships in softball). One former Trinity coach described this self-interest dynamic in the information-sharing process. "It really came down to your dean of admission and your president, when they sit in that meeting and say to the rest of the conference, 'This is what we're going to do. Go screw.' It's how strong your dean of admissions is going to be with the colleagues who are going to call him out on it." There was no penalty for policy violations, said the coach. "It's frowned upon, but you're not getting kicked out for it. Trinity was and still is giving money to international students." "My first few years at Trinity," the coach continued, "we had a dean who had been there for a long time. He was great. He was like a duck. Water rolled off his back like it was no big deal. He was willing to take some heat—not all the time—but he would say, 'Hey, we're Trinity, we're not Amherst. We've gotta do this to keep the lights on.'" Trinity's financial concerns were real, as tuition and room and board accounted for two-thirds of the college's operating budget, and Trinity was running an annual deficit of $8 million.[8]

This changed, said the coach, when the admissions dean became "a guy who was not as interested in athletics as a priority, so he wasn't willing to sit there and take the heat." The new dean, Angel Pérez, who came from the Claremont Colleges in California, was hired to bring in more tuition revenue to address Trinity's financial losses and to diversify the student body.[9] "I never sat in those meetings, I never had to take the fire," said the former Trinity coach, "but it was clear that schools that had strong leadership and were okay with what they were doing may have gotten barked at a little bit, but so what? 'This is our institutional priority,' they'd say, 'and we have to take these kids.' Conn has to do that, too. There's a few schools that have to do that, but maybe not to the level of Conn and Trinity."

In an extensive 2003 interview for the Williams College Oral History Project, former Williams head football coach Dick Farley observed, "There are some schools that are more focused on certain sports. They're giving more tips to their sports than we are to ours. So I can tell you that Middlebury in hockey and Middlebury in lacrosse are doing substantially more than Williams is." Farley then wondered, "Is it fair to evaluate the hockey and lacrosse at Williams in the same way as another sport where the tip system is a little bit more equitable? There are some teams here that have a lot easier time getting tips for the NCAA playoffs than other sports."[10] And as the former Trinity coach pointed out, NESCAC's lack of enforcement and infractions mechanisms meant that unless a school or a coach pulled a complete Ned Harkness, schools were unlikely to be called out for it.

With more schools looking to feed their own self-interests through on-field success, presidents viewed the balance between self-interest and altruism as out of kilter, and in trying to compete with the successful, some schools felt the need to respond by "recruiting more vigorously" or by disputing and questioning admissions actions. In turn, some presidents broke from the collectivism of conference operations and moved on their own to decrease the number of admissions slots dedicated to incoming prospective student-athletes. In 2001, Bowdoin president Barry Mills was the first to announce such a move, saying that his school would aim to reduce to seventy-nine from ninety-nine the number of matriculated student-athletes (out of an incoming class of 450) coaches had rated as "desirable."[11] At Amherst, the number of athletic admissions was reduced to seventy-five from ninety-four for the entering classes in 2004 and 2005 and to sixty-six in 2006. Said Amherst admissions dean Tom Parker: "When you start to say 94 of [our entering class] are there because of athletics, that's too many."[12] Williams president Morton Schapiro, while happy to be portrayed as the Ephs' number one fan in the popular sports media, nonetheless acted to cut Williams's slots from as many as ninety to sixty-six.[13] Wesleyan president Douglas Bennet stated that NESCAC presidents had a mission, which was "to go back to the high ground in admissions and compete with each other with teams composed as our student bodies are composed." "Our standard is that an individual's athletic excellence should be given weight in the selection process, but no more weight than other non-academic factors," he concluded.[14]

Bennet said the decrease at Wesleyan would be 10 to 20 percent (which meant sixty-six students would be admitted for whom athletics was a "primary credential"), but he admitted that he didn't know if other schools would adhere to these standards: "We don't know whether others will follow us; that's not why we're doing this."[15] Colby president William Adams also supported the change in policy, saying that there was enough evidence of discrepancies between the academic performance of recruited athletes and that of the rest of the student body: "I'm sorry if coaches disagree, but it's simply an empirical fact. It's not a matter of which there is very much doubt."[16] "By making clear our values and taking a certain type of position with respect to athletics and the escalating pressures of intercollegiate athletics," he offered, "I think NESCAC can do something important."[17]

One question was whether, as a result of these actions, such reductions would put schools at a competitive disadvantage. Bowdoin's Mills admitted that such a move would be "risky" for his school if other NESCAC schools declined to follow suit,[18] as the school's teams may then begin to lose to other conference schools as students turned away from Bowdoin to matriculate elsewhere in NESCAC. Case in point, Bates AD Suzanne Coffey indicated her school would not alter its admissions policies.[19]

The Impact of Admissions Process Formalization

The commissioner of a New England Division III conference observed that admissions processes at NESCAC schools and those of schools in other conferences "are like night and day. Most [non-NESCACs] have rolling admission and need athletics for enrollment purposes. They are somewhat desperate for applications and admit all who are in the neighborhood academically." One former NESCAC AD gave a number of frank assessments on the mechanics of recruiting, noting that since "the number of applicants that athletic departments can support has decreased," the conference has adopted a process developed at Williams in the 1990s, a system where coaches can submit candidates for evaluation to admissions. "Each school may vary slightly," but generally the coach is required to submit a prospect's transcript through junior year, along with standardized testing and the school's academic profile. He or she is then informed where the candidate stands relative to the overall applicant pool. "This was based on the academic reader rating from admissions," said the AD. "If you make the assumption (which I would), that recruited athletes deserve significant credit for extracurricular activities, admissions essentially has all of the information they would normally get to evaluate a candidate with the exception for recommendations. At [my school], my coaches understood that it was very important that they evaluate the character of those they were going to support. In practice, that is as important for the team as it is for the school."

Dick Farley verified the establishment of an approach to athletic recruiting at Williams that was systematic rather than intuitive and idiosyncratic, because "a lot of alumni" were "complaining about the quality of some of our athletic teams at Williams, that they weren't doing as well as they should." At the time, as Farley described, the Williams admissions office, "without a whole lot of input from the Athletic Department, chose the class without giving a whole lot of weight possibly to the athletic prowess of a certain kid."[20] What resulted was a system where "they divvied up what they called 'tips,' ... probably 72 or 74 'tips,' ... probably 15 in football, five for hockey." Farley defined the tips process as the "ability of the coach to have some input into the admissions process. ... [I]f you said he was a tip athlete that basically meant that the criteria academically was very strong but that individual probably would not have been admitted to Williams unless a coach had put him on a list and indicated strong interest."[21] Former Williams head men's hockey coach Bill McCormick corroborated this system, noting that the number of tips for hockey was six.[22] Farley said that in 2003 total athletics tips was eighty-one out of an admitted class of five hundred. "That's where the faculty gets upset," said Farley. "They feel those 81 kids should be kids [with SATs of] 1500 with straight A's."[23]

The process would continue, said Farley, when athletics would get "readings back," where admissions would give an academic reading of "admissible, not admissible, and whether we should continue to recruit." This was done through an admissions office liaison for every sport to foster communication. "If we have quarterbacks in the program and we don't need a quarterback, we probably don't put that kid on the list," said Farley, adding, "I think Williams was on top of the gang when this happened, because in subsequent conversations with some of my colleagues in NESCAC, they felt we had an unfair advantage by having what they called input into the process."[24] But there was also pressure on coaches to induce prospects to commit. "Yield is very important in the Admissions Office," said Farley, "so they would like us to make sure that we're very close to having a youngster say that he will come to Williams if he's admitted."[25]

Beyond the system in place at Williams, Farley, like many Pentagonal and NESCAC coaches and administrators throughout the decades, indicated that competitor schools weren't following the rules pertaining to the awarding of financial aid: "I think people are playing a game with financial aid." He said,

> There are certain schools that don't have the endowment Williams does, and they will do what I call preferential packaging.... We have found that certain schools seem to have different financial aid packages than Williams.... There are some schools in the conference who give kids that are pretty good athletes a few more dollars.... I've also heard from enough kids over the years indicating to me that X, Y, or Z school have been a little bit better in terms of financial aid.[26]

Farley went on to describe one such situation.

> There was a very good football player going to a very strong opponent of ours and in talking with the parents over the phone I subsequently found out that the financial aid award to that youngster was about $7,500 more and I subsequently found out, by doing a little work ... [that] this youngster's sister was going to a prep school where he had just finished, and Williams ... does not take into account that your sister might be in a prep school. So we were $7,500 off in a financial aid practice. He subsequently went to this other school, which is over the hill from Williams. He is a very good athlete and we lost him in part because the other institution was willing to give him $7,500 a year. ... [W]e didn't think that Williams should underwrite prep school experiences.[27]

Questions about the aid processes across NESCAC persisted from outside the conference. One non-NESCAC Division III men's basketball coach in the region noted that he could never match the aid packages of NESCAC schools. As Division III signatories, NESCACs couldn't offer athletically related aid, but many offers weren't significantly different. "From what I know and what I've seen," said the coach, "the NESCACs will prioritize kids financially. They'll find a way to put them in some sort of leadership scholarship or some sort of scholarship-based package that other kids are getting normally through academics and extracurricular stuff, but not necessarily athletics. They're finding a way to put some of their priority athletic kids in those spots and get them an extra $15,000. That's where the biggest gap is for me. There was a year we went up against Conn College for three kids, we lost them all, and our packages were off by $15,000 each. Hard to blame a kid for that."

One former NESCAC AD disputed this, however, claiming, "Athletics has zero impact on [financial aid] packaging. I suspect those outside of NESCAC don't believe that, but it's true. I know we didn't at [my school] and I never saw any evidence that it was happening at other schools." This former AD did allow that financial aid packages differed from school to school, but "other than encouraging families to speak directly with admissions if they had questions about their package, we didn't get involved." The AD also rejected the notion that NESCAC schools gave merit money for academic achievement. "That has become very common at schools across the country," said the AD, "but to the best of my knowledge not at NESCACs."

As to how the "Williams process" was applied across NESCAC, one former NESCAC AD explained that once coaches had the evaluations from admissions, the coaches decided whom they wanted to support; that the school limited the number of athletic prospects who could be admitted played a role in their decision. "The number came from a formula primarily based on how many sports a school sponsored," said the AD. "The formula was a little wacky, but in the end, it has proven to be pretty fair. In the end, the goal is that the athletic population mirror the general population in terms of academics." The AD also emphasized that the early evaluations "were not and are not an offer of admission. Recruits were expected to thoughtfully complete applications." "If something surfaced between the read and the offer from admissions," said the AD, "it could change the decision. For example, if grades went down in the fall of senior year, the applicant got in trouble, or a recommendation revealed a character flaw. It didn't happen often, but it did happen."

The current NESCAC admissions playbook is based on the Ivy League Academic Index (AI) model, crafted by William Bowen while president at Princeton, melded with the practices implemented at Williams under Tom Parker. The result is a system where student-athlete ratings are based on a tabulation of class rank, test scores, and GPA, and these ratings determine where exceptions can be made for athletics prospects; common meetings among NESCAC presidents and admissions personnel review these exceptions. According to former Middlebury president Ron Liebowitz, NESCAC presidents "were warned specifically by Bill Bowen, who created the Ivy banding system, to stay away from their banding system because it's easily cheated on, and it is."

But in 2002, the NESCACs created a banding system nonetheless, based on each school's applicant pool, which allowed for more flexibility than the Ivies' AI but limited weaker academic applicants.[28] Bowdoin AD Tim Ryan noted that because NESCAC institutions recognized the "important role that athletics play on our campuses," the banding system was put in place "to help ensure that institutions are able to develop athletic programs that are competitive within the conference," or rather, to keep schools from stacking their admissions decks. To that point, former Bowdoin head men's ice hockey coach Terry Meagher conceded that when NESCAC became a playing conference in the early to mid-2000s, recruiting became "as intense as I've seen it since I started here 30 years ago. It's always been a part of what we do—for this program we've always recruited very extensively and we've had a thorough model—but across the board it's as competitive as I've ever seen it."[29] The following is a general outline of how the bands are delineated:

> **A Band:** SAT Scores 700+ average, all above 670; SAT II 710; GPA: 92+ GPA, with grades almost All A's; Class Rank: Top 5%; Courses taken: 4+ APs, Honors classes.
> **B Band:** SAT scores 650+ average, all above 620; SAT II 640; GPA: 88+ GPA, Mix of A's and B's; Class Rank: Top 15%; Courses taken: A few AP Courses, Honors classes.
> **C Band:** SAT scores 630+ average, all above 590; SAT II 600; GPA: 85+ GPA, Mix of A's, B's, occasional C's; Class Rank: Top 20%; Courses taken: Honors classes.[30]

Tom Parker saw the creation of the banding system as tacit acknowledgment of the preferential treatment of athletes. "When it was on the table exactly what we do, it wasn't as bad as some faculty thought," said Parker. "Once the admissions deans fully understood the differentiation between the bands based on academic achievement, we had to line up the other schools, which turned out to be a pretty big task."[31] In addition, the practical implementation of the system had, according to Ron Liebowitz, "bizarre and disastrous" implications for school presidents, who were once again—by choice—thrust into athletics management actions few of them anticipated or savored. "At our fall meeting in Boston," recounted Liebowitz, "I had to get a driver and a car so I could read through all the admissions crap in the three-and-a-half-hour drive. I got information on every single player on every single NESCAC team at every school—without names—their GPAs and their test scores, and we got to see whether they were an A band [highest qualified academically], B band [middle], or C band [lowest]. It drove me insane because each school had a different band." "It did even out to some extent," said Liebowitz, "but the system was tied to the average academic performance of the full applicant pool, so the Williams bands were much different from the Conn College bands or the Trinity bands. I felt it was a little unfair to Williams and Amherst, but that's how it went. It didn't hurt Williams competitively, though." A Williams coach's observations bore this out. "I'd be out on the road and see a good player with 1250 scores, and I'd report back to the head coach, and he'd say, 'That's not good enough.'" "A score of 1250 for us is really low," said the coach. A prospect with a 4.0 GPA and a 1350 was good, "but what's that 4.0? What classes did he take? Were they APs? And what school did he go to?" "I'm a product of the public school system," said the coach, "so I have no problem with public schools, but we had a kid read my first year who had a 4.0 and a 31 ACT, and I'm thinking it's not a bad fit, but the kid was inadmissible for us because the school and the classes he took weren't strong enough."

A former Trinity coach verified that "from institution to institution there are variables," and Trinity dean of admission Angel Pérez confirmed these differences when he observed that when he arrived, Trinity had been "taking some students who probably should not have been admitted, but we were taking them because they could pay. So the academic quality of our student body was dropping," and it led to a scenario where there were a "growing number of affluent students who couldn't keep up in class and weren't interested in trying."[32] As a result, said the former Trinity coach, "a C band kid was a C band kid at all the schools, but a B band kid at Williams might be an A band kid at Trinity." "Those B band ones were such a tight one to figure out and navigate. A band was pretty obvious, and there was a wider spread of what the A band was at the schools. B band was the narrowest sliver, then the C band was wide, too. It was easier to find A bands and C bands than it was to find B bands." The coach described one further element of the system, where a prospect's testing might be right on the A band border, but if the prospect got a grade of C in a freshman-year class, "that might drop a kid down to a C band." "At Trinity I'd get maybe one C band a year," said the coach, "but that wasn't guaranteed. Other places had a C band kid guaranteed. As much as you wanted unlimited C bands because it makes recruiting easier, you're also offering a NESCAC education to a kid who might not otherwise get it. So once you went below the threshold and said, 'We're going to dip a little bit,' that all depended on your director of admission."

Other Stakeholder Perspectives on Recruiting

So how has NESCAC athletic recruiting continued to evolve? Former Bowdoin women's soccer coach John Cullen said that he left coaching in 2007 because he "didn't want to be in a position to pressure a sophomore in high school to make a commitment to college." The question, therefore, became: What was the recruiting process like for coaches, prospects, and families as a result of this heightened level of formalization? To examine this, the author interviewed several coaches and parents of current students. These perspectives on NESCAC recruiting over two periods of time were particularly enlightening, reflecting the shift from the recruiting process of the late 1960s and even the mid–1980s to the highly formalized contemporary process contributing to the cultivation of the hothouse generation, but the lesson learned was the same: adults were exploiting kids for their own ends, so kids learned to do the same.

A Former Student-Athlete Experience

One former NESCAC athlete attended a large public high school in central New York, where his football program "was intense. It was a full-year program, and we had a varsity team, a JV team, and two freshman teams. So it was a bit of a factory. We had a depth chart hung up in the hallway, and you moved up or down the depth chart depending on how you did in practice that day."

"So there was part of me that was proud to be part of that program," he said, "but by the time I was a senior, I was thinking, 'I like playing football, and I think football can help me go to college,' but at the same time I was not sure I wanted the same level of intensity of football in college." This realization helped formulate his college search, which, when combined with his academic performance, was augmented by the fact that his coach "was on the cutting edge of using scouting services, where we would fill out every form with GPA and SATs. He would send that out for us, and the combination of that along with where I played football led some coaches to reach out."

"Nobody in my family had gone to college," he said, "so I was just figuring it out on my own as a high school teenager. I didn't have parents looking over my shoulder or asking me about my grades or if I did my homework. I think they saw that I was on a good path. They were always supportive and complimented me on my grades, but they were all about 'schoolwork is important' and 'you need to do well in the classroom.' At the time, the only schools I knew that were academically strong were Ivy League schools, so I was basically just looking at those schools. And even those schools at the time had spring football and were intense in their own way."

Because of that view of the academic landscape, at first he was "pretty far down the path with Princeton. They had shown a lot of interest in me and I'd gone to visit a couple times." However, other schools were in the mix as well. "We used to have college coaches visit us at my high school," he said, "and you'd get pulled out of class to come talk with them. So I remember once my coach came and pulled me out of class, and he said, 'There's a coach here, and you're the kind of guy who might be interested in talking with him.' And I said okay. So I go in and the coach is showing slides (on a slide projector) of their facilities. And I asked, 'What's the name of your school again?' And he said, 'Phillips Exeter.' And I said, 'I gotta stop you. Are you a college?' And he said, 'No, but we have something called a postgraduate year.' And I said, 'I don't mean to be disrespectful at all, but I just spent four years trying to get out of high school, and it sounds like you're trying to talk me into another year of high school. So I don't want to waste your time, but I'm not going to high school anymore.'"

He then recalled his first NESCAC contact. "One night I got this phone call, and it was one of the coaches from Amherst, and he said, 'We'd like to talk to you about coming to Amherst.' And embarrassingly I said at the time—because there's an Amherst, New York, near Buffalo—'Thanks, I really appreciate your interest, but I'm really doing all I can to get out of here, and I don't want to be in central New York anymore.' And he said, 'What are you talking about?' And I said, 'Aren't you near Buffalo?' and he said, 'I'm at Amherst College.' And I said, 'Sorry, I don't know Amherst College.' To his credit, he said, 'Here's what you should do: go to your guidance counselor and look up Amherst College, and do a little research, and I'll call you next week, and we'll start over.' And I said, 'Okay, that sounds good.'"

"So I went to the guidance counselor and researched it," the player said, "and I was like, 'Oh my gosh, from what it says in [the Peterson's college guide], this might be just what I'm looking for.' It was a smaller school—half the size of my high school—because one of the things I didn't like about my high school was that it was just gigantic and sort of anonymous. And it's really good academically, and it was a little different than some of these other schools I had talked about." When the Amherst coach called back, the player said, "Yeah, I'm interested. What do we do? Where do we go from here?" The player also broadened his search to include Hamilton, as it was "close to home and that's where some smart kids from my school went."

After the follow-up conversation with the Amherst coach, the player was invited to come to campus in February, "but I had no way of getting there because both my parents worked. They said, 'We have a kid coming to visit from Buffalo, so if you want to get in the car with that guy, you could do that. We'll ask him to pick you up on the way.' I said okay."

The player said,

> When I talked to that kid, he was stopping at Williams the day before going to Amherst. "Are you okay coming to Williams with me?" he asked. I said sure. So I looked up Williams in the guidance office book and saw they had a rivalry with Amherst, so I thought, "Okay, I'll look at them, too."
>
> So I sent Williams head coach Bob Odell a videotape—like you did back then—and told him I'd be coming through with this other kid and that I'd be happy to talk with him. So when we got to Williams, Odell sits down with me and says, "I looked at your tape and saw you. We have one running back who's already committed to us, and if you tell me right now that Williams is your first choice, I'll support your application and we can get you in, but you've gotta tell me right now." And I said, "Today?" And he said, "Yeah." I hadn't even known what Williams was, I was going there to find out if I should apply, and Odell said, "You can apply, and we can get you in if you say yes today."

However, this was in February, past the admissions application deadline. "My response to Odell was 'I think that's completely unfair for you to ask me to do that right now, and if that's the way you're approaching this, I don't want to play for you.'" Odell responded, "Hey, we all have choices we make, and I wish you the best of luck." "The next year I remember we went to play Williams," the player recalled, "and I remember the vibe on the field was 'If we beat them, that coach was getting fired.'" Amherst won 10–7, the sixth straight win for Amherst in the series, and Odell, a former Pennsylvania football player who came in second in the Heisman Trophy vote in 1943 and was elected to the College Football Hall of Fame in 1992, was fired, replaced by his assistant Dick Farley. "And I remember at the time thinking, 'Well, I guess things all worked out for the best for me.'"

So the pair then headed to Amherst, and the player enjoyed the fact that "it was half the size of my high school, so everybody knew I was there visiting because it's not that big a community. And the guys I was staying with, everywhere we went, everybody knew them, and everyone was really friendly to me." "At my high school," said the player, "the starters on the football team—the guys with me in the huddle—I never saw those guys during the academic day. None of those guys were in any of my classes. They were not on the college prep track. I always took the AP and honors courses, and those guys didn't. Maybe one or two of them would. And when I went to Amherst, it was like everybody there you could have a conversation with them, they all seemed reasonably bright and good guys. And I was like, 'Oh my gosh, this is what I've been looking for.'"

But the player was still looking at Princeton, along with Cornell. "Cornell called me and said, 'Okay, this is it, we're coming down to it, I need to know: Is Cornell where you want to go?' ... And being a kid," said the player, "I was honest with everybody. I told Princeton I wanted to go there, and I told everyone else, 'I'm interested in Princeton.'" But what happened with Princeton could be characterized as "every parent's worst nightmare."

Princeton had assigned the player an alumnus who lived in the area to take him out to lunch and to dinner, and the Princeton assistant coach who was recruiting the player was the speaker at his high school football banquet. He recalled,

> There was another kid in my class—a baseball player—who was also being recruited, and three or four days before decisions went out, this local alum called me and congratulated me on getting in.... And then the Princeton coach called and asked me and the other kid whether we wanted to room together. And then the letter came in the mail telling me I didn't get in. And then I asked them afterward, "What happened, you called me two days ago asking me where I wanted to live?" And they told me that the admissions office screwed them over. Me and the other kid—the baseball player—neither one of us got in.
>
> Was the coach telling me the truth? Who knows? But I was in a class of a thousand, and I was like number forty in class rank, so maybe the Princeton admissions office said we can't deny kids one through ten to take the fortieth. Probably more likely the coach just said, "I'm not going to push that hard for this kid." The only thing I couldn't understand is why the coach would continue to call me two days before the decisions came out if he wasn't really backing me, because usually contacts would tail off at that point.

"So it turned out I didn't get into any Ivy League schools," recalled the player, "but I did get into Amherst and Hamilton. I don't think I applied to Williams after the coach told me he wasn't going to support me if I did commit right then." Hamilton responded with a financial aid package that was better than Amherst's, meeting his full stated need. "So my parents said, 'You're going to he place with the better financial aid package. That's the way it goes. Get to like it.'"

"So both schools called me and said, 'Congratulations—what do you think?'" Hamilton called first, and the player said, "Hey, it looks like I'm coming to Hamilton." And when Amherst called, "I said, 'Sorry, I can't come because I can't afford it.' And the coach said, 'What are you going to do?' I said, 'I'm going to go to Hamilton because they gave me a better aid award.' And he said, 'Well, what was their award?' I forget the exact amount, but I had to pay about $10,000 to go to Amherst and $5,000 to go to Hamilton. And so the Amherst coach said, 'Okay, interesting. I'll call you back tomorrow.' So he called me back, and now Amherst was only asking me to pay $3,000. So he came in a little under Hamilton. So I thought, 'I like Amherst better, great. That works. I'll go to Amherst.'"

"So then I called Hamilton back," said the player, and he told them, "Hey, just a heads-up, I want to let you know that Amherst came in with a little bit more money, I like the school better, I'm going to go to Amherst." And the assistant coach told him, "Well, this isn't going to go over well with the head coach, and you're going to have to tell him this news. He's right here, let me put him on." And the head coach Steve Frank got on "and just started yelling at me. My dad was sitting there, and at that point I was thinking, 'I can't take this whole process anymore,' because the way in which Princeton treated me, and it really drove home that these people don't care, so part of me was like, 'So why should I care, so I'll just go where I want to go, since they're just doing whatever they want to do.' So when the Hamilton coach started yelling at me, I just gave the phone to my dad and I said, 'Dad, could you just talk to this guy?' And I just left the room."

In assessing the impact of Amherst's recruiting process, the player said, "I don't have any stats to back this up, but maybe [recruiting kids like me] was why Amherst was pretty good in football, because they didn't just swim in the same waters as everyone else. They found me from upstate New York, and one of my roommates was from Detroit, Michigan. We were not the normal, New England-y kid you found at Amherst. I would not have been at Amherst if it weren't for football, and I felt like the teams we played, their recruitment circles were a little tighter."

A Current Prospect Experience

The Amherst football player's experience from the late 1980s indicated an increase in formalization of the athletic recruiting processes within NESCAC. This trend only accelerated in the ensuing AP Era, as evidenced by the experience of a current NESCAC student-athlete, as told by a parent, a former recruited NESCAC student-athlete.

"For me," said the parent, "the biggest change from my experience was that my child's whole recruiting process happened coach-to-kid on my kid's phone. It was all texting from all different coaches. Half the time my spouse and I didn't know who my kid was texting with or what texts my kid got, because it wasn't coming in on the home phone or coming through us. My kid spoke directly with a coach on the phone only a handful of times."

Chapter 8. Recruiting

"If you're on the phone with a coach," said the parent, "it's a two-way conversation, and you can ask questions, and you can detect tone and enthusiasm. When you are just texting back and forth, a coach never has to say anything but can imply enthusiasm with a couple of exclamation points or an emoji. And a coach can have a volume of texts going through but not say anything in a way you can't get away with in a two-way conversation. Because more than anything, you have adults who do this for a living and their livelihood depends on it, and you have kids who are naive and haven't been through this before, and it's easy to read into a text what you want to from it."

The parent observed that the schools "my kid really wanted to go to never fully committed but never walked away either. And no matter how my kid asked or phrased the question, there's a way over text that a coach could play it. There was a time when my kid was thinking, 'Okay, Trinity likes me, Trinity wants me, so maybe I'll just go to Trinity,' and then the Amherst coach sent him a text with three exclamation points, and my kid thinks, 'I guess I'm still in it with Amherst, because the coach didn't have to put exclamation points on there, and the fact that he did must mean the coach still wants me.'" Said the parent: "What am I going to say? What I've learned from that process is if you ever finding your kid saying, 'I think they want me,' then that school doesn't want you, because either you know it, and the school is very clear about it, or it's just degrees of positivity that keep you hanging on. There was no one my kid dealt with who said, 'We're not interested.' Nobody said, 'You're not good enough.'"

In terms of contacts, the current recruit mostly responded to coaches' inquiries. "My kid did a little bit of outreach with sending highlights out to people, and I think he had a pretty tight window of schools he was interested in. [An Ivy League school] figured that my kid was a borderline player for them, and I think the coach kinda thought, 'For where we want to go as a program, I'm not sure I want to use one of my spots on this kid, but this kid could definitely be on the team.'" The parent noted that the coach went as far as to say, "You have a jersey, you have a number, you have a roster spot, you just have to get in, and based on what I'm seeing, that's likely." "So when schools like Kenyon, Trinity, and a couple others said, 'You're our guy,'" the parent recalled, "my kid was honest and said, 'I can't commit to you right now until I see this [Ivy League] thing through and see what happens.'"

But the prospect was deferred admission at the Ivy school after applying early decision. "We got the vibe that they were saying, 'We'll defer you now, but we'll take you regular decision,'" said the parent. "And the whole time the coach said, 'I'm shocked you didn't get in [early], but I've seen this happen before.' Right up until the end the coach—who was a straight shooter—said, 'I'm not going to use one of my slots on you, but I think you can play. If you can get in, you could definitely be a second- or third-team All-Ivy kind of player.'"

So the prospect was now part of the regular admissions pool, and, observed the parent, "if you're not an early app to one of the other schools, now you're one of the 'walk-ons.'" Because of this, the prospect's high school coach contacted other colleges to let them know of the prospect's availability. "It turned out a poor Division I program in a supercompetitive league had a new coach looking to create a powerhouse there, and they needed bodies," said the parent. "So they called and said, 'We think we can get you in, we need bodies, and you can play here.' And it was one of the schools my kid was going to apply to anyway."

During a subsequent campus visit, the coaches "were very honest and said they wanted to get better and to play at a high level. And my kid kind of liked that, but for him the school was kind of an unknown, and I think he always thought NESCAC was where he wanted to go," said the parent. "The school was just not in his universe, and a little bit of him wondered, 'Do I want to be at a program that was starting from the ground up?' So I think my kid felt the need for an extra year, committed to the school, and then went to do a PG year."

But this meant that during the upcoming summer, the prospect had to play in competitive recruiting events. "His club team played in a couple of tournaments, and we decided maybe he could do one of these prospect days," said the parent. "The school that my kid loved from the beginning was [a NESCAC school], because they're the best team in the conference, it's not too far from home, and it's a great school. So I said, 'Okay, you can go to their prospect day.'" While the coaches at the school had never contacted the prospect, another NESCAC had very early in the process, but the prospect didn't consider the school because its program wasn't competitive. The prospect had text conversations with coaches at several other NESCACs, with variations of interest on the part of both parties.

At the desired school's prospect day, the parent said, "It was hot. I left and came back for the last half hour, and it was the best I've ever seen my kid play. And I thought, 'Wow, that's awesome.' Granted, my kid's a year older as an end-of-September birth, so my kid's on the older side of the cohort. So that was the very end of June." Recruiting bylaws prohibited coaches from talking to prospects prior to July 1, but on July 1 or 2, the school's head coach texted the prospect. "My kid was shocked. It was July 4 weekend, and the coach asked how quickly could we get to campus. My kid says, 'I can get there July 5.' So I'm thinking, 'Here we go again. My poor kid's gonna get jerked around,' but at least at this point my kid's jaded enough to think, 'Here's another one of these frickin' coaches.' But my kid thought, 'I've never toured the campus, so I'll go.'" The school had received the prospect's transcript and test scores.

"So after the visit my kid called me and said, 'The coach toured us around campus, and the coach just offered me a spot,'" said the parent. "My kid was in disbelief, because … this is how it was supposed to happen: go to a prospect day, they like me, July 1 comes, they call me, I go to campus, and they offer me a spot. So my kid responded to the coach, 'Done. Yes. I'm going.'"

This prospect's experience was typical, according to the parent of another current NESCAC athlete. "The entire recruiting class at my kid's school was accepted early decision, and that's pretty much how they all do it. And the other amazing thing to me is that I don't think I've ever heard of a kid in [my kid's sport] who's had multiple NESCAC offers from the top tier of schools. So the coaches must talk. I've never heard a kid in August say, 'I've got to decide where I want to apply early, because I've got offers from Williams and Amherst.' The kids who go to Amherst never had an option to go anywhere else because they never got an offer from anyone else."

Two former NESCAC coaches provided their perspectives on this parent's observation. "Every coach complains about every other coach," said one coach. "I can remember the July 1 offer date thing, but there was always the Middlebury 'wink' and the Amherst 'wink,' so that caused problems in our recruiting world because these kids were committing before July 1. At Trinity it didn't bother me because we weren't getting that kid anyway, so let them commit early so I know who I can go after. They're not choosing Trinity over Amherst or Middlebury. It's not going to happen." As to why Trinity couldn't lure such prospects, another former Trinity coach identified "watercooler talk" as the culprit. "Our first couple years we were pretty good, and we would talk to kids about, say Bowdoin. We beat Bowdoin three years in a row, and the kid would say, 'I'm still going to go there because Bowdoin's just a better school.' In reality, Bowdoin *is* a very good school, but the difference was the parents standing around the watercooler at work and saying, 'Oh, my kid's going to Bowdoin,' or 'My kid's going to Amherst.' That was very much the reality and we beat our heads against that wall for three years." The coach recalled a conversation with an alumnus at an annual golf event. "We'd just started recruiting against Centennial Conference schools, and we're getting better kids," said the coach, but the alumnus responded, "You should win that battle against Amherst every time." "And I told the alum, 'Listen, it just doesn't happen.' And the alumnus responds, 'Trinity is a much better school than Amherst.'" "And I'm thinking to myself, 'Okay, it's great to have an alum feel that way, but I can show you five years of data that disproves that.'"

Parental Involvement and the Power of Athletics in the Admissions Process

Eugene Tobin noted that the Bowen books identified how current and prospective students' parents were "aware of the 'signaling effects' of such admission practices." A current NESCAC athlete's parent offered this perspective on how parents are impacted by the athletics recruiting process. "I see why parents are nuts about this process," said the parent. "Parents have zero control over it, and the athletic thing provides probably the only piece of certainty in the process." For example, a coach told his child, "We've reviewed your transcript, we've run your test scores by our admissions office, you're an A band kid for us, you apply early, you'll get in. Don't get any C's, don't get arrested, and you'll get in." "And here's the funny thing," said the parent, "my kid applied the year before, because when he wasn't getting recruited since he was waiting for [an Ivy school, he figured], 'I'll apply to all these schools, and if I get in, I'll just walk on.' And my kid applied to the NESCAC school and got denied. And a few months later, with the same grades—the grades in the middle of senior year aren't that different from the grades at the end of the year—and the same test scores, the school took him when my kid was on the coach's list."

"So as a parent, with these high and unrealistic expectations around the college process," said the parent, "you start to figure out that the regular decisions are a total crapshoot. There's a random factor to the NESCAC/Ivy college process that is scary for them, and athletics provides one of the only sure ways in. So it just makes parents think, 'Shoot, my kid should have spent more time at athletics practice.'"

"People like to think that the physical lottery winner piece exists at LSU and Alabama, but not at Colby," said the parent.

NESCAC schools have always sought to cultivate the notion that athletics is the "sweatiest of the liberal arts," just another component to an idealized educational experience, while simultaneously using athletics in the pursuit of institutional goals and objectives. In many recruiting scenarios, as Tufts's John Casey aptly summarized, the battle of idealism versus realism has also meant NESCAC schools have pursued policies of athletics self-interest to survive or thrive in its environment. As Bowdoin's Roger Howell presciently commented on the cusp of NESCAC formation, "Recruiting is, and will continue to be, a difficult problem." This message was not lost on Ian Ward, a recent Bowdoin student writing for the newspaper there, who also noticed the athletic divide referred to in the Bowen books on his campus. "Most non-athletes are either completely ambivalent about or vaguely dismissive of the whole concept of varsity sports in the first place," Ward wrote, "and I see no reason to believe this will ever change.

Despite this fact, Bowdoin remains an institution that is thoroughly shaped by its desire to attract and retain varsity athletes. No aspect of the College, from admissions to academic affairs to alumni relations, remains untouched by this commitment."[33]

While one is tempted to summarize these comments simply by saying "the more things change, the more they stay the same," intercollegiate athletics historian Ronald Smith offered this view: "As Thomas Fuller said more than three centuries ago: 'Old actions return again, furbished over with some new and different circumstances.'"[34] In the case of NESCAC recruiting, it is more accurate to say that as NESCAC athletics has become the big-time of the small-time, the more athletics recruiting has impacted, for better or worse, member schools' admissions processes, refurbishing old actions in new and different circumstances.

Epilogue
The Cultivation of a New Image Era

At the conclusion of his 1994 *Sports Illustrated* piece, Douglas Looney offered this summary encomium on the conference's approach to intercollegiate athletics management: "Is the NESCAC way the wave of the future? Probably not. Robert Kirkpatrick, a retired vice president of Wesleyan, shakes his head. 'They just can't seem to control the mentality of winning that comes from alumni.... Could it be,' suggests Kirkpatrick, 'that Division I-A is the voice in the wilderness and we are reality?'"[1]

These comments, captured after the start of the inchoate AP era, evoke several questions. Was it NESCAC's BP era to which Looney referred, even as he noted significant changes in the wind, specifically the epochal decision to allow team participation in NCAA championships? And what did Kirkpatrick mean by reality? Was he saying that the manner in which NESCAC operates its athletics programs is somehow more real, or was he saying that NESCAC athletics is the real—meaning more appropriate—manner in which programs should be operated?

Based on the review of events and actions in this book, could either Looney or Kirkpatrick have envisioned what NESCAC athletics and the manner in which they were managed would become once the implications and practices of the AP era were fully realized? Some have argued that what NESCAC became—the small-time's version of the big-time—is what the rest of intercollegiate athletics already was. Ronald Smith, whose perspectives have been cited throughout the book, wrote in his study of what is now the Division III Wisconsin Intercollegiate Athletic Conference that "the competitive spirit which has been manifested in many aspects of American life [is] no more clearly shown than on the athletic fields of American colleges,"[2] even within the context of what we would now define as a small-time intercollegiate athletics conference. Smith continued: "An institution is the product of the rime and the nature of the individuals concerned with its development.... If intercollegiate athletics continue to play an important role in the social life of institutions ... they are likely to create problems for which solutions will be sought."[3]

NESCAC athletics were never as pure and simple as Looney portrayed them, and, to Smith's point on seeking solutions for athletics problems, Tufts's John Casey surmised that "the ongoing struggle within NESCAC has always been between idealism versus realism." NESCAC and its members have always sought to craft an ideal image of intercollegiate athletics participation as the "sweatiest of the liberal arts," managed and controlled entirely by school presidents, and to tame the reactions that occurred when these notions were challenged—either by internal forces (such as recruiting conflicts with member schools), external forces (such as the demands and expectations wrought by youth sport specialization), or a combination of both (such as the decision to opt for team participation in NCAA postseason play for image and equity reasons). The creation of Division III proved to be a slow-burning catalyst to NESCAC's image transformation, as the BP-era image—based on connections to the foundational era of intercollegiate athletics, the forced or elected departure from the nascent big-time, and the widely recognized elite, academically selective, small liberal arts college sheen—morphed into the AP era's demonstrated competitive success against the D-III cohort outside the conference.

While this book functions mainly as a review of the impacts of the individual and collective actions of NESCAC schools—from the establishment of intercollegiate athletics programs in the 1800s, to the retreat from the big-time in the early 1900s, to the formulation of the Pentagonal Agreement in the mid-1950s, to the decision to expand it to create NESCAC in 1971, to the allowance of full postseason participation in 1993—it is also meant to serve as an instrument to examine how the member schools and conference might continue to act in response to changes in the ever-immiscible intercollegiate athletics environment. What does the continuing evolution of NESCAC's institutional expectations of its athletics programs mean to the cultivation of its ideal image? While issues will evolve and others as yet unknown will emerge, NESCAC's immediate future "idealism versus realism" struggles include the effort to promote institutional diversity through athletic recruiting, reactions to calls for student-athlete compensation, and managing the inevitable decline of football. The actions NESCAC managers take in response to these may well lead to the establishment of another era in NESCAC's evolution, but as to what form that era takes is to be determined.

Using Athletics Recruiting to Achieve Institutional Diversity Goals

On NESCAC campuses, somewhere on the walls or in the trophy cases of athletics facilities, one can often find a display of team pictures spanning across the decades. Viewing these as one walks along, one will notice the following: squads and coaches seated on bleachers or standing on the steps of a venerable athletics building; the emergence of sports other than football and baseball in the mid–1950s and of female faces somewhere in the 1970s; the disappearance of sports like gymnastics and wrestling in the 1990s. But regardless of year, sport, or gender, the racial composition of the overwhelming majority of the players and coaches reflect little change from of those who attended these hilltop colleges generations ago.

While NESCAC is not alone in this regard, its teams are less diverse than most. NCAA data reports that while 61 percent of all student athletes in 2017–18 were white, at elite colleges, according to a 2018 article in the *Atlantic*, "that number is even higher: 65 percent in the Ivy League, not including international students, and 79 percent in the Division III New England Small College Athletic Conference." "Put another way," wrote Saahil Desai, "college sports at elite schools are a quiet sort of affirmative action for affluent white kids, and play a big role in keeping these institutions so stubbornly white and affluent…. It's a particular quirk of the American higher-education system that ultimately has major ramifications for who gets in—and who doesn't—to selective colleges."[4] A detailed piece reviewing the admissions process at Trinity in the *New York Times Magazine* in 2019 confirmed this state of affairs for all of NESCAC. According to author Paul Tough, because the popular sports in the league are less likely to be played at low-income schools, "most of the recruited athletes are actually more likely to be white and wealthy."[5]

Desai continued: "The processes that funnel rich white athletes to selective colleges aren't going anywhere in the short term, but in a possible future in which colleges can no longer consider race in admissions, there could be renewed public pressure for these schools to clear the musty cobwebs of the admissions process that undermine their self-proclaimed ethos as America's engines of social mobility."

"It's curious to me that these elite universities are holding on to these policies, because I think they expose the contradictions of what universities do in admissions," commented Harvard professor Natasha Warikoo. "They're blatantly privileging already privileged groups."[6]

Soon after the *Atlantic* piece, in another national press moment contributing to the NESCAC ideal image, veteran *New York Times* sportswriter Bill Pennington outlined Amherst's efforts to use its intercollegiate athletics program to further an institutional goal in his article "Elite College Spares No Cost to Diversify Team Rosters" (published online as "The Real Cost of Diversifying College Rosters"). Pennington was well versed in the mechanics of small liberal arts college athletics recruiting, having penned a multipart series in 2005–2006, including one on the creation of the NESCAC athletics admissions banding system (see Chapter 8). Pennington had also written about the rise and fall of Division IV in 2007. Of the genesis of the Amherst article, Pennington stated that the school "did not reach out to me. I've been covering youth sports issues at the *Times* for about twenty years, so I've been well aware of how the modern economics of the youth sports model shuts out tens of millions of less affluent families. I've written on the edges of the phenomenon but I've also been searching for ways to explore how certain institutions or coaches are trying to combat the situation and the outcomes it causes."[7]

Through basic research and a Google Alert, Pennington became aware that NESCAC had recently relaxed recruiting budget restrictions in hopes of making roster diversity more likely. "I kept an eye on that and pursued it in a few places. In late 2017, I came across Amherst president Biddy Martin's missive to the Amherst community, which included a passage about how they were going to make diversifying team rosters an overarching priority. I got in touch with Amherst a few months later." What Pennington found was that while Amherst had been lauded for its campus-wide diversity (with a student body 45 percent students of color, 43 percent non-Hispanic white, and 9 percent international students), the demographic profile of its athletic teams did not match that of the overall student population (23 percent of student-athletes were people of color). A major challenge in diversifying athletics rosters is the fact that, as reported in a 2014 study published by Utah State University, U.S. families spend an average of $2,292 on youth sports, while many spend as much as 10.5 percent of their gross income annually—sometimes more than $20,000—on expenditure for personal trainers, travel, and private teams.[8] This spending trend is likely to continue as high schools offer fewer athletics participation opportunities in an effort to stem the spread of COVID-19 and parents look to private clubs and organizations to fill the gap.

In response to this data, Amherst's Martin, a scholar of German studies with a master's from Middlebury and a former chancellor at the University of Wisconsin and provost at Cornell, took another step in NESCAC's presidential control model, advancing a new notion of the NESCAC ideal when she wrote an online message to the Amherst community announcing that the institution would embark on a "mission to prove that its sports rosters could be reshaped to include underrepresented ethnic and socioeconomic groups."[9] Since that point, Amherst coaches, "with a slightly augmented recruiting budget," noted Pennington, "have since looked beyond the most popular, suburban-based youth sports tournaments and frequently taken the less-traveled path to far-flung locales, small urban gyms and foreign countries ... and expanded an existing program that flies prospective minority applicants to the Amherst campus to substantially include recruited athletes." Of the initiative, Martin stated, "In terms of resources, we're talking thousands of dollars, or tens of thousands of dollars, but we're not talking millions of dollars," adding, "What matters more than money to travel is the effort, the awareness and the commitment to diversity."[10]

Pennington's assessment of "a slightly augmented recruiting budget" invites review, given that many NESCAC schools dedicate a deceptively low percentage of their athletics expenditures to recruiting. One former Trinity coach offered this comparison: "The restrictions that NESCAC has on athletic recruiting spending are insane. I think it was limited to around $30,000 per department. Trinity had twenty-nine varsity programs. Do the math. My recruiting budget at my current school is ten times what I had at Trinity." As a result, coaches spend money out of their own pockets to cover overages. So if Amherst augmented its recruiting budgets "slightly," the chances are it was an increase in the range of tens of thousands of dollars.

Whatever the precise amount, it was certainly the smallest of drops in the bucket for Amherst, with an endowment of well over $2 billion (behind only Williams among NESCACs), but Pennington reported, "Coaches at other small colleges suggested in off-the-record conversations that diversity recruiting is demonstrably easier for Amherst because of its deep financial resources.... About 55 percent of its students receive need-based scholarships and the average aid package is nearly $56,000.... [In addition,] 21 percent of the students at Amherst came from households whose annual income ranks in the top 1 percent nationwide." This meant that a fifth of Amherst's students demonstrated no financial aid need whatsoever, so Amherst could spread the money to other students more liberally. This was also a significant competitive advantage for Amherst and some within NESCAC, as they were affluent enough to meet the full need of any prospect, which was in effect the equivalent of a Division I full athletic grant-in-aid. Under that scenario, Amherst would do well to target full-need prospects of any race, because it was in a position to be able to meet full need. A former Tufts coach highlighted the importance of the financial aid advantage: "Because in NESCAC there are variations to those who are need-blind [meaning that the school will make admissions decisions without considering an applicant's ability to pay, as well as meet any demonstrated need for which a candidate qualifies, either by grant or loan] and those who say they are need-blind but really aren't. The schools I believed were need-blind were Amherst, Williams, Middlebury, and Bowdoin. For a long time, all the other schools were claiming they were need-blind, but that was clearly not the case at many."

The issues with selectivity and aid also underscore that the NESCACs in general, and in this case Amherst in particular, occupy a rarified space in the competitive market to attract and retain students. As increasing numbers of schools—especially small private colleges—face dire enrollment projections that may well force them to

Amherst president Biddy Martin announced that the institution would embark on a "mission to prove that its sports rosters could be reshaped to include underrepresented ethnic and socioeconomic groups." Courtesy Amherst College Office of Media Communications.

cease operation, the NESCACs are so secure financially that they can continue to pick and choose its students, while others scrap and scrounge for each body they can get.

There is also the sense that targeting populations of color may be a way for Amherst to circumvent the particulars of the admissions banding system and admit a greater number of prospects, since, according to a former Trinity coach, such prospects "did not count in our banding. You had the A, B, C bands, and you had SOC—student of color—who would not count in the band." This coach noted that Trinity's admissions office "quite often wanted me to get students of color who had been to prep school because they'd have a better chance to succeed. Yeah, well, guess what? The rest of friggin' NESCAC wants that, too!" "And that's about resources spent," said the coach. "It's a times-ten effort for me to get a student of color, and my resources are not what Amherst's are, and Amherst is saying we're going to overspend to get these kids, whether that's in recruiting or financial aid or whatever it might be. And that's their priority. I'm not saying it's a bad priority, but that's the reality." To this point, Trinity dean of admission Angel Pérez commented that part of his job since arriving at the school has been educating the community "about the fact that you can't have it all—selectivity and better academic quality and more socioeconomic diversity and more revenue—at the same time. You've got to pick which goals you're going to pursue."[11]

On the resources Amherst can spend to yield prospects, Pennington wrote that at an annual diversity weekend each fall, the college pays airfare and expenses to visit the campus for more than one hundred prospective students, nearly 15 percent of whom are athletic prospects identified by Amherst coaches. In many cases those athletes eventually choose to matriculate, and as a result, while just 11 percent of Amherst athletic recruits were students of color in 2002, its most recent athletics recruiting class was 32 percent athletes of color.[12]

The question for the rest of NESCAC is whether Amherst's approach and resources spent will cause others in the conference, unwilling or unable to make the same resources commitments, to call for Amherst to scale back the enhanced financial support of its diversity efforts. While Trinity made the same play for international squash prospects at the turn of the century, is Amherst going to do the same to spend what it takes to attract and yield its targeted prospects? And if the rest of NESCAC doesn't like it, what are they prepared to do about it? It was one thing for presidents and ADs to take a hard line (a charge led by Williams) to expel Union in 1977, but is it conceivable to have NESCAC without Amherst? And if Amherst left, Wesleyan and Williams would likely soon follow to give rise to a renewed twenty-first-century Little Three.

But Amherst's embracing of athletics diversity has not been seamless. In 2020, three members of the men's lacrosse team—Rodrigo Castro, Dylan Finazzo, and Matt Solberg—chanted the N-word outside of a Black teammate's campus residence while his Black roommate and another Black student were in the room. According to student witnesses, the three lacrosse players "screamed and chanted '[N-word! N-word! N-word! Goodnight, n-word!]'" The student, "understandably upset … came out to the common room and a physical altercation ensued." In the immediate aftermath of the release of the names of the three perpetrators, students began sharing photos of them taken from the Amherst Athletics Flickr with the caption "Hold. Them. Accountable."[13]

As a result, the college announced probation for the men's lacrosse team until June 30, 2021, and a ban from NCAA postseason play, among additional disciplinary measures. It also concluded that "a change in leadership for the lacrosse team will be necessary," leading to the termination of ten-year head coach Jon Thompson. In an email to the college community, Martin announced plans to address the "culture and actions" of the men's lacrosse team, saying that the incident was "only the most recent in a list of deeply troubling cases involving some team members over the years," including that members of the team were found to have drawn a swastika on an unconscious person at a party, and other team members made transphobic comments at a meeting of the school's College Republicans chapter. "Probation is a significant part of our overall plan to address the culture of the lacrosse team, but not the only part," wrote Amherst AD Don Faulstick. "In the end, we felt that probation struck a good balance between sending a strong message to the team and recognizing that not all members of the team have been involved in the most egregious behaviors."[14] The team collectively submitted an open letter to the campus student newspaper, asking "that each member of our team be evaluated based on their engagement with and commitment to the Amherst community at large.... We think individually; we act individually; and we deserve to be judged individually."[15]

In another statement, Martin admitted:

> We have not yet done all we can to create an environment that is truly inclusive and free from the harm of racism. We have had success in increasing educational opportunity and enrolling a student body that more nearly reflects the richness of difference in the world. We have focused on the work of inclusion, but we are not where we need to be. We know that it is not enough to bring talented students from many backgrounds together if the educational environment is not supportive of the success and flourishing of them all. Recent incidents and accounts of student and alumni experiences give abundant evidence of that fact. As you would expect, I am hearing from a large number of students and alumni, with a wide range of perspectives on how we should move forward. I am doing my best to listen and reflect, knowing how important it is that we can move forward as a community.[16]

And Amherst will not be alone in these community culture challenges. *The Game of Life* coauthor James Shulman predicted as much when he noted that with athletics recruiting, "you don't want the kids all from one region of the country or from the same socioeconomic class because then the campus tensions get worse." The issue with Amherst was that the nonathlete population was more diverse than the athletics teams, which is often the reverse case at many schools, especially Division I, where students of color are more largely represented on athletics teams, most notably football and men's basketball. And other NESCAC schools may soon see the same reactions as they pursue prospects of color, as one former NESCAC student-athlete, now a high school football coach, highlighted using the recruiting of a recent player, who is Latino, as an example: "He's a nice kid, but he's never made it through a full football season healthy, but he does seem to have some possible potential. And he has pretty good grades, an okay tester. So he's got the golden ticket, he can go anywhere. He was offered by every school in NESCAC."

A Coming Existential Crisis? Reacting to Calls for Student-Athlete Compensation

Many have argued that the core challenge to the legitimacy of the NCAA's efforts to govern intercollegiate athletics is its approach to and definition of "amateurism." Indeed, part of its elemental "Basic Purpose," printed on the first page of each of its divisional manuals, is to "retain a clear line of demarcation between intercollegiate athletics and professional sports."[17] As noted in the opening paragraphs of this book, the basis of American intercollegiate athletics was the Victorian idea of gentlemanly fair play, an ethos that was "the watchword of the gentleman amateur," an amateur being anyone who did not play for pay.[18] Initially, this notion was employed to bar working-class participants, first in England and later in the United States. But while the notion of the modern "gentleman [or -woman] amateur" student-athlete who plays merely for the love of the game persists, the fact remains that operational challenges to this notion are as old as intercollegiate athletics itself, especially when one recalls that in the very first intercollegiate event, the victorious rowers from Harvard received a prize and expenses for both crews were paid for by race promoters. Given this, it can be argued that those rowers from Harvard and Yale—the very first intercollegiate athletics participants in this country—were professional.

At the time of this writing, the NCAA faces the most pivotal moment in this centuries-long amateurism debate as it and member institutions craft responses to state laws, most notably in California, that allow student-athletes to receive compensation in the form of control over their names, images, or likenesses (NIL). While there have been calls for such measures for decades, the advent of actual state legislation is another thing entirely. Consider the comments on the issue by NCAA president Mark Emmert at the organization's 2020 annual conference: "Do I believe college sports is going to blow up? No, I don't.... The existential crisis to me is, can we respond in a way that makes sense for our students and supports the college sports model?"[19] This is while the NCAA has, as described by the *New York Times*, "lurched into a campaign—on Capitol Hill, before a think tank, at the Justice Department and in news media interviews—to stave off simmering public discontent and more drastic government interventions." University of Pennsylvania AD M. Grace Calhoun suggested that while the NCAA could ease obstacles for student-athletes to earn income, the moves should only go so far: "We're dealing with student-athletes, and when you look at the principles we've established, we won't cross that line from them being students to turning into employees."[20]

But many stakeholders respond simply, "Why not?" since many non-athlete students already work on college campuses in various capacities. "What about doing what's right for the kids on whose backs schools generate millions of dollars?" is a common refrain. While there are many significant legal issues to consider, most notably the fact that paying students to play would enact workers' compensation and taxable income issues, and severe financial implications for schools and athletics departments, one might wonder how this would impact Division III, where the demands of the small-time are believed to pale in comparison to those in the big-time.

For NESCAC, all the above factors are in play, but there is more at stake: How could NESCAC preserve its ideal image, based so squarely on the Oxbridge fair play ethos, if men's squash players at Trinity are playing for prize money, or EA Sports seeks to release a NESCAC men's basketball video game and compensate the players for the use of their likenesses? For NESCAC, the issue is as much about preserving its ideal image, and it's not an abstract construct. Could the funding given to students of color in the athletics recruiting process, as practiced by Amherst to promote institutional diversity, be seen as financial compensation for athletic ability? Currently, that might violate NCAA bylaws, but if there were no such bylaws, then there would be no such concern. It was made clear during the postseason expansion debate that some considered the team sport ban to be detrimental to the conference. If the NCAA were to allow student-athlete compensation for athletics participation, could NESCAC afford to say, "No, we won't allow it, because our student-athletes play only for the love of the game?" Forget whether this would cost NESCAC in the recruiting wars (it would)—how could the conference's ideal image survive if the conference opted to deny resources to needy students who could access them through outside endorsements or other forms of compensation? And if compensation were denied from needier students, would that mean that the demographic profiles of NESCAC teams no longer reflected racial, ethnic, and income diversity?

There is some precedent for this conundrum, albeit under the current NCAA structural and conceptual guidelines. In 2013, Williams men's golfer Dylan Dethier became involved in yet another Williams postseason imbroglio. Dethier had written a book, scheduled to come out just prior to the NCAA championship tournament, and when a Williams athletics department staff member called the NCAA for a rules compliance interpretation, Dethier learned he "had been kicked out of the NCAA." Dethier stated:

The process behind this quick-trigger decision was never fully explained, but by my best understanding a straw poll had been taken around the NCAA's compliance offices. Nobody [from the NCAA] had spoken to me (they never did) and [I] had no real idea what they were suspending me for, but no matter. What I was doing sounded like it was probably in violation. That was enough.... I was deemed to have used my athletic ability for commercial gain (only the NCAA's corporate partners are allowed to profit from said ability). In their defense, I was a college golfer, and the book involved golf. In my defense, well, everything else.[21]

The book, *18 in America*, was set to come out one week later, on May 13, and the NCAA championships were to begin the next day. Dethier described the book as the story of the year he spent between high school and college, living in his car, driving around the country, and playing at least one round of golf in every state in the contiguous United States. "The book is about people who play golf and where they play it—but it's much more about a teenager surviving in his Subaru, plus it preceded my time at Williams College and had nothing to do with my golf ability anyways. A 20-handicapper could have written the same story."[22]

Less than twenty-four hours before the start of the competition, Dethier heard from the NCAA. "I was being offered a plea deal of sorts," he recalled, where he would be temporarily reinstated for the duration of the tournament, after which he would "essentially admit guilt and complete 30 hours of community service in exchange for reinstatement for my senior year. I couldn't believe it. I didn't think I was guilty, I didn't think my guilt could be determined by an office who hadn't read or even seen the book in question, and I definitely didn't feel like I should be making any plea deals. Still, I readily agreed." He continued: "I'd never considered it could affect my eligibility.... I'd done nothing wrong, and more to the point, I was a DIII golfer. There was no way anybody would care."[23] While he thought the relative lack of attention paid to his sport would allow him to avoid scrutiny, Dethier's statement is very much in keeping with the generally held perception of the small-time Division III as inherently violation-free, so therefore by definition he couldn't be a rule breaker.

Regardless of one's response to the NCAA's enforcement apparatus and treatment of Dethier, it is important to bear in mind that NCAA compliance staffers only interpret bylaws and determine appropriate sanctions, while the actual rules are approved by member institutions. One could also argue that Dethier was given a break when allowed to compete, then to address the violation after the fact, although his recollections don't reflect this perspective. As for the coming changes in amateurism rules, Dethier commented, with some allowances toward the complicated nature of the issue, that student-athletes should retain the rights to their likenesses or at least receive a percentage of revenue generated by those likenesses. "At the Division III level, the old rules around likeness are unnecessarily restrictive," he wrote. "Nobody's going to become a millionaire selling Williams College hoops jerseys. From the NESCAC's perspective, I think they should allow student-athletes to profit from their likenesses—but perhaps not their likenesses as it relates specifically to being a member of their current team?"

Nonetheless, if and when the NCAA moves to allow future Dylan Dethiers the right to publish books and profit from their sale, or to endorse sporting equipment, or to appear in video games, all NCAA members, from Division I on down, will have to consider how to accommodate this new reality. While the allowance for postseason play gave way to NESCAC's AP era, the move either to allow or to restrict professionalism will have significant impact and potentially trigger an existential crisis in how NESCAC's next image era will be perceived.

Dr. David Ridpath, a professor of sport business at Ohio University and president of the Drake Group, a network of academics dedicated to intercollegiate athletics reform, states flatly that "NILs are going to happen. There's going to be a federal law, or there's going to be a hodgepodge of state laws or a uniform state law." "It reminds me when Title IX enforcement was starting," he recounted, "where there was all this gloom and doom and all these awful things were going to happen. And instead of fighting this and being reactive, it's time to be proactive and say, 'How are we going to make this work?'" The Drake Group has sought to advance this issue through congressional oversight of intercollegiate athletics in place of the NCAA.

NESCAC executive director Andrea Savage points to a growing trend of government in higher education and the implications for NESCAC on the compensation issue. "I think we're seeing a lot more involvement, and it's certainly impacting what we are going to be doing and how things are going to play out in the coming years," said Savage. "The concepts are just coming together from the NCAA on what each division is going to do. It's not necessarily going to be the same. There are some overarching principles that are going to guide those conversations, but how they play out in each division is going to be different, and it's certainly going to impact Division III, and it's going to impact it in different ways than Division I and in some similar ways as Division I athletes, depending on what sport it is, and where you're located and a whole host of different things."

But Savage did not mince words about the impact of NILs. "It's certainly going to impact the way we operate and the ways in which student-athletes are able to use their name, image, and likeness, and now have some students making half a million dollars and somebody else on the team making nothing," she presaged. What those dollar figures will be for NESCAC athletes will become apparent soon enough.

Managing the End of Football

When NESCAC chose to permit team sports to participate in NCAA championships in 1993, football was conspicuously absent from the inclusion. Williams football co-captain Bobby Walker told Looney that excluding football was "very unfair to us, but I know they are concerned football will grow into what they fear most,"[24] that fear being, according to Paul Sweeney at Tufts, "that the marquee college sport of football could subvert the NESCAC ideal of the scholar-athlete with the lure of big gate receipts and pressure from alumni to field championship-contending teams ... [resulting in] lower admissions standards and an escalation of recruiting and program intensity."[25] While it is less clear how the NESCAC ideal would be threatened by the lure of gate receipts, since the NESCACs routinely forgo admission fees to sporting events, Sweeney's premise that football's status as the marquee sport in American intercollegiate athletics is accurate, and decision makers were indeed concerned about stakeholder pressures. The earliest conflicts among the Pentagonals arose from recruiting irregularities among football coaches, and various NESCAC athletics administrators have maintained, as noted by former Amherst AD Peter Gooding, that "football in many respects is the main problem in small colleges in terms of how it distorts admissions. ... [A] lot of the bullshit we spent our time on was usually something to do with football. Someone cheating or someone doing something so they could win two games."

As a result of the continued playoff ban and the decision to adopt round-robin scheduling as part of the never implemented one-school-per-sport postseason proposal in 1998, NESCAC football has existed in its own competitive bubble. All other Division III programs begin play prior to or around Labor Day, play several games with teams from other conferences, and seek to participate in the Division III national championship game in mid–December, while NESCAC football teams play nine games a season, with the first game on the third Saturday in September, the last on the second Saturday of November, and only against other NESCACs. Given these parameters, one could conclude that football is the last so-called pure BP-era NESCAC sport.

It is also debatable whether NESCAC football coaches really want to play in the postseason. In 2003, former Williams head coach Dick Farley intimated as much when he stated that football "is set up in an ideal situation where the last two games in the year are almost like playoff games.

The first round of the playoffs is Wesleyan and the final game is Amherst." "There's not a football team in America that I or anybody on this team has any interest in playing after Amherst," said Farley, added that it would be a waste "to go play Rowan or RPI or someone.... When I came [here, longtime Williams coach] Tony Plansky drilled into me, 'Little Three.' He thought Little Three was the ultimate."[26]

As Farley's statement came as the NESCACs were establishing national dominance in multiple sports, it is of interest whether current NESCAC coaches, seeing the successes many of their colleagues have attained, long for postseason opportunities. It also may be that when faced with the reality of matching up against longtime powers such as Mount Union University, the University of Mary Hardin–Baylor, and the University of Wisconsin–Whitewater (which have collectively won twenty of the last twenty-four titles), these coaches are well aware that the likelihood of a NESCAC team beating any of these schools is remote. Whatever coaches and players say publicly on the issue, they are doing so with the virtual certainty that they will never be permitted to test the extra-NESCAC waters.

While this restricted, in-house approach might have been intended to lessen competitive pressures for NESCAC football schools, the actual result has led to something else entirely, namely, a significant competitive delineation between the haves (Amherst, Trinity, and Williams), the have-somes (Middlebury, Tufts, and Wesleyan), and the have-nots (Bates, Bowdoin, Colby, and Hamilton). In describing the phenomenon, a former president of one of the have-nots paraphrased an African proverb: "When elephants fight, the grass gets trampled." In this case, when the Mammoths and Jumbos (and the Bantams, Cardinals, Ephs, and Panthers) fight, the Bobcats, Continentals, Mules, and Polar Bears get trampled.

The glare of the persistent underperformance of the football have-nots glows even harsher with the fact that the have-not football programs, unlike those in every other NESCAC sport, aren't free to eke out a few wins against nonconference teams. One former have-not AD indicated that the implications of this status are real. "We've got alumni who can't stand our lack of success," said the AD. "I understand we have to be successful to then raise the money, to then hire the coaches. And it's not okay to be winless in football. It's just not okay. So when we lose to [a rival], I get the call. So Monday mornings in the fall for a while have been hell. And the president feels that way, too, because we wink at each other sometimes in the fall and say, 'Did you have a pleasant Monday?' because [the president] gets those calls, too."

While Hamilton's struggles have been in place for nearly as long, the issues are most acutely felt by Colby, Bates, and Bowdoin, the former State

Series associates now part of the so-called CBB. Consider the following, as reported in 2014:

> Bowdoin and Colby haven't had winning seasons since 2005, but winning is still important to the players and coaches at those schools. "It matters to me," said Dave Caputi, in his 15th season as Bowdoin's coach. "It matters absolutely. It always matters. [Winning] is very important. I think we attract a good group of kids. There have been some years we have been closer to being good than others. We just have to make sure we're doing the best things we can as a football staff to make sure our kids are successful."[27]

Caputi, a former assistant at Williams, announced midway through the 2014 season that he would resign at the end of the season and moved on to an assistant post at Middlebury. His final record as Bowdoin head coach: 35–85.

More from that 2014 article:

> Jon Michaeles, the Colby coach, said there are different ways to gauge success. "Everybody has a different definition of success and what they want out of the program," he said. "With our kids we define success by their and our collective commitment to reaching their full potential. Bear in mind that finishing in the upper echelon of NESCAC is very important to us and winning a CBB championship is a tangible goal that we set every year. We don't spend a lot of time talking about wins and losses, we focus on the process but it is something we value, for sure."[28]

Michaeles resigned at the end of the 2017 season with a record of 14–35 and moved on to the assistant position at…. Bowdoin.

Looney wrote in his *Sports Illustrated* piece that "no one can ever remember a NESCAC coach being fired for not winning."[29] That observation is clearly a remnant of the NESCAC's BP era, which Peter Gooding reinforced when he said, "My last five years as an AD, I grew tired of meeting with parents and athletes who wanted a coach fired because the team didn't make the NCAAs." Alumni responses can be equally demanding and prescriptive, as a 2017 letter to the Bowdoin student newspaper from Bowdoin football alumnus Dan Spears (whose brother Tim teaches at Middlebury) illustrates, claiming that football success could be achieved if Bowdoin were to

- hire a dynamic harsd-charging head coach who played NESCAC football and has a track record of building football programs from scratch.
- give him the opportunity to build his own roster by recruiting players from outside of the competitive Northeast Corridor.
- show patience as he defines a new culture.

Fortunately, President Rose and Director of Athletics Tim Ryan have already chosen to exercise that option and although the record doesn't show it, Coach J.B. Wells is in the process of creating the foundation that will bring long-term success to the program. Changing a culture is akin to pushing a rock up hill, but Wells has shown many of us that he is a strong and capable leader.[30]

Spears added this coda to his analysis: "Finally, we should never quantify success solely through wins and losses. Bowdoin Football is far more about learning the value of hard work and discipline and building lifelong relationships."[31] While this may be true and was also highlighted by former head coaches Caputi and Michaeles, it is far more in line with the BP-era image of NESCAC; the realities of the AP era are quite different. To that point, the rock Wells was pushing rolled back over him when Rose and Ryan chose to fire him at the end of the 2018 season, and in 2019, his replacement, B.J. Hammer (with an aggressive-sounding, hard-charging name at least), also went winless. An additional challenge for Bowdoin's football fortunes: Hammer was named as a defendant in a federal sexual harassment lawsuit filed by a former player at Allegheny College, alleging that the school ignored reports of sexual misconduct and discrimination when Hammer was head coach there prior to coming to Bowdoin. The filing alleges that Samantha Simonetta, a female kicker for Allegheny, reported multiple instances of sexual assault and harassment by fellow players to Hammer's staff during the 2018 off-season.[32]

While past performances of the have-nots have been poor, the future of football at these schools looks equally grim. Youth football participation rates are down across the country and are decidedly lower in the regions and at the secondary schools from which NESCACs traditionally recruit prospects. Increasingly, private secondary schools are shuttering their football programs because of this decline, and those struggling to maintain programs are doing so with greatly reduced rosters. One can debate the reasons for this decline (fear of concussions being primary) and whether they are justified, but the numbers don't lie. Additionally, more Division III colleges in the region have added football to attract male students. This means more schools vying for fewer qualified prospects, which has also forced Ivy League programs to entice prospects formerly targeted by NESCAC schools. To this point, Bowdoin head coach Hammer had this assessment of his 2019 roster: "We're not very good. When you're not very fast and you're not very physical, that happens." He added, "There's a reason Bowdoin's won one game over a three or four year period. I've been coaching for 20 years and I can tell you when you're outmanned and when you're not outmanned, and that's been the case."[33]

The Football Endgame

The managerial realities of NESCAC football are this: For how much longer will the have-nots suffer through abject won-loss records? One former NESCAC AD said, "I think Colby will invest in football and give it five years and then decide to pull the plug if it doesn't get better." To that end, Colby replaced Michaeles with former University of Maine head coach Jack Cosgrove, the winningest football coach in school history, who was dismissed from that post after the 2015 season. On his hiring, Cosgrove told a former Colby football alumnus that he had met with Colby president David Greene and that "it was the first time in all of my years coaching that I sat down for dinner with a president to discuss needs." As for the adjustment to NESCAC recruiting, Cosgrove noted that unlike at Maine, "the challenge is can they get in, are their academic credentials good enough to get in here? You have to be able to see in the young man you're recruiting that he's going to compete in the classroom like he does as a football player, so that's an area I hope to establish some credibility with here." Cosgrove also stated the need to establish a Division I–level work ethic with his new team: "I frankly told them to change our results they had to change their ways." "I felt like that if I missed a lift [Coach Cosgrove] was going to find out some way," said Jake Schwern, a senior running back, "so I definitely wanted to stay on top of everything."[34]

So if all the coaching efforts fail to reverse the fortunes of the have-nots, what will their ADs and presidents do? Keep the coaching carousel circling and hope that Wesleyan alumnus Bill Belichick tires of the NFL and wants to reimagine himself in NESCAC? Any solution to the have-nots' plight will require a concerted and coordinated effort among conference administrators, as occurred in the early 2000s when football rosters were capped at seventy-five. Otherwise, alternatives actions might include the following.

The have-nots drop football: When programs have struggled mightily for decades, or even centuries, coaches, ADs, and presidents are quick to say that wins and losses are only secondary to the life lessons learned through athletic participation, but these types of bromides feel especially forced when the AP-era reality is that so many other programs at NESCAC schools annually compete for national championships. It would be interesting to see, in this time of declining football participation, how many of the children and grandchildren of these decision makers play football. That number may be all the data they need to inform their decision. Two small, private Midwestern liberal arts schools—Earlham College and Grinnell College—have served as the canary in the coal mine, with Earlham ending its program in 2018 and Grinnell suspending play in 2019 because of low roster numbers. Certainly it would be a difficult decision to drop a sport, but wrestling used to be a common sport on NESCAC campuses, and now only Wesleyan and Williams sponsor intercollegiate programs, while gymnastics programs are nonexistent. The move to drop football would most certainly need to be done in consort, as coordinated actions, a standard element of conference membership, to help defuse the inevitable blowback from certain—but by no means all—stakeholder groups. The financial realities forced on colleges large and small as part of the post–COVID-19 landscape—whatever they might be—will likely push many schools toward dropping costly athletic programs, and there is nothing more costly than football.

The have-nots secede: In 2019, Bates was 2–7 (with wins versus Bowdoin and Hamilton), Colby was 2–7 (with wins over Bates and Bowdoin), and Bowdoin was 0–9. All three lost to Trinity, by a combined score of 155–14. Hamilton was a comparatively competitive 4–5 (with wins versus Bowdoin and Colby; from 2015 to 2019, ten of its fifteen wins have come at the expense of the CBB) but still hasn't had a winning season since 1996. In lieu of dropping football, Bates, Bowdoin, Colby, and Hamilton could craft a joint statement announcing the creation of a separate football conference and make overtures to other programs—NESCAC and/or others—to join them, or they could join another existing grouping. Macalester College in St. Paul, Minnesota—which once lost fifty straight games—made a similar move in 2002, shifting football play from the Minnesota Intercollegiate Athletic Conference (MIAC) to the Midwest Conference, a grouping of schools in Illinois, Iowa, and Wisconsin, while remaining a member of the MIAC in all other sports. This move would not be a complete surprise, as former Williams president John Chandler noted that the prolonged lack of success led the Maine schools to consider pulling football out of the conference in the early 1980s.

The have-nots ban the haves: Consider the following: in May 2019, ninety-nine years after helping found the MIAC, the University of St. Thomas (UST) was notified by the other conference members that after extensive discussions UST would be "involuntarily removed from membership." After weeks of speculation, conference commissioner Dan McKane notified UST of the decision, saying that it was the only way to save the conference. "The MIAC would have collapsed in a year if this action didn't occur," McKane said. "There was no vote. The membership, the presidents, discussed this over the past several months and agreed this is the best way to keep the conference intact, with a two-year transition for St. Thomas," added McKane.[35] The effort to oust UST was conducted in secret, with officials of the MIAC and its other schools declining to comment. Said UST athletic director Phil Esten: "It's [a] sad day. We're disappointed with the outcome. We had hoped to find a way to stay in the MIAC. Ultimately, it was just absolutely inevitable that wasn't going to happen."[36]

UST was kicked out because its teams were too good. The four-sentence news release announcing the move said the MIAC Presidents'

Council cited athletic competitive parity as its primary concern for the move, but football appeared to be the catalyst. In 2016, under the leadership of head coach Glenn Caruso, the Tommies beat conference rivals Carleton, Hamline, and St. Olaf by a combined score of 244–0. In 2017, that gap was shaved to 190–0 but included a 97–0 victory over St. Olaf in the regular-season finale.[37] Soon thereafter, a number of MIAC schools began discussing the possibility of expulsion.

But UST's football hegemony wasn't the only issue. Tommies squads had racked up fifteen Division III national titles since 1973, more than any other conference school. In addition, the past decade's UST teams had been MIAC champion or cochampion fifty-seven times in the sports of baseball, men's and women's basketball, football, men's and women's hockey, softball, and volleyball. The next highest title winner? Gustavus Adolphus with fifteen.[38] So the MIAC had their Union hockey moment, but unlike the Union divorce debate on who did what when, there was no doubt: the MIAC kicked UST out. In response, in a quasi-Union-like move, UST petitioned the NCAA to be immediately allowed to join the Division I Summit League in all sports. After UST's expulsion, Macalester announced its return to the MIAC in football in 2021.

The relevant question to be gleaned from this is whether football will serve to break up NESCAC. Do the have-nots, along with the have-somes, have the power to expel the haves? Could the haves and the have-somes field a full football schedule if the have-nots jump ship? Is there anything ADs and presidents can do to boost the fortunes of the have-nots in the face of the uncontrollable and inevitable demographic shifts facing all football-playing colleges? Would the NESCAC release the have-nots from the strictures of the banding system for the have-nots to begin recruiting a wider range of prospects? And if so, how would this move be seen on campuses where football players are already perceived as academically inferior to other students?

Managing the Changes

The presidential response to the football question and the others outlined in this chapter will define the next era of NESCAC managerial relations. James Shulman—along with coauthor William Bowen, seen by some stakeholders as one of NESCAC's historical bogeymen—offered this observation on the power of sport and its role in relation to the conference: "The one feeling I've had about sports over the years is that we're going to need it," said Shulman, adding, "It helps with alumni and it brings people back to campus. And [to manage challenges], you're going to need

Epilogue: The Cultivation of a New Image Era 229

a sense of identity and community and all those good things that come from sports. How you do them and who you invest in is another question." "But we could do fine without recruiting," he stated. "I'm not saying realistically it would happen, but you could fill a soccer team pretty easily at Bowdoin these days. You could play a lot of sports without recruiting student-athletes to play them."

As this book has highlighted, questions like those raised by Shulman with recruiting have always existed in NESCAC, and to address them have come managerial decisions and indecisions seeking to cultivate the conference's ideal athletic image. As a result, the future NESCACs were big-time for a short time, were small-time for a long time, and are now the small-time's big-time. However strong the conference's image might be, NESCAC athletics will never be immune to the stakeholder expectations that are an inextricable part of the American intercollegiate athletics equation. To that end, NESCAC executive director Andrea Savage noted that to create some sort of accord, "it demands listening, understanding, building relationships, and building consensus with your members—presidents, ADs, coaches, admissions, student-athletes—all your stakeholders." Savage describes her work with member institutions "as seeing around the corner to see what's coming and knowing what your institutions need before they know they need it. It's not to say that I have the ability to do that all the time, but the ability to be able to see those things and to serve the membership in that way would help anyone in this position, as is the case with any leadership position."

Savage does not oversimplify this process, however, and knows "you're not going to make everyone happy all the time, but if it's clear what is guiding your decisions and the actions you take, then people will understand. They may not like it, but at least having that foundation, whether it's a common philosophy for the conference and what drives the conference decisions, or a personal philosophy around the way you operate, people will know what to expect, can understand why those decisions are made." Ultimately, this decision-making process will always demand that current and future conference stakeholders face the inevitable: the constant need to cultivate a conference image that maintains athletics as the "sweatiest of the liberal arts" and achieves national levels of success. To that end, the struggle between idealism and realism will no doubt continue.

Chapter Notes

Introduction

1. Douglas S. Looney, "Pure and Simple," *Sports Illustrated*, October 31, 1994, 74.

2. Michael MacCambridge, *The Franchise: A History of Sports Illustrated Magazine* (New York: Hyperion, 1997), 355.

3. *Ibid.*, 241.

4. *Ibid.*, 276, 293.

5. Michael Jaffe, "Holy (Purple) Cow!: After 32 Years of Self-Imposed Exile from Postseason Play, Williams Can Once Again Compete for the National Title," *Sports Illustrated*, November 29, 1993, https://www.webcitation.org/6Jzsg7RnQ?url=http://sportsillustrated.cnn.com/vault/article/magazine/MAG1138299/.

6. Looney, "Pure and Simple," 74.

7. *Ibid.*, 77.

8. *Ibid.*, 74.

9. *Ibid.*, 77.

10. Joe MacDonald, "How It All Began," *Nothing but NESCAC* (blog), July 19, 2016, https://nothingbutnescac.com/?page_id=80.

11. "Which Colleges Have the Largest Endowments?" *Chronicle of Higher Education*, January 31, 2019, https://www.chronicle.com/article/Which-Colleges-Have-the/245587.

12. Chris Miller, *The Real Animal House: The Awesomely Depraved Saga of the Fraternity That Inspired the Movie* (New York: Little, Brown, 2006), 135–36.

13. David Remnick, *King of the World: Muhammad Ali and the Rise of an American Hero* (New York: Random House, 1998).

14. Rachael Hanley, "Amherst Announces Mammoths Mascot," Amherst College, April 3, 2017, https://www.amherst.edu/news/news_releases/2017/4-2017/amherst-announces-mammoths-mascot.

15. Derek Bok, "Intercollegiate Athletics," in *Contemporary Issues in Higher Education: Self-Regulation and the Ethical Roles of the Academy*, edited by John B. Bennett and J.W. Peltason (New York: Macmillan, 1985), 124.

16. Paul Venable Turner, *Campus: An American Planning Tradition* (New York: Architectural History Foundation, 1984).

17. Winton U. Solberg, *Creating the Big Ten: Courage, Corruption and Commercialization* (Urbana: University of Illinois Press, 2018).

18. Richard Holt, *Sport and the British: A Modern History* (Oxford: Clarendon, 1990), 98.

19. Solberg, *Creating the Big Ten*, 2.

20. Frederick Rudolph, *Mark Hopkins and the Log: Williams College, 1836–1872* (New Haven: Yale University Press, 1956), 165.

21. David F. Allmendinger, *Paupers and Scholars: The Transformation of Student Life in Nineteenth-Century New England* (New York: St. Martin's Press, 1975).

22. John R. Thelin, *A History of American Higher Education*, 3rd ed. (Baltimore: Johns Hopkins University Press, 2019), 24.

23. *Ibid.*, 56.

24. George E. Peterson, *The New England College in the Age of the University* (Amherst, MA: Amherst College Press, 1964), 84.

25. C. Miller, *The Real Animal House*, 36.

26. nescacghost, "If Schools in the NESCAC Were High School Stereotypes...," Let'sRun.com, March 18, 2013, https://www.letsrun.com/forum/flat_read.php?thread=5094021).

27. Arthur M. Cohen and Carrie B. Kisker, *The Shaping of American Higher Education: Emergence and Growth of the Contemporary System*, 2nd ed. (San Francisco: Jossey-Bass, 2010); Paul H. Mattingly, *American Academic Cultures: A History of Higher Education* (Chicago: University of Chicago Press, 2017); Brian M. Ingrassia, "Conceptualizing 'Small-Time' College Athletics: The Fracture of the 'Little Nineteen' Conference in the 1930s," *Journal of Sport History* 47, no. 3 (Fall 2020): 191–209.

28. Peterson, *The New England College*, 5–7.

29. Dick Friedman, *The Coach Who Strangled the Bulldog: How Harvard's Percy Haughton Beat Yale and Reinvented Football* (Lanham, MD: Rowman & Littlefield, 2018), 39.

30. Mattingly, *American Academic Cultures*.

31. Friedman, *The Coach Who Strangled the Bulldog*, 34.

32. Mattingly, *American Academic Cultures*, 238, 258.

33. Clark Kerr, *The Gold and the Blue: A Personal Memoir of the University of California, 1949–1967*, vol. 1 (Berkeley: University of California Press, 2001), 12–13.

34. James S. Coles, memorandum to Malcolm Morrell, February 29, 1956.

35. John Sawyer, "NESCAC Philosophy: Remarks at NESCAC Presidents' Executive Committee Meeting," New England Small College Athletic Conference, May 1971, 2–3.

36. K. Velez, "The New England Small College Athletic Conference, 1971–1997: A Retrospective," unpublished manuscript, Williams College, 1997, 7.

37. Robert J. Higgs, *God in the Stadium: Sports and Religion in America* (Lexington: University of Kentucky Press, 1995), 102.

Chapter 1

1. Frederick Rudolph, *The American College and University: A History*, rev. ed. (Athens: University of Georgia Press, 1990), 151.

2. Ronald A. Smith, *Pay for Play: A History of Big-Time College Athletic Reform* (Chicago: University of Illinois Press, 2011), 17.

3. Ronald A. Smith, *Sports and Freedom: The Rise of Big-Time College Athletics* (New York: Oxford University Press, 1988), 15.

4. Rudolph, *The American College and University*, 153.

5. Frank Prentice Rand, *Yesterdays at Massachusetts State College, 1863–1933* (Amherst, MA: Associate Alumni of Massachusetts State College, 1933), 129.

6. R. Smith, *Pay for Play*, 1.

7. R. Smith, *Sports and Freedom*.

8. Henry D. Sheldon, *Student Life and Customs*, rev. ed. (New York: Arno Press, 1969), 195, 230.

9. Rudolph, *The American College and University*, 154–55.

10. Dean A. Sullivan, ed., *Early Innings: A Documentary History of Baseball, 1825–1908* (Lincoln: University of Nebraska Press, 1995).

11. Francis X. Dealy, *Win at Any Cost: The Sell Out of College Athletics* (New York: Carol Publishing Group, 1990), 59.

12. Sullivan, *Early Innings*.

13. R. Smith, *Sports and Freedom*.

14. James Axtell, "The Death of the Liberal Arts College," *History of Education Quarterly* 11, no. 4 (Winter 1971): 339–52.

15. R. Smith, *Sports and Freedom*.

16. Patrick B. Miller, "The Manly, the Moral, and the Proficient: College Sport in the New South," *Journal of Sport History* 24, no. 3 (Fall 1997): 292.

17. R. Smith, *Pay for Play*, 26; see also Solberg, *Creating the Big Ten*.

18. "Academic Standards," 1994.

19. Roger R. Tamte, *Walter Camp and the Creation of American Football* (Urbana: University of Illinois Press, 2018).

20. Louis C. Hatch, *The History of Bowdoin College* (Portland, ME: Loring, Short & Harmon, 1927).

21. Andrew McIlwaine Bell, *The Origins of Southern College Football: How an Ivy League Game Became a Dixie Tradition* (Baton Rouge: Louisiana State University Press, 2020).

22. Michael Oriard, *King Football: Sport and Spectacle in the Golden Age of Radio and Newsreels, Movies and Magazines, the Weekly and Daily Press* (Chapel Hill: University of North Carolina Press, 2001), 67.

23. Rudolph, *The American College and University*, 378.

24. Friedman, *The Coach Who Strangled the Bulldog*, 163–64.
25. Gregory S. Sojka, "Evolution of the Student-Athlete in America," *Journal of Popular Culture*, 16, no. 4 (Spring 1983): 56.
26. Rudolph, *The American College and University*, 383.
27. David B. Potts, *Wesleyan University, 1910–1970: Academic Ambition and Middle-Class America* (Middletown, CT: Wesleyan University Press, 2015), 137, 142.
28. *Ibid.*, 270, 290.
29. *Ibid.*, 35, 139.
30. Herbert R. Brown, *Sills of Bowdoin: The Life of Kenneth Charles Morton Sills, 1879–1954* (New York: Columbia University Press, 1964), 312–13.
31. John J. Miller, *The Big Scrum: How Teddy Roosevelt Saved Football* (New York: Harper, 2011), 150.
32. Peterson, *The New England College*, 202.
33. Randy Roberts and Johnny Smith, *War Fever: Boston, Baseball, and America in the Shadow of the Great War* (New York: Basic Books, 2020).
34. August Heckscher, *Woodrow Wilson: A Biography* (Newtown, CT: American Political Bibliography Press, 2007).
35. Richard I. Miller, *The Truth about Big-Time Football* (New York: William Sloane, 1953).
36. Thelin, *A History of American Higher Education*, 209.
37. *Ibid.*, 11–12, 34.
38. Brown, *Sills of Bowdoin*, 251.
39. R. Smith, *Pay for Play*.
40. Peterson, *The New England College*, 83.
41. Potts, *Wesleyan University*.
42. R. Smith, *Pay for Play*, 59.
43. John M. Carroll, *Red Grange and the Rise of Modern Football* (Urbana: University of Illinois Press, 1999), 98–99.
44. Murray Sperber, *Shake Down the Thunder: The Creation of Notre Dame Football* (New York: Henry Holt, 1993).
45. Raymond Schmidt, *Shaping College Football: The Transformation of an American Sport, 1919–1930* (Syracuse: Syracuse University Press, 2007), 217.
46. Howard J. Savage et al., *American College Athletics* (New York: Carnegie Foundation for the Advancement of Teaching, 1929), 32.
47. R. Smith, *Pay for Play*, 69.
48. Ronald A. Smith, personal communication to author, April 19, 2020.
49. Savage, *American College Athletics*, 79–80.
50. *Ibid.*, 124–26.
51. *Ibid.*, 83.
52. John R. Thelin, *Games Colleges Play: Scandal and Reform in Intercollegiate Athletics* (Baltimore: Johns Hopkins University Press, 1996), 27–28.
53. Schmidt, *Shaping College Football*, 233.
54. *Ibid.*
55. Thelin, *Games Colleges Play*.
56. R. Smith, *Pay for Play*.
57. Ronald A. Smith, personal communication to author, April 19, 2020.
58. Rudolph, *Mark Hopkins and the Log*, viii.

Chapter 2

1. Dan Covell, "'And We're Dropping Them?' Managing Transitions in Intercollegiate Football at Bowdoin College, 1946–1964," *Sport History Review* 45, no. 1 (2014): 59–78; Matthew Katz and Chad Seifried, "And Then There Were Three: The NCAA's Struggle for Reorganization and the Emergence of Division III Athletics," *Sport History Review* 45, no. 2 (2014): 145–70.
2. Brad Austin, *Democratic Sports: Men's and Women's College Athletics during the Great Depression* (Fayetteville: University of Arkansas Press, 2015).
3. *Ibid.*, xix, 68–69.
4. Benjamin G. Rader, *American Sports: From the Age of Folk Games to the Age of Televised Sports*, 6th ed. (Upper Saddle River, NJ: Pearson; Prentice Hall, 2009).
5. R. Miller, *The Truth about Big Time Football*, 117.
6. Friedman, *The Coach Who Strangled the Bulldog*, xiv.
7. Kenneth C.M. Sills, letter to Victor Schmidt, October 27, 1951.
8. Katz and Seifried, "And Then There Were Three," 148.
9. *Ibid.*
10. Annual Report of the Director of Athletics, submitted to President Kenneth C.M. Sills, Bowdoin College, April 21, 1950, 7–8.
11. William G. Bowen and Sarah A.

Levin, *Reclaiming the Game: College Sports and Educational Values* (Princeton: Princeton University Press, 2003).

12. Jerome Quarterman, "Managerial Role Profiles of Intercollegiate Athletic Conference Commissioners," *Journal of Sport Management* 8, no. 2 (1994): 129.

13. Thelin, *Games Colleges Play*, 14, 129.

14. Erik Kjeldsen, "The Manager's Role in the Development and Maintenance of Ethical Behavior in the Sport Organization," *Journal of Sport Management* 6, no. 2 (1992): 102.

15. Michael Oriard, *Bowled Over: Big-Time College Football from the Sixties to the BCS Era* (Chapel Hill: University of North Carolina Press, 2009), 277.

16. Kyle V. Sweitzer, "Institutional Ambitions and Athletic Conference Affiliation," *New Directions for Higher Education* 148, no. 148 (Winter 2009): 55.

17. R. Smith, *Sports and Freedom*, 140.

18. R. Smith, *Pay for Play*, 58–59.

19. *Ibid.*

20. Malcolm Morrell, minutes of the ninth annual meeting of the representatives of liberal arts colleges, January 12, 1945.

21. Malcolm Morrell, letter to Kenneth Sills, October 19, 1939.

22. Potts, *Wesleyan University*.

23. *Ibid.*, 144.

24. *Ibid.*, 364.

25. Alden Whitman, "James P. Baxter 3d Dies; Ex-President of Williams," *New York Times*, June 19, 1975, 38.

26. Charles Cole, letter to Kenneth Sills, May 16, 1951.

27. James P. Baxter III, letter to Charles Cole, May 21, 1951.

28. Victor L. Butterfield, letter to Charles Cole, May 19, 1951.

29. Charles Cole, letter to Kenneth Sills, May 21, 1951.

30. Charles Cole, letter to Kenneth Sills, November 13, 1951.

31. *Ibid.*

32. Malcolm Morrell, letter to Kenneth Sills, November 16, 1951.

33. *Ibid.*

34. James S. Coles, memorandum to Malcolm Morrell, February 29, 1956.

35. James S. Coles, letter to Charles Cole, James Baxter III, and Victor Butterfield, February 17, 1956.

36. Henry Beach Needham, "The College Athlete: How Commercialism Is Making Him a Professional," *McClure's Magazine*, June 1905, 121.

37. Malcolm Morrell, letter to James Coles, February 3, 1954.

38. *Ibid.*

39. Charles Cole, letter to James Coles, April 11, 1955.

40. Victor Butterfield, letter to James Coles, May 23, 1955.

41. Thelin, *Games Colleges Play*, 108.

42. Malcolm Morrell, letter to James Coles, November 11, 1955.

43. *Ibid.*

44. James Coles, letter to John Sawyer, August 8, 1966.

45. P. Samuelson, "Banquet Speakers, Watters, Pelham Search for Well-Balanced Students," *Williams Record*, February 6, 1959.

46. James Coles, letter to Charles Cole, March 6, 1959.

47. Charles Cole, letter to James Coles, March 7, 1959.

48. James Coles, letter to Charles Cole, April 7, 1959.

49. Charles Cole, letter to James Coles, April 11, 1959.

50. Charles Cole, letter to James Coles, December 18, 1959.

51. James Coles, letter to Charles Cole, December 23, 1959.

52. Malcolm Morrell, letter to James Coles, January 7, 1960.

53. Charles Cole, letter to James Coles, January 4, 1960.

54. James P. Baxter III, letter to James Coles, April 4, 1960.

55. James Coles, letter to Victor Butterfield, March 3, 1960.

56. Charles Cole, letter to James Baxter III, March 3, 1959.

57. James Coles, letter to Charles Cole, James Baxter, III, and Victor Butterfield, March 3, 1959.

58. Charles Cole, letter to James Coles, March 4, 1959.

59. James Coles, letter to A. Shirley Gray, February 20, 1967.

60. *Ibid.*

61. Hugh McCurdy, memorandum to Victor L. Butterfield on the meeting of athletic directors of Amherst, Bowdoin, Wesleyan, and Williams, June 4, 1964.

62. *Ibid.*

63. John Sawyer, letter to Victor Butterfield, June 17, 1964.

64. Victor Butterfield, letter to John Sawyer, June 22, 1964.
65. Calvin Plimpton, letter to Victor Butterfield, September 22, 1964.
66. Victor Butterfield, letter to James Coles, Calvin Plimpton, and John Sawyer, October 19, 1964.
67. Calvin Plimpton, letter to Victor Butterfield, October 29, 1964.

Chapter 3

1. Ronald D. Mott, "The 100-Year Debate," *NCAA News*, January 4, 1995, 10–11; Allen L. Sack and Ellen J. Staurowsky, *College Athletes for Hire: The Evolution and Legacy of the NCAA's Amateur Myth* (Westport, CT: Praeger, 1998). Stephen Hardy, personal communication, May 1, 2021.
2. R. Smith, *Pay for Play*, 202.
3. Jack Falla, *NCAA: Voice of College Sports—A Diamond Anniversary History, 1906-1981* (Mission, KS: National Collegiate Athletic Association, 1981).
4. Jay W. Helman, "A History of American Intercollegiate Academic Eligibility: Educational Compromises to Competitive Interests," PhD diss., Pennsylvania State University, 1989.
5. Falla, *NCAA*, 132–33.
6. Murray Sperber, *Onward to Victory: The Crises That Shaped College Sports* (New York: Henry Holt, 1998).
7. *Proceedings of the 41st Annual Convention of the National Collegiate Athletic Association* (Kansas City: National Collegiate Athletic Association, 1947), 77, 87.
8. *Proceedings of the 42nd Annual Convention of the National Collegiate Athletic Association* (Kansas City: National Collegiate Athletic Association, 1948), 212.
9. R. Smith, *Pay for Play*, 97.
10. Paul R. Lawrence, *Unsportsmanlike Conduct: The National Collegiate Athletic Association and the Business of College Football* (New York: Praeger, 1987).
11. Ibid.
12. Ibid.
13. Sack and Staurowsky, *College Athletes for Hire*, 96.
14. Falla, *NCAA*.
15. Walter Byers, *Unsportsmanlike Conduct: Exploiting College Athletes* (Ann Arbor: University of Michigan Press, 1995), 158.

16. R. Smith, *Pay for Play*, 129.
17. Ibid.
18. "Bowdoin College Will Not Subject Its Scholarship Policy to NCAA Control." Press release. Bowdoin College News Service, January 24, 1966.
19. Ibid.
20. R. Smith, *Pay for Play*, 129.
21. "Bowdoin College Will Not Subject Its Scholarship Policy to NCAA Control."
22. Frank Litsky, "2-Day Track Meet Will Open Today," *New York Times*, March 11, 1966, 15; "N.C.A.A. Championships Are Slated for Next Week," *New York Times*, March 6, 1966, 8.
23. Edward Born, "A 16,000 Seat Proposal," *Bowdoin Alumnus*, March 1966.
24. Charles C. Calhoun, *A Small College in Maine: Two Hundred Years of Bowdoin* (Brunswick, ME: Bowdoin College, 1993), 231; "F. Alexis Schulten '66," Bowdoin Athletics, accessed April 6, 2021, https://athletics.bowdoin.edu/sports/2020/5/20/information-history-hall-schulten.aspx.
25. "F. Alexis Schulten '66."
26. Peter Pappas and Gary Graham, Polar Bearings, *Bowdoin Orient*, September 25, 1964, 6.
27. James Coles, confidential memorandum to Malcolm Morrell, February 1, 1966.
28. Ibid.
29. Charles Watts, letter to James Coles, February 7, 1966.
30. Vincent Barnett, Jr., letter to James Coles, February 10, 1966.
31. Gordon S. White, Jr., "N.C.A.A. Gives 57 Colleges Extension on Scholastic Code," *New York Times*, February 18, 1966, 14.
32. Ibid.
33. "410 Colleges Meet N.C.A.A. 1.6 Standard," *New York Times*, February 20, 1966, 15.
34. "Ivy League to Accept N.C.A.A. Academic Norm," *New York Times*, February 24, 1966, 16.
35. Ibid.
36. "Ivy Teams Will Shun N.C.A.A. Title Play," *New York Times*, March 6, 1966.
37. "Ivy Ace Penn Scratches from NCAA Hoop Event," *Portland (ME) Press Herald*, February 26, 1966, 10.
38. "Ivy Teams Will Shun N.C.A.A. Title Play."

39. Everett D. Barnes, "19th Hole: The Readers Take Over," *Sports Illustrated*, February 21, 1966, 75.
40. James Coles, letter to Everett D. Barnes, February 25, 1966.
41. "Dean Reaffirms Bowdoin Stand," *Portland (ME) Press Herald*, March 10, 1966, 22.
42. *Ibid.*
43. James Bradner, Jr., letter to Frank Sabasteanski, March 1966.
44. Joseph S. Tiede, letter to editor, *Bowdoin Alumnus*, July 1966.
45. "An Interim Agreement," press release, Yale University News Bureau, February 20, 1967.
46. James Coles, letter to Marcus L. Plant, February 23, 1967.
47. Marcus L. Plant, letter to James Coles, March 1, 1967.
48. James Coles, letter to Marcus L. Plant, March 3, 1967.
49. Barnes, "19th Hole."
50. Marcus L. Plant, letter to James Coles, March 1, 1967.
51. Kingman Brewster, letter to John Sawyer, September 29, 1967.
52. *Bowdoin College Bulletin: Catalogue for the Sessions of 1967-1968*, no. 366 (Brunswick, ME: Bowdoin College, September 1967), 75.
53. *Ibid.*, 63.
54. James Coles, memorandum to Bowdoin College director of financial aid and director of admissions regarding establishment of the Arthur D. and Francis J. Welch Scholarship fund, December 1, 1966.
55. *Bowdoin College Bulletin: Catalogue for the Sessions of 1968-1969*, no. 370 (Brunswick, ME: Bowdoin College, September 1968), 77.
56. Vincent Welch, letter to Walter Moulton, November 5, 1970.
57. Walter Moulton, letter to Vincent Welch, October 26, 1970.
58. Daniel Stuckey, letter to Richard Moll, 1970.
59. Walter Moulton, letter to Vincent Welch, November 28, 1970.
60. J.S. Drummond, letter to Henry Flynn, Jr., February 5, 1968.
61. Marcus L. Plant, special memorandum to chief executive officers, faculty representatives, and directors of athletics on the subject of council-sponsored amendment to 1.6 legislation, December 1, 1967.
62. "N.C.A.A. Council-Sponsored Amendment to 1.600 Rule," National Collegiate Athletic Association, November 30, 1967.
63. "New 'Triple Option' May Be Submitted," *NCAA News*, June 1, 1978, 4.
64. Daniel Stuckey, letter to Athern Daggett, January 15, 1968.
65. "Institutional Predictive Formula for Freshmen," Office of the Dean of the College, Bowdoin College, February 2, 1968.
66. *Ibid.*
67. *Ibid.*
68. Walter Byers, letter to A. LeRoy Greason, March 14, 1968.
69. "Olympians on Campus," *Bowdoin Alumnus*, July 1972, 18.
70. "F. Alexis Schulten '66."

Chapter 4

1. Don Russell, "An Athletic Conference," June 3, 1969.
2. Benjamin Katz, "NESCAC Schools Band Together to Create Forum," *Williams Record*, November 17, 1998.
3. Nils Wessell, letter to James Coles, February 20, 1954.
4. M. Conroy, D. Estridge, and P. Rich, "Turmoil, Triumph—and a Call for Change," in *Jumbo Footprints: A History of Tufts Athletics, 1852-1999*, edited by Rocco J. Carzo et al. (Medford, MA: Tufts University, 2005), 136-65.
5. Richard M. Freeland, *Academia's Golden Age: Universities in Massachusetts, 1945-1970* (New York: Oxford University Press, 1992).
6. James Coles, letter to Nils Wessell, March 3, 1954.
7. James Coles, letter to Charles Cole, March 3, 1954.
8. R.M. Hurst, Polar Bearings, *Bowdoin Orient*, November 11, 1953, 4.
9. Wayne Somers, ed., *Encyclopedia of Union College History* (Schenectady, NY: Union College Press, 2003).
10. *Ibid.*, 70.
11. "Little Ivy League?" *Bowdoin Orient*, December 16, 1959, 2.
12. Looney, "Pure and Simple," 67.
13. S.F. Parkyn, letter to the editor,

Notes—Chapter 4

Hartford (CT) Courant, November 20, 1983, 8.
14. James English, letter to Wayne Loveland, November 28, 1983.
15. Chris Lincoln, *Playing the Game: Inside Athletic Recruiting in the Ivy League* (White River Junction, VT: Nomad Press, 2004), 242.
16. James Coles, letter to Robert Livingston, November 20, 1962.
17. James Coles, letter to Major General E.N. Harmon, December 10, 1964.
18. James Coles, memorandum to Victor Butterfield, Calvin Plimpton, and John Sawyer, December 10, 1964.
19. Calvin Plimpton, letter to James Armstrong, December 14, 1964.
20. Calvin Plimpton, letter to Major General E.N. Harmon, December 15, 1964.
21. Victor Butterfield, letter to Major General E.N. Harmon, December 15, 1964.
22. Victor Butterfield, letter to James Armstrong, December 16, 1964.
23. James Armstrong, letter to Victor Butterfield, January 4, 1965.
24. James Coles, letter to Victor Butterfield, Calvin Plimpton, and John Sawyer, January 4, 1967.
25. Ibid.
26. James Coles, letter to Robert Shulze, January 4, 1967.
27. John Sawyer, letter to James Coles, January 16, 1967.
28. A. LeRoy Greason, Jr., letter to James Coles, February 2, 1967.
29. John Sawyer, letter to James Coles, January 25, 1967.
30. James Coles, memorandum on agenda for meeting of athletic directors of the four colleges to director of athletics, May 17, 1967.
31. Athern Daggett, memorandum to members of the Governing Boards Committee on Physical Education, July 24, 1968.
32. Dick Mersereau, Polar Bearings, *Bowdoin Orient*, January 13, 1967, 12.
33. Ibid.
34. E.E. Richardson et al., eight-team athletic conference, July 1, 1968.
35. Roger Howell, Jr., memorandum to acting president Athern Daggett on proposed athletic league, May 27, 1968.
36. Potts, *Wesleyan University*, 406.
37. Athern Daggett, letter to Calvin Plimpton, June 25, 1968.
38. Thomas Hedley Reynolds, letter to Athern Daggett, July 10, 1968.
39. Thomas Hedley Reynolds, letter to Athern Daggett, July 11, 1968.
40. Edwin Etherington, letter to Thomas Hedley Reynolds, July 18, 1968.
41. Edwin Etherington, letter to Harold Martin, July 1, 1968.
42. Edwin Etherington, letter to Robert Strider, July 31, 1968.
43. Edwin Etherington, letter to Athern Daggett, July 31, 1968.
44. Athern Daggett, letter to Edwin Etherington, August 6, 1968.
45. Daniel Stuckey, letter to Athern Daggett, August 19, 1968.
46. Athern Daggett, letter to Daniel Stuckey, August 23, 1968.
47. Athern Daggett, memorandum to members of the Governing Boards Committee on Physical Education, July 24, 1968.
48. Athern Daggett, memo on staff conference held on August 26, 1968, August 26, 1968.
49. John Sawyer, memorandum to Athern Daggett, Edwin Etherington, and Calvin Plimpton, September 19, 1968.
50. Ibid.
51. Calvin Plimpton, letter to Edwin Etherington, November 14, 1968.
52. Daniel Stuckey, letter to Athern Daggett, October 15, 1968.
53. Edwin Etherington, memorandum to Athern Daggett, Calvin Plimpton, and Jack Sawyer on the subject of athletic league proposal, October 30, 1968.
54. Ibid.
55. Roger Howell, Jr., letter to Athern Daggett, November 7, 1968.
56. Athern Daggett, letter to Edwin Etherington, November 11, 1968.
57. Athern Daggett, letter to Edwin Etherington, December 2, 1968.
58. John Sawyer, letter to Edwin Etherington, November 12, 1968.
59. John Sawyer, memorandum to Athern Daggett, Edwin Etherington, and Calvin Plimpton, December 27, 1968.
60. Ibid.
61. Roger Howell, Jr., letter to Philip Calhoun, January 7, 1969.
62. Daniel Stuckey, letter to Roger Howell, Jr., January 28, 1969.
63. Roger Howell, Jr., letter to Daniel Stuckey, July 2, 1969.
64. Robert Strider, letter to Calvin

Plimpton, Thomas Hedley Reynolds, Roger Howell, Jr., James Armstrong, Theodore Lockwood, Burton Hallowell, Edwin Etherington, and John Sawyer, March 3, 1969.

65. John Sawyer, letter to Robert Strider, March 6, 1969.

66. "That Impenetrable Athletic Policy," *Colby Echo*, November 7, 1969, 3, https://digitalcommons.colby.edu/cgi/viewcontent.cgi?article=3190&context=colbyecho.

67. Roger Howell, Jr., letter to Robert Strider, March 14, 1969.

68. Calvin Plimpton, letter to Robert Strider, March 18, 1969.

69. Daniel Stuckey, letter to Roger Howell, Jr., May 14, 1969.

70. Edwin Etherington, letter to Frank Thoms, December 23, 1969.

71. Edwin Etherington, letter to Calvin Plimpton, John Sawyer, and Roger Howell, Jr., December 23, 1969.

72. Edwin Etherington, draft of athletic conference agreement, December 23, 1969.

73. *Ibid.*

74. Roger Howell, Jr., letter to Edwin Etherington, January 9, 1970.

75. John Sawyer, memorandum to Frank Thoms, Jr., February 24, 1970.

76. Richard Costello, letter to John Sawyer, October 19, 1972.

77. John Sawyer, note to Roger Howell, Jr., May 31, 1972.

78. Roger Howell, Jr., letter to John Sawyer, June 1, 1972.

79. Richard Costello, letter to John Sawyer, October 19, 1972.

80. John Sawyer, letter to Richard Costello, October 23, 1972.

81. Athletic Conference Agreement, May 4, 1970, 3-4.

82. *Ibid.*

83. James Armstrong, letter to Roger Howell, Jr., May 4, 1970.

84. *Ibid.*

85. Press release on formation of New England Small College Athletic Conference, Middlebury College, March 21, 1971.

86. Special report of the Faculty Committee on Athletics, Bowdoin College, May 8, 1970, 1.

87. Roger Howell, Jr., letter to James Armstrong, June 23, 1970.

88. James Armstrong, memorandum to the presidents on the subject of proposed New England Small College Athletic Conference, August 13, 1970.

89. James Armstrong, letter to Roger Howell, Jr., November 27, 1970.

90. James Armstrong, memorandum to the presidents of the New England Small College Athletic Conference on the subject of report on Hanover meeting, November 27, 1970.

91. John Sawyer, letter to James Armstrong, November 17, 1970.

92. *Ibid.*

93. Roger Howell, Jr., letter to John Sawyer, 1970.

94. John Sawyer, note to Roger Howell, Jr., November 25, 1970.

95. A. LeRoy Greason, Jr., note to Roger Howell, Jr., December 2, 1970.

96. John Sawyer, remarks to the first meeting of conference athletic directors and presidents executive committee, New England Small College Athletic Conference, May 24, 1971.

97. Frank Thoms, minutes of joint meeting between ADs and executive committee, New England Small College Athletic Conference, May 24–25, 1971.

98. J. Cicia, "A Breakout Decade for Women," in *Jumbo Footprints: A History of Tufts Athletics, 1952–1999*, edited by Rocco J. Carzo et al. (Medford, MA: Tufts University, 2005), 170.

99. Lee M. Levison, "Origins of the New England Small College Athletic Conference," unpublished manuscript, Trinity College, 1981, 7.

100. Bowen and Levin, *Reclaiming the Game*, 31.

Chapter 5

1. Martin Friedlander, "For the Times: Hair Today ... Gone Tomorrow," *Bowdoin Orient*, November 8, 1968, 8.

2. Conroy, Estridge, and Rich, "Turmoil, Triumph—and a Call for Change," 160.

3. *Miller v. Gillis*, 315 F. Supp. 94 (N.D. Ill. 1969).

4. Rick Perlstein, *Nixonland: The Rise of a President and the Fracturing of America* (New York: Scribner, 2008), 378.

5. "Unrest Is Found to Be Widespread among Faculty Members as well as Students; Many Groups Are Split," *Chronicle of Higher Education*, September 15, 1969.

Notes—Chapter 5

6. Roger Howell, Jr., *Report of the President to the Trustees and Overseers* (Brunswick, ME: Bowdoin College, 1970), 7.
7. Calhoun, *A Small College in Maine*, 232.
8. D. Huntington, "True Grit," *Bowdoin Alumnus*, March 1970, 8.
9. Eric Hoover, "A Manly Old Guide to the Ivy League," *Chronicle of Higher Education*, September 12, 2014, 22.
10. Richard Williams, "Kirkland College 52 Years Later," Clinton Historical Society, December 18, 2019, https://clintonhistory.org/kirkland-college-52-years-later.
11. Nancy Weiss Malkiel, *"Keep the Damned Women Out": The Struggle for Coeducation* (Princeton: Princeton University Press, 2016).
12. Katherine Rorer, "The Process of Co-education at Amherst College and Trinity College," student paper, Trinity College, May 3, 2012, https://commons.trincoll.edu/edreform/2012/05/the-process-of-co-education-at-amherst-college-and-trinity-college.
13. Potts, *Wesleyan University*, 89.
14. E.J. Shea, "Clubs Teams and a Quest for Belonging," in *Jumbo Footprints: A History of Tufts Athletics, 1852–1999*, edited by Rocco J. Carzo et al. (Medford, MA: Tufts University, 2005), 23–32.
15. R. Smith, *Pay for Play*.
16. Gerald R. Gems, *For Pride, Profit, and Patriarchy: Football and the Incorporation of American Cultural Values* (Latham, MD: Scarecrow Press, 2000).
17. Welch Suggs, *A Place on the Team: The Triumph and Tragedy of Title IX* (Princeton: Princeton University Press, 2005), 23.
18. Pamela Grundy, *Learning to Win: Sports, Education, and Social Change in Twentieth-Century North Carolina* (Chapel Hill: University of North Carolina Press, 2001), 41.
19. E.J. Shea, "A Lead Position—Scholarship First, then Sports," in *Jumbo Footprints: A History of Tufts Athletics, 1852–1999*, edited by Rocco J. Carzo et al. (Medford, MA: Tufts University, 2005), 67.
20. Conroy, Estridge, and Rich, "Turmoil, Triumph—and a Call for Change."
21. Auban Haydel and Kit Lasher, *The Fairest College? Twenty Years of Women at Amherst* (Amherst, MA: Amherst College, 1997), 129.
22. Ibid., 137.
23. Sally LaPointe, "The State of Women's Athletics," memorandum to Roger Howell, Jr., Bowdoin College, May 23, 1977, https://research.bowdoin.edu/forty-years-the-history-of-women-at-bowdoin/athletics/letter-from-sally-lapointe-to-president-howell.
24. Jillyan Henrikson, "A Female Athlete in a Men's Athletic World: A Discussion with Beth Richardson, '79," Forty Years: The History of Women at Bowdoin, November 4, 2011, https://research.bowdoin.edu/forty-years-the-history-of-women-at-bowdoin/athletics/interview-beth-cantara-richardson-79.
25. Jillyan Henrikson, "What about the Female Athletes? A Discussion with Richard (Dick) Mersereau, '69," Forty Years: The History of Women at Bowdoin, October 21, 2011, https://research.bowdoin.edu/forty-years-the-history-of-women-at-bowdoin/athletics/interview-richard-mersereau-bowdoin-women%E2%80%99s-basketball-coach.
26. Thelin, *A History of American Higher Education*, 318, 320.
27. Cicia, "A Breakout Decade for Women," 186.
28. Looney, "Pure and Simple," 79.
29. "Basketball Tourney Permit Denied by League," press release, Union College News Release, February 15, 1972.
30. Somers, *Encyclopedia of Union College History*, 70.
31. Jan K. Ludwig, "Bonner, Thomas Neville," in *Encyclopedia of Union College History*, edited by Wayne Somers (Schenectady, NY: Union College Press, 2003), 116.
32. Ibid.
33. Ibid.
34. Ibid., 117.
35. "Men's Hockey History," Cornell University Athletics, http://www.cornellbigred.com/sports/2009/4/6/MICE_0406094147.aspx?path=mhockey.
36. Pat Putnam, "No Heels in the Achilles," *Sports Illustrated*, February 7, 1977, https://vault.si.com/vault/1977/02/07/no-heels-in-the-achilles.
37. MacCambridge, *The Franchise*, 3, 5–6, 188.
38. "Guys and Dolls among the Ivy," *Sports Illustrated*, October 31, 1960, 25–26.
39. Ibid., 29–30.

40. *Ibid.*, 28–29.
41. Mark Mulvoy, "The Poison Ivy in the Ivy League," *Sports Illustrated*, January 2, 1967, 44–46.
42. Stephen Hardy and Andrew C. Holman, *Hockey: A Global History* (Urbana: University of Illinois Press, 2018), 50.
43. John Sawyer, letter to James Coles, January 16, 1967.
44. Putnam, "No Heels in the Achilles."
45. *Ibid.*
46. *Ibid.*
47. *Ibid.*
48. Olin Robison, letter to Thomas Bonner, February 12, 1976.
49. Thomas Kershner, letter to Thomas Bonner, February 20, 1976.
50. Thomas Bonner, letter to Olin Robison, February 20, 1976.
51. Olin Robison, letter to Thomas Bonner, March 5, 1976.
52. Ludwig, "Bonner, Thomas Neville," 117.
53. *Ibid.*
54. *Ibid.*, 118.
55. "Williams Reported Harkness," *Holyoke (MA) Transcript-Telegram*, March 18, 1977, 15.
56. Somers, *Encyclopedia of Union College History*, 392.
57. *Ibid.*
58. Alan Nelson, "Admissions," in *Encyclopedia of Union College History*, edited by Wayne Somers (Schenectady, NY: Union College Press, 2003), 15.
59. Somers, *Encyclopedia of Union College History*, 392.
60. *Ibid.*, 394.
61. Francis J. Connolly, "Chaos at 60 B," *Harvard Crimson*, September 16, 1977, https://www.thecrimson.com/article/1977/9/16/chaos-at-60-b-pif-harvards/.
62. Ludwig, "Bonner, Thomas Neville," 119.
63. Edward A. Gargan, "Union Reshapes Winning Attitude," *New York Times*, September 16, 1984.
64. Looney, "Pure and Simple," 79.
65. Robert Sproull, letter to Colin Campbell, September 30, 1974.
66. Bob Peck, letter to Colin Campbell, January 20, 1975.
67. Potts, *Wesleyan University*, 89.
68. Paul P. Marthers, *"Eighth Sister No More": The Origins and Evolution of Connecticut College* (New York: Peter Lang, 2011).
69. Oakes Ames, letter to Jean Mayer, July 6, 1981.
70. Rocky Carzo, update to Jean Mayer on NESCAC athletic directors meeting of September 21, 1981, September 23, 1981.
71. Jeanette Hersey, letter to Rocky Carzo, September 4, 1981.
72. Oakes Ames, letter to James English, January 25, 1982.
73. James English, letter to Oakes Ames, January 29, 1982.
74. Minutes of the NESCAC meeting, April 13, 1982, 2.
75. Marthers, *"Eighth Sister No More,"* 5, 226.
76. *Ibid.*, 226–27.
77. *Ibid.*, 230, 232, 234.
78. *Ibid.*, 134.
79. Malkiel, *"Keep the Damned Women Out,"* 228.
80. Marthers, *"Eighth Sister No More,"* 134.
81. E. Carlson, "The World According to Darp," in *Passages of Time: Narratives in the History of Amherst College*, edited by Douglas C. Wilson (Amherst, MA: Amherst College Press, 2007), 259–60.
82. *Ibid.*, 262.
83. S. Clay and M.I. Alaimo, "One Hell of a Decade," in *Jumbo Footprints: A History of Tufts Athletics, 1852–1999*, edited by Rocco J. Carzo et al. (Medford, MA: Tufts University, 2005), 219.
84. Letters, *Sports Illustrated*, November 21, 1994, 15.

Chapter 6

1. Looney, "Pure and Simple," 79.
2. *Ibid.*, 80.
3. *Ibid.*
4. Velez, "The New England Small College Athletic Conference," 18.
5. *Ibid.*
6. Henry H. Hubbard III, letter to James English, March 23, 1984.
7. James English, letter to Henry H. Hubbard III, April 3, 1984.
8. *Ibid.*
9. "NESCAC Presidents Lift Ban on NCAA Team Competition for Three-Year Trial," New England Small College Athletic Conference, 1993.

10. *Ibid.*
11. Looney, "Pure and Simple," 79.
12. Paul Sweeney, "The Scholar-Athlete Standard Endures," in *Jumbo Footprints: A History of Tufts Athletics, 1852–1999*, edited by Rocco J. Carzo et al. (Medford, MA: Tufts University, 2005), 249.
13. *Report on Varsity Athletics*, Williams College Ad Hoc Faculty Committee on Athletics, May 2002, 7.
14. J. Seelye Bixler, letter to Clarence Houston, January 14, 1957.
15. J. Seelye Bixler, letter to James Coles, Arthur Hauk, and Charles Phillips, January 14, 1957.
16. Malcolm Morrell, letter to James Coles, April 3, 1958.
17. Charles Phillips, letter to J. Seelye Bixler, January 18, 1957.
18. James Coles, letter to J. Seelye Bixler, January 18, 1957.
19. James Coles, letter to Frank Gardner, April 7, 1958.
20. Earl H. Smith, *Mayflower Hill: A History of Colby College* (Hanover, NH: University Press of New England, 2006), 103.
21. Katz and Seifried, "And Then There Were Three," 150.
22. Jaffe, "Holy (Purple) Cow."
23. James Coles, letter to Victor Butterfield, February 21, 1961.
24. Hugh McCurdy, memorandum to Calvin Plimpton, James Coles, Victor Butterfield, and John Sawyer regarding points of the October 11, 1961, agreement among Amherst, Bowdoin, Wesleyan, and Williams concerning intercollegiate athletics, as amended by suggestions from Bowdoin and Williams, November 6, 1961.
25. James Coles, letter to Victor Butterfield, December 11, 1961.
26. Michael Rosenberg, *War as They Knew It: Woody Hayes, Bo Schembechler, and America in a Time of Unrest* (New York: Grand Central, 2008), 158.
27. Frank Thoms, memorandum to Hugh McCurdy, Malcolm Morrell, and Red Richardson regarding proposed revisions and release of athletic agreements among Amherst, Bowdoin, Wesleyan, and Williams as formulated at meeting on October 11, 1961, October 31, 1961.
28. Asa Smith, Polar Bearings, *Bowdoin Orient*, January 18, 1962, 3.
29. *Ibid.*
30. "Pentagonal Conference Upholds Post-Season Rule," *Bowdoin Orient*, March 1, 1962.
31. Hugh McCurdy, memorandum to Victor L. Butterfield on the meeting of athletic directors of Amherst, Bowdoin, Wesleyan, and Williams, June 4, 1964.
32. John Sawyer, letter to Victor Butterfield, June 17, 1964.
33. *Ibid.*
34. Victor Butterfield, letter to James Coles, Calvin Plimpton, and John Sawyer, October 19, 1964.
35. Hugh McCurdy, minutes of meeting of athletic directors of Amherst, Bowdoin, Wesleyan, and Williams at Brunswick, Maine, May 30–31, 1966, June 7, 1966.
36. James Coles, letter to Victor Butterfield, Calvin Plimpton, and John Sawyer, January 4, 1967.
37. John Sawyer, letter to James Coles, January 16, 1967.
38. Calvin Plimpton, letter to Robert Strider, March 18, 1969.
39. Red Richardson, letter to Donald Russell, Frank Thoms, and Daniel Stuckey, April 23, 1969.
40. Ray Bicknell et al., letter to Daniel Stuckey, May 7, 1969.
41. Edwin Etherington, letter to Calvin Plimpton, John Sawyer, and Roger Howell, December 23, 1969.
42. Roger Howell, letter to Edwin Etherington, Calvin Plimpton, and John Sawyer, February 3, 1970.
43. Dude, "East Snowed, East Buried," *Bowdoin Orient*, March 6, 1970, 8.
44. "New England Small College Athletic Conference—Operational Policies," New England Small College Athletic Conference, August 23, 1971, 1–2.
45. Don Russell, minutes of joint meeting between ADs and executive committee, New England Small College Athletic Conference, May 22, 1972, 2.
46. *Ibid.*
47. Cicia, "A Breakout Decade for Women."
48. Minutes of NESCAC presidents' meeting, February 3, 1986, 1.
49. "Let Them Play," *Williams Record*, May 7, 1996, 2.
50. James L. Shulman and William G. Bowen, *The Game of Life: College Sports and Educational Values* (Princeton: Princeton University Press, 2001), xvi.
51. "Let Them Play."

52. *Ibid.*
53. Quarterman, "Managerial Role Profiles of Intercollegiate Athletic Conference Commissioners."
54. "Statement from the Commission on Post-Season Athletic Competition," Williams College, September 1998, 2.
55. *Ibid.*
56. "Prep School President Commits Suicide," Associated Press, January 11, 2008, https://groups.google.com/forum/#!topic/alt.obituaries/-s4pLXKYijY.
57. *Ibid.*
58. "Statement of Presidents of the New England Small College Athletic Conference," New England Small College Athletic Conference, 1997.
59. *Ibid.*
60. "The Future of NESCAC in the NCAA Postseason," Orient Forum, *Bowdoin Orient*, November 7, 1997, 9.
61. Velez, "The New England Small College Athletic Conference," 8.
62. Mike Szostak, "College Picks," *Providence (RI) Journal*, November 8, 1997.
63. Lincoln, *Playing the Game*, 221.
64. Jaffe, "Holy (Purple) Cow."
65. "NESCAC Presidents Adopt New Mission Statement and Make Decisions Regarding Post-Season Competition," New England Small College Athletic Conference, April 23, 1998, 2.
66. Minutes of NESCAC presidents' meeting, January 27, 1988, 1.
67. *Ibid.*
68. "NESCAC Presidents Adopt New Mission Statement."
69. "NCAA Forum Follow-Up: Statement from Williams College Council," Williams College, 1998.
70. *Ibid.*
71. Katz, "NESCAC Schools Band Together to Create Forum."
72. *Ibid.*
73. Welch Suggs, "Postseason Play Creates Tensions for an Unusual Athletics Conference," *Chronicle of Higher Education*, June 18, 1999, 46.
74. Brian Katten, personal communication to author, March 22, 1999.

Chapter 7

1. Scott Cacciola, "Best Division III School: Williams College," *Sports Illustrated*, October 7, 2002, 67.
2. Albert Chen, "A Little Goes a Long Way," *Sports Illustrated*, November 27, 2000, 40.
3. Eric Bergofsky, "Perpetual Panther Power," Letters, *Sports Illustrated*, October 28, 2002, 14.
4. Lincoln, *Playing the Game*, 196–97.
5. Matthew L. Wald, "Trinity's New Hand at the Helm," *New York Times*, June 21, 1981, https://www.nytimes.com/1981/06/21/nyregion/trinity-s-new-hand-at-the-helm.html.
6. Faye S. Wolfe, "The Man to Do It: Making Sense of the Relationship between Trinity College and Hartford," *UMASS Magazine*, Winter 1998, https://www.umass.edu/umassmag/archives/1998/winter_98/wint98_f_trinity.html.
7. Peter J. Knapp, *Trinity College in the Twentieth Century: A History* (Hartford, CT: Trinity College, 2000), 502.
8. Paul Wachter, "Squashing the Ivies," *New York Times Magazine*, February 20, 2011, 37.
9. Wolfe, "The Man to Do It."
10. Lincoln, *Playing the Game*, 196–97.
11. Mark Beech, "A Global Racquet," *Sports Illustrated*, March 1, 2004, 30.
12. Lincoln, *Playing the Game.*
13. Wachter, "Squashing the Ivies," 39.
14. *Ibid.*, 38.
15. Lincoln, *Playing the Game*, 203, 207–208.
16. *Ibid.*, 197–98, 213.
17. "Trinity Men's Squash Tops Yale in Dramatic Fashion for 13th Straight National Title," Bantam Sports, February 27, 2011, https://bantamsports.com/news/2011/7/7/7_7_2011_3442.aspx.
18. Paul Wachter, "After 14-Year Run, Squash Juggernaut Loses a Match," *New York Times*, January 20, 2012.
19. "Paul Assaiante," Bantam Sports, https://bantamsports.com/staff-directory/paul-assaiante/145.
20. Lincoln, *Playing the Game*, 214.
21. "Trinity Athletic Teams Excited About New Facilities and Fields," Trinity College, March 27, 2017, https://bantamsports.com/sports/2020/5/28/Information-Athletics-51617.aspx.
22. Lincoln, *Playing the Game*, 197.
23. Andrea Estes and Scott Allen, "Ex-UH President under Scrutiny Again," *Honolulu Star-Advertiser*, August 20, 2013, https://www.staradvertiser.com/2013/08/

20/hawaii-news/ex-uh-president-under-scrutiny-again/.

24. "Former Trinity President Settles in Massachusetts College Spending Probe," Associated Press, April 30, 2015, https://www.courant.com/education/hc-evan-dobelle-settlement-0430-20150430-story.html.

25. Shulman and Bowen, *The Game of Life*, xxvi.

26. Ibid., xxxv.

27. Jimmy Golen, "Small Colleges Weigh Academics, Athletics," *Bangor (ME) Daily News*, January 10, 2002.

28. Shulman and Bowen, *The Game of Life*, xvii.

29. Hal S. Scott, "What Game Are They Playing?," review of *The Game of Life*, by James L. Shulman and William G. Bowen, *Journal of College and University Law* 28, no. 3 (2002): 720.

30. Ibid., 721.

31. Ibid., 722.

32. Ibid.

33. Ibid., 723.

34. Ibid., 724.

35. Timothy B. Spears, *Spirals: A Family's Education in Football* (Lincoln: University of Nebraska Press, 2018), 137–38.

36. Bill Pennington, "Division III Seeks Harmony between Field and Classroom," *New York Times*, February 13, 2007.

37. L. Jon Wertheim, "Green Mountain Giant: Tiny Middlebury Produces Teams to Match Its Impressive Facilities," *Sports Illustrated*, November 30, 1998, 45.

38. Ibid.

39. Ibid.

40. "'Not Even Comparable': New Baseball/Softball Complex Opens," Colby College, April 4, 2016, https://www.colby.edu/news/2016/04/04/new-baseballsoftball-complex not even comparable/.

41. Wertheim, "Green Mountain Giant," 45.

42. Ibid.

43. Ronald D. Liebowitz, "Striking the Balance," *Middlebury Magazine*, Winter 2008, 26–27.

44. Ibid.

45. Pennington, "Division III Seeks Harmony."

46. Looney, "Pure and Simple," 77.

47. Pennington, "Division III Seeks Harmony."

48. John Dzik, "Richer Colleges, Better Teams," *Chronicle of Higher Education*, July 13, 2007, https://www.chronicle.com/article/richer-colleges-better-teams.

49. *The NCAA Division III Membership Survey: Findings*, National Collegiate Athletic Association, April 9, 2008, https://www.ncaa.org/sites/default/files/2008 DIII_Division_III_Membership_Survey_Report_20180420.pdf.

50. J. Copeland, "News Analysis: What's Next in Division III," *NCAA News*, April 9, 2008.

51. Looney, "Pure and Simple," 70.

52. "Jak Knelman," Elite Prospects, https://www.eliteprospects.com/player/37827/jak-knelman.

53. William H. Baaki, "Second Circuit Refuses to Second-Guess College Hockey Coach," *Sports and Entertainment Law Insider* (blog), June 27, 2014, https://sportslawinsider.com/litigation/second-circuit-refuses-to-second-guess-college-hockey-coach/ (site discontinued).

54. Ibid.

55. Ibid.

56. "Middlebury and Coach Beaney Respond to Jak Knelman's Lawsuit," NESCAC Hockey, June 15, 2011, https://nescachockey.wordpress.com/2011/06/15/middlebury-and-coach-beaney-respond-to-jak-knelmans-lawsuit/.

57. Ibid.

58. Ibid.

59. Ibid.

60. Baaki, "Second Circuit Refuses to Second-Guess College Hockey Coach."

61. Ibid.

62. "Middlebury's Beaney to Step Down as Hockey Coach," Middlebury College, March 4, 2015, http://www.middlebury.edu/newsroom/node/492118#:~:text=MIDDLEBURY%2C%20Vt.,successful%20careers%20in%20collegiate%20history.

63. Looney, "Pure and Simple," 78.

64. Rob Mahoney, "How Did the NBA Overlook One of the Best Shooters in Basketball?" *Ringer*, September 17, 2020, https://www.theringer.com/nba/2020/9/17/21439778/duncan-robinson-miami-heat-boston-celtics-playoffs.

65. "Catching Up with the Miami Heat's Duncan Robinson Who Played His First Year at Williams," Williams College, December 6, 2019, https://ephsports.williams.edu/sports/mbkb/2019-20/releases/2019 1206jnrc0l (URL discontinued).

66. Ricky O'Donnell, "Duncan Robinson Is Redefining What an NBA Player Can Be," *SB Nation*, March 6, 2020, https://www.sbnation.com/nba/2020/3/6/21166068/duncan-robinson-miami-heat-three-point-shooting-impact-stats-highlights.

67. "Undrafted Duncan Robinson Breaks Heat's 3-Pointer Mark," ESPN, March 6, 2020, https://www.espn.com/nba/story/_/id/28853493/undrafted-duncan-robinson-breaks-heat-3-pointer-mark.

Chapter 8

1. Roger Howell, memorandum to Athern Daggett on proposed athletic league, May 27, 1968.

2. John F. Rooney, Jr., *The Recruiting Game: Toward a New System of Intercollegiate Sports*, 2nd rev. ed. (Lincoln: University of Nebraska Press, 1987), 118.

3. *2019–20 NCAA Division III Manual* (Indianapolis, IN: National Collegiate Athletic Association, 2019), 70.

4. *The Second-Century Imperatives: Presidential Leadership, Institutional Accountability* (Indianapolis, IN: National Collegiate Athletic Association, 2006), 1.

5. Jacques Steinberg, *The Gatekeepers: Inside the Admissions Process of a Premier College* (New York: Viking, 2002), x.

6. *Ibid.*, 71.

7. Meeting of the presidents of Amherst, Bowdoin, Wesleyan, and Williams on athletic policies and agreements, report and proposed agenda, June 12, 1967, 1–2.

8. Paul Tough, "What College Admissions Offices Really Want," *New York Times Magazine*, September 10, 2019, https://www.nytimes.com/interactive/2019/09/10/magazine/college-admissions-paul-tough.html.

9. *Ibid.*

10. Richard Farley, interview by Charles Alberti, Williams College Oral History Project, July 22, 2003, 53.

11. Scott Smallwood, "Bowdoin College to Admit Fewer Athletes; Other Members of Conference Consider Similar Change," *Chronicle of Higher Education*, December 10, 2001, https://www.chronicle.com/article/bowdoin-college-to-admit-fewer-athletes-other-members-of-conference-consider-similar-change/.

12. Golen, "Small Colleges Weigh Academics, Athletics."

13. David D. Field, "Athletic Admissions Details," *EphBlog*, October 10, 2017, http://ephblog.com/2017/10/10/athletic-admissions-details/ (blog discontinued).

14. "Return to the Higher Ground," *Wesleyan University Magazine*, Spring 2002, 22.

15. *Ibid.*

16. Travis Lazarczyk, "Athletics & Academics," *Morning Sentinel* (central Maine), May 12, 2002.

17. Golen, "Small Colleges Weigh Academics, Athletics."

18. Smallwood, "Bowdoin College to Admit Fewer Athletes."

19. Golen, "Small Colleges Weigh Academics, Athletics."

20. Richard Farley, interview by Charles Alberti, July 22, 2003, 22.

21. *Ibid.*, 23.

22. William E. McCormick, interview by Charles Alberti, Williams College Oral History Project, July 24, 2002, 9.

23. Richard Farley, interview by Charles Alberti, July 22, 2003, 41.

24. *Ibid.*, 23–24.

25. *Ibid.*, 24.

26. *Ibid.*, 26.

27. *Ibid.*, 31–32.

28. Chris Meade, "Lacrosse Recruiting in the NESCAC," Tier One Athletics, February 26, 2013, http://www.tier1athletics.org/2013/02/26/lacrosse-recruiting-in-the-nescac/.

29. Sam Weyrauch, "Banded Together: Recruited Athletes with Sub-Average Academics Can Receive Preference in Admissions," *Bowdoin Orient*, March 28, 2014, https://bowdoinorient.com/bonus/article/9151.

30. Meade, "Lacrosse Recruiting in the NESCAC."

31. Bill Pennington, "One Division III Conference Finds That Playing the Slots System Pays Off," *New York Times*, December 25, 2005, https://www.nytimes.com/2005/12/25/sports/ncaafootball/one-division-iii-conference-finds-that-playing-the.html.

32. Tough, "What College Admissions Offices Really Want."

33. Ian Ward, "Farewell, Bowdoin Football," *Bowdoin Orient*, November 22, 2019,

https://bowdoinorient.com/2019/11/22/farewell-bowdoin-football/.

34. Ronald A. Smith, "From Normal School to State University: A History of the Wisconsin State University Conference," PhD diss., University of Wisconsin, 1969, 319, 327.

Epilogue

1. Looney, "Pure and Simple," 80.
2. R. Smith, "From Normal School to State University," 326.
3. Ibid., 319, 327.
4. Saahil Desai, "College Sports Are Affirmative Action for Rich White Students," *Atlantic*, October 23, 2018, https://www.theatlantic.com/education/archive/2018/10/college-sports-benefits-white-students/573688/.
5. Tough, "What College Admissions Offices Really Want."
6. Desai, "College Sports Are Affirmative Action for Rich White Students."
7. Bill Pennington, personal communication to author, November 13, 2019.
8. Joe Drape, "Shut Out, and Not Expecting a Quick Rally," *New York Times*, April 20, 2020.
9. Bill Pennington, "The Real Cost of Diversifying College Rosters," *New York Times*, November 9, 2019, https://www.nytimes.com/2019/11/07/sports/college-sports-diversity-amherst.html.
10. Ibid.
11. Tough, "What College Admissions Offices Really Want."
12. Pennington, "The Real Cost of Diversifying College Rosters."
13. Olivia Gieger and Natalie De Rosa, "Racist Incident Prompts Men's Lacrosse Probation, Coach Termination and BSU Activism for Greater Accountability," *Amherst Student*, March 27, 2020, https://amherststudent.com/article/racist-incident-prompts-mens-lacrosse-probation-coach-termination-and-bsu-activism-for-greater-accountability.
14. Ibid.
15. "Amherst Lacrosse Letter to the College Community," *Amherst Student*, March 27, 2020, https://amherststudent.com/article/amherst-lacrosse-letter-to-the-college-community.

16. Gieger and De Rosa, "Racist Incident Prompts Men's Lacrosse Probation."
17. *2019–20 NCAA Division III Manual*, 1.
18. Holt, *Sport and the British*, 98.
19. Alan Blinder and Billy Witz, "N.C.A.A. Talks Change, but It's a Hard Conversation," *New York Times*, January 25, 2020.
20. Ibid.
21. Dylan Dethier, "The Strange Saga of a Division III Golfer Who Got Kicked Out of the NCAA," *Golf*, October 4, 2019, https://golf.com/news/features/division-3-golf-dylan-dethier-ncaa/.
22. Ibid.
23. Ibid.
24. Looney, "Pure and Simple," 79.
25. Sweeney, "The Scholar-Athlete Standard Endures," 249.
26. Richard Farley, interview by Charles Alberti, July 22, 2003, 53.
27. Mike Lowe, "Time to Talk Football for Maine's College Coaches," *Portland (ME) Press Herald*, August 1, 2014, https://www.pressherald.com/2014/08/01/time-to-talk-football-for-maines-college-coaches/.
28. Ibid.
29. Looney, "Pure and Simple," 76.
30. Dan Spears, "Defending the Football Program," *Bowdoin Orient*, December 8, 2017, https://bowdoinorient.com/2017/12/08/defending-the-football-program/.
31. Ibid.
32. Ian Ward, "Head Football Coach Sued in Title IX Lawsuit," *Bowdoin Orient*, April 10, 2020, https://bowdoinorient.com/2020/04/10/head-football-coach-sued-in-title-ix-lawsuit/.
33. Ian Ward, "Faced with More of the Same, Bowdoin Football Takes the Long View," *Bowdoin Orient*, October 4, 2019, https://bowdoinorient.com/2019/10/04/faced-with-more-of-the-same-bowdoin-football-takes-the-long-view/.
34. Ernie Clark, "It's Game Time Again for Jack Cosgrove," *Bangor (ME) Daily News*, September 13, 2018, https://bangordailynews.com/2018/09/13/sports/college/its-game-time-again-for-jack-cosgrove/.
35. John Shipley, "It's Official: St. Thomas Has Been Kicked Out of MIAC," *St. Paul (MN) Pioneer Press*, May 22, 2019, https://www.twincities.com/2019/05/

22/st-thomas-kicked-out-of-miac-tommies-football-university/.

36. Randy Johnson, "St. Thomas Vows to 'Attack What's Next' After Being Kicked Out of MIAC," *Minneapolis Star Tribune*, May 23, 2019, http://www.startribune.com/st-thomas-vows-to-attack-what-s-next-after-being-kicked-out-of-miac/510270892/.

37. Shipley, "It's Official."

38. *Ibid.*

Bibliography

Allmendinger, David F. *Paupers and Scholars: The Transformation of Student Life in Nineteenth-Century New England.* New York: St. Martin's Press, 1975.

"Amherst Lacrosse Letter to the College Community." *Amherst Student,* March 27, 2020. https://amherststudent.com/article/amherst-lacrosse-letter-to-the-college-community.

Annual Report of the Director of Athletics. Submitted to President Kenneth C.M. Sills. Bowdoin College, April 21, 1950.

Austin, Brad. *Democratic Sports: Men's and Women's College Athletics during the Great Depression.* Fayetteville: University of Arkansas Press, 2015.

Axtell, James. "The Death of the Liberal Arts College." *History of Education Quarterly* 11, no. 4 (Winter 1971): 339–52.

Baaki, William H. "Second Circuit Refuses to Second-Guess College Hockey Coach." *Sports and Entertainment Law Insider* (blog), June 27, 2014. https://sportslawinsider.com/litigation/second-circuit-refuses-to-second-guess-college-hockey-coach/ (site discontinued).

Barnes, Everett D. 19th Hole: The Readers Take Over. *Sports Illustrated,* February 21, 1966, 75.

"Basketball Tourney Permit Denied by League." Press release. Union College News Release, February 15, 1972.

Beech, Mark. "A Global Racquet." *Sports Illustrated,* March 1, 2004, 30.

Bell, Andrew McIlwaine. *The Origins of Southern College Football: How an Ivy League Game Became a Dixie Tradition.* Baton Rouge: Louisiana State University Press, 2020.

Bergofsky, Eric. "Perpetual Panther Power." Letters, *Sports Illustrated,* October 28, 2002, 14.

Bidgood, Jess. "At Amherst College, Some Say It's the Mascot's Turn to Embrace Diversity." *New York Times,* October 31, 2015. https://www.nytimes.com/2015/11/01/us/at-amherst-some-say-its-the-mascots-turn-to-embrace-diversity.html.

Blinder, Alan, and Billy Witz. "N.C.A.A. Talks Change, but It's a Hard Conversation." *New York Times,* January 25, 2020.

Bok, Derek. "Intercollegiate Athletics." In *Contemporary Issues in Higher Education: Self-Regulation and the Ethical Roles of the Academy,* edited by John B. Bennett and J.W. Peltason, 123–46. New York: Macmillan, 1985.

Born, Edward. "A 16,000 Seat Proposal." *Bowdoin Alumnus,* March 1966.

Bowdoin College Bulletin: Catalogue for the Sessions of 1967-1968. No. 366. Brunswick, ME: Bowdoin College, September 1967.

Bowdoin College Bulletin: Catalogue for the Sessions of 1968-1969. No. 370. Brunswick, ME: Bowdoin College, September 1968.

"Bowdoin College Will Not Subject Its Scholarship Policy to NCAA Control." Press release. Bowdoin College News Service, January 24, 1966.

Bowen, William G., and Sarah A. Levin. *Reclaiming the Game: College Sports and Educational Values.* Princeton: Princeton University Press, 2003.

Brown, Herbert R. *Sills of Bowdoin: The Life of Kenneth Charles Morton Sills, 1879–1954.* New York: Columbia University Press, 1964.

Byers, Walter. *Unsportsmanlike Conduct: Exploiting College Athletes.* Ann Arbor: University of Michigan Press, 1995.

Cacciola, Scott. "Best Division III School: Williams College." *Sports Illustrated,* October 7, 2002, 67.

Calhoun, Charles C. *A Small College in Maine: Two Hundred Years of Bowdoin.* Brunswick, ME: Bowdoin College, 1993.

Carlson, E. "The World According to Darp." In *Passages of Time: Narratives in the History of Amherst College,* edited by Douglas C. Wilson, [PAGES TK]. Amherst, MA: Amherst College Press, 2007. [AU: Check.]

Carroll, John M. *Red Grange and the Rise of Modern Football.* Urbana: University of Illinois Press, 1999.

"Catching Up with the Miami Heat's Duncan Robinson Who Played His First Year at Williams." Williams College, December 6, 2019. https://ephsports.williams.edu/sports/mbkb/2019-20/releases/20191206jnrc01 (URL discontinued).

Chen, Albert. "A Little Goes a Long Way." *Sports Illustrated,* November 27, 2000, 38, 40.

Cicia, J. "A Breakout Decade for Women." In *Jumbo Footprints: A History of Tufts Athletics, 1952–1999,* edited by Rocco J. Carzo et al., 169–203. Medford, MA: Tufts University, 2005.

Clark, Ernie. "It's Game Time Again for Jack Cosgrove." *Bangor (ME) Daily News,* September 13, 2018. https://bangordailynews.com/2018/09/13/sports/college/its-game-time-again-for-jack-cosgrove/.

Clay, S., and M.I. Alaimo. "One Hell of a Decade." In *Jumbo Footprints: A History of Tufts Athletics, 1852–1999,* edited by Rocco J. Carzo et al., 207–41. Medford, MA: Tufts University, 2005.

Cohen, Arthur M., and Carrie B. Kisker. *The Shaping of American Higher Education: Emergence and Growth of the Contemporary System.* 2nd ed. San Francisco: Jossey-Bass, 2010.

Connolly, Francis J. "Chaos at 60 B." *Harvard Crimson,* September 16, 1977. https://www.thecrimson.com/article/1977/9/16/chaos-at-60-b-pif-harvards/.

Conroy, M., D. Estridge, and P. Rich. "Turmoil, Triumph—and a Call for Change." In *Jumbo Footprints: A History of Tufts Athletics, 1852–1999,* edited by Rocco J. Carzo et al., 136–65. Medford, MA: Tufts University, 2005.

Copeland, J. "News Analysis: What's Next in Division III." *NCAA News,* April 9, 2008.

Covell, Dan. "'And We're Dropping Them?': Managing Transitions in Intercollegiate Football at Bowdoin College, 1946–1964." *Sport History Review* 45, no. 1 (2014): 59–78.

Covell, Dan, and Claude Catapano. "'Whatever This Intangible Spirit Is': Hockey and Institutional Culture at Bowdoin College, 1956–1973." *Sport History Review* 46, no. 2 (2016): 193–213.

Dealy, Francis X. *Win at Any Cost: The Sell Out of College Athletics.* New York: Carol Publishing Group, 1990.

"Dean Reaffirms Bowdoin Stand." *Portland (ME) Press Herald,* March 10, 1966, 22.

Desai, Saahil. "College Sports Are Affirmative Action for Rich White Students." *Atlantic,* October 23, 2018. https://www.theatlantic.com/education/archive/2018/10/college-sports-benefits-white-students/573688/.

Dethier, Dylan. "The Strange Saga of a Division III Golfer Who Got Kicked Out of the NCAA." *Golf,* October 4, 2019. https://golf.com/news/features/division-3-golf-dylan-dethier-ncaa/.

Drape, Joe. "Shut Out, and Not Expecting a Quick Rally." *New York Times,* April 20, 2020.

Dude. "East Snowed, East Buried." *Bowdoin Orient,* March 6, 1970, 8.

Dzik, John. "Richer Colleges, Better Teams." *Chronicle of Higher Education,* July 13, 2007. https://www.chronicle.com/article/richer-colleges-better-teams.

Estes, Andrea, and Scott Allen. "Ex-UH President under Scrutiny Again." *Honolulu Star-Advertiser,* August 20, 2013. https://www.staradvertiser.com/2013/08/20/hawaii-news/ex-uh-president-under-scrutiny-again/.

"F. Alexis Schulten '66." Bowdoin Athletics. Accessed April 6, 2021. https://athletics.bowdoin.edu/sports/2020/5/20/information-history-hall-schulten.aspx.

Falla, Jack. *NCAA: Voice of College Sports—A Diamond Anniversary History, 1906–1981.* Mission, KS: National Collegiate Athletic Association, 1981.

Farley, Richard. Interview by Charles Alberti. Williams College Oral History Project, July 22, 2003.

Field, David D. "Athletic Admissions Details." *EphBlog*, October 10, 2017. http://ephblog.com/2017/10/10/athletic-admissions-details/ (blog discontinued).

"Former Trinity President Settles in Massachusetts College Spending Probe." Associated Press, April 30, 2015. https://www.courant.com/education/hc-evan-dobelle-settlement-0430-20150430-story.html.

"410 Colleges Meet N.C.A.A. 1.6 Standard." *New York Times*, February 20, 1966, 15.

Freeland, Richard M. *Academia's Golden Age: Universities in Massachusetts, 1945–1970*. New York: Oxford University Press, 1992.

Friedlander, Martin. "For the Times: Hair Today. Gone Tomorrow." *Bowdoin Orient*, November 8, 1968, 8.

Friedman, Dick. *The Coach Who Strangled the Bulldog: How Harvard's Percy Haughton Beat Yale and Reinvented Football*. Lanham, MD: Rowman & Littlefield, 2018.

"The Future of NESCAC in the NCAA Postseason." Orient Forum. *Bowdoin Orient*, November 7, 1997, 9.

Gargan, Edward A. "Union Reshapes Winning Attitude." *New York Times*, September 16, 1984.

Gems, Gerald R. *For Pride, Profit, and Patriarchy: Football and the Incorporation of American Cultural Values*. Latham, MD: Scarecrow Press, 2000.

Gieger, Olivia, and Natalie De Rosa. "Racist Incident Prompts Men's Lacrosse Probation, Coach Termination and BSU Activism for Greater Accountability." *Amherst Student*, March 27, 2020. https://amherststudent.com/article/racist-incident-prompts-mens-lacrosse-probation-coach-termination-and-bsu-activism-for-greater-accountability.

Golen, Jimmy. "Small Colleges Weigh Academics, Athletics." *Bangor (ME) Daily News*, January 10, 2002.

Grundy, Pamela. *Learning to Win: Sports, Education, and Social Change in Twentieth-Century North Carolina*. Chapel Hill: University of North Carolina Press, 2001.

"Guys and Dolls among the Ivy." *Sports Illustrated*, October 31, 1960, 26–31.

Hanley, Rachael. "Amherst Announces Mammoths Mascot." Amherst College, April 3, 2017. https://www.amherst.edu/news/news_releases/2017/4-2017/amherst-announces-mammoths-mascot.

Hardy, Stephen, and Andrew C. Holman. *Hockey: A Global History*. Urbana: University of Illinois Press, 2018.

Harvey, Giles. "The Royal We." *New York Times Magazine*, November 10, 2019, 28–31, 53–54.

Hatch, Louis C. *The History of Bowdoin College*. Portland, ME: Loring, Short & Harmon, 1927.

Haydel, Auban, and Kit Lasher. *The Fairest College? Twenty Years of Women at Amherst*. Amherst, MA: Amherst College, 1997.

Heckscher, August. *Woodrow Wilson: A Biography*. Newtown, CT: American Political Bibliography Press, 2007.

Helman, Jay W. "A History of American Intercollegiate Academic Eligibility: Educational Compromises to Competitive Interests." PhD diss. Pennsylvania State University, 1989.

Henrikson, Jillyan. "A Female Athlete in a Men's Athletic World: A Discussion with Beth Richardson, '79." Forty Years: The History of Women at Bowdoin, November 4, 2011. https://research.bowdoin.edu/forty-years-the-history-of-women-at-bowdoin/athletics/interview-beth-cantara-richardson-79.

———. "What about the Female Athletes? A Discussion with Richard (Dick) Mersereau, '69." Forty Years: The History of Women at Bowdoin, October 21, 2011. https://research.bowdoin.edu/forty-years-the-history-of-women-at-bowdoin/athletics/interview-richard-mersereau-bowdoin-women%E2%80%-99s-basketball-coach.

Higgs, Robert J. *God in the Stadium: Sports and Religion in America*. Lexington: University of Kentucky Press, 1995.

"Hockey Crisis of 1977." Schaffer Library, Union College, 2020. https://libguides.union.edu/ArchivesandSpecialCollections/HockeyCrisis#:~:text=In%201977%2C%20the%20Union%20College,from%20Union's%20administration%20and%20students.&text=Coach%20Harkness%20took%20

Bonner%20at,against%20the%20rules%20of%20NESCAC.

Holt, Richard. *Sport and the British: A Modern History*. Oxford, UK: Clarendon, 1990.

Hoover, Eric. "A Manly Old Guide to the Ivy League." *Chronicle of Higher Education*, September 12, 2014, 22.

Howell, Roger, Jr. *Report of the President to the Trustees and Overseers*. Brunswick, ME: Bowdoin College, 1970.

Huntington, D. "True Grit." *Bowdoin Alumnus*, March 1970, 8.

Hurst, R.M. Polar Bearings. *Bowdoin Orient*, November 11, 1953, 4.

Ingrassia, Brian M. "Conceptualizing 'Small-Time' College Athletics: The Fracture of the 'Little Nineteen' Conference in the 1930s." *Journal of Sport History* 47, no. 3 (Fall 2020): 191–209.

"Institutional Predictive Formula for Freshmen." Office of the Dean of the College, Bowdoin College, February 2, 1968.

"An Interim Agreement." Press release. Yale University News Bureau, February 20, 1967.

"Ivy Ace Penn Scratches from NCAA Hoop Event." *Portland (ME) Press Herald*, February 26, 1966, 10.

"Ivy League to Accept N.C.A.A. Academic Norm." *New York Times*, February 24, 1966, 16.

"Ivy Teams Will Shun N.C.A.A. Title Play." *New York Times*, March 6, 1966.

Jaffe, Michael. "Holy (Purple) Cow: After 32 Years of Self-Imposed Exile from Postseason Play, Williams Can Once Again Compete for the National Title." *Sports Illustrated*, November 29, 1993. https://www.webcitation.org/6Jzsg7RnQ?url=http://sportsillustrated.cnn.com/vault/article/magazine/MAG1138299/.

"Jak Knelman." Elite Prospects. https://www.eliteprospects.com/player/37827/jak-knelman.

Johnson, Randy. "St. Thomas Vows to 'Attack What's Next' After Being Kicked Out of MIAC." *Minneapolis Star Tribune*, May 23, 2019. http://www.startribune.com/st-thomas-vows-to-attack-whats-next-after-being-kicked-out-of-miac/510270892/.

Katz, Benjamin. "NESCAC Schools Band Together to Create Forum." *Williams Record*, November 17, 1998.

Katz, Matthew, and Chad Seifried. "And Then There Were Three: The NCAA's Struggle for Reorganization and the Emergence of Division III Athletics." *Sport History Review* 45, no. 2 (2014): 145–70.

Kerr, Clark. *The Gold and the Blue: A Personal Memoir of the University of California, 1949–1967*. Vol. 1. Berkeley: University of California Press, 2001.

Kjeldsen, Erik. "The Manager's Role in the Development and Maintenance of Ethical Behavior in the Sport Organization." *Journal of Sport Management* 6, no. 2 (1992): 99–113.

Knapp, Peter J. *Trinity College in the Twentieth Century: A History*. Hartford, CT: Trinity College, 2000.

LaPointe, Sally. "The State of Women's Athletics." Memorandum to Roger Howell, Jr. Bowdoin College, May 23, 1977. https://research.bowdoin.edu/forty-years-the-history-of-women-at-bowdoin/athletics/letter-from-sally-lapointe-to-president-howell.

Lawrence, Paul R. *Unsportsmanlike Conduct: The National Collegiate Athletic Association and the Business of College Football*. New York: Praeger, 1987.

Lazarczyk, Travis. "Athletics & Academics." *Morning Sentinel* (central Maine), May 12, 2002.

"Let Them Play." *Williams Record*, May 7, 1996, 2.

Letters. *Sports Illustrated*, November 21, 1994.

Levison, Lee M. "Origins of the New England Small College Athletic Conference." Unpublished manuscript. Trinity College, 1981.

Liebowitz, Ronald D. "Striking the Balance." *Middlebury Magazine*, Winter 2008, 26–27.

Lincoln, Chris. *Playing the Game: Inside Athletic Recruiting in the Ivy League*. White River Junction, VT: Nomad Press, 2004.

Litsky, Frank. "2-Day Track Meet Will Open Today." *New York Times*, March 11, 1966, 15.

"Little Ivy League?" *Bowdoin Orient*, December 16, 1959, 2.

Looney, Douglas S. "Pure and Simple." *Sports Illustrated*, October 31, 1994, 66–80.

Lowe, Mike. "Time to Talk Football for

Maine's College Coaches." *Portland (ME) Press Herald,* August 1, 2014. https://www.pressherald.com/2014/08/01/time-to-talk-football-for-maines-college-coaches/.

Ludwig, Jan K. "Bonner, Thomas Neville." In *Encyclopedia of Union College History,* edited by Wayne Somers, 115–20. Schenectady, NY: Union College Press, 2003.

MacCambridge, Michael. *The Franchise: A History of* Sports Illustrated *Magazine.* New York: Hyperion, 1997.

MacDonald, Joe. "How It All Began." *Nothing but NESCAC* (blog), July 19, 2016. https://nothingbutnescac.com/?page_id=80.

Mahoney, Rob. "How Did the NBA Overlook One of the Best Shooters in Basketball?" *Ringer,* September 17, 2020. https://www.theringer.com/nba/2020/9/17/21439778/duncan-robinson-miami-heat-boston-celtics-playoffs.

Malkiel, Nancy Weiss. *"Keep the Damned Women Out": The Struggle for Coeducation.* Princeton: Princeton University Press, 2016.

Marthers, Paul P. *"Eighth Sister No More": The Origins and Evolution of Connecticut College.* New York: Peter Lang, 2011.

Mattingly, Paul H. *American Academic Cultures: A History of Higher Education.* Chicago: University of Chicago Press, 2017.

McCormick, William E. Interview by Charles Alberti. Williams College Oral History Project, July 24, 2002.

Meade, Chris. "Lacrosse Recruiting in the NESCAC." Tier One Athletics, February 26, 2013. http://www.tier1athletics.org/2013/02/26/lacrosse-recruiting-in-the-nescac/.

"Men's Hockey History." Cornell University Athletics. http://www.cornellbigred.com/sports/2009/4/6/MICE_0406094147.aspx?path=mhockey.

Mersereau, Dick. Polar Bearings. *Bowdoin Orient,* January 13, 1967, 12.

"Middlebury and Coach Beaney Respond to Jak Knelman's Lawsuit." NESCAC Hockey, June 15, 2011. https://nescachockey.wordpress.com/2011/06/15/middlebury-and-coach-beaney-respond-to-jak-knelmans-lawsuit/.

"Middlebury's Beaney to Step Down as Hockey Coach." Middlebury College, March 4, 2015. http://www.middlebury.edu/newsroom/node/492118#:~:text=MIDDLEBURY%2C%20Vt., successful%20careers%20in%20collegiate%20history.

Miller, Chris. *The Real Animal House: The Awesomely Depraved Saga of the Fraternity That Inspired the Movie.* New York: Little, Brown, 2006.

Miller, John J. *The Big Scrum: How Teddy Roosevelt Saved Football.* New York: Harper, 2011.

Miller, Patrick B. "The Manly, the Moral, and the Proficient: College Sport in the New South." *Journal of Sport History* 24, no. 3 (Fall 1997): 285–316.

Miller, Richard I. *The Truth about Big-Time Football.* New York: William Sloane, 1953.

Miller v. Gillis, 315 F. Supp. 94 [N.D. Ill. 1969].

Mott, Ronald D. "The 100-Year Debate." *NCAA News,* January 4, 1995, 10–11.

Mulvoy, Mark. "The Poison Ivy in the Ivy League." *Sports Illustrated,* January 2, 1967, 44–46.

"N.C.A.A. Championships Are Slated for Next Week." *New York Times,* March 6, 1966, 8.

"N.C.A.A. Council-Sponsored Amendment to 1.600 Rule." National Collegiate Athletic Association, November 30, 1967.

The NCAA Division III Membership Survey: Findings. National Collegiate Athletic Association, April 9, 2008. https://www.ncaa.org/sites/default/files/2008DIII_Division_III_Membership_Survey_Report_20180420.pdf.

"NCAA Forum Follow-Up: Statement from Williams College Council." Williams College, 1998.

Needham, Henry Beach. "The College Athlete: How Commercialism Is Making Him a Professional." *McClure's Magazine,* June 1905, 115–28.

Nelson, Alan. "Admissions." In *Encyclopedia of Union College History,* edited by Wayne Somers, 11–15. Schenectady, NY: Union College Press, 2003.

nescac ghost. "If Schools in the NESCAC Were High School Stereotypes." Let's Run.com, March 18, 2013. https://www.letsrun.com/forum/flat_read.php?thread=5094021.

"NESCAC Presidents Adopt New Mission Statement and Make Decisions Regarding Post-Season Competition." New England Small College Athletic Conference, April 23, 1998.

"NESCAC Presidents Lift Ban on NCAA Team Competition for Three-Year Trial." New England Small College Athletic Conference, 1993.

"New England Small College Athletic Conference—Operational Policies." New England Small College Athletic Conference, August 23, 1971.

"New 'Triple Option' May Be Submitted." *NCAA News*, June 1, 1978, 4.

"'Not Even Comparable': New Baseball/Softball Complex Opens." Colby College, April 4, 2016. https://www.colby.edu/news/2016/04/04/new-baseball-softball-complex-not-even-comparable/.

O'Donnell, Ricky. "Duncan Robinson Is Redefining What an NBA Player Can Be." *SB Nation*, March 6, 2020. https://www.sbnation.com/nba/2020/3/6/21166068/duncan-robinson-miami-heat-three-point-shooting-impact-stats-highlights.

"Olympians on Campus." *Bowdoin Alumnus*, July 1972, 18–19.

Oriard, Michael. *Bowled Over: Big-Time College Football from the Sixties to the BCS Era*. Chapel Hill: University of North Carolina Press, 2009.

———. *King Football: Sport and Spectacle in the Golden Age of Radio and Newsreels, Movies and Magazines, the Weekly and Daily Press*. Chapel Hill: University of North Carolina Press, 2001.

Pappas, Peter, and Gary Graham. Polar Bearings. *Bowdoin Orient*, September 25, 1964, 6.

Parkyn, S.F. Letter to the editor. *Hartford (CT) Courant*, November 20, 1983, 8.

"Paul Assaiante." Bantam Sports. https://bantamsports.com/staff-directory/paul-assaiante/145.

Pennington, Bill. "Division III Seeks Harmony between Field and Classroom." *New York Times*, February 13, 2007.

———. "One Division III Conference Finds That Playing the Slots System Pays Off." *New York Times*, December 25, 2005. https://www.nytimes.com/2005/12/25/sports/ncaafootball/one-division-iii-conference-finds-that-playing-the.html.

———. "The Real Cost of Diversifying College Rosters." *New York Times*, November 9, 2019. https://www.nytimes.com/2019/11/07/sports/college-sports-diversity-amherst.html.

"Pentagonal Conference Upholds Post-Season Rule." *Bowdoin Orient*, March 1, 1962.

Perlstein, Rick. *Nixonland: The Rise of a President and the Fracturing of America*. New York: Scribner's, 2008.

Peterson, George E. *The New England College in the Age of the University*. Amherst, MA: Amherst College Press, 1964.

Potts, David B. *Wesleyan University, 1910–1970: Academic Ambition and Middle-Class America*. Middletown, CT: Wesleyan University Press, 2015.

"Prep School President Commits Suicide." Associated Press, January 11, 2008. https://groups.google.com/forum/#!topic/alt.obituaries/-s4pLXKYijY.

Proceedings of the 41st Annual Convention of the National Collegiate Athletic Association. Kansas City, MO: National Collegiate Athletic Association, 1947.

Proceedings of the 42nd Annual Convention of the National Collegiate Athletic Association. Kansas City, MO: National Collegiate Athletic Association, 1948.

Putnam, Pat. "No Heels in the Achilles." *Sports Illustrated*, February 7, 1977. https://vault.si.com/vault/1977/02/07/no-heels-in-the-achilles.

Quarterman, Jerome. "Managerial Role Profiles of Intercollegiate Athletic Conference Commissioners." *Journal of Sport Management* 8, no. 2 (1994): 129–39.

Rader, Benjamin G. *American Sports: From the Age of Folk Games to the Age of Televised Sports*. 6th ed. Upper Saddle River, NJ: Pearson; Prentice Hall, 2009.

Rand, Frank Prentice. *Yesterdays at Massachusetts State College, 1863–1933*. Amherst, MA: Associate Alumni of Massachusetts State College, 1933.

Remnick, David. *King of the World: Muhammad Ali and the Rise of an American Hero*. New York: Random House, 1998.

Report on Varsity Athletics. Williams College Ad Hoc Faculty Committee on Athletics, May 2002.

"Return to the Higher Ground." *Wesleyan*

University Magazine, Spring 2002, 22–23.
Roberts, Randy, and Johnny Smith. *War Fever: Boston, Baseball, and America in the Shadow of the Great War*. New York: Basic Books, 2020.
Rooney, John F., Jr. *The Recruiting Game: Toward a New System of Intercollegiate Sports*. 2nd rev. ed. Lincoln: University of Nebraska Press, 1987.
Rorer, Katherine. "The Process of Co-education at Amherst College and Trinity College." Student paper. Trinity College, May 3, 2012. https://commons.trincoll.edu/edreform/2012/05/the-process-of-co-education-at-amherst-college-and-trinity-college.
Rosenberg, Michael. *War as They Knew It: Woody Hayes, Bo Schembechler, and America in a Time of Unrest*. New York: Grand Central Publishing, 2008.
Rudolph, Frederick. *The American College and University: A History*. Rev. ed. Athens: University of Georgia Press, 1990.
———. *Mark Hopkins and the Log: Williams College, 1836–1872*. New Haven: Yale University Press, 1956.
Sack, Allen L., and Ellen J. Staurowsky. *College Athletes for Hire: The Evolution and Legacy of the NCAA's Amateur Myth*. Westport, CT: Praeger, 1998.
Samuelson, P. "Banquet Speakers, Watters, Pelham Search for Well-Balanced Students." *Williams Record*, February 6, 1959.
Savage, Howard J., et al. *American College Athletics*. New York: Carnegie Foundation for the Advancement of Teaching, 1929.
Sawyer, John. "NESCAC Philosophy: Remarks at NESCAC Presidents' Executive Committee Meeting." New England Small College Athletic Conference, May 1971.
Schmidt, Raymond. *Shaping College Football: The Transformation of an American Sport, 1919–1930*. Syracuse: Syracuse University Press, 2007.
Scott, Hal S. "What Game Are They Playing?" Review of *The Game of Life*, by James L. Shulman and William G. Bowen. *Journal of College and University Law* 28, no. 3 (2002): 719–55.
The Second-Century Imperatives: Presidential Leadership, Institutional Accountability. Indianapolis, IN: National Collegiate Athletic Association, 2006.
Shea, E.J. "Clubs Teams and a Quest for Belonging." In *Jumbo Footprints: A History of Tufts Athletics, 1852–1999*, edited by Rocco J. Carzo et al., 23–32. Medford, MA: Tufts University, 2005.
———. "A Lead Position—Scholarship First, then Sports." In *Jumbo Footprints: A History of Tufts Athletics, 1852–1999*, edited by Rocco J. Carzo et al., 55–67. Medford, MA: Tufts University, 2005.
Sheldon, Henry D. *Student Life and Customs*. Rev. ed. New York: Arno Press, 1969.
Shipley, John. "It's Official: St. Thomas Has Been Kicked Out of MIAC." *St. Paul (MN) Pioneer Press*, May 22, 2019. https://www.twincities.com/2019/05/22/st-thomas-kicked-out-of-miac-tommies-football-university/.
Shulman, James L., and William G. Bowen. *The Game of Life: College Sports and Educational Values*. Princeton: Princeton University Press, 2001.
Smallwood, Scott. "Bowdoin College to Admit Fewer Athletes; Other Members of Conference Consider Similar Change." *Chronicle of Higher Education*, December 10, 2001. https://www.chronicle.com/article/bowdoin-college-to-admit-fewer-athletes-other-members-of-conference-consider-similar-change/.
Smith, Asa. Polar Bearings. *Bowdoin Orient*, January 18, 1962, 3.
Smith, Earl H. *Mayflower Hill: A History of Colby College*. Hanover, NH: University Press of New England, 2006.
Smith, Ronald A. "From Normal School to State University: A History of the Wisconsin State University Conference." PhD diss. University of Wisconsin, 1969.
———. *Pay for Play: A History of Big-Time College Athletic Reform*. Chicago: University of Illinois Press, 2011.
———. *Sports and Freedom: The Rise of Big-Time College Athletics*. New York: Oxford University Press, 1988.
Sojka, Gregory S. "Evolution of the Student-Athlete in America." *Journal of Popular Culture*, 16, no. 4 (Spring 1983): 54–67.
Solberg, Winton U. *Creating the Big Ten: Courage, Corruption and Commercialization*. Urbana: University of Illinois Press, 2018.

Somers, Wayne, ed. *Encyclopedia of Union College History*. Schenectady, NY: Union College Press, 2003.

Spears, Dan. "Defending the Football Program." *Bowdoin Orient*, December 8, 2017. https://bowdoinorient.com/2017/12/08/defending-the-football-program/.

Spears, Timothy B. *Spirals: A Family's Education in Football*. Lincoln: University of Nebraska Press, 2018.

Sperber, Murray. *Onward to Victory: The Crises That Shaped College Sports*. New York: Henry Holt, 1998.

———. *Shake Down the Thunder: The Creation of Notre Dame Football*. New York: Henry Holt, 1993.

"Statement from the Commission on Post-Season Athletic Competition." Williams College, September 1998.

"Statement of Presidents of the New England Small College Athletic Conference." New England Small College Athletic Conference, 1997.

Steinberg, Jacques. *The Gatekeepers: Inside the Admissions Process of a Premier College*. New York: Viking, 2002.

Suggs, Welch. *A Place on the Team: The Triumph and Tragedy of Title IX*. Princeton: Princeton University Press, 2005.

———. "Postseason Play Creates Tensions for an Unusual Athletics Conference." *Chronicle of Higher Education*, June 18, 1999.

Sullivan, Dean A., ed. *Early Innings: A Documentary History of Baseball, 1825–1908*. Lincoln: University of Nebraska Press, 1995.

A Summary of an Agreement among the Presidents of Amherst College, Bowdoin College, Wesleyan University and Williams College Concerning Intercollegiate Athletics and Related Activities. Middletown, CT: Wesleyan University, 1969.

Sweeney, Paul. "The Scholar-Athlete Standard Endures." In *Jumbo Footprints: A History of Tufts Athletics, 1852–1999*, edited by Rocco J. Carzo et al., 245–67. Medford, MA: Tufts University, 2005.

Sweitzer, Kyle V. "Institutional Ambitions and Athletic Conference Affiliation." *New Directions for Higher Education* 148, no. 148 (Winter 2009): 55–63.

Szostak, Mike. "College Picks." *Providence (RI) Journal*, November 8, 1997.

Tamte, Roger R. *Walter Camp and the Creation of American Football*. Urbana: University of Illinois Press, 2018.

"That Impenetrable Athletic Policy." *Colby Echo*, November 7, 1969. https://digitalcommons.colby.edu/cgi/viewcontent.cgi?article=3190&context=colbyecho.

Thelin, John R. *The Cultivation of Ivy: A Saga of the College in America*. Cambridge, MA: Schenkman Publishing, 1976.

———. *Games Colleges Play: Scandal and Reform in Intercollegiate Athletics*. Baltimore: Johns Hopkins Press, 1996.

———. *A History of American Higher Education*. 3rd ed. Baltimore: Johns Hopkins University Press, 2019.

Tiede, Joseph S. Letter to editor. *Bowdoin Alumnus*, July 1966.

Tough, Paul. "What College Admissions Offices Really Want." *New York Times Magazine*, September 10, 2019. https://www.nytimes.com/interactive/2019/09/10/magazine/college-admissions-paul-tough.html.

"Trinity Athletic Teams Excited About New Facilities and Fields." Trinity College, March 27, 2017. https://bantamsports.com/sports/2020/5/28/Information-Athletics-51617.aspx.

"Trinity Men's Squash Tops Yale in Dramatic Fashion for 13th Straight National Title." Bantam Sports, February 27, 2011. https://bantamsports.com/news/2011/7/7/7_7_2011_3442.aspx.

Turner, Paul Venable. *Campus: An American Planning Tradition*. New York: Architectural History Foundation, 1984.

2019–20 NCAA Division III Manual. Indianapolis, IN: National Collegiate Athletic Association, 2019.

"Undrafted Duncan Robinson Breaks Heat's 3-Pointer Mark." ESPN, March 6, 2020. https://www.espn.com/nba/story/_/id/28853493/undrafted-duncan-robinson-breaks-heat-3-pointer-mark.

"Unrest Is Found to Be Widespread among Faculty Members as well as Students; Many Groups Are Split." *Chronicle of Higher Education*, September 15, 1969.

Velez, K. "The New England Small College Athletic Conference, 1971–1997: A Retrospective." Unpublished manuscript. Williams College, 1997.

Wachter, Paul. "After 14-Year Run, Squash

Juggernaut Loses a Match." *New York Times,* January 20, 2012.

———. "Squashing the Ivies." *New York Times Magazine,* February 20, 2011, 36–39.

Wald, Matthew L. "Trinity's New Hand at the Helm." *New York Times,* June 21, 1981. https://www.nytimes.com/1981/06/21/nyregion/trinity-s-new-hand-at-the-helm.html.

Ward, Ian. "Faced with More of the Same, Bowdoin Football Takes the Long View." *Bowdoin Orient,* October 4, 2019. https://bowdoinorient.com/2019/10/04/faced-with-more-of-the-same-bowdoin-football-takes-the-long-view/.

———. "Farewell, Bowdoin Football." *Bowdoin Orient,* November 22, 2019. https://bowdoinorient.com/2019/11/22/farewell-bowdoin-football/.

———. "Head Football Coach Sued in Title IX Lawsuit." *Bowdoin Orient,* April 10, 2020. https://bowdoinorient.com/2020/04/10/head-football-coach-sued-in-title-ix-lawsuit/.

Wertheim, L. Jon. "Green Mountain Giant: Tiny Middlebury Produces Teams to Match Its Impressive Facilities." *Sports Illustrated,* November 30, 1998, 45.

Weyrauch, Sam. "Banded Together: Recruited Athletes with Sub-Average Academics Can Receive Preference in Admissions." *Bowdoin Orient,* March 28, 2014. https://bowdoinorient.com/bonus/article/9151.

"Which Colleges Have the Largest Endowments?" *Chronicle of Higher Education,* January 31, 2019. https://www.chronicle.com/article/Which-Colleges-Have-the/245587.

White, Gordon S., Jr. "N.C.A.A. Gives 57 Colleges Extension on Scholastic Code." *New York Times,* February 18, 1966, 14.

Whitman, Alden. "James P. Baxter 3d Dies; Ex-President of Williams." *New York Times,* June 19, 1975, 38.

Williams, Richard. "Kirkland College 52 Years Later." Clinton Historical Society, December 18, 2019. https://clintonhistory.org/kirkland-college-52-years-later.

"Williams Reported Harkness." *Holyoke (MA) Transcript-Telegram,* March 18, 1977, 15.

Wolfe, Faye S. "The Man to Do It: Making Sense of the Relationship between Trinity College and Hartford." *UMASS Magazine,* Winter 1998. https://www.umass.edu/umassmag/archives/1998/winter_98/wint98_f_trinity.html.

Index

Numbers in **_bold italics_** refer to pages with illustrations

academics and athletics 5, 8, 12, 13, 16, 17, 18, 27, 37, 52, 82, 92, 94, 129, 141, 221; *see also* idealism; realism
Achilles, H. Laurence 110
Achilles Center 110, 112, 116
Adams, William 193
Adamski, Bryan 165
admissions 160, 163, 170, 192, 194, 198, 204, 207, 214; *see also* banding; diversity; tips; *see also* individual institutions
Alfond, Harold 189
Ali, Muhammad 9
Allegheny College 224
Altman, Koby 9
alumni 2, 9, 10, 11, 13, 24, 26, 27, 31–33, 37–43, 47–48, 51, 61, 62, 66, 68, 69, 73, 74, 78, 79, 85, 86, 98, 100, 103, 111, 112, 118, 120, 122, 123, 126, 129, 130, 132, 133, 137, 148, 154, 161, 163, 164, 165, 170–175, 178, 182, 187–191, 194, 202, 208, 209, 216, 221–223, 225, 227
Alumni Gym (Bates) 173
Amateur Athletic Union (AAU) 61
American College Testing 59
American Council on Education 46
American Southwest Conference 176
Ames, Oakes 123, 127
Amherst, Lord Jeffery 10
Amherst College 5, 6, 12, 23, 24–25, 79, 103, 106, 112, 123, 127–128, 129–130, 191, 215–216, 221–222; admissions 9, 21, 160–162, 175, 193, 198, 211–212; alliances 15, 18, 26, 39–44, 76–77, 80, 84–86, 96, 98–99, 154; control 24, 29, 30, 155; eligibility 33, 62–63, 70; endowment, 9, 213; financial aid 33; postseason 92, 138–139, 142, 146–147, 150, 152, 156; practice 52; recruiting 46–51, 52–53, 186–188, 200–203, 203–206, 213–215; schedule 90 124–125; *see also* names of athletic directors, coaches, presidents
Anaheim Ducks 130

Animal House 9
Apple, Henry 31
archery 105
Arlanson, Harry 76, 83
Armstrong, James 80, 116
Assaiante, Paul 160–164
Associated Press 76
athletic directors 1, 19, 41, 45, 53, 67, 74, 81, 83, 84, 88–89, 93–94, 117, 142, 175; *see also* names of individuals
The Atlantic Magazine 211, 212
Auerr, Allen 69–70
automatic qualifiers (AQ) 156
autonomy 16–17, 20–21, 33, 60, 75, 96
Aydelotte, Franklin 14

Babson College 173
badminton 105
Baldwin Wallace University 130
"banding system" 21, 162, 197–198, 207, 211, 214, 227
Bantams 10, 163–164, 222; *see also* Trinity University
Barnes, Everett D. "Eppy" 60
Barnum, P.T. 10
Bartlett, Scott 180
Bartlett, Wendy 164, 165
baseball 12, 24–25, 30–31, 41, 44, 83, 88, 92, 128, 132, 136–138, 145, 165, 173, 202, 210, 227
basketball 6, 20, 36–37, 56, 59, 64, 70, 83, 92, 105, 107, 108, 109, 125, 135, 145, 151–152, 156–157, 183–184, 191, 216
Bates College 5, 31, 79, 128, 168, 173, 222, 226; admissions 9, 193; alliances 4, 41, 74 84–89, 91, 125; financial aid 33; postseason 137–138; recruiting 188; schedule 87, 90, 125, 152; *see also* names of athletic directors, coaches, presidents
Baxter, James Phinney III 43, 50, 78, 82, 139
Baylor University 116

257

Index

Beal, Richard 130
Beaney, Bill 20, 173, 171, 177–182, *183*
Belichick, Bill 9, 225
Bell, Andrew 26
Bennet, Douglas 193
Benton, Otis 25
Berenson, Senda 105
Berger-Sweeney, Joanne 78
Bergeron, Katherine 78
Bergofsky, Eric 160, 167
Bergofsky, Julia *160*
Bicknell, Ray 108
Biddiscombe, John 133, 134
Big Conference 39, 183–184
"Big Three" 41; *see also* Harvard; Princeton; Yale
"big-time" [programs] 6–7, 14–17, 25, 29, 35, 36, 39, 41, 46, 56, 59, 61, 109, 113, 174, 174, 208–210, 218, 228
Bixler, J. Seelye 136–138, 145
Bobcats 10, 222; *see also* Bates College
Bok, Derek 169
Bonner, Thomas 109, 164
Born, Edward 61
Boschert, Sherry 106
Bossidy, John Collins 42
Boston College 32, 58, 114
Boston, Concord, and Montreal Railroad 24
Boston Globe 130
Boston University 62, 123
Bowdoin College 5, 13, 25, 27, 31, 37, 47–48, 101–103, 129–130, 170, 222–224, 226, 227; admissions 9, 83, 107–108, 115, 206; alliances 15, 18–19, 26, 39, 40, 41, 43, 44, 76, 77, 80, 81, 83–84, 86, 88–89, 91–93, 96–98; control 25, 29, 140–141; eligibility 56, 60–64, 65–67, 82; financial aid 7, 27, 33, 67, 69–72, 213; postseason 61–62, 83, 99, 135–136, 137–138, 139, 140, 142–144, 156; practice 36, 44; recruiting 27, 46, 47, 48–51, 156–157, 185, 186, 187–188, 193, 197, 198, 207–208; schedule 42, 87, 152; *see also* names of athletic directors, coaches, presidents
Bowdoin College Bulletin 68
Bowen, William G. "Bill" 38, 134. *167*; Academic Index model 196, 197, 207, 227; study of athletics on NESCAC campuses 166–171, 174, 190
bowling 105
Bradley, John, 101
Bradley University 36
Bradner, James, Jr. 65–66
Brand, Myles 185
Brandeis University 122, 177
Brewster, Kingman 66, 68
Brown Conference (1898) 39
Brown University 9, 45, 49, 81, 105, 106
Bryn Mawr College 31

Buckley, Ryan 150
Bucknell University 63
Budweiser 129
Bullock, J.E. 40
Butt, Charlie 188
Butterfield, Victor 27, 43–55, 80–81, 85, 139–141

Cacciola, Scott 159
Cahill, Tom 110
Calhoun, M. Grace 217
Camels 10; *see also* Connecticut College
Campbell, Colin 122, 123, 129, 166
Canadian players *see* international players
Canisius College 36
Caputi, Dave 223, 224
Cardinals 10, 27, 179, 222; *see also* Wesleyan University
Carleton College 171, 226
Carlson, Tucker 9
Carlton, Amy 176
Carnegie Foundation for the Advancement of Teaching 31–33, 39
Carnegie Report (1929) 18, 30, 31, 34–35, 169
Caruso, Glenn 226
Carzo, Rocky 124, 129
Casey, John 12, 18, 207, 210
Castro, Rodrigo 215
Cavanaugh, Frank 32
Chace, William 133
Chadbourne, Paul 23
championships 2, 8, 10, 16, 20, 37, 42, 43, 60, 63, 67, 88, 95–96, 100, 134, 142, 152, 176–177, 225; *see also* individual institutions, postseason; NCAA championships
Chandler, John 92, *93*, 96, 98–99, 109, 118, 123, 144, 146, 226
Cherington, Ben 9
Chicago Conference (1985) 39
Chicago Steel 179
Chouinard, Ray 69
Chronicle of Higher Education 155, 176
Cisneros, Henry 161
The Citadel 58
civil rights 101; *see also* diversity; Title IX
Civil War 25
Claflin, John 24
Claremont Colleges 192; *see also* names of individual institutions
Clarkson University 112
Cleary, Bill 78
Clemson University 58
coaches 1–2, 8, 15, 21, 25, 27, 28, 38, 41, 44–45, 47, 55, 67, 76, 82, 83, 99–100, 101–102, 108, 118, 129, 132, 135, 136, 141–142, 154, 157, 170, 175, 178, 180, 222, 225, 228; faculty status 19, 31, 33; recruiting 46, 48, 50–51, 53–54, 81, 114, 121, 139, 191, 193–96, 100–

Index

200, 203–206, 210, 213; women coaches 105–107, 136; *see also* names of coaches
coeducation 13, 19, 52, 102–103, 108, 123, 125, 127, 188
Coffey, Suzanne 193
Colby College 5, 13, 106, 108, 128, 173, 222, 223, 224, 226; admissions 9, 193, 207; alliances 5, 41, 74, 77, 83–86, 88, 89, 92, 96, 104; control 165, 148; financial aid 70–71, 189; postseason 83, 136, 137–138, 151, 156; recruiting 115, 186, 188–189; schedule 87, 90, 152; *see also* names of athletic directors, coaches, presidents
Cole, Charles 43–44, 46–51, 76, 139
Coleman, Richard 16–17
Coles, James Stacy "Spike" 45–51, 53, 60, 71, 75, 80, 137–142
Colgate University 9, 63, 106, 179
College Football Hall of Fame 201
College of the Holy Cross 138
Colorado College 171
Columbia University 23, 27, 30, 43, 45, 53, 86, 102, 129
compensation 21, 217, 218–220
Conant, James 33
Connecticut College 5, 7, 13, 123, 126, 173; admissions 192, 196, 198; alliances 19, 28, 122–125, 127–128; endowment 126; postseason 152; schedule 124; *see also* names of athletic directors, coaches, presidents
Connecticut College for Women 123
Continentals 10, 222; *see also* Hamilton College
Coolidge, Calvin 9
Coombs, Jack 9
Coombs Field 173
Cooper, Kevin 180
Corey, C. Nels 49
Cornell Agricultural College 115
Cornell University 26, 43, 78, 82, 110, 111, 114–115, 120, 202, 212
Cosgrove, Jack 224
Costello, Richard 96
Cotter, Bill 125, 148
Covell, Waldo 73
COVID 184
Cowie, Marcus 163
cross country 37, 113, 132, 137, 138, 159, 172
Cullen, John 108, 135, 199
Curtiss, John D. 78

Daggett, Athern 71, 83–89
Daley, Arthur 77
Darden, Colgate, Jr. 58
Dartmouth College 2, 9, 12–13, 15, 26, 39; joins Ivy League 40, 44, 51, 78–79, 114, 123, 127, 160, 186–187
Davidson, Carter 109

Dayton Arena 173
deaths 25, 28
DeFrantz, Anita 9
Delvecchio, Alex 111
Desai, Saahil 211
Dethier, Dylan 218–220
diversity 52, 60, 162, 169, 173, 190, 210–216, 218
Dobelle, Evan 160–**163**, 164–165
Dorrance, Chris 187
Doyle, Bill 163
Doyle, Brandon 174, 180
Drake Group 2
Dunbar, Don 187
Dunbar, Scott 187–188
Dupree, Marcus 5
Dutcher, Dan 176–177
Dzik, John 176

EA Sports 218
Earlham College 225
Eastern College Athletic Conference (ECAC) 1, 43, 96, 99, 111, 142–144
Edwards, Bob 166
Eliot, Charles 28
Elkins, 21
Ellis, Dorothea "Dorie" 105
Ellis, Faith 105
Emily Dickenson College [fictitious] 9
Emmert, Mark 217
endowments 2, 9, 110, 126, 160, 176, 195, 233
English, James 79, 121, 124, 132, 160
entertainment 14, 26, 129
Ephs 10, 159, 183, 193, 222; *see also* Williams College
Equity and Excellence in American Higher Education 170
Erickson, Herb 101
ESPN 5, 129, 164
Esten, Phil 226
Etherington, Edwin "Ted" 85–95, 122, 142–143
Evansville University 138

Faber College [fictitious] 9
facilities 6, 73, 76, 106, 108, 111, 115, 123, 128, 160, 165, 172–173, 178, 200, 210; *see also* named facilities
faculties 1, 6, 13, 14, 23, 25–26, 28–29, 38, 39, 50, 57, 72, 80, 86, 92, 96–98, 102, 110, 118, 120, 123, 126, 134, 136, 138, 140, 144, 146, 147–148, 159, 161, 168, 170, 181–182, 187, 188, 191, 194, 197
Fainstein, Norman 127
Fairbanks, Chuck 6
Family Guy 9
Farley, Dick 176, 192, 194–195, 201, 221–222
Faulstick, Don 78, 216
Fauver, Edgar 27

Index

fencing 105
field hockey 1, 2, 105, 107, 124, 152, 159, 172
"Fighting Methodists" 10; *see also* Wesleyan
Finazzo, Dylan 215
Flood, George 100
football 1, 2, 6, 13, 14, 15, 17, 21, 24-33, 36-37, 40-41, 43, 48-50, 52, 61, 69-71, 75, 77, 82-84, 87, 88, 90, 92, 104, 106, 110, 112-113, 121, 123, 128, 129, 133-134, 139, 149, 151-152, 172, 178, 188-191, 195, 199-200, 201, 203, 210, 216, 221-227
Ford Foundation 125
Fordham University 32
foreign players *see* international players
Fortune Magazine 102
Frank, Steve 203
Franklin & Marshall College 31
fraternities 24, 61, 113, 169, 189
Fuller, Thomas 208

Galbraith, Drew 78
Game of Life: College Sports and Educational Values 166
Garfield, Harry 27
Garfield, James 9
Gaudiani, Claire 7
Gerety, Tom 7-8, 12, 160, 174
Gilchrist, Mickey 180
Gingold, Eric 6
Goheen, Robert 64
golf 9, 131, 205, 218, 219
Gooding, Peter 120-121, 125-128, 134-135, 150-151, 154-158, 221, 223
Goodwin, Doris Kearns 9
Gowen, Dick "Red" 49
Graddock, Mason 180
Grange, Harold "Red" 30
Greason, A. LeRoy, Jr. 70-72, 82, 86, 98-99
Green Bay Packers 130
Greene, David 173, 225
Griffin, Meg 9
Grinnell College 225
Gumbel, Bryant 9
Gustavus Adolphus College 227
gymnastics 24, 25, 211, 225

hair grooming 101-102
Hallock, Wiles 63
Hallowell, Burton 75
Hamilton College 5, 99, 103, 173, 226; admissions 9, 166, 202-203; alliances 74, 92, 95, 122, 127; postseason 150; recruiting 203; schedule 152; *see also* names of athletic directors, coaches, presidents
Hamline University 226
Hammer, B.J. 224
hammer throw 19, 60, 61-62
Hardy, Erland 3, 100, *103*

Hardy, Stephen "Steve" 3, 16, 82, *103*, 110-111, 114-116, 120, 132, 186
Harkness, Nevin "Ned" 82, 110-*114*, 115-121, 192
Harmon, Major General E.N. 10, 80
Hartford (CT) 79, 160-161
Hartford Courant 79, 164
Harvard Business School 168
Harvard College 11
Harvard Divinity School 137
Harvard Law School 167
Harvard School of Public Health 124
Harvard University 9, 11, 13, 24, 25-26, 28, 33-34, 43, 52, 53, 78, 82, 91, 114, 115, 120, 123, 125, 160, 163, 167, 169, 211, 217
Hatch, Bob 125
Haverford College 76, 146
Heath, Jack 188
Hebert, Guy 10, 130
Heisman Trophy 201
Hersey, Jeanette 124
"hilltop colleges" 12-14, 16, 40, 75, 160, 211
Hobart College 76
hockey *see* field hockey; ice hockey
Holiday Magazine 42
Holt, Charlie 186
"hothouse generation" 177-178, 182, 200
Houston, Clarence "Pop" 136
Howard, Heidi 172
Howell, Roger, Jr. 69-70, 84-86, 89, 91-99, 102, 109, 142-144, *147*, 185, 207
Hull, Roger 122
Hutcherson, Austin 184
Hyde, William 28

ice hockey 1, 19, 22, 28, 82, 99-100, 101, 103, 136, 142-144, 145, 159-160, 164, 165, 172, 173, 175, 179-182, 188, 190, 192; controversy 109-122
idealism 4, 7, 12, 14, 16-18, 32-33, 39, 47, 50, 52, 55-61, 95, 100, 128-130, 133-138, 146, 149, 152, 159, 166-175, 180, 207, 210-211, 218, 228
injuries 25, 26, 28, 105
intercollegiate athletic conference 19, 38, 76
Intercollegiate Lawn Tennis Association 25
international players 114-115, 119, 120, 161-162, 164, 212, 163-164
Ithaca College 131
Ivy League 15, 16, 19, 38-4, 46, 55, 59, 63, 68, 77, 79, 81-82, 104, 108, 112, 114, 115, 120, 133, 161-162, 164, 184, 197, 200, 202, 204, 211, 224
Ivy League Academic Index 196

Jackson College (Tufts) 104-105
John Joseph Magee Memorial Track 73
Jones, James 165
Joseph, Donald 188
Journal of College and University Law 167
Jumbos 10, 145, 222; *see also* Tufts University

Index

Kalamazoo College 165
Katten, Brian 29, 155
Katz, Matthew 37
Kelley, Jack 115
Kendrick, Nathaniel 65
Kennedy, John F. 43
Kent State University 98, 102, 143
Kentucky Wesleyan College 138
Kenyon, Chip 172
Kenyon College 171, 204
Kerr, Clark 14
Kershner, Thomas 117
Kings College 23
Kirkland College (Hamilton) 103
Kirkpatrick, Robert 209
Knelman, James "Jak" 20, 177–184
Kunzelmann, Sue 113
Kurth, Karl 145

lacrosse 106–108, 125, 145–148, 152, 159, 168, 172, 173, 174, 215
Lane, David 188–*190*
LaPointe, Sally 107
Lawrence University 186
Lehigh University 33, 63
Levin, Sarah 38, 174
Levy, Zafi 163
Liebowitz, Ronald 171–177, 196–198
Liston, Sonny 9
Little East Conference 95
Little Eight League 83
Little Four 43; *see also* Bowdoin; Middlebury; Trinity; Wesleyan
Little Ivy League "Little Ivies" 2, 19, 42, 76–79
Little Six League 83
Little Three 41–42, 50, 75, 78, 86, 90, 92, 215, 222; *see also* Amherst; Wesleyan; Williams
Livingston, Robert 80
Loomis, Frederic Brewster 10
Looney, Douglas 4–8, 30, 113, 122, 130–136, 159, 167, 173–178, 182, 209–210, 215, 221, 223
Lord Jeffs 10
Louisiana State University 207
Lowell, Abbott Lawrence 13
Loyola Marymount University 30
Luce, Charles "Charlie" 123–*126*

Macalester College 226–227
MacCambridge, Michael 112
MacDonald, Duncan 113
Madden, John 129
Maker, Mike 183
Maldonado, Tom 180
Mammoths 10, 222; *see also* Amherst College
Mangini, Eric 9
Marist College 183
Marsh, Allison W. "Eli" 40

Marthers, Paul 123, 126–127
Martin, Elizabeth "Biddy" 212, **215**
Martin, Harold 85, 109–110
Mason, Chris 146
Massachusetts Institute of Technology 26
Massachusetts State College Athletic Conference 95
Mayer, Jean 123–125
McCabe, Ben 111
McClure's Magazine 45
McCormick, Bill 118–119, 194
McCurdy, Hugh 52, 141
McGee, Dick "Max" 125, 189–190
McKane, Dan 226
McKenna, Jamie 180
McNitt, Jim 187
Meagher, Terry 197
media 1, 17, 19, 20, 32, 38, 57, 76, 96, 113, 126, 128, 134, 147, 150, 155, 159, 164, 193, 217; *see also* names of student and national publications; networks; news outlets
Melendy, Lisa 42, 78, 175
Melling, John 101
Mellon Foundation 33, 166
men's lacrosse *see* lacrosse
Merrimack College 144
Mersereau, Dick 84, 108
Miami Heat 183
Michaeles, Jon 223–224
Michigan State University 119, 131
Middlebury College 1, 5, 7, 8, 9, 116–118, 173, 178, 222; admissions 9, 115, 196–197; alliances 74, 76, 77, 79, 89–81, 83, 84, 85, 89–90, 92, 96, 97; championships 159, 172, 174–175, 191–192; control 16, 20, 25; eligibility 43, 63; financial aid 213; lawsuit 179–182; postseason 83, 87–88, 135; recruiting 170, 175, 187, 206; schedule 87, 124–125, 152, 160; *see also* names of athletic directors, coaches, presidents
Middlesex Community College 165
Midwest Conference 226
Mills, Barry 193
Minnesota Intercollegiate Athletic Conference (MIAC) 226
Moll, Richard "Dick" 68, 70
Montville, Leigh 130
Moore, Harold 28
Moore, Sammy 29
Morgan, Edward 68
Morrell, Malcolm "Mal" 37, 40, 44, 46–51, 62, 66, 137–138, 141–142
Morrison, Charlie 120
Morrone, Joe 187
Moulton, Walter 68–70
Mount Holyoke College 123
Mount Union University 222
Mules 10, 190, 222; *see also* Colby College

262　　　　　　　　　　　　Index

Mulvoy, Mark 113–115
Murphy, Tom 152, 159

Name Image or Likeness (NIL) *see* compensation
National Basketball Association (NBA) 9, 20, 183–184
National Collegiate Athletic Association (NCAA): Division I 11, 17, 78, 106, 109, 112, 116, 118, 120, 122, 125, 150, 158, 172, 179, 183, 205, 213, 216, 220, 225; Division I-A 209; Division I Summit League 227; Division III 2, 6, 7–8, 14, 18, 20, 55. 65, 67, 79, 112, 116, 121, 127, 129–130, 131–135, 145, 148, 151, 157, 158, 160, 165, 171–172, 174–177, 193, 195, 211, 218, 219, 221, 224, 227; Division IIIA (proposed) 171; Division IV (proposed) 20, 174–177, 211; Division X (proposed) 171, 174
National Football League (NFL) 9
National Hockey League (NHL) 9, 111, 115, 130, 180
NCAA Council 37, 64, 71
NCAA Men's Basketball Tournament 64, 66, 80, 136, 138, 140, 156
Nebraska Wesleyan 172, 176
Needham, Henry Beach 45–46
New England College Conference on Athletics 44
New England Small College Athletic Conference (NESCAC): background 5–10; founding 95–99, future 210–228; influence on NCAA Division III; *see also* individual institutions
New England State College Athletic Conference 2, 74, 96
New England State Teacher's College Conference 95
New Haven Register 77
New Trier High School 188
New York Herald Tribune 77
New York State Agriculture Experiment Station 115
New York Times 63–64, 76–77, 119, 121, 164, 172, 175, 211, 217
New York Times Magazine 163, 211
New York University 28, 33, 36
New York Yankees 172
Newhall, Dick 87
Norris family 111
Northeastern Conference 94
Norwich University 80, 84, 112, 124

Ocorr, Dave 122
Odell, Bob 129, 201
Ohio State University 65, 139–140
Ohio University 220
Olympic Games (Munich, 1972) 73
Olympic Games (Paris, 1924) 61

Olympic Games (Tokyo, 1964) 61
one point six rule 33, 59–61, 62–73, 80, 142; *see also* Schulten, Alex
The Oneida 24
Oni, Miye 184
"orbits of competition" 38
Oregon College of Education 80
Oriard, Michael 26, 38
Orleans, Jeff 63, 79
Ostendarp, Jim 49, 129
Oxbridge 11, 17, 218

PAC-12 Conference 36
Pacific Coast Intercollegiate Athletic Conference 36
Panthers 10, 180, 222; *see also* Amherst College
parents 1, 3, 48, 129, 146, 157, 158, 159, 160, 167, 170, 175, 177–178, 187, 195, 199, 201–202, 203–206, 207, 212, 224
Parker, Tom 150, 166, 193, 196–197
Patton, Laurie 78
Payne, Harry "Hank" 146–149, **147**, 155, 159
Peary, Robert 10
Peck, Bob 87, 92, 118- 120, 122, 125, 138
Pembroke College (Brown) 105
Pemper, Stephanie 156–157
Penders, Tom 145
Pennington, Bill 211–215
Pentagonal Agreement 1, 8, 15, 19, 29, 35–53, 60, 62, 67, 72, 74–77, 81, 90, 94, 138, 139, 143–144, 186, 190, 210; *see also* names of institutions
Pérez, Angel 192, 198, 214
Peterson's Guide to Four-Year Colleges 200
Phillips, Charles 137
Phillips Academy (Andover) 186, 188
Phillips Exeter Academy 183, 187–188, 200
Piedmont College 176
Pierce, Franklin 9
Plansky, Tony 222
Plant, Marcus 66, 68
Plimpton, Calvin 5–54, 80, 85–86, 88, 92–94, 98–99, 139, 142
Plummer, Dale 173
"Poison Ivy of the Ivy League" 113; *see also* Harkness, Nevin "Ned"
Polar Bears 10, 143, 144, 222; *see also* Bowdoin College
polo 25
Pomona College 171
postseason play (before 1993) 2, 8, 30, 36–37, 95, 97, 134–137, 142, 143–145; individual sports 132, 139; team sports 19, 103, 109, 132, 139; *see also* individual and team sports
postseason play (after 1993) 140, 145, 147, 149–151, 152, 154–155, 157, 169, 171, 210, 215, 220; *see also* individual and team sports

Index 263

Potts, David 41
Pouncey, Peter 129
Prefontaine, Steve 73
presidents and athletics 2, 14, 16, 19, 25, 29, 32, 40, 41, 47, 52, 53, 74
Princeton University 12, 23, 25–26, 28, 33, 39, 41, 42, 64, 69, 78–79, 97, 123, 133–134, 160, 163, 164, 166, 168, 196, 200, 202, 203
Providence Journal 150
"Purity Code" *see* Sanity Code
Putnam, Pat 112–113, 114, 118, 120

Quarterman, Jerome 147
Quinn, Dick 130
Quinn, Erin 79

Radcliffe College 105
Rapelye, Janet Lavin 166
realism 1, 7–8, 12, 18, 20, 135, 153, 207, 209, 210, 214, 220, 222, 225, 228
Reclaiming the Game: College Sports and Educational Values 20, 168, 171
The Record 48
recruiting 7–8, 15, 16, 18–20, 21, 31, 41, 44–54, 57, 59, 74–75, 81, 95, 131–133, 135, 136, 140, 151, 161, 163, 172, 176, 185–208, 210, 212- 213, 216, 218, 221, 223, 225, 227–228; *see also* individual institutions
Reilly, Russ 152, 172
Rensselaer Polytechnic Institute 110, 112, 115–116, 222
Report of the State of Athletics at Tufts University (1970) 76
Reynolds, Thomas Hedley 85, 87, 98–99
Richardson, Red 141–142
riding 105
Ridpath, David 220
Robert Morris University 3
Robinson, Duncan 9, 20, 182–184, **185**
Robison, Olin 116–117
Rockne, Knute 30–31
Rooney, John F. 185
Roosevelt, Theodore 28
Rose, Clayton 223–224
Rose Bowl 140
Roth, Michael 78
Rowan University 222
rowing 9, 11, 33, 173, 217
Rudolph, Frederick 11, 24, 33–34
Russell, Don 74–75, 94
Rutgers University 122
Ryan, Tim 197, 223–224

Sabasteanski, Frank 65
St. Lawrence University 112, 190
St. Olaf College 226
St. Paul's School (New Hampshire) 69

Sakala, Richard 109, 121
Salem State University 112
"Sanity Code" 57–59, 121
Samuelson, Joan Benoit 9
Savage, Andrea 153, 156, 220, 228
Savage, Howard 31–33
Sawyer, John 16, 52–53, 68, 88, 90–**93**, 94–99, 116, 118, 139
scandals 36, , 59, 109, 118, 120–121, 128, 136, 168, 221
Schapiro, Morton 158, 193
Schmidt, Victor 36
Scholastic Aptitude Test 9, 59, 72, 120, 149, 189, 194, 198–199
Schulten, Frederick Alexis "Alex" 19, 54, 55, 60–**62**, 63–67, 73, 132, 142
Schulten, T. Tarpy 61
Schulze, Robert 81
Schwemm, Heather 106
Schwern, Jake 225
Scott, Hal 167–168
Seifried, Chad 37
The Shape of the River: Long-Term Consequences of Considering Race in College and University Admissions 169
Sheehy, Harry 42, 78, 128, 138, 150, 152, 155, 156, 175
shinny 22
show jumping 9
Shulman, James 33, 166–170, 216–217, 227–228
Shulpe, Jay 120
Sills, Kenneth 27, 29, 36, 40, 43–44, 46
Simmons College 105
Simonetta, Samantha 224
"sinful seven" 58
Skidmore College 124
skiing 83, 87, 88
"small-time" [programs] 8, 10, 17, 25, 34, 35, 56, 174, 208, 209, 228
Smith, Red 77, 95
Smith, Ronald 31, 33, 39, 59, 208–209
Smith College 105, 123
Snyder, Dave 186
softball 108, 128 165, 191, 227
Solberg, Matt 215
Somers, Wayne 77, 118
Spears, Dan 224
Spears, Tim 224
Spencer, Clayton 78
Spicer, Sean 9
Sports Illustrated 1, 5–6, 8, 64, 67, 112, 128, 131, 138, 151, 159, 164, 178, 209, 223
Springfield College 138
Sproull, Robert 122
squash 2, 20, 80, 107, 112, 160–164, 166, 172, 173, 191, 215, 218
Stagg Bowl 121

Index

stakeholders 2, 5, 8, 10, 12, 15, 17–19, 25, 41, 51, 55, 59, 61, 65, 83, 100, 102, 116, 121, 128, 132, 136, 144, 145, 147, 150, 154, 156, 159, 165, 169, 174, 178, 186, 190–191, 218, 227–228; *see also* alumni; athletic directors; coaches; faculties; parents; presidents; students; trustees
Stanford University 32, 159, 168
Steinberg, Jacques 190
Stephenson, Richard 127
Stewart, Joan 152
Stott, Sandy 186–187
Stover at Yale 13
Strider, Robert 86, 91–92, 98, 123
Stuckey, Daniel 69–70, 72, 86, 88–89, 91, 93–94, 98–99, 143
student athletes 11–13, 16–17, 20, 23–25, 33, 46–50, 52–53, 55–57, 60, 64–72, 84, 90, 93, 100, 114, 120, 122–124, 133, 135, 142, 147, 150, 156, 158, 178–181, 187, 191, 192, 193, 198, 199, 207, 211, 214–215, 217–218, 220, 224, 227
students 8, 10, 25, 26, 30, 32, 30, 39, 76, 82, 98, 102–103, 113, 115, 118, 120, 124, 126, 134, 138–141, 144, 146, 155, 159, 161, 166–167, 169–170, 171, 174–176, 212–213; *see also* names of college newspapers
Sturtevant, Mary 107–108
Sullivan, John 180
Swarthmore College 14, 76
Sweeney, Paul 133–134, 221
swimming 23, 60, 105, 130, 131, 132, 145, 156
Switzer, Barry 5–6
Szostak, Mike 150

Talbott, Dave 162–164
Tassell, Van 29
tennis 2, 25, 69–70, 105, 131, 137, 156, 160
Thelin, John R. 107
Thompson, Jon 215
Thoms, Frank 93–94, 140–141
Thornton Academy 188
Tiede, Joseph 66
"tips" 192, 194
Title IX of the Education Amendments of 1972 19, 103, 104–108, 220
Tobin, Eugene 99–100, 122, 127, 135, 147, 170, 207
Tootell, Frederic 61
Tough, Paul 211
Tower, John 104
Townsend, Charlie 180
track and field 60, 73, 137, 156, 189
Trinity College 5, 20, 31, 79, 103, 123, 160, 165, 168, 173, 192, 222, 226; admissions 9, 160, 162, 163, 192, 198, 204, 211, 214; alliances 5, 25, 43, 74, 76–77, 84–85, 89–90, 92, 96; championships 164–165, 166, 172, 191; eligibility 30, 43, 63; financial aid 31-3, 192, 218; postseason 132, 136, 145, 156, 162, 163, 172, 206, 213, 215; schedule 83–84, 87, 124; *see also* names of athletic directors, coaches, presidents
Trout, Charles "Chuck" 187
trustees 40, 52, 82, 92, 98, 102, 104, 110, 119, 148, 191
Tufts Alumni Review 83
Tufts University 5, 25, 31, 76, 99, 104, 106–108, 222; admissions 9, 76, 166; alliances 5, 74, 76, 84, 88–92, 94; championships 191; postseason 36, 136, 144–145, 156; recruiting 48, 75; schedule 83–84, 129–130; *see also* names of athletic directors, coaches, presidents
Twelve-College Exchange 123

Union College (New York) 19, 109, 110, 113, 116, 160, 215; admissions 119–120, 121; alliances 73, 76–77, 90, 92, 95, 96, 118, 122; championships 116, 120; control 100; men's hockey team photo 114; postseason 109, 145; recruiting 19, 109, 115, 118–119, 121, 136, 162; schedule 87, 92, 116–117; *see also* names of athletic directors, coaches, presidents
United Press International 9
U.S. Coast Guard Academy 84
U.S. District Court for the District of Vermont 180
U.S. Military Academy 1, 36, 59, 110, 161
U.S. Naval Academy 110, 157
University of Alabama 32, 207
University of California 14
University of California at Berkeley 102
University of Cambridge 12
University of Chicago 29
University of Colorado 6
University of Hawaii 165
University of Illinois 30, 184
University of Indiana 25
University of Iowa 32
University of Maine 27, 41, 224
University of Maine at Portland-Gorham 2, 96
University of Mary Hardin-Baylor 222
University of Maryland 58
University of Massachusetts 161
University of Miami 6
University of Michigan 80, 183–184
University of Minnesota 25
University of Mount Union 222
University of New Hampshire 3, 105, 109–110, 116
University of Notre Dame 26, 30–31
University of Oklahoma 5
University of Oregon College of Education 80

Index 265

University of Oxford 11, 85, 116, 129
University of Pennsylvania 25–26, 64, 78, 160, 201, 217
University of Rhode Island 145
University of Rochester 76, 122, 138
University of St. Thomas 226–227
University of South Carolina 58
University of Southern California 30–31, 158
University of Southern Maine 2, 96
University of Texas 36, 145, 158
University of Vermont 144
University of Virginia 25, 58
University of Washington 3
University of Wisconsin 25, 212
University of Wisconsin-Oshkosh 131
University of Wisconsin-Whitewater 183, 222
University School (Ohio) 188
Utah State University 212
Utah Jazz 184

Vassar College 124, 125, 127
Villanova University 58
violence 28, 28, 168; *see also* deaths; injuries
Virginia Military Institute 58
Virginia Polytechnic Institute 58

Wachter, Paul 163
Waldrep v. Texas Employers Insurance Association 179
Walker, Bobby 133, 221
Wall Street Journal 128
Wall Street Stock Market Crash (1929) 32
Wallace, Lisa-Ann 173
Walsh, Christy 30–31
Walsh, Mike 157
Ward, Ian 207
Ward, John 99
Warikoo, Natasha 211
Washington and Lee University 157, 171
Washington State University 36
Watson, Sidney J. "Sid" 7, 101, 108, 144, 186
Watson Arena 173
Watters, Len 48
Watts, Charles 63
Wayne State University 120
weight throw 61
Welch, Francis J. 68
Welch, Vincent 68
Welch, Vincent D. 68
Welch Scholarship 68–70, 80
Wellesley College 123
Wells, J.B. 223–224
Wertheim, L. Jon 172, 174
Wesleyan University 5, 13, 25, 27, 31, 103–104, 123 128–130, 222; admissions 9, 166, 190, 193; alliances 15, 18, 25, 29, 39–40, 41–42, 74, 77, 88, 96; control 30, 141; eligibility 26, 30, 33, 43, 62–63; financial aid 215; postseason 131, 133, 139–140, 152; recruiting 44, 46–47, 50–51, 52, 186; schedule 83–84; *see also* names of athletic directors, coaches, presidents
Westover School 113
Wessell, Nils 75–76
West Virginia University 183
Westfield State University 165
Whalen, Mike 78
Wheaton College (Illiinois) 138
Wheaton College (Massachusetts) 123
White, Gordon S., Jr. 63–64
White Mules 10
Whitmore, Dick 70–71, 73, 125, 128, 134, 156
Whittier Field 27, 73
Wieland, Ralph "Cooney" 114
Will, George 9
Williams, Ephraim 10
Williams College 5, 13, 24, 25, 31, 34, 79, 82, 103, 108, 112–113, 123, 127, 129, 134, 159, 173, 191–192, 221–223; admissions 9, 115, 121, 163, 166, 175, 193–196, 198, 206; alliances 15, 18–19, 26, 29, 39–40, 41–42, 44, 77–78, 94, 96, 98, 109, 215; championships 8, 130–132, 145, 158; control 30, 148; eligibility 26, 33, 63–64; endowments 9, 213; financial aid 33, 45, 71, 21, 213–214; postseason 36, 83, 133, 136, 138, 140, 142, 146–147, 149–150, 151, 154, 156, 167, 218–219; recruiting 46, 47, 48, 50, 118–119, 139, 187–188, 201; schedule 83–84, 90, 151–152; *see also* names of athletic directors, coaches, presidents
Williamson, Jay 9
Wilner, Jeff 130
Wilson, Barbara-Jan 190
Wilson, Woodrow 28
Winkin, John 88, 92, 138
winning 150, 164, 165, 181, 184, 186, 209, 222–223, 224, 226
Wippman, David 78
Wisconsin Intercollegiate Athletic Conference 209
Wittenberg University 138–139
women's lacrosse *see* lacrosse
Woodward Academy 149
Worcester Polytechnic Institute 124
wrestling 225
Wylde, Peter 9
Wyman, Thomas 129

Yale University 10–13, 24–26, 28–29, 33–34, 39, 41–42, 52, 64, 66, 68, 70, 78, 79, 82, 85, 114, 123, 137, 146, 153, 160, 162–164, 168, 170, 184, 217

Zuppke, Bob 30

www.ingramcontent.com/pod-product-compliance
Lightning Source LLC
Chambersburg PA
CBHW032034300426
44117CB00009B/1061